Books and Prints at the Heart of the Catholic Reformation in the Low Countries (16th–17th centuries)

Library of the Written Word

VOLUME 104

The Handpress World

Editor-in-Chief

Andrew Pettegree (*University of St Andrews*)

Editorial Board

Ann Blair (*Harvard University*)
Falk Eisermann (*Staatsbibliothek zu Berlin – Preußischer Kulturbesitz*)
Shanti Graheli (*University of Glasgow*)
Earle Havens (*Johns Hopkins University*)
Ian Maclean (*All Souls College, Oxford*)
Alicia Montoya (*Radboud University*)
Angela Nuovo (*University of Milan*)
Helen Smith (*University of York*)
Mark Towsey (*University of Liverpool*)
Malcolm Walsby (*ENSSIB, Lyon*)
Arthur der Weduwen (*University of St Andrews*)

VOLUME 83

The titles published in this series are listed at *brill.com/lww*

Books and Prints at the Heart of the Catholic Reformation in the Low Countries (16th–17th centuries)

Edited by

Renaud Adam
Rosa De Marco
Malcolm Walsby

BRILL

LEIDEN | BOSTON

Cover illustration: Albert & Isabella Clara Eugenia, *Placcaet* [...] *opt collecteren* [...] *op die waeren ende coopmanschappen* (Brussels: Rutger Velpius & Hubert Anthoine Velpius, 1610). © Arenberg Auctions, Brussels

The Library of Congress Cataloging-in-Publication Data is available online at https://catalog.loc.gov
LC record available at https://lccn.loc.gov/2022003658
LC ebook record available at https://lccn.loc.gov/2022003659

Typeface for the Latin, Greek, and Cyrillic scripts: "Brill". See and download: brill.com/brill-typeface.

ISSN 1874-4834
ISBN 978-90-04-50437-0 (hardback)
ISBN 978-90-04-51015-9 (e-book)

Copyright 2023 by Koninklijke Brill NV, Leiden, The Netherlands.
Koninklijke Brill NV incorporates the imprints Brill, Brill Nijhoff, Brill Hotei, Brill Schöningh, Brill Fink, Brill mentis, Vandenhoeck & Ruprecht, Böhlau, V&R unipress and Wageningen Academic.
All rights reserved. No part of this publication may be reproduced, translated, stored in a retrieval system, or transmitted in any form or by any means, electronic, mechanical, photocopying, recording or otherwise, without prior written permission from the publisher. Requests for re-use and/or translations must be addressed to Koninklijke Brill NV via brill.com or copyright.com.

This book is printed on acid-free paper and produced in a sustainable manner.

PRINTED BY DRUKKERIJ WILCO B.V. - AMERSFOORT, THE NETHERLANDS

Contents

List of Figures   VII
List of Tables   XI
List of Abbreviations   XII
Notes on Contributors   XIII

1   Books and Prints at the Heart of the Catholic Reformation in the Low
     Countries (16th–17th Centuries)   1
     Renaud Adam, Rosa De Marco and Malcolm Walsby

PART 1
Book Production and Book Business

2   A Window of Opportunity: Framing Female Owner-Managers
     of Printing Houses in Sixteenth-Century Antwerp   9
     Heleen Wyffels

3   The Printing Industry and the Counter-Reformation in Brussels under
     Archduke Albert and Archduchess Isabella (1598–1633)   23
     Renaud Adam

4   Successful Strategies for Creating a Devotional Best Seller: Canisius's
     Manuale Catholicorum Published by the Plantin Press   46
     Dirk Imhof

5   International Sales of Tridentine Emblems Books by the Antwerp
     Officina Plantiniana: The Case of Father Joannes David at the Beginning
     of the Seventeenth Century   61
     Renaud Milazzo

PART 2
Publishing Enterprises

6   A French Book in the Low Countries: Matthieu de Launoy's *Déclaration
     et Réfutation* and Its Reissues in Douai, Cambrai and Antwerp
     (1578–1579)   81
     Alexander Soetaert

VI   CONTENTS

7   'Per Modum Compendii a Leonardo Damerio Leodiensi in Lucem Editum': Odo van Maelcote, Léonard Damery, the *Astrolabium Aequinotiale*, and the Parallactic Print between Italy and the Southern Netherlands in the Age of Galileo   101
      Ruth Sargent Noyes

8   An Imperial Crusade? Public Opinion in Antwerp and the Response to the Bohemian Crisis   131
      Paul Arblaster

9   Printed Christian *hilaritas* under Archdukes Albert and Isabel (1598–1621)   155
      Johan Verberckmoes

PART 3
Prints and Iconography

10   Militant Printers' Marks across the Southern Low Countries (1561–1640): A Survey at the Heart of the *Emblematic Era*   179
      Rosa De Marco

11   The Counter-Reformation and Its Rebranding through Images: The Frontispieces of Books Printed in Antwerp   216
      Annelyse Lemmens

12   Thesis Prints Dedicated to Archduke Leopold William of Austria, in the Service of the *Pietas Austriaca*   239
      Gwendoline de Mûelenaere

13   The Iconography of the Last Supper in Géronimo Nadal's *Evangelicæ historiæ imagines*   268
      Valentine Langlais

Index   295

Figures

3.1 Book production in Brussels, 1598–1633: global production by four-year intervals 26

3.2 Book production in Brussels, 1598–1633: market shares of active printers 29

3.3 Book production in Brussels, 1598–1633: breakdown by categories 33

3.4 Book production in Brussels, 1598–1633: paper requirements of the different literary categories 35

3.5 Book production in Brussels, 1598–1633: breakdown by language 36

3.6 Etienne Ydens, *Histoire du saint Sacrement de Miracle* (Brussels: Rutger Velpius, 1605): title-page (©Royal Library of Belgium, Brussels, LP 9547 A) 42

4.1 Petrus Canisius, *Manuale catholicorum* (Antwerp: Christopher Plantin, 1588): title page (© Plantin-Moretus-Museum, Antwerp, MPM A 1288) 48

4.2 Petrus Canisius, *Manuale catholicorum*, Antwerp, Christopher Plantin, 1588: pp. 70–71 (beginning of the 4th Exercice) (© Plantin-Moretus-Museum, Antwerp, A 1288) 51

4.3 Petrus Canisius, *Handt-boeck der catholijcken*, Antwerp, Jan Moretus I, 1604, pp. 170–171 (beginning of the 7th exercice) (© Plantin-Moretus-Museum, Antwerp, A 889) 53

4.4 Sale of a colored copy to Martin Ginderhoven on 18 May 1605 (© Plantin-Moretus-Museum, Antwerp, Arch. 177, Journal 1605, fol. 78v) 56

4.5 Petrus Canisius, *Le manuel des catholiques*, Antwerp, Balthasar Moretus II, 1662, pp. 174–175 (beginning of the 8th exercice) (© Plantin-Moretus-Museum, Antwerp, O.B 1.4) 58

5.1 Market share of the various David's emblem books at the Frankfurt Fairs from 1606 to 1610 according to the Cahiers de Francfort kept at the Plantin-Moretus Museum in Antwerp 66

5.2 Sales of Joannes David's emblem books at the Frankfurt fairs between 1606 and 1610 67

5.3 Montage of two separate sheets of the Veridicus Christianus, emphasising the relationship between image and text. Jan David, *Veridicus christianus* (Antwerp: ex officina Plantiniana, 1601) 69

5.4 Sales by cities of emblem books published by the Officina plantiniana at the Frankfurt fairs (spring and autumn) between 1606 and 1610 according to the Cahiers de Francfort kept at the Plantin-Moretus Museum in Antwerp 73

7.1 Léonard Damery after Odo van Maelcote, *Equinoctial astrolabe*, in *Astrolabium aequinoctiale, Odonis Malcotij Bruxellensis e Societate Iesu. Per modum compendij a Leunardo Damerio Leodiensi in lucem editum* (Brussels: Rutger Velpius, 1607). Burin engraving (© Royal Library of Belgium, Brussels, VH 8.416 A 1) 115

VIII FIGURES

7.2 Lambert Damery after Odo van Maelcote, stereographic astrolabe, *c.*1600–1610. Engraved brass (© Musée de la Vie Wallonne, Liège, MVW 4000035) 118

7.3 Ferdinand Arsenius after Odo Van Maelcote, "Astrolabium Hemisphaericum ad lat. 66 ½ / Odo Malcot invenit Ferd. Arssenius Sculp" (Aequinoctial austral-boreal tympanum printing plate, latitude 66 ½ [=arctic circle]), *c.*1610 (terminus post quem). Copper, burin-engraved (© Musée des arts et métiers-Cnam, Paris, 00914-0000) 119

7.4 Valerian Regnard after Odo van Maelcote, *Hemisphaeria AEquinoctialia*, in *Astrolabiorum seu Vtriusque planispherij vniuersalis, et particularis vsus. Per modum compendij traditus à Valeriano Regnartio Belga* [...] (Rome: Bartholomaeus Zannettus, 1610). Burin engraving (© Biblioteca Angelica, Rome, h.5.16) 123

7.5 Ferdinand Arsenius after Odo Van Maelcote, *Hemisphaeria AEquinoctialia* terrestrial austral hemisphere plate, in *Astrolabiorum seu Vtriusque planispherij vniuersalis, et particularis vsus* [...], *c.*1610 (terminus post quem). Burin engraving (© Zentralbibliothek Zürich, Zürich, NE 1951) 124

10.1 Cornelis I Galle after Paul Peter Rubens, Plantin's Mark in Silvestro Pietrasanta, *De symbolis heroicis libri IX* (Antwerp: Balthasar Moretus (© University Library of Liege, Liège, 374B) 179

10.2 Hendrick Goltzius, *Portrait of Christopher Plantin*, 1581–1585. Copper engraving, 20,4 × 13,4 cm (© Rijksmuseum, Amsterdam, RP-P-1884-A-7748) 183

10.3 Guillaume La Rivière's mark, the wide river, in Maximilien de Wignacourt, *Discours sur l'estat des Pays Bas, auquel sont déduictes les causes de ses troubles et calamitez et leurs remèdes* (Arras: Guillaume de La Rivière, 1593) (© University of Gent) 187

10.4 Guillaume La Rivière's mark, at the address of The Good Shepherd, from the dictionary compiled by Ferdinand van der Haeghen, *Marques typographiques des imprimeurs et libraires qui ont exercé dans les Pays Bas, et marques typographiques des imprimeurs et libraires belges établis à l'étranger* (2 vols., Ghent: C. Vyt, 1894), II. 8 188

11.1 *Engraved title page*, Lodovico Guicciardini, *Descrittione di tutti i Paesi Bassi, altrimenti detti Germania Inferiore* (Antwerp: Christophe Plantin, 1581 (© Plantin Moretus Museum, Antwerp, A1342) 218

11.2 *Frontispiece*, Lodovico Guicciardini, *Descrittione di tutti i Paesi Bassi, altrimenti detti Germania Inferiore* (Antwerp: Christophe Plantin, 1581) 220 (© Plantin Moretus Museum, Antwerp, A1342) 220

11.3 Cesare Baronio, *Annales ecclesiatici a Christo nato ad annum 1198* (12 vols., Antwerp: Officina Plantiniana, 1597–1607): engraved title page (© Plantin Moretus Museum, Antwerp, 2–173.1) 225

11.4 Jerónimo Nadal, *Evangelicae historiae imagines ex ordine Evangeliorum, quae tot anno in Missae Sacrificio recitantur, in ordinem temporis vitae Christi digestae*

FIGURES IX

(Antwerp: s.l., 1593): frontispiece (© Plantin Moretus Museum, Antwerp, A 3808) 229

11.5 Jerónimo Nadal, *Adnotationes et meditationes in Evangelia quae in sacrosancto Missae sacrificio toto anno leguntur* (Antwerp: Martinus Nutius, 1595): engraved title page (© Plantin Moretus Museum, Antwerp, A 555) 230

11.6 Jan David, *Veridicus Christianus* (Antwerp: Officina Plantiniana, 1601): engraved title page (© Katholieke Universiteit Leuven, Leuven, BRES-R5A14986) 233

11.7 Jan David, *Occasio arrepta, neglecta, huius commoda, illius incommoda* (Antwerp: Officina Plantiniana, 1605): engraved title page (© Plantin Moretus Museum, Antwerp, A 1205) 235

12.1 Cornelis II Galle, *Portrait of Archduke Leopold William of Austria crowned by two angels*, ca 1652. Engraving, 26,7 × 17 cm (© Rijksmuseum, Amsterdam, RP-P-1904-380) 242

12.2 Petrus Clouwet after Jean-Baptiste Van Heil, *Universal Philosophy*, thesis frontispiece with a portrait of Archduke Leopold William of Austria, 1655. Engraving, 41,2 × 26,5 cm (© Royal Library of Belgium, Brussels, SI 11514) 245

12.3 Adrien Lommelin after Antoine Sallaert, *Synopsis theologica*, title page for a thesis defended by Humbert de Precipiano, Jesuit college of Louvain, 1648. Engraving, 39,3 × 24,1 cm (© Rijksmuseum, Amsterdam, RP-P-1908-702) 249

12.4 E. de Boulonnois after F.A. Marienhof, "Serenissimo Principi Leopoldo Guilielmo pacis ac tranquillitatis publicae auctori", in P.D.F., *À son Altesse Leopolde Guillaume* [...] *panegirique* [...], s.l., ca 1651, 16 pp., 24,5 × 37,5 cm (© Royal Library of Belgium, Brussels, VH 26.867 C) 253

Fig. 12.5 and 12.6. Paul Pontius after Abraham van Diepenbeeck, Thesis of Claudius, Count of Collalto, dedicated to Archduke Ferdinand of Austria, University of Louvain, 1645. Engraving, 102,5 × 68 cm (© Rijksmuseum, Amsterdam, RP-P-OB-70.060 and 061) 254

12.7 Theodore van Thulden after Peter Paul Rubens, *Temple of Janus*, in Caspar Gevartius (ed.), *Pompa Introitus Ferdinandi Austriaci Hispaniarum Infantis...*, Antwerp, 1641, pl. 117A (© Rijksmuseum, Amsterdam, RP-P-OB-70.270) 256

12.8 Theodore van Thulden after Peter Paul Rubens, *Portico of the Emperors* (Matthias and Ferdinand II), in Caspar Gevartius (ed.), *Pompa Introitus Ferdinandi Austriaci Hispaniarum Infantis...*, Antwerp, 1641, pl. 50A (© Rijksmuseum, Amsterdam, RP-P-OB-70.262) 257

12.9 Jacob Neeffs after Philippe Fruytiers, *Austriaco Burgundico*, title page for a thesis dedicated to Leopold William of Austria, undated (c.1647–1656). Engraving, 22,3 × 17,2 cm (© Royal Library of Belgium, Brussels, SI 28961) 258

12.10 Anonymous, *Timore Domini concessa divinitus Israeli sapientia, felicitas, gloria* [...], frontispiece for the libretto of a stage play given to Leopold William of Austria, Antwerp, 1648. Etching, 20,5 × 15 cm (© KU Leuven, Tabularium, inv. A 16018 n°5) 261

12.11 Adrien Lommelin after Abraham van Diepenbeeck, *Decor Carmeli*, thesis (?) broadside dedicated to Leopold William of Austria, ca 1650–1655. Engraving, 100 × 40 cm (Antwerp, St Charles Borromeo church, © IRPA, inv. 57750)   264

13.1 Johannes Wierix after Bernardino Passeri, *Feria v. Maioris Hebdom*, 1593, woodcut, 232 × 145 mm (© Rijksmuseum, Amsterdam, RP-P-OB-67.223)   270

13.2 Johannes Wierix after Bernardino Passeri, *Cœna commvnis, et Lavatio Pedum*, 1593, woodcut, 232 × 145 mm (© Rijksmuseum, Amsterdam, RP-P-OB-67.224)   271

13.3 Johannes Wierix after Bernardino Passeri, *Sanctissimi Sacramenti, et Sacrificii Institvtio*, 1593, woodcut, 232 × 145 mm (© Rijksmuseum, Amsterdam, RP-P-OB-67.225)   272

13.4 Johannes Wierix after Bernardino Passeri, *De Gestis post sacram Commvnionem*, 1593, woodcut, 231 × 144 mm (© Rijksmuseum, Amsterdam, RP-P-OB-67.226)   273

13.5 Jacob Corneliszoon van Oostsanen, *Christ and the apostles celebrating the Passover*, 1523, woodcut, 110 × 78 mm (© The British Museum, London, 1859.0709.2865)   275

13.6 Jacob Corneliszoon van Oostsanen, *The Institution of the Eucharistic sacrament*, 1523, woodcut, 110 × 78 mm (© The British Museum, London, 1859.0709.2865)   276

13.7 Johannes Wiei, after Pieter van der Borcht, *The Last Supper*, 1571, etching, 114 × 73 mm (© The British Museum, London, 1875.0710.116)   286

13.8 Antoine II Wierix after Bernardino Passeri, *Eodem die apparet Iesvs dvobvs discipvlis evntibvs emavnta*, 1593, woodcut, 233 × 146 mm (© Rijksmuseum, Amsterdam, RP-P-OB-67.265)   287

13.9 Pieter Paul Rubens, *The Last Supper*, 1620, oil on panel, 43,8 × 44,1 cm (© The Art Museum, Seattle, 61.66)   291

13.10 Philips Galle after Jan van der Straet, *The Last Supper*, 1585, etching, 198 × 269 mm (© Boijmans van Beuningen Museum, Rotterdam, L1966/56–3)   292

Tables

4.1 Plantin editions of Canisius's *Manuale* in Latin, Dutch and French and their basis selling price 52

4.2 Balthasar I and Jan Moretus II editions of Canisius's *Manuale* in Latin, Dutch and French and their basis selling price 57

10.1 An attempt to systematically assess the influence between emblems and printers' marks in the Low Countries (sixteenth–seventeenth centuries) 203

Abbreviations

Bibliotheca catholica   *Bibliotheca catholica neerlandica impressa 1500–1727*
(The Hague: Martinus Nijhoff, 1954).

BT   Elly Cocx-Indestege, Geneviève Glorieux and Bart Op de Beeck, *Belgica Typographica, 1541–1600. Catalogus librorum impressorum ab anno MDXLI ad annum MDC in regionibus quæ nunc Regni Belgarum partes sunt* (4 vols., Nieuwkoop: De Graaf, 1968–1994).

DPD   Peter van Huisstede and J.P.J. Brandhorst, *Dutch Printer's Devices. 15th–17th Century: A Catalogue* (3 vols., Nieuwkoop: De Graaf Publishers, 1999).

ICC-ODIS   *Impressa catholica cameracensia. A Database on the Religious Book and its Networks in the Ecclesiastical Province of Cambrai (1559–1659)*, on line: <https://www.arts.kuleuven.be/nieuwetijd/english/odis/ICC_search>.

ISTC   *Incunabula Short-Title Catalogue*, on line: <http://data.cerl.org/istc/_search>.

NB   Andrew Pettegree, Malcolm Walsby, *Netherlandish Books. Books Published in the Low Countries and Dutch Books Printed Abroad Before 1601* (2 vols.; Leiden-Boston: Brill, 2011).

NK   Wouter Nijhoff, Maria Elizabeth Kronenberg, *Nederlandsche bibliographie van 1500 tot 1540* (3 vols., The Hague: M. Nijhoff, 1923–1971).

PP   Léon Voet, *The Plantin Press at Antwerp (1555–1589). A Bibliography of the Works Printed and Published by Christopher Plantin at Antwerp and Leiden* (6 vols., Amsterdam: Van Hoeve, 1980–1983).

STCV   *Short Title Catalogue Flanders*, on line: <www.stcv.be>.

USTC   *Universal Short Title Catalogue*, on line: <https://www.ustc.ac.uk>.

VD 16   *Verzeichnis der im deutschen Sprachbereich erschienenen Drucke des 16. Jahrhunderts*, on line: <http://www.vd16.de>.

Notes on Contributors

Renaud Adam

works for the auction house Arenberg Auctions (Brussels) and is scientific collaborator for the Modern History Department of the University of Liège, where he also taught History of the book in the Renaissance from 2012 until 2019. His research focusses on the book culture and its industry in the Low Countries during the Early Modern Period. He published a.o. *Vivre et imprimer dans les Pays-Bas méridionaux (des origines à la Réforme)* (2 vols., Turnhout, Brepols, 2018), *Lectures italiennes dans les pays wallons à la première modernité (1500–1630)*, with Nicole Bingen (Turnhout, Brepols, 2015) and *Itinéraires du livre italien à la Renaissance. Suisse romande, anciens Pays-Bas et Liège*, edited with Chiara Lastraioli (Paris, Classiques Garnier, 2019).

Paul Arblaster

D.Phil. (Oxford, 2000), is a historian and translator who has taught at the Centre for European Studies of the KU Leuven and at the Maastricht School of Translation and Interpreting. He currently teaches at the Marie Haps Faculty of Translation and Interpreting, Université Saint-Louis Bruxelles, and the Louvain School of Translation and Interpreting. His research has focused on communication, translation and news publishing in the sixteenth and seventeenth centuries, and on martyrdom, exile and monasticism in the religious conflicts of the period. He is the author of *Antwerp & the World: Richard Verstegan and the International Culture of Catholic Reformation* (Leuven, 2004); *From Ghent to Aix: How They Brought the News in the Habsburg Netherlands, 1550–1700* (Leiden, 2014); and *A History of the Low Countries* (third edition, fully revised and updated, London, 2019).

Rosa De Marco

has a master in conservation of cultural heritage and holds a PhD in history of modern art from the University of Burgundy. She is a scientific collaborator at the Modern History Department of the University of Liège where she has been hosted as a *Marie Skłodowska-Curie* research fellow. Her researches focus on baroque ceremonies and the relationship between text and image in the European arts. She is currently preparing a monograph from her thesis, on Jesuit Festivals in France (1586–1643), and a further volume, *Emblems in European stages*, for the series Glasgow Emblem Studies.

Dirk Imhof

has a master in classics and in library sciences. In 2008 he obtained his doctorat in history at the University of Antwerp with a thesis on the Antwerp publisher Jan Moretus I (1543–1610). He is curator of the rare books and archives at the Plantin-Moretus Museum in Antwerp. His research focuses on book history in Antwerp in the early modern period and the Plantin Press in particular. Together with Karen Bowen he published *Christopher Plantin and Engraved Book Illustrations in Sixteenth-Century Europe* (Cambridge University Press, 2008). His bibliography of the editions of Jan Moretus I, *Jan Moretus and the Continuation of The Plantin Press: A Bibliography of the Works Published and Printed by Jan Moretus I in Antwerp (1589–1610)*, (Leiden: Brill), appeared in 2014.

Valentine Langlais

is a PhD student at the University of Montpellier and the University of Geneva. Graduate of the Ecole du Louvre, she is currently working on a thesis titled "Painting the Eucharist: the iconography of the Last Supper in Dutch and Flemish painting (1560–1660)". Her field of research is the religious iconography in the Flemish and Dutch art and, more specifically, the links between painting and the religious and political context of the Netherlands in the wake of the crisis of iconoclasm in the 16th century, and then during the 17th century. Alongside her research, she is also working as a lecturer at the University of Montpellier and teaching Renaissance art in Europe.

Annelyse Lemmens

is Phd student in History of art at the Université catholique de Louvain and former fellow of the F.R.S.-FNRS (2010–2014). Member of the GEMCA (UCLouvain) since 2010, she also beneficiated from a short-term fellowship at the Warburg Institute (London). Her researches are centred on the statuses, functions and uses of the frontispiece in Antwerp between 1585 and 1640. Her interest concerns especially the evolution of the structures of the frontispieces in the sixteenth and seventeenth centuries and the link between the liminal image and the book. Influenced at first by visual semiotic, her last interventions led her to consider her object of study from the angle of visual rhetoric.

Renaud Milazzo

obtained his Ph.D. in History, Art History and Archaeology at the University of Versailles Saint-Quentin-en-Yvelines with a thesis about the emblem book market in Europe over the period between 1531–1750 (Tutor: Prof. Chantal Grell). His dissertation will soon be published in the series Bibliologia by

Brepols (Turnhout, Belgium). Dr Milazzo has published articles on topics related to the sale of emblem books printed by Christopher Plantin and Jan Moretus I, based on the archives of the Museum Plantin-Moretus in Antwerp. He joined the EMoBookTrade project team in July 2018 (Università deli Studi di Milano) through the special project EMoEuropeBookPrices (funded by FARE-MIUR, Italy) with the goal of studying the manuscript catalogue of book prices recorded by Christopher Plantin and Jan Moretus I (1555–1593 ca.) at the Museum Plantin-Moretus in Antwerp.

Gwendoline de Mûelenaere
is a postdoctoral researcher in history of art at Ghent University, in Belgium. Her current project focuses on illustrated lecture notebooks from the Old University of Louvain. She intends to analyze the features and the functioning of such images in order to assess their role in the transmission of knowledge, and to survey their socio-symbolic stakes from an art historical perspective. Prior to that, she obtained a PhD at the Université catholique de Louvain, under the supervision of Prof. Ralph Dekoninck. She carried out an iconological study of thesis prints produced in the Southern Low Countries in the seventeenth and eighteenth centuries. Her research interests include early modern prints, the history of education in the Southern Netherlands, the role of the Jesuits in the creation of images produced in academic frameworks, allegorical and emblematic languages, text/image relationships, frame and framing issues.

Ruth S. Noyes
Novo Nordisk Foundation Mads Øvlisen Fellow at the National Museum of Denmark, holds a PhD in the History of Art from Johns Hopkins University. A Fellow of the American Academy in Rome, she has received over 10 postdoctoral research grants, awards and fellowships, including the Rome Prize (2014) and Marie Skłodowska-Curie EU Fellowship (2019). Author of numerous articles and essays, she published her first monograph with Routledge in 2017 and is currently preparing two further monographs.

Alexander Soetaert
earned his PhD in Early Modern History from the University of Leuven (KU Leuven). In 2019, he was a postdoctoral fellow at the Leibniz-Institute for European History in Mainz, Germany. His main research interests concern transregional history, early modern book history and hagiography and the history of the Walloon provinces of the Low Countries. His PhD thesis on the

Catholic printing press in the Ecclesiastical Province of Cambrai has been published in the series of the Royal Flemish Academy of Belgium for Science and the Arts under the title *De katholieke drukpers in de kerkprovincie Kamerijk. Contacten, mobiliteit en transfers in een grensgebied (1559–1659)* (Leuven: Peeters, 2019). Together with Violet Soen, Johan Verberckmoes and Wim François, he also published the volume *Transregional Reformations: Crossing Borders in Early Modern Europe* (Refo500 Academic Series, Göttingen, 2019).

Johan Verberckmoes

is Professor of early modern cultural history at the Faculty of Arts, KU Leuven. His research focuses on humour and laughter as cultural movers from the 16th to the 18th century. He is currently preparing a book on the humour of ordinary people in the 17th and 18th century based on joke collections and egodocuments. His other main research interest is the history of intercultural contacts in the context of the Spanish Habsburg territories as part of the worldwide Spanish and Portugese empires in the 16th and 17th century. His latest book is *Ontmoetingen in het Westen. Een wereldgeschiedenis* (Encounters in the West, A World History), Pelckmans Pro 2019.

Malcolm Walsby

is Professor of book history at Enssib in Lyon, director of the Gabriel Naudé research centre, and co-founder of the Universal Short Title Catalogue. He is the author of a number of monographs and articles on 15th-, 16th- and 17th-century French history. Most recently, he has published *L'imprimé en Europe occidentale, 1470–1680* and *Booksellers and Printers in Provincial France 1470–1600* (2020 and 2021). He has also edited volumes on European book history as well as bibliographies on French and Netherlandish books. A specialist of the archaeology of the book and the economics of the book trade, he is currently developing an international research project on the creation and use of Sammelbände in Europe.

Heleen Wyffels

is a PhD-fellow of the Research Foundation-Flanders (FWO) based at the University of Leuven. She is preparing a doctoral thesis on women printers in the Habsburg Low Countries (sixteenth and seventeenth centuries), under the supervision of Violet Soen and Johan Verberckmoes. Before starting her PhD, Heleen Wyffels studied history at the University of Leuven and arts and heritage at Maastricht University.

CHAPTER 1

Books and Prints at the Heart of the Catholic Reformation in the Low Countries (16th–17th Centuries)

Renaud Adam, Rosa De Marco and Malcolm Walsby

The use and the impact of the printing press in promoting the Catholic Reformation in the early modern Habsburg Low Countries has not received the attention it deserves. In contrast, the use of books and prints by Protestants – often considered as the first phenomenon of mass media in history – has been widely studied and has generated a rich and plentiful bibliography.[1] Yet the Spanish monarchy and local authorities, the Catholic Church, the universities of Douai and Louvain, and the new religious orders within these territories seized the opportunities offered by printers and booksellers to strengthen their missions: to restore Spanish authority, ensure dissemination of the decrees of the Council of Trent, fight all kinds of heresy, and contribute to pastoral and pedagogical activities. Though there are studies on a few core figures, such as Christophe Plantin or the Verdussen family,[2] or a few important publishing enterprises, such as the Plantin *Biblia Regia* or the *Imago Primi Saeculi* by Moretus, many other less well-known cases are still as yet unstudied.[3] The main target of this book is to shed light on the extent, dynamism and underlying mechanisms of the processes set up to support Catholic Reform. The thirteen essays gathered in this volume offer an interdisciplinary approach to understand the complexity of the phenomenon through religious history, book history, art history and cultural history. Each part focuses on specific fields: book

---

1 Among the rich and plentiful bibliography on the subject, see Mark Ulin Edwards, *Printing, Propaganda and Luther* (Berkeley: University of California Press, 1994); Ilja M. Veldman, *Images for the Eye and Soul. Function and Meaning in Netherlandish Prints (1450–1650)* (Leiden: Primavera Pers, 2006); Andrew Pettegree, *Brand Luther 1517. Printing, and the Making of the Reformation* (New York: Penguin Press, 2015).

2 Leon Voet, *The Golden Compasses: A History and Evaluation of the Printing and Publishing Activities of the 'Officina Plantiniana' at Antwerp* (2 vols., Amsterdam-London-New York: Vangendt, 1969–1972); Stijn Van Rossem, *Het Gevecht met de Boeken. De uitgeversstrategieën van de familie Verdussen* (Antwerp, unpublished PhD, 2014).

3 Frederico Pérez Castro, Leon Voet, *La Biblia Políglota de Amberes* (Madrid: Fundación universitaria española, 1973); John W. O'Malley, *Art, Controversy, and the Jesuits: The 'Imago Primi Saeculi' (1640)* (Philadelphia: Saint Joseph's University Press, 2015).

© KONINKLIJKE BRILL NV, LEIDEN, 2023 | DOI:10.1163/9789004510159_002

production and dissemination, the actors of the Counter-Reformation and their networks, and prints and iconography.

•••

The first part of the volume focuses on Catholic book production and bookselling in the Low Countries. While such publications are well documented for the fifteenth and the sixteenth century and studies on publishers' editorial policies are flourishing, there is still a severe lack of data regarding some aspects of book production.[4] Some of the social facets of the book world have been neglected (such as the key role played by widows); and dissemination, circulation and bookselling need to be further investigated. Four chapters dealing with these matters intend to fill some of these historiographical gaps. Heleen Wyffels explores the contribution of women to the production of Catholic books and images in Antwerp during the sixteenth century. This case is an opportunity to study the options available to printers' widows and provides quantitative analysis of widows' printing houses. Renaud Adam reconsiders the case of Brussels under the reign of Archduke Albert and Archduchess Isabella (1598–1633). The history of this printing centre during the seventeenth century has been unjustly ignored by scholars for many years, which has affected our vision of the role played by Brussels printers in the dissemination of the Counter-Reformation. Dirk Imhof examines the publishing history of Petrus Canisius's *Manuale catholicorum*, printed by the Plantin Press. This prayer book, essential to the Counter-Reformation, quickly became an extremely successful text with numerous editions. Imhof's chapter documents the publication of this work from the first edition to the middle of the seventeenth century. He discusses the evolution of its illustration and investigates the sale of a selection of editions. Renaud Milazzo looks at the issue of the international emblem book trade at the beginning of the seventeenth century through the prism of the Plantin company's archives.

The second part is dedicated to the actors of the Counter-Reformation and their networks (both within and beyond the Low Countries) through the study of some relevant publishing enterprises. Four chapters focus on authors who, through their writings, participated in the struggle led by the Habsburgs

---

4   NB; USTC; Andrew Pettegree, 'Printing in the Low Countries in the Early Sixteenth Century', in *The Book Triumphant. Print in Transition in the Sixteenth and Seventeenth Centuries*, eds. Graham Kemp, Malcolm Walsby (Leiden-Boston: Brill, 2011), pp. 3–25; Chiara Ruzzier, Xavier Hermand, Ezio Ornato, *Les stratégies éditoriales à l'époque de l'incunable: le cas des anciens Pays-Bas* (Turnhout: Brepols, 2012); Renaud Adam, *Vivre et imprimer dans les Pays-Bas méridionaux (des origines à la Réforme)* (2 vols.; Turnhout: Brepols, 2018).

BOOKS AND PRINTS AT THE HEART OF THE CATHOLIC REFORMATION 3

against all forms of heresy. Alexander Soetaert examines how the Catholic Party appropriated *La déclaration et réfutation des fausses suppositions*, written by Matthieu de Launoy and Henri Pennetier (both former Huguenot ministers who had converted to Catholicism). First published in Paris in 1577, it was reissued four times in the Low Countries. This editorial history enables him to reassess the role played by the Walloon provinces in the exchange of news and books between France and the Low Countries. Exploring the nature of a network of scientists by examining the relationship between the Jesuit astronomer-mathematician Christoph Clavius, from Rome, and the young Jesuit Odo van Maelcote, from Liège, Ruth S. Noyes studies Catholic Reformation confessionalised science and the material culture of the converting [im] prints in the Low Countries ca 1600. Paul Arblaster examines two aspects of the Habsburg response to the Bohemian crisis of 1618–1620 in Antwerp: the licensing of the city's first newspaper and the establishment of a confraternity to support the maintenance of the legitimate authority of the Catholic princes. He studies how and why rhetoric and imagery of crusades were deployed, and argues that its use was limited by concerns about the institutional and fiscal implications that 'crusading' still bore within the Habsburg monarchy more broadly. Johan Verberckmoes's contribution challenges the instrumental uses of humour during the rule of the Archdukes in the first decades of the seventeenth century. He analyses the rediscovery of *hilaritas* in the production of contemporary biographies and news on the Archdukes, as well as contemporary advice on laughter in books and prints.

It is well known that images were used as didactic vehicle for spreading Lutheran theses. From the end of the fifteenth century, images were employed to criticise the perceived excesses and moral abuses of the Roman Church and the use of sacred imagery, often in a grotesque and satirical way that met with great success among all levels of society.[5] To appeal to the souls and show evidence of dogmas through the pedagogical power of images, Catholic reaction to the Reformers' attacks became a theological legitimisation of the sacred image, emphasising the necessary discernment between image and idol, and reaching a wide audience thanks to an ambition publication strategy.[6] The third part of the book explores the production, use and impact of illustrated books and broadsheets in the Catholic campaign against the Protestant reformers.

---

5 Veldman, *Images for the Eye and Soul*, passim.
6 Ralph Dekoninck, '*Ad Imaginem*'. *Statuts, fonctions et usages de l'image dans la littérature spirituelle jésuite du XVIIe siècle* (Genève: Droz, 2005); Walter S. Melion, *The Meditative Art: Studies in the Northern Devotional Print, 1550–1625* (Philadelphia: Saint Joseph's University Press, 2010).

Images enabled Catholic authors to challenge their opponents. Jerome Nadal's *Evangelicae historiae imagines* (Antwerp, 1593), or Jan David's *Veridicus christianus* (Antwerp, 1601) were the best-known and most influential illustrated books of catechetical and polemical literature.[7] However, the scope of their content is still far from fully understood, as Valentine Langlais demonstrates in her essay. She focuses on the Nadal's visual strategy to explain the scriptural and ritual roots of the sacrament of the Eucharist. Prints were also a very effective way of magnifying the promotion and political support of the Catholic conquest, namely during public events such as thesis defences currently the subject of much new research in France.[8] Gwendoline de Mûelenaere suggests that printed thesis dedicated to Archduke Leopold-William, governor of the Spanish Low Countries from 1647 to 1656, used allegorical expressions of Christian virtues to affirm and frame his princely authority and Roman Catholic aspirations. Two other contributions explore particular visual and verbal elements in the paratext. These have a commercial and aesthetic value, arousing the interest of the reader through their enigmatic word-image amalgam and in particular in the choices of decorated title-pages or frontispieces and the publishers' devices. The analysis of a series of frontispieces produced in Antwerp at the turn of the seventeenth century allows Annelyse Lemmens to show how this ornamental element could guide the reader and both change the perception of the book as a material object and emphasise its significance. Building on recent studies on the publisher's device as a complex medium sharing strong links with emblematic expression,[9] Rosa De Marco focuses on devices (end sixteenth to early seventeenth centuries) from the Southern Low Countries, a territory where device indexing projects are still lacking.

The contributions collected in this book allow us to rethink the state of Catholic book culture, the industry and its actors in the early modern Low

---

7   Ralph Dekoninck, Agnès Guiderdoni-Bruslé, M. van Vaeck (eds.). *Emblemata Sacra. Rhétorique et herméneutique du discours sacré dans la littérature en images* (Turnhout: Brepols, 2007); Walter S. Melion, *Annotations and Meditations on the Liturgical Gospels* (3 vols., Philadelphia: Saint Joseph's University Press, 2003–2014); Imhof 2014, Melion 2003–2014, Dekoninck, Guiderdoni, Vaeck 2007); Dirk Imhof, *Jan Moretus and the Continuation of the Plantin Press: A Bibliography of the Works Published and Printed by Jan Moretus I in Antwerp (1589–1610)*, (2 vols., Leiden: Brill, Hes & De Graaf., 2014).

8   Véronique Meyer, *L'illustration des thèses à Paris dans la seconde moitié du XVIIᵉ siècle: peintres, graveurs, éditeurs* (Paris: Commission des travaux historiques, 2002); Id., *Pour la plus grande gloire du roi. Louis XIV en thèses* (Rennes: PUR, 2017).

9   Michaela Scheibe, Anja Wolkenhauer (eds.), *Signa Vides. Researching and Recording Printers' Devices* (London: Consortium of European Research Libraries, 2015); Bernhard F. Scholz, Anja Wolkenhauer (eds.), *Typographorum Emblemata The Printer's Mark in the Context of Early Modern Culture* (Berlin: De Gruyter Saur, 2018).

Countries within an interdisciplinary framework. They provide a new understanding of book production under the Archdukes by focusing on the social aspects of book world, on the nature of the trade and the international dissemination of books and prints, as well as on the role played by the Walloon provinces. It reassesses the role of Antwerp in relation to other typographical centres and improves our understanding of the visual culture of the book. It also challenges our knowledge of the relationship of books and prints with the Jesuits and other religious orders. As a whole, these essays highlight the efficacious manner in which the handpress book industry was able to support the Catholic strategy in the Spanish Low Countries and underline the mutually beneficial relationship between proponents of the Counter-Reformation and the typographic world. As such, they represent an important contribution to our understanding of sociocultural and socioeconomic realities of the Catholic Low Countries.

This book brings together the proceedings of a two-day conference held at the University of Liège on 23 and 24 February 2017. The editors would like to thank the Foundation for the protection of cultural, historical and craft heritage (Lausanne) for supporting the symposium in Liège and the edition of this book. This work has been also supported by the European Commission (Marie Skłodowska-Curie Actions-COFUND Programme).

PART 1

Book Production and Book Business

∵

CHAPTER 2

A Window of Opportunity: Framing Female Owner-Managers of Printing Houses in Sixteenth-Century Antwerp

Heleen Wyffels

1   Introduction

The role of women in early modern printing houses intrigues a growing number of book historians.[1] However, the question of how we should assess their presence in the book trade remains a matter of debate. As Beatrice Beech has rightly observed, the sources do not permit us to assess women as workers in printing shops because the evidence thereof remains anecdotal.[2] Indeed, the daily routine of a printing firm is likely to remain obscure in the absence of extensive business archives such as those of the Antwerp *Officina Plantiniana*. Beech and other historians therefore turned their attention to women acting as owner-managers of early modern printing houses. In practice, this means that they predominantly analyse the role of widows, who appear at the head of printing houses more often than other women do.[3] Wills, business contracts, and legal action, show these female owner-managers inheriting, overseeing and passing on their firms. In terms of content, the production of their printing houses does not seem to have differed significantly from that of male-headed businesses,[4] but female owner-managers do seem to diverge from gendered

---

1   This article was written as part of a PhD fellowship of the Research Foundation – Flanders (FWO).

   See for example: Rémi Jimenes, *Charlotte Guillard. Une femme imprimeur à la Renaissance* (Rennes: Presses Universitaires de Rennes 2017); Helen Smith, *Grossly Material Things: Women and Book Production in Early Modern England* (Oxford: Oxford University Press, 2012); Hannie van Goinga, 'Schaduwbeelden: vrouwen in het boekenvak in de vroegmoderne tijd: een nieuw terrein van onderzoek', *Jaarboek Voor Nederlandse Boekgeschiedenis*, 12 (2005), pp. 13–27; Susan Broomhall, *Women and the Book Trade in Sixteenth-Century France* (Aldershot: Ashgate 2002).

2   Beatrice Beech, 'Women printers in Paris in the sixteenth century', *Medieval Prosopography*, 10 (1989), p. 76.

3   I use the term owner-manager as proposed by Beech. See Beech, 'Women printers in Paris', p. 76.

4   Heleen Wyffels, 'Weduwen-drukkers in 16de-eeuws Antwerpen. Samengebracht in een bio-bibliografisch repertorium', *De Gulden Passer*, 95 (2017), pp. 235–236. The data were compiled on the basis of NK, BT, STCV and USTC.

© KONINKLIJKE BRILL NV, LEIDEN, 2023 | DOI:10.1163/9789004510159_003

patterns which traditionally assign to men work that required training – for some tasks even literacy – and work that needed relatively large investments but had the potential of yielding good profits.[5]

This chapter argues that a debate about whether or not the printing trade was a favourable environment for female entrepreneurship would benefit from a re-examination of the impact of family and women's life cycles on the careers of female owner-managers. By analysing how widows became owner-managers, this article seeks to contribute to our understanding of the ways in which women navigated this particular male-dominated craft. Reconsidering the negotiation of inheritance and the re-organisation of the family business after the death of an owner-manager could prove to be a fruitful addition to the debate about the place of women in the printing trade. This chapter proposes to understand the moment of succession after the death of an owner-manager as a focal point of agency for widows. It focuses on sixteenth-century Antwerp, the most prolific printing town of the Southern Low Countries in the sixteenth century.[6] Because of the high concentration of male and female printers, it serves as an excellent case study for a first analysis of the opportunities available to widows in this region.

2 The Printing House, an (un)Favourable Environment for Women?

The early modern book trade has often been framed implicitly as either a favourable or an unfavourable environment for women. In 1999, the Swiss book dealer Axel Erdmann published a catalogue of his book collection, consisting of works published or printed in Europe between 1501 and 1601, which features publications about women as well as books where women contributed as, amongst others, authors, illustrators or publishers. The catalogue frames this collection as if shattering the silence expected of women in sixteenth-century Europe, an imagery that could easily be applied to the

---

5 Merry Wiesner-Hanks, '*A learned task and given to men alone*: the Gendering of Tasks in Early Modern Germany', *Journal of Medieval and Renaissance Studies*, 25 (1995), pp. 104–106; Marjolein van Dekken, *Brouwen, branden en bedienen. Productie en verkoop van drank door vrouwen in de Noordelijke Nederlanden, circa 1500–1800* (Amsterdam: Aksant, 2010), pp. 19, 243–246. See also Ariadne Schmidt, 'Labour Ideologies and Women in the Northern Netherlands, c.1500–1800', *International Review of Social History*, 56 (2011), pp. 66–67.

6 Andrew Pettegree, 'Printing in the Low Countries in the Early Sixteenth Century', in Malcolm Walsby and Graeme Kemp (eds), *The Book Triumphant: Print in Transition in the Sixteenth and Seventeenth Centuries* (Leiden: Brill, 2011), pp. 9–11 and 13–16.

historiography of women printers.[7] Earlier work on this subject might be seen in the light of an endeavour to acknowledge women's contribution to history. This first body of literature therefore emphasises the life and work of exceptional female owner-managers who boasted long and fruitful careers, like the Parisian Charlotte Guillard (–1557).[8] A second strand of research interested in specific women is concerned with the production and dissemination of heterodox texts. It casts printers as powerful agents through a focus on their contribution to the diffusion of heterodox thought and their subsequent evasion of or conviction by the authorities.[9]

Aside from interest in either women's history or religion, scholars might gravitate towards publicly successful woman printers due to the greater quantity of sources compared to their less visible colleagues. Thus, these women make for interesting case studies.[10] At least, this seems to have been part of the reason why the print maker Volcxken Diericx (–1600) has to this point received more than average scholarly attention compared to other female printers in sixteenth-century Antwerp, even eclipsing her second husband in the process.[11]

By focusing on exceptional owner-managers, this research could unintentionally give the reader the impression that the book trade was a favourable

---

7   Alex Erdmann, *My Gracious Silence. Women in the Mirror of 16th Century Printing in Western Europe* (Luzern: Gilhofer & Ranschburg GmbH, 1999). See especially the catalogue's introduction by Merry Wiesner-Hanks (pp. VIII–XXIV) and the title of the second part of the catalogue on female writers and artisans *Triumph over Silence* (p. 99). Mary Duggan, 'Review: My Gracious Silence', *Libraries & Culture*, 39 (2004), pp. 95–96.

8   For example, Beatrice Beech, 'Charlotte Guillard: A Sixteenth-Century Business Woman', *Renaissance Quarterly*, 36 (1983), pp. 345–367. More recently, see Jimenes, *Charlotte Guillard*.

9   For example: Maureen Bell, 'Seditious Sisterhood: Women Publishers of Opposition Literature at the Restoration', in Kate Chedgzoy, Melanie Hansen and Suzanne Trill (eds), *Voicing Women: Gender and Sexuality in Early Modern Writing* (Keele: Keele University Press, 1996), pp. 185–195; Victoria Christman, 'The Coverture of Widowhood: Heterodox Female Publishers in Antwerp, 1530–1580', *Sixteenth Century Journal*, 42 (2011), pp. 77–97.

10   Although there certainly are studies on all female printers in a region, like: Romeo Arbour, *Les femmes et les métiers du livre en France, de 1600 à 1650* (Paris: Garamond, 1997); Romeo Arbour, *Dictionnaire des femmes libraires en France (1470–1870)* (Geneva: Droz, 2003); Deborah Parker, 'Women in the Book Trade in Italy, 1475–1620', *Renaissance Quarterly*, 49 (1996), pp. 509–541; Helen Smith, *Grossly Material Things: Women and Book Production in Early Modern England* (Oxford: Oxford University Press, 2012).

11   Lydia de Pauw-de Veen, 'Archivalische gegevens over Volcxken Diericx, weduwe van Hieronymus Cock', *De Gulden Passer*, 53 (1975), pp. 15–247; Erik Duverger (ed.), *Antwerpse kunstinventarissen uit de zeventiende eeuw* (14 vols., Brussel: KVAB, 1984–2009), I. 17–37; Joris Van Grieken, Ger Luijten and Jan Van der Stock (eds), *Hieronymus Cock: de renaissance in prent* (Brussels: Mercatorfonds, 2013), pp. 14–19, 22–23, 26–27, 78–79 and 82–83.

environment for female entrepreneurs. For example, women like the publisher Jeanne Giunta (1522?–1584) are, according to Natalie Zemon Davis, "the closest we come in sixteenth century Lyon to the high-level female entrepreneur". In this passage Davis seems to hint at a greater potential for businesswomen in the book trade compared to the other trades featuring in her acclaimed *Women in the Crafts in Sixteenth-Century Lyon*, even though she certainly remains aware of the limited number of women who did become high-level entrepreneurs.[12] Susan Broomhall has worded the same observation, that there was a modest number of successful female entrepreneurs in the book trades, very differently. She stresses the limited scope for the training of women in this male environment. Because families did not imagine their daughters running the business on their own in the future, they did not see why girls should need thorough training in this area. Broomhall also suggests the business role for most widows was that of emergency ad interim in a moment of crisis in the family line. Furthermore, according to her, most widows did not continue their husbands' trade due to debt or second marriages. This led her to conclude that women were not very welcome in the book trade after all.[13]

3   Widowhood as a Window of Opportunity in a Moment of Crisis

While it is certainly true that the number of women who worked in the printing trade remained limited to often invisible daughters and wives – Voet found evidence for only one female wage earner in the rich archives of the *Officina Plantiniana*[14] – it remains unclear precisely how the women who did

---

12   She also mentions that women could primarily find recognition within their neighbourhood but that the printing trade was an exception due to its imprints carrying women's names beyond the neighbourhood. Natalie Zemon Davis, 'Women in the Crafts in Sixteenth-Century Lyon', *Feminist Studies*, 8 (1982), pp. 31 and 66–67.

13   Susan Broomhall, *Women and the Book Trade in Sixteenth-Century France* (Aldershot: Ashgate, 2002), pp. 52–69. Deborah Parker however, suggests that many printer's widows had to continue working precisely because of outstanding debts that could only be paid back by generating an income through their work in the printing house. See Parker, 'Women in the Book Trade in Italy, 1475–1620', p. 522.

14   She was the daughter of collator Merten Gilles and worked from 1583 to 1584 at the *Officina Plantiniana*. Léon Voet, *The Golden Compasses: a History and Evaluation of the Printing and Publishing Activities of the Officina Plantiniana at Antwerp* (2 vols, Amsterdam: Vangendt – London: Routledge & Kegan Paul – New York: Abner Schram, 1969–1972), II. 331. Parker also found that women rarely received payment for work in a printing house. She gives two examples, one of which is about a Venetian printer leaving two of his wife's nieces a sum in his will for their work in his shop. Whether the women were paid for their labour while he was alive, remains uncertain. In any case, these examples again illustrate the

A WINDOW OF OPPORTUNITY

become owner-managers negotiated the transition from invisibility to visibility – a change that was also often visible on the imprints they produced. A first observation is that most women mentioned in these imprints were widows. Although it remains uncertain how many daughters remain hidden behind the rather anonymous designation 'heirs', the presence of a widow seems to have mostly been mentioned explicitly.

Probably, this practice stemmed from the particular status accorded to widows. Although women's possibilities to earn a living through their labour – and master's widows access to profitable work – differed significantly on a local level and were influenced by economic and institutional changes,[15] widowhood placed a woman at the head of the household, acting as a kind of 'deputy husband'.[16] This was also translated into legislation, where, according to Laura Van Aert, the "nuclear family, or what was left of it, was accorded absolute priority, even over the incapable legal status of women". Hence, the power of mother-widows was considerable. Furthermore, Antwerp widows, like many of their peers elsewhere, had the right to continue their husband's trade.[17]

A striking feature of the careers of the 32 widow-printers of sixteenth-century Antwerp is the considerable diversity in terms of the period of time the widow

---

importance of family ties for women's work in the book trade. Parker, 'Women in the Book Trade in Italy, 1475–1620', pp. 519–520.

15 Janine Lanza, *From Wives to Widows in Early Modern Paris: Gender, Economy, and Law* (Aldershot: Ashgate, 2007), pp. 181–184; 222–224 and 228; Sheilagh Ogilvie, *A Bitter Living: Women, Markets, and Social Capital in Early Modern Germany* (Oxford: Oxford University Press, 2006), pp. 6–13 and 206–268; Scarlett Beauvalet-Boutouyrie, *Etre veuve sous l'Ancien Régime* (Paris: Belin, 2001), pp. 264–269; Ariadne Schmidt, 'Women and Guilds: Corporations and Female Labour Market Participation in Early Modern Holland', *Gender & History*, 21(2009), pp. 170–189.

16 Laural Ulrich has coined the term for wives and Martha Howell has also taken it up. One could argue that the term might be extended to widows, who – in the perpetual absence of their husband – took over his responsibilities to ensure the smooth running of family and business. See Laural Thatcher Ulrich, *Good Wives. Image and Reality in the Lives of Women in Northern New England, 1650–1750* (New York: Oxford University Press, 1982), pp. 36–37; Martha Howell, *The Marriage Exchange: Property, Social Place, and Gender in Cities of the Low Countries, 1300–1550* (Chicago: The University of Chicago Press, 1998), pp. 18, 237–238. Also see Ariadne Schmidt, *Overleven na de dood. Weduwen in Leiden in de Gouden Eeuw* (Amsterdam: Prometheus-Bert Bakker, 2001), pp. 74–79.

17 Laura Van Aert, 'The Legal Possibilities of Antwerp Widows in the Late Sixteenth Century', *The History of the Family*, 12 (2007), pp. 288 and 293. For examples from elsewhere, restrictions on widow's right to continue their husbands trade, and a certain flexibility in practice, see, for example, Beauvalet-Boutouyrie, *Etre veuve sous l'Ancien Régime*, pp. 276–277; van Dekken, *Brouwen, branden en bedienen*, pp. 246–248.

was active, the productivity of the firm, and the nature of its production.[18] All of them share the loss of a husband, but between Broomhall's poor widows giving up the printing house entirely and Davis's high-level female entrepreneurs, there are a myriad ways in which printers' widows participated in the book trade. The stories of two widows from important Antwerp printing houses, Steelsius and Plantin-Moretus, just after their husbands died, should shed some light on the negotiations that ensued at such times of crisis. Families had to re-negotiate the way they managed the printing house and distributed its profits after the death of the patriarch. In such cases, both inheritance law and ideas about family hierarchy would have played a role in determining the position women could take up. To my knowledge, the cases of Steelsius and Plantin-Moretus are the only instances where formal agreements between family members in sixteenth-century Antwerp were drawn up (and preserved). This suggests that these agreements were usually made orally within the family and that only in the case of discord and serious negotiation did the need for a formal contract arise. In other families, similar negotiations might have led to a smoother implementation of new arrangements.

4   Negotiating Shares: Anna van Ertborn

Anna Van Ertborn (–1575) married into an established and productive printing house in 1542, as her husband Joannes Steelsius I was a well-known printer. As a widow, she published around 180 books, predominantly religious texts in Latin with a number of Spanish titles. Part of these publications were meant for export to Spain, so van Ertborn and Steelsius's heirs avoided Bible translations and other work in danger of being censured on the Iberian Peninsula.[19]

Van Ertborn's claim to the property of the printing house as a widow would depend on marriage and inheritance laws. During the sixteenth century, Antwerp's laws shifted from favouring kin to favouring the conjugal couple and

---

18   For names and short biographies, see: Heleen Wyffels, 'Weduwen-drukkers in 16de-eeuws Antwerpen', pp. 231–260.

19   Prosper Verheyden, 'Uit het huis van Steelsius', *Tijdschrift Voor Boek- En Bibliotheekwezen*, 8 (1910), pp. 126–129; César Manrique Figueroa, *Cultural Trade Between the Southern Netherlands and New Spain. A History of Transatlantic Book Circuits and Book Consumption in the Early Modern Age* (KU Leuven, unpublished PhD, 2012), pp. 104–105 and 150; Pedro R. León, 'Brief Notes on some 16th-Century Antwerp Printers with Special Reference to Jean Steelsius and his Hispanic Bibliography', *De Gulden Passer*, 54 (1976), 85–87.

the longest living spouse.[20] After Steelsius's death in 1562, his widow became sole guardian of their children and – when she accepted the inheritance – retained her own belongings in addition to half of the communal belongings as well as the urban advantage (*stadts voordeel*), an optional set of personal belongings from the communal fund.[21] The couple's will does not seem to have survived, but it might have altered van Ertborn's rights.[22]

Apart from the widow, there were probably eleven children in the Steelsius household, who would also have had a stake in the future of the printing house. Joannes Steelsius I's first marriage to Margriete Hillen had resulted in two sons and a daughter. Anna van Ertborn, his second wife, probably had at least six children.[23] Steelsius's eldest son from his first marriage, Joannes II, obtained a degree in law, but his brother Frans trained as a printer. Their sister Yda married Nicolaas van der Veken. The only mention of him in connection to the book trade is a note from Plantin, who mentioned that he delivered some books to Joannes Steelsius I through his son-in-law in 1558. Van Ertborn's eldest daughter, Johanna, married the printer Petrus I Bellerus and van Ertborn's son Gillis became a printer as well. Her daughter Marie married Arnout sConincx, who started out as a grocer but turned to bookselling and later printing. Magdalena Steelsius however, took the silk trader Bernard Cordier as her second husband and probably left the printing trade.[24]

With one widow and several children from two marriages interested in the book trade, it seems that deciding on the reorganisation of the Steelsius printing house necessitated some negotiation. Frans Steelsius – who must have been in his mid-20s – apparently wanted to continue in his father's footsteps, whilst Johanna Steelsius had already married Petrus Bellerus, and her

---

20   Kaat Cappelle, '*In de macht, plicht en momboorije van heuren man*. De rechtspositie van de getrouwde vrouw in Antwerpen en Leuven (16ᵈᵉ eeuw)', *Pro Memorie*, 18 (2016), pp. 51–61 and 67.

21   *Ibidem*, pp. 50, 52, 55–58, 67–68; Van Aert, 'The Legal Possibilities of Antwerp Widows', pp. 286 and 293.

22   Antwerp, City Archives, *Aldermens' registry no. 307*, fols. 138v–139r: mention of a lost will of Anna van Ertborn and Joannes Steelsius I, [March?] 1566.

23   Lode Van den Branden traced nine children (five sons and three daughters) for van Ertborn, but Verheyden and Rouzet together mention only six. Brussels, Royal Library of Belgium, *Notes of Van den Branden*, file of Steelsius; Prosper Verheyden, 'Uit het huis van Steelsius', *Tijdschrift Voor Boek- en Bibliotheekwezen*, 8 (1910), pp. 127–128; Anne Rouzet, *Dictionnaire des imprimeurs, libraires et éditeurs des XVᵉ et XVIᵉ siècle dans les limites géographiques de la Belgique actuelle* (Nieuwkoop: B. de Graaf, 1975), pp. 43–44 and 207–209.

24   KBR, *Notes of Van den Branden*, file Steelsius; Verheyden, 'Uit het huis van Steelsius', pp. 127–128; Rouzet, *Dictionnaire des imprimeurs*, pp. 43–44 and 207–209.

brother Gillis was only about 14 years old.[25] Therefore, it was probably the widow Anna van Ertborn and her stepson Frans who needed to come to an agreement and they enlisted the help of a notary to draw up a contract formalising the arrangements for the coming three years, a document signed on 14 July 1562.[26] Possibly, the Steelsius and/or Hillen families wanted to safeguard Frans's interests in this way against the (presumed) threat from his stepmother and her children(-in-law). The Verdussen family, also active in Antwerp, seems to have thought along these lines. In his dissertation, Stijn van Rossem shows that the Verdussens focused on training up sons and did not often marry their daughters to men in the book trade during the seventeenth century. Indeed, Hieronymus Verdussen III considered one of the exceptions to this rule, his in-law Guilielmus Lesteens, a threat.[27]

The contract of 1562 stipulated a division of the risk and profit of the printing house for the next three years. Anna van Ertborn would take on five sixths and Frans Steelsius the remaining sixth. This unequal division points to the considerable negotiation power on the part of the widow. A similar example is mentioned by Janine Lanza: in 1751, the Parisian widow-printer Moreau could negotiate a favourable deal with her son because she controlled the resources – equipment and client base – and because her son would have a greater chance of success in securing a place as master in the guild if he had these assets to back his claim. Their contract stipulated that the son would take on the daily running of the workshop but that the widow would retain authority over the management of the business.[28] Van Ertborn seems to have enjoyed a similar position during the negotiations and retained a great measure of control over the firm.

Although Frans took on a sixth of risk and profit, he was not yet considered capable of running the business with his stepmother because the contract stipulated that her son-in-law, Petrus, would take care of the day-to-day management. During the aforementioned three years, he would in return train Frans

---

25 Johanna Steelsius was born around 1544 and was about 22 years old when her father died. Petrus Bellerus was born around 1531. Lode van den Branden, 'Archiefstukken betreffende het Antwerpse boekwezen in de vijftiende en zestiende eeuw', in Francine De Nave (ed.), *Liber Amicorum Léon Voet* (Antwerp: Vereeniging der Antwerpsche Bibliophielen, 1985), pp. 180–181; Rouzet, *Dictionnaire des imprimeurs*, pp. 207–209.

26 Antwerp, City Archives, *Protocol of Stephanus Claeys van Loemel, no. 544 (1561–1562)*, fol. 22r–22v: contract between Anna van Ertborn and Frans Steelsius concerning the printing house and bookshop 'in den Scilt van Bourgoignen', 14 July 1562.

27 Stijn van Rossem, *Het gevecht met de boeken: de uitgeversstrategieën van de familie Verdussen (Antwerpen, 1589–1689)* (University of Antwerp, unpublished PhD, 2014), pp. 44–48.

28 Lanza, *From Wives to Widows in Early Modern Paris*, pp. 147–149.

A WINDOW OF OPPORTUNITY   17

in the trade. If there had been any unease in the family about potential rivalry between Frans Steelsius and Petrus Bellerus, it seems to have been justified. After the death of Anna van Ertborn in 1576, it was Petrus and his wife Johanna who took over the whole firm, whereas Frans continued in the book trade but not as printer. His stepbrother Gillis Steelsius set up as book trader and moved on to printing under his own sign, that of the Salamander.[29] Johanna Steelsius survived her husband and became manager-owner of the Steelsius-Bellerus firm in around 1600, like her mother had before her.[30]

5   **Family First: Jeanne Rivière**

Little historical interest has been paid to Jeanne Rivière (–1596), the widow of the most iconic of Antwerp printers, Christophe Plantin. She is portrayed as meek, boring and utterly uninterested in her husband's famous printing house. This vein of characterisation might stem from Justus Lipsius's description of Rivière as a good housewife who knew nothing more than she ought to for this task. Léon Voet casts her as a 'loyal helpmate' to her husband with a 'somewhat care-worn appearance'.[31] This fits nicely into a narrative focussing on the two great men of the *Officina Plantiniana*, Christophe Plantin and Jan Moretus I, but glosses over the fact that Rivière held a position of potential great influence in the history of the printing house. She might have been set aside too easily.

From Plantin's death in 1589 until her own in 1596, the imprints of the printing house ran as follows: "ex officina Plantiniana, apud viduam, & Ioannem Moretum".[32] During this period of shared imprints and after Rivière's death, religious books came to dominate the production of the *Officina Plantiniana* and constituted nearly half of the firm's total production, amongst them the liturgical publications the firm would become famous for.[33] Without further

---

29   Rouzet, *Dictionnaire des imprimeurs*, p. 208.
30   Rouzet, *Dictionnaire des imprimeurs*, p. 11.
31   Voet, *The Golden Compasses*, I. 139.
32   Dirk Imhof, *Jan Moretus and the Continuation of the Plantin Press. A Bibliography of the Works Published and Printed by Jan Moretus I in Antwerp (1589–1610)* (2 vols., Leiden: Brill, 2014), I., pp. 2–3.
33   Dirk Imhof stresses that these liturgical books only comprised a fifth of the production under Jan Moretus and hence constitute an important sub-category but not the only type of work published by the firm. Imhof, *Jan Moretus*, I, pp. xxxix–lxxxv; Jan Materné, 'The Officina Plantiniana and the dynamics of the Counter-Reformation, 1590–1650', in S. Cavaciocchi (ed.), *Produzione e commercio della carta e del libro secc. XIII–XVIII. Atti della Ventitresima settimana di studi, 15–20 aprile 1991* (Firenze: Le Monnier, 1992), pp. 481–490.

evidence, the imprints would seem to suggest that widow and son-in-law worked together to continue the firm. However, archival sources tell another story.

Plantin's and Rivière's wills from 1584 and 1588 (with a codicil dated 1589) designated the longest surviving spouse as universal heir, which meant in effect that the highly valuable inheritance would not have been divided amongst Plantin's daughters (and sons-in-law) until Rivière's death.[34] This was not exceptional, as many couples entrusted the care of children and inheritance to the surviving spouse by appointing them universal heirs.[35] In practice, the last will of Plantin threatened to split the family and they had to negotiate a new agreement. On his deathbed, perhaps stemming from a final wish to see his life's work preserved as a whole, the famous printer had confirmed the arrangements of his 1588 will, which greatly favoured one of his sons-in-law above the others. Jan Moretus I was married to Martina Plantin, the second daughter, and had been a loyal and steadfast employee of his father-in-law for 32 years. Therefore, Moretus was well suited to manage the firm he already knew so well.[36]

Needless to say, other heirs took issue with this new plan and it took several months to negotiate a settlement that satisfied everyone reasonably well. Martina and Jan took over the Antwerp branch of the printing house and compensated the other heirs. Interestingly, Jeanne Rivière gave up her share in the inheritance almost completely, only retaining an annuity and the right to remain in her home at the Vrijdagmarkt. In contrast to her daughters, she indeed seems to have forsaken any active participation in the family business while her husband was alive and so perhaps she was glad to hand it over to experienced hands after his death. The settlement ensured that she would have a comfortable retirement while also keeping the peace in her family.[37]

---

34   Maurice Van Durme (ed.), *Supplément à la correspondance de Christophe Plantin* (Antwerp: Nederlandsche boekhandel, 1955), pp. 297–301; Voet, *The Golden Compasses*, I. 162–163; Museum Plantin-Moretus, *Arch. 1181*, no. 4 and 5: wills and codicil of Christophe Plantin and Jeanne Rivière, 14 May 1588 and 7 June 1589.

35   Van Aert, 'The Legal Possibilities of Antwerp Widows', p. 287; Barbara Diefendorf, 'Widowhood and Remarriage in Sixteenth-Century Paris', *Journal of Family History*, 7 (1982), p. 386.

36   Voet, *The Golden Compasses*, I. 162–168; Imhof, *Jan Moretus and the Continuation of the Plantin Press*, I. XXI–XXVIII; Dirk Imhof 'Keeping the Plantin Press Together: Jan Moretus and the Inheritance of Christophe Plantin', *Bulletin Du Bibliophile*, 1 (2011), pp. 119–128.

37   Voet, *The Golden Compasses*, I. 162–168; Imhof, *Jan Moretus and the Continuation of the Plantin Press*, I. XXI–XXVIII; Dirk Imhof 'Keeping the Plantin Press Together', 1 (2011), pp. 119–128.

A WINDOW OF OPPORTUNITY

Given this solution, the naming practice in their imprints did not mirror actual involvement in the printing house at all. It remains up for speculation why Rivière was not simply removed from the imprints after she resigned any official post in the firm.[38] Removing her would have obscured a visible link between the new and the old owner-manager and, thus, reduce the impression of a continuation of the qualitative work customers had come to expect from Plantin. In addition, it could perhaps have been interpreted as offensive to remove the widow from her rightful place, given that Moretus was not a son but only a son-in-law.

Jeanne Rivière is without question the best documented case in sixteenth-century Antwerp of a widow not taking on responsibilities as owner-manager.[39] Next to debt or remarriage as reasons not to take on responsibilities in the firm, Rivière's case illustrates a third one: the next generation. In big firms like the *Officina Plantiniana*, a lot of capital was tied up in stock and ongoing projects. In addition, they had invested in privileges and market shares. These investments and potential profits meant that the family was heavily invested in keeping the printing house running.[40] Therefore, it mattered less who did the actual work, as long as it was done. Avoiding discord and prolonged litigation was crucial and in that perspective, Jeanne Rivière played her role as part of the family perfectly.

6 Re-negotiating Responsibilities

Once a division of responsibilities and income had been decided upon, the arrangement was not set into stone and could be adapted to meet the requirements of changing conditions.[41] One such change was undoubtedly children growing up and taking up more responsibilities. For example, the coming of age of Jan van Liesvelt, who lost his father when he was executed in 1545, is

---

38   Imhof, *Jan Moretus and the Continuation of the Plantin Press*, I. 2.

39   The exact number of women who did so remains uncertain. The same goes for daughters. Broomhall mentions daughters giving up their claims, like the Parisian Claudine and Marguerite Gimbre who renounced their claim on their parents' estate in 1581 in return for an annual and lifelong pension. See Broomhall, *Women and the Book Trade*, p. 60.

40   Lanza mentions for example that Parisian printers almost saw mastership as property in a source from 1777, but that they could not simply hand it down to the next generation due to regulations. It was therefore the accoutrements of mastership i.e. tools, goods, and raw materials that preoccupied artisanal families. See Lanza, *From Wives to Widows in Early Modern Paris*, pp. 43–44.

41   This was also noted by Beauvalet-Boutouyrie, who gives the example of a widow-printer in Paris. See Beauvalet-Boutouyrie, *Etre veuve sous l'Ancien Régime*, pp. 278–279.

likely to have altered the business relationship with his mother Marie Ancxt (–*c*.1566?) as his input in the firm augmented.[42] Gaspard Bellerus I, nephew of Petrus Bellerus I, worked in the printing house of his mother Elisabeth Commers (*c*.1530–1616) for several years before acquiring his own admission privilege from the Privy Council in 1613. In his request, he used his experience in his families' firm as an argument to his advantage.[43]

Another change that had a big impact upon the career of women was marriage. A widow who remarried might, depending on the trade of her new spouse, continue or leave the family business.[44] Mechtelt van den Wouwere (–1612) for example, sold stock, tools and house to Hieronymus Verdussen I upon her remarriage in 1594, but probably remained a book seller for another five years.[45] A widow's business experience, tools, and commercial network could also be an asset to bring to a new marriage.[46] Five of the nine Antwerp widow-printers who remarried chose a new husband within the book trade and one print maker married an engraver and later a painter.[47] For three printers, remarriage and their children reaching adulthood followed a revealing pattern. Lynsken Berckmans (–after 13 September 1592), Elizabeth Pauwijns (imprints 1571–1572) and Engele Wouters (imprints 1534–1535?) all took over the firm from their first husbands before remarrying after a short period of time. At the death of their second husbands, their sons from first marriages – now adults – took over from their stepfathers.[48] These women experienced widowhood with both small children and adult sons, and seem to have adapted their work to these changing circumstances.

---

42 Rouzet, *Dictionnaire des imprimeurs*, p. 128; Heleen Wyffels, 'Marie Ancxt', *Impressae. The Family Networks of Widow Printers* (*Antwerp, Louvain, and Douai, 16th and 17th centuries*), record 142503 (last modified: 8 December 2017). It will become available at: http://www .odis.be/lnk/PS_142503. This database is being compiled for the Ph.D.-project *Women and Work in Early Modern Printing Houses. Antwerp, Douai, and Leuven (1500–1700)*.

43 Brussels, State Archives of Belgium, *Privy Council* (*Spanish period*), 1276/A, no. 29: file admission privilege Gaspard Bellerus, 4 February 1613.

44 Davis, 'Women in the Crafts in Sixteenth-Century Lyon', p. 58; Schmidt, *Overleven na de dood*, pp. 234–237 and 243.

45 Antwerp, City Archives, *Aldermen registry no. 416*, fol. 317r–317v: sale of tools from Mechtelt Van den Wouwere to Hieronymus Verdussen I, 30 September 1595; Antwerp, City Archives, *Aldermen registry no. 416*, fols. 317v–319v: sale of real property from Mechtelt Van den Wouwere to Hieronymus Verdussen I, 16 January 1596; Van Rossem, *Het gevecht met de boeken*, pp. 82 and 249.

46 Lanza, *From Wives to Widows in Early Modern Paris*, pp. 148–149.

47 Elizabeth Pauwijns, Lynsken Berckmans, Johanna Grapheus, Myncken Liefrinck, Volcxken Diericx and Enghele Wouters.

48 Rouzet, *Dictionnaire des imprimeurs*, pp. 108, 204, 215 and 250.

7 Conclusion. Gender and Family Shaping the Printing House

Factors that shaped a widow's possibilities fall into two categories. First, there were concerns all new mangers-owners shared, like the financial situation of the business, its reputation and commercial profile, economic and political climate. Secondly, other factors were more susceptible to be influenced by gendered ideas about work and would make for differences in experience between the women printer and her male colleague, like her marital status, her education and training, her work identity, her familiarity with the running of such a firm, and her position within the family.[49] This last factor seems to have been of significant importance. The organisation of the trade in family businesses meant that husbands and wives, sons(-in-law), daughters(-in-law), and other family members worked together to secure a livelihood through their firm. It is generally accepted that women worked in their family businesses, but this labour often remains obscured due to the nature of the sources. Only by surviving their husbands or fathers did women become visible as owner-managers of printing houses.

Additionally, gendered ideas about work were not in favour of overt female entrepreneurship where women acted as heads of printing houses. The examples from sixteenth-century Antwerp show that this did not make it impossible for women printers to run one. The organisation of the work in the form of a family business in combination with the widow's place in the family hierarchy seem to have created windows of opportunity at the death of a spouse. Widowhood placed a woman at the head of the family and often involved extensive rights over family property. Except for printing houses on the verge of bankruptcy, the family had a lot to gain from continuing the firm, because a considerable amount of its capital would have been invested in tools, stock, and ongoing projects. Hence, widowhood in combination with a prospering printing house gave women a strong bargaining position in the firm. It allowed them to derive sufficient income to sustain themselves and their children. This resulted in various patterns of collaboration between widows, daughters(-in-law), and sons(-in-law). Continually renegotiated, the relationship between family members induced changes in the organisation of work at the level of individual firms over time.

The cases of Jeanne Rivière and Anna van Ertborn indicate that when considering the transmission of printing houses from one owner-manager to another, we ought to take into account the role women played in a family's

---

49 Davis, 'Women in the Crafts in Sixteenth-Century Lyon', pp. 49, 52 and 56; van Dekken, *Brouwen, branden en bedienen*, pp. 23–26.

strife to consolidate its commodities more seriously than we have done thus far. Rivière's case also suggests that it is necessary to widen our understanding of female agency to include other scenarios besides simply taking full control of a printing house. Given her rights to the inheritance as a widow, Rivière probably had to make a conscious choice on what she wanted to do with that power. Provided there are sufficient sources, an analysis of family dynamics after the death of an owner-manager – coupled with a broader sample of women who did not take up the role of owner-manager in their printing house – might therefore result in a more nuanced picture. This would enable us to contextualise visibly successful female printers and take into account constraints on female entrepreneurship while not downplaying the contribution of women to the production of printed texts and images.

CHAPTER 3

The Printing Industry and the Counter-Reformation in Brussels under Archduke Albert and Archduchess Isabella (1598–1633)

Renaud Adam

In early September 1598, while the personnel of the Palace of Coudenberg, seat of the government in Brussels, awaited the end of Philip II's long agony, another household, situated nearby, was readying itself for an event of a very different nature.[1] Catherine Velpius, daughter of the printer Rutger Velpius and wife of his successor, Hubert Anthoine I, was about to give birth, providing her first son, born two years earlier, with a brother.[2] Little Guillaume was finally born on 15 October, a fortnight before the lavish celebrations held in the Church of St Gudula on 30 and 31 October 1598 to mark the death of Philip II.[3]

If the historical resonance of these two events is somewhat unequal, the Anthoine-Velpius family did have something in common with the sovereign rulers of the Spanish Netherlands: their adherence to the Counter-Reformation movement. The dynasty of printers founded by Rutger Velpius and active until 1689, when its last representative passed away, played a major role in the typographic industry of Brussels – an industry which provided the actors of the Counter-Reformation with an essential means of diffusing their ideas.[4]

---

1   The stages of the protracted illness of Philip II, deceased on 13 September 1598, are traced in: Henry Kamen, *Philip of Spain* (New Haven-London: Yale University Press, 1997), pp. 313–316; Geoffrey Parker, *Imprudent King: A New Life of Philip II* (New Haven-London: Yale University Press, 2015), pp. 353–356.
2   Rutger Anthoine was born on the 12 February 1596 (Brussels, Archives of the City, St Gudula, Parish registers, Baptismal certificates, 79, fol. 129).
3   Brussels, Archives of the City, St Gudula, Parish registers, Baptismal certificates, 79, fol. 342. A description of the commemorative service, including the oration delivered by the Bishop of Namur, was published in 1599 by Rutger Velpius under the title *Certaine relation des obseques faicts a Philippe II* (USTC 4221).
4   On this family of printers, see Paul E. Claessens, 'Deux familles d'imprimeurs brabançons: les Velpius et les Anthoine-Velpius (1542 à 1689)', *Brabantica*, 2 (1957), pp. 333–347; Anne Rouzet, *Dictionnaire des imprimeurs, libraires et éditeurs belges des XVe et XVIe siècles dans les limites géographiques de la Belgique actuelle* (Nieuwkoop: De Graaf, 1975), pp. 1–2, 230–232, 242; Koen De Vlieger-De Wilde, *Directory of Seventeenth-Century Printers, Publishers and Booksellers in Flanders* (Antwerp: Vereniging van Antwerpse bibliofielen, 2004), no. 184–189, 222–223.

© KONINKLIJKE BRILL NV, LEIDEN, 2023 | DOI:10.1163/9789004510159_004

24

Looking beyond the particular role of the Anthoine-Velpius family, the aim of this chapter is to assess the extent to which the whole body of printers active in Brussels during the joint reign of Archduke Albert and Archduchess Isabella (1598–1621), and then under Isabella alone (1621–1633), contributed to the Counter-Reformation.[5] The focus on the first third of the seventeenth century is motivated by the fact that these decades not only represent the apogee of the Counter-Reformation in the Spanish Netherlands, but also correspond to a marked growth of the Brussels book industry.[6]

Unfortunately, while books enable authors to continue making their voices heard across the centuries, none of the printers in question left personal accounts of their politico-religious aims and motivations. To glean an idea of their involvement in the Counter-Reformation movement, we are thus obliged to concentrate our inquiry on their typographic production. We shall proceed in three steps: firstly, a general presentation of the printers active in Brussels during the first third of the seventeenth century, their production and the legislation regulating it; secondly, a closer look at the various kinds of religious texts produced during this period; thirdly, a detailed examination of a particularly significant publication within the Counter-Reformation context: Etienne Ydens's *Histoire du saint Sacrement de Miracle*.

1   The Printed Book in Early Seventeenth-Century Brussels: Printers, Production and Legislation

On setting out to explore the typographical production of early seventeenth-century Brussels, we were immediately confronted by a major problem: the

---

5   On the reigns of the archducal couple, see notably Alexandre Pasture, *La restauration religieuse aux Pays-Bas catholiques sous les archiducs Albert et Isabelle (1596–1633)* (Louvain: Uystpruyst, 1933); Werner Thomas and Luc Duerloo (eds), *Albert & Isabella 1598–1621: Essays* (Turnhout: Brepols, 1998); Paul Janssens (ed.), *La Belgique espagnole et la Principauté de Liège 1585–1715* (2 vols., Brussels: La Renaissance du livre, 2006); Luc Duerloo, *Dynasty and Piety: Archduke Albert (1598–1621) and Habsburg Political Culture in an Age of Religious Wars* (Farnham-Burlington: Ashgate, 2012); Dries Raeymaekers, *One Foot in the Palace: The Habsburg Court of Brussels and the Politics of Access in the Reign of Albert and Isabella 1598–1621* (Louvain: Leuven University Press, 2013); Pierre-François Pirlet, *Le confesseur du Prince dans les Pays-Bas espagnols* (Louvain, Leuven University Press, 2018).

6   The history of the Brussel printing industry in the seventeenth century sorely needs to be updated. In the meantime, the most pertinent general studies are Auguste Vincent, 'La typographie bruxelloise aux XVIIe et XVIIIe siècles', in *Histoire du livre et de l'imprimerie en Belgique. Des origines à nos jours* (6 vols., Brussels: Musée du livre, 1923–1934), IV. 9–41; Auguste Vincent, 'L'imprimerie à Bruxelles jusque 1800', in *Le livre, l'estampe, l'édition en Brabant du XVe au XIXe siècle* (Gembloux: Duculot, 1935), pp. 31–48.

THE PRINTING INDUSTRY AND THE COUNTER-REFORMATION 25

glaring absence of high-performance bibliographical tools with which to compile an inventory of the works in question.[7] Contrary to the preceding centuries, no comprehensive bibliography exists for this period.[8] In June 2016, the launch of the beta version of the *Universal Short-Title Catalogue* (USTC) for the period 1601–1650 provided a stopgap. Though far from complete, this offered valuable assistance in accomplishing the painstaking work of reconstituting the catalogue of the Brussels presses during the reign of the archducal couple – an objective we had originally begun working towards in the framework of a research project initiated in 2011.[9] The nucleus of this initial research project was the rich collection of early seventeenth-century printed works preserved in the Royal Library of Belgium.[10] This was subsequently complimented by the consultation of a number of specialised biographies, as well as the catalogues of various libraries located in France, Spain, Germany, Austria, the Netherlands and America, whose collections include works printed in Brussels during the same period. These efforts enabled us to compile a list of slightly under 1,100 preserved works (1,061 to be exact), as well as to identify a certain number of works which have not survived.[11] Notable examples of the latter category include two works by Crisóstomo Henríquez, *Vitas sanctorum Patrum Eremi Dunensis, libros duos* and *Lilia Cistercii*, respectively printed in 1626 and 1626–27 by Jan van Meerbeeck, and which we know about thanks to descriptions given by Carolus Visch in his *Bibliotheca scriptorum sacri ordinis Cisterciensis*

---

7   In 1915, a bibliographic project aimed at taking stock of Brussels book production from the end of the 15th century to 1830 was initiated by several librarians of the Royal Library of Belgium. Unfortunately, this undertaking was abandoned due to career evolutions implying the prioritisation of other projects. See Claude Sorgeloos, 'Un projet de *Bibliographie bruxelloise* (1915)', *In Monte Artium. Journal of the Royal Library of Belgium*, 9 (2016), pp. 127–142.

8   For the 15th and 16th centuries respectively, see the ISTC and the USTC. Complementary bibliographies for these same centuries include: NK, BT, NB.

9   This research project (*Ex officinibus bruxellensis: Printers and Society in Brussels, 17th–18th Century*), was carried out in the Royal Library of Belgium. It was funded for the period 2011–2013 by the Belgian Science Policy Office. We hope to publish the resulting bibliography soon.

10   Between 1999 and 2003, some 30,000 texts printed in Brussels in the 17th and 18th centuries and preserved in Royal Library of Belgium were systematically catalogued. More recent acquisitions have been integrated. The catalogues entries are consultable online: http://www.kbr.be.

11   For the mid-seventeenth century, David F. McKenzie gives the figure of one third of losses: David F. McKenzie, 'The economics of print, 1550–1750: Scales of production and conditions of constraint', in *Produzione e commercio della carta e del libro, secc. XIII–XVIII: atti della "Veintitresima Settimana di studi", 15–20 aprile 1991* ([Florence]: F. Le Monnier [1992]), p. 394.

(published in Cologne, 1656).[12] The original catalogue of the Brussels printers would also have comprised a considerable number of official documents which, ephemeral by nature, have likewise failed to come down to us.[13] Furthermore, it is only reasonable to surmise that a certain number of books and documents printed in Brussels in the early seventeenth century are quietly gathering dust in obscure libraries and archives around the world, unbeknownst to interested bibliographers. In brief, the figures we are working with here are inevitably indicative rather than absolute.

Taking 1,100 as a low approximation of the total number of books printed in Brussels between 1598 and 1633, we can calculate the average number of books produced per year at a little over thirty. Annual production was not, however, constant, as the following graph, tracing production by four-year intervals, illustrates:

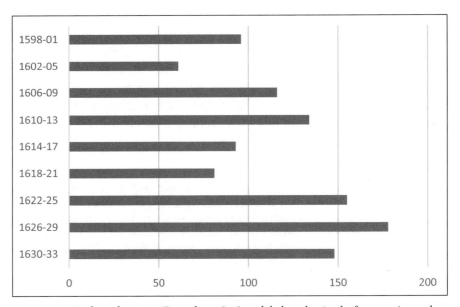

FIGURE 3.1   Book production in Brussels, 1598–1633: global production by four-year intervals

---

12 Carolus de Visch, *Bibliotheca scriptorum sacri ordinis Cisterciensis* (Cologne: Johannes Busaeus, 1656), pp. 67–68.
13 On this subject, see Saskia Limbach, 'Tracing Lost Broadsheet Ordinances Printed in Sixteenth-Century Cologne', in Flavia Bruni and Andrew Pettegree (eds), *Lost Books: Reconstructing the Print World of Pre-Industrial Europe* (Leiden: Brill, 2016), pp. 488–503.

THE PRINTING INDUSTRY AND THE COUNTER-REFORMATION   27

As we can see, after a slight decline in the earliest years, production increased during the first decade of the seventeenth century, then fell off again until 1618–1619, which were the least productive years. Only 38 works were produced in these two years together, while the years 1610–1611 saw over twice as many (84). The rise in prosperity that accompanied the Twelve Years' Truce (1609–1621) does not seem to have had a direct impact on the Brussels printing industry.[14] On the other hand, the renewal of hostilities with the Dutch Republic following this truce corresponded with a clear rise of typographic activities: from 1622 to 1633, some 480 works were printed, i.e. 45 per cent of the total number of works issued from Brussels presses in the period 1598–1633.

The third decade of the seventeenth century was also marked by a wave of new printing houses. Until then, the market had been dominated by only two families: the Anthoine-Velpiuses and the Mommaerts, both active in Brussels since 1585. The founders of these dynasties, Rutger Velpius and Jan Mommaert I, on launching their enterprises, had shrewdly taken advantage of the gap left by the death of the sole printer active in Brussels during the second half of the sixteenth century: Michiel van Hamont.[15] They had also benefitted from the retaking of the town by the troops of Alexander Farnese, Governor of the Spanish Netherlands, on 10 March 1585, which put an end to the Calvinist regime inaugurated a few years earlier.[16] The two printers' particular object of rivalry was the lucrative position of official court printer vacated by Michiel van Hamont.[17] Jan Mommaert I's hopes of obtaining this position rested on his

---

14   On the Twelve Years' Truce, see Simon Groenveld, *Het twaalfjarig bestand, 1609–1621. De jongelingsjaren van de Republiek der Verenigde Nederlanden* (The Hague: Haags Historisch Museum, 2009); Randall Lesaffer (ed.), *The Twelve Years' Truce (1609): Peace, Truce, War and Law in the Low Countries at the Turn of the 17th Century* (Leiden: Brill Nijhoff, 2014).

15   On Michiel van Hamont (active 1554–1583), see Rouzet, *Dictionnaire des imprimeurs*, pp. 87–88; Edmond Roobaert, 'Michiel van Hamont. Hellebaardier van de keizer, rederijker en drukker van de koninklijke ordonnanties en plakkaten', in Frank Daelemans and Ann Kelders (eds), *Miscellanea in memoriam Pierre Cockshaw (1938–2008)* (2 vols., Brussels: Archives et Bibliothèques de Belgique, 2009), I. 465–485; Renaud Adam, '*Men and books under watch*: the Brussels' Book Market in the Mid-Sixteenth Century Through the Inquisitorial Archives', in Shanti Graheli (ed.), *Buying and Selling: The Early Book Trade and the International Marketplace* (Leiden: Brill, 2019), pp. 303–321.

16   On the Calvinist regime in Brussels – surprisingly little studied, contrary to other towns like Ghent of Antwerp –, see Olivier Cammaert, 'L'iconoclasme sous la République calviniste à Bruxelles', in Monique Weis (ed.), *Des villes en révolte. Les 'Républiques urbaines' aux Pays-Bas et en France pendant la deuxième moitié du XVIe siècle* (Turnhout: Brepols, 2010), pp. 47–52.

17   Throughout the Ancien Régime, the status of official court printer represented a highly sought-after economic advantage for printer families. On this subject, see Sébastien Afonso, 'L'imprimé officiel: enjeu et objet de rivalités entre imprimeurs dans les villes du sud des Pays-Bas méridionaux au XVIIe siècle', in Renaud Adam, etc. (eds), *Urban Networks and the Printing Trade in Early Modern Europe (15th–18th Century): Papers*

close friendship with Michiel van Hamont (who had notably served as a witness at his wedding[18]) and for a while his chances looked promising.[19] Finally, however, it was Rutger Velpius who availed himself of the coveted title, apparently on account of his unflagging faithfulness to the Spanish court. Velpius had started out in the printing business by opening a workshop in Louvain in 1556. In 1580, when Alexandre Farnese transferred the seat of government to Mons, Velpius followed him.[20] He set up Mons's first press, entirely dedicated to the Catholic cause.[21] Then, when Farnese moved to Brussels in 1585, Velpius again relocated. It was only natural that such fidelity was rewarded by his appointment as official court printer. This position, which included the exclusive right to reproduce all the documents issued by the central government, enabled Rutger Velpius, then his successor Hubert Anthoine I and, after 1630, Anthoine's widow, to dominate the Brussels book industry. The family, obviously well aware of the advantage it gave them, took care to request the renewal of the appointment every time the end of its term drew near, at least every ten years. The Anthoine-Velpiuses had succeeded in turning the printing of official acts into a dynastic monopoly.[22] The following graph plainly illustrates the Anthoine-Velpius ascendancy:

Presented on 6 November 2009, at the CERL Seminar Hosted by the Royal Library of Belgium (London: CERL, 2010), pp. 53–75.

18 Brussels, Archives of the City, Our Lady of the Chapel, Parish registers, Marriage records, 1575–1598, fol. 30r.

19 Brussels, State Archives, Spanish Private Council, 1276, 9.

20 On the Mons period, see Christine Piérard and Pierre Ruelle, *Les premiers livres imprimés à Mons: fac-similés de la 'Kakogeitnia' de Libert Houthem et du 'Renart decouvert' attribué à Jean Richardot, sortis des presses de Rutger Velpius, en 1580* (Mons: Société des bibliophiles belges, 1966).

21 The catalogue of Velpius's Mons press includes the official ban of outlawry issued by Philip II against William I, Prince of Orange, printed in 1580: *Sommaire et substance du ban et proscription contre Guillaume de Nassau, prince d'Oranges* (USTC 13596).

22 Rutger Rescius and Hubert Anthoine I worked together from 1601 onwards. They requested the renewal of their joint status of official court printer on the 17 August 1609 (Brussels, State Archives, Spanish Private Council, 1276, 134). Rutger Rescius died around 1614–1615. Hubert Anthoine I succeeded him and asked for renewing his grant on 9 August 1625 (Brussels, State Archives, Spanish Private Council, 1277, 93). On 7 November 1634, Hubert Anthoine II obtained the right to print, for a period of ten years, all the edicts, statutes and regulations issued by the court, as his predecessors had been doing for sixty years (Brussels, State Archives, Spanish Private Council, 1278, 77). This privilege was accorded for another ten-year term on 9 May 1645, on 9 February 1658, and again on 27 March 1666 (Brussels, State Archives, Spanish Private Council, 1278, 77; 1279, 94; 1280, 36). After the death of Hubert Anthoine II at the end of October 1670 (Brussels, Archives of the City, St Gudula, Parish registers, Death certificates, 1669–1683, fol. 66v), his son Marcel Anthoine-Velpius obtained the same privilege for ten years (Brussels, State Archives,

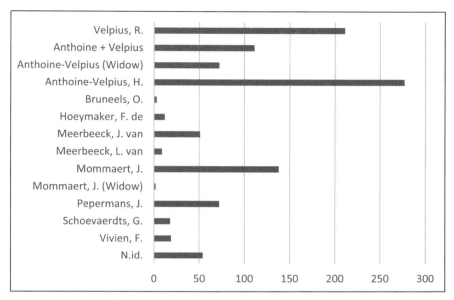

FIGURE 3.2 Book production in Brussels, 1598–1633: market shares of active printers

The catalogue of the Anthoine-Velpius press represents almost 65 per cent of the works published in Brussels during the reign of the archducal couple. All the other printers active at the time occupied considerably smaller parts of the market. Jan Mommaert I (who was succeeded by his widow, Martine van Strael, in September 1631) was the second most important printer in Brussels in the early decades of the seventeenth century, yet his business only represented a little over 13 per cent of the market.[23] Olivier Bruneels managed to make a small name for himself in the years 1608–1609, but disappeared thereafter.[24]

Spanish Private Council, 1280, 36). He died seven years later without heir and was buried on 30 March 1677 (Brussels, Archives of the City, St Gudula, Parish registers, Death certificates, fol. 243r). Four days later, on 4 June 1677, Jean-Théodore Anthoine-Velpius addressed a petition to the Privy Council asking to succeed his brother (Brussels, State Archives, Spanish Private Council, 1280, 3). On 16 May 1689, following the death of the last family representative, Jean-Théodore Anthoine-Velpius, the position of official court printer passed to Eugène-Henry Frickx (Brussels, State Archives, Spanish Private Council, 1280, 10).

23 On Mommaert and his wife, see Paul E. Claessens, 'Deux familles d'imprimeurs brabançons: les Mommaert et les Fricx (1585 à 1777)', in *Brabantica*, 3 (1958), pp. 205–220; Rouzet, *Dictionnaire*, pp. 152–153; De Vlieger-De Wilde, *Directory of Seventeenth-Century Printers*, n° 210.

24 Little is known about Olivier Bruneels. Auguste Vincent, in his glimpse of the history of books in Brussels during the 17th and 18th centuries, refers to him as a simple publisher active between 1608 and 1614 (Vincent, 'La typographie bruxelloise', p. 36). The

As mentioned, around the 1620s, a number of new printers set up in Brussels. Ferdinand de Hoeymaker opened his press in 1619, followed a year later by Jan Mommaert I's nephew, Jan Pepermans.[25] Neither rose to heights of the Anthoine-Velpius press, nor even that of the Mommaerts. In fact, the Hoeymaker press closed down after only five years of activity; the Pepermans after fifteen. In 1624, another hopeful young entrepreneur, Jan van Meerbeeck, set up business.[26] And in 1632 his brother (?) similarly invested in the typographical adventure – possibly with the aim of taking the place of Jan, who ceased his activities in 1632.[27] The two new printers who met with the best success were Govaerdt Schoevaerdts and François Vivien, respectively active from 1625 and 1627.[28] Both managed to gain a real foothold in the market and their presses continued to function until the early 1660s.

Before considering the contents of the publications issued from the Brussels presses in the first thirty years of the seventeenth century, it is necessary to evoke rapidly the legislation which regulated the printing industry at the time. This legislative aspect was very much an actual concern and one which the sovereign rulers took a direct interest in. On 11 March 1616, the archducal couple notably issued an edict laying down a strict set of rules for printers to abide by.[29] The earliest regulations of this kind issued by the Habsburgian

---

USTC includes several books signed with the Hispanicised form of his name, *Olivero Brunello* (USTC 1506460, 1436008, 1514809). The archives of the Private Council contain a document, dated 7 November 1607, granting the "sworn printer" and bookseller Olivier Bruneels the right to print, in both Spanish and French, Francisco López de Úbeda's *Book of Entertainment of the Picaro Justina* (Brussels, State Archives, Spanish Private Council, 1276, 125). The Spanish version issued in 1608 (USTC 5023841). No copy of the French version has been preserved, if indeed it was ever published: it was not uncommon for printers to request the right to publish texts in several languages, and then omit to publish one or several of the projected translations.

25   On these two printers, see Vincent, 'La typographie bruxelloise', p. 36; Claessens, 'Deux familles d'imprimeurs brabançons', p. 209; De Vlieger-De Wilde, *Directory of Seventeenth-Century Printers*, n° 202, 212.

26   Vincent, 'La typographie bruxelloise', p. 36; Bernard Antoon Vermaseren, *De katholieke Nederlandsche geschiedschrijving in de XVIe en XVIIe eeuw over den opstand* (Maastricht: Van Aelst, 1941), pp. 213–214, 247–248; De Vlieger-De Wilde, *Directory of Seventeenth-Century Printers*, no. 207.

27   Vincent, 'La typographie bruxelloise', p. 36.

28   François Van Ortroy, 'Schoevaerdts (Godefroid)', in *Biographie nationale* [*de Belgique*] (44 vols., Brussels: Bruylant, 1866–1986), XXI. 812–820; Vincent, 'La typographie bruxelloise', p. 36; André-M. Goffin, *L'imprimerie à Namur de 1616 à 1636* (Namur: Vieux-Quartier), 1981, pp. 30–34; De Vlieger-De Wilde, *Directory of Seventeenth-Century Printers*, no. 215, 224.

29   The document was printed and distributed by Hubert Anthoine I in French and Dutch, under the following titles: *Ordonnance, statut et placcart de Noz Souverains Seigneurs et Princes les Archiducqz d'Austrice, Ducqs de Brabant &c. Sur le faict de l'imprimerie, vente &*

THE PRINTING INDUSTRY AND THE COUNTER-REFORMATION

authorities date back to early sixteenth century, when a commercial dispute between two typographs led to the first conferral of the exclusive privilege in the Southern Low Countries (1512).[30] Over the following decades, as the Reformation movement gained ground, the government of the Southern Low Countries began to impose increasingly restrictive regulations on the printing industry. On the 28 September 1520, the first regulations against heresy were ordained in Antwerp.[31] Penned in a single day by Mercurino Gattinara, Grand Chancellor of the Holy Roman Empire, Luís Marliano, Bishop of Tuy, and Erard de La Marck, Prince-Bishop of Liège, the text was based on the pontifical bulls *Inter sollicitudines* and *Exsurge domine*, brought from Rome by the papal nuncio, Girolamo Aleandro. A few days later, the first auto-da-fé of Reformation books was organized in Louvain. Then, on the 22 March 1521, a law was issued in Mechelen prohibiting the printing, sale, acquisition, possession and reading of Lutheran books throughout the Netherlands, under pain of the confiscation of all belongings and other unspecified punishments. Less than two months later, on 8 May 1521, Charles v promulgated the Edict of Worms, which extended the prohibition to all works attacking the Roman Church, the pope, the ecclesiastical community and the University of Louvain. In the wake of this, the legislation against the heretics was progressively completed by the edicts of 1526, 1529, 1540, 1546 and 1550, then, under Philip II, those of 1556, 1562, 1568, 1570, 1571 and 1572.

While clearly demonstrating the authorities' desire to stamp out heresy, this relentless issuing of edicts inevitably raises questions about their efficiency. The archducal couple, it would seem, were perfectly aware of the challenge

---

apport de plusieurs sortes de livres, refrains, & images en ce Pays de Pardeça (USTC 1507533); *Ordonnantie ende placcaet vande Eertshertogen Onse Souvereine Princen Hertogen van Brabant, &c. ghemaeckt op het stuck van het drucken, vercoopen ende inbrenghen van verscheyden soorten van boecken, refereynen ende beelden, in de Landen van herwaertsovere* (USTC 1001796).

30 On printing legislation in the Early Modern Southern Netherlands, see André Puttemans, *La censure dans les Pays-Bas autrichiens* (Brussels: Académie royale de Belgique, 1935), pp. 13–27; Aline Goosens, *Les inquisitions modernes dans les Pays-Bas méridionaux (1520–1633)* (2 vols., Brussels: Éditions de l'Université de Bruxelles, 1997–1998), I. 50–171; Jeroom Machiels, *Privilège, censure et index dans les Pays-Bas méridionaux jusqu'au début du XVIIIᵉ siècle* (Brussels: State Archives, 1997), pp. 72–113; Renaud Adam, 'The Profession of Printer in the Southern Netherlands before the Reformation: Considerations on Professional, Religious and State Legislations', in Wim François, Violet Soen and Dries Vanysacker (eds), *Church, Censorship and Reform in the Early Modern Habsburg Netherlands* (Turnhout: Brepols, 2017), pp. 13–25; Renaud Adam, 'La contrefaçon dans les anciens Pays-Bas (XVᵉ–XVIIᵉ siècles)', *Histoire et civilisation du livre. Revue internationale*, 13 (2017), pp. 17–37.

31 No copy of the document has been preserved; its contents have been established thanks to the contents of the edict of 1521. See Goosens, *Les inquisitions modernes*, pp. 48–49.

that curtailing the liberty of the presses represented, since their 1616 edict was headed by the following words:

> as we are duly made aware of the excesses and disturbances occurring abroad by the daily accounts issued by our country's presses, as well as the importation and sale in these establishments of all kinds of books, slogans and images, not only contrary to our holy faith and Catholic and Apostolic religion, but also to all decent behaviour[32]

Drawing on previous edicts, the body of the text comprises 16 principal rules. Printers were under obligation to register with the competent authorities: failure to do so was punishable by exile and a heavy fine (300 guilders). They were likewise obliged to prove both their technical competence as printers and their attachment to Catholic orthodoxy. No book could be printed without permission from the central governmental and religious authorities, and all books were to contain, either on the first or last page, a summary of the visit of control effectuated by the religious authorities, together with the official text of authorisation. Each and every publication also had to include the name of the printer and the date and place of printing – this with an aim to stemming the ever-increasing tide of anonymously-penned books. Shopfronts too were targeted: all printers were obliged to hang the sign of a printing press over their establishments. Finally, in order to ensure that no "indecent or scandalous" text was sold on the open market, books imported from abroad were obligatorily submitted to inspection by the religious authorities prior not only to their sale, but before the undoing of their packaging. To the same end, all books printed in the Dutch Republic were purely and simply prohibited.

While the legislative arsenal mobilised to control the printing profession was undeniably restrictive, it did not lessen book production in Brussels. As mentioned, during the reign of Albert and Isabella, some 1100 publications issued from the town's presses – almost half the number printed in Douai, one of Europe's major publishing centres at the time, and well above that of towns such as Liège (which produced some 550 works) or Louvain (which only managed 500).[33]

---

32   "comme nous sommes deuement advertis des excez et désordres qui se commentent journellement en nos pays de par-deçà par l'imprimerie, vente et apport en iceux de plusieurs sortes de livres, refrains et images, non seulement contraires à notre sainte foy et religion catholique, apostolique romaine, mais aussi à toutes bonnes mœurs", quoted by Jean Barthelemy Vincent, *Essai sur l'histoire de l'imprimerie en Belgique, depuis le XVme jusqu'à la fin du XVIIIme siècle* (Brussels, J. Delfosse, 1867), pp. 163–164.

33   Sources: USTC & Renaud Adam, Nicole Bingen, *Lectures italiennes dans les pays wallons à la première Modernité (1500–1630)* (Turnhout: Brepols, 2015), p. 44.

What type of works were printed in Brussels? And in what proportions? To answer these questions, we inventoried the town's production in five main categories, organised in four-year intervals, are shown in the following table:

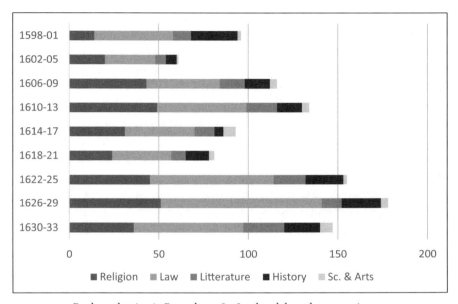

FIGURE 3.3   Book production in Brussels, 1598–1633: breakdown by categories

Publishing activity in Brussels under the archducal couple was clearly dominated by legal texts. The 445 works in this category amount to just under half the total production. The vast bulk of these were official documents issued either by the central government or local or regional institutions (making it easy to understand why the Anthoine-Velpius family were careful to renew their exclusive privilege to print this kind of document). Running second were religious texts: the 310 works we have been able to inventory represent a little over a quarter of the total publications for this period (we shall consider these religious works in more detail below). In joint third place come literary and historical works (each represented by some 100–150 works). The literary works include prose, poetry, theatre and epistolary volumes, as well as numerous treatises and manuals, notably on how to perfect one's own language or learn foreign ones. Approximately half of the historical works deal with recent events: military exploits, political affairs such as the assassination of the King of France, accounts of ceremonial entrances, etc. They also include numerous texts written by historians of the Low Countries – notably Jean-Baptiste Gramaye, Aubertus Miraeus and Antonius Sanderus – and several works on Central Europe – cradle of the Habsburg dynasty –, the Far East and America. The categories least represented are science and the arts: only thirty or so works between them. Treatises on military arts are not however lacking, though this is hardly surprising, since the period under consideration fell in the midst of the Eighty Year War, during which Brussels was the main base of the Flemish army.[34] Finally, a particularly noteworthy publication was the catalogue of Charles de Croÿ III's library, printed on the occasion of its sale in 1615 by Rutger Velpius and Hubert Anthoine I, and the first of its kind in the Spanish Low Countries. The sole remaining copy is today in the private collection of the Dukes of Arenberg in Enghien (Belgium).[35]

To appraise fully the respective importance of these different categories of the Brussels presses catalogue, it is necessary to deal in precise quantities. To do so, we are obliged to consider the units we use to take account these presses' output. Using the titles of published works as units certainly enables us to gain a certain picture of their production. This method overlooks, however, the material requirements of different types of works. Small devotional books written in a popular vein, for example, did not require anything like the same quantity of raw materials as bibles, nor, consequently, the same financial outlay.[36] A more accurate method than the title-counting one is that based on the number of sheets needed for a given book. This reduces the countable unit to what actually passed through the press. The notion of "sheet" is a very precise one: contemporary contracts were not worded in terms of either "pages" or "folios"; what counted was the number of sheets of paper, that is to say, the actual volume of paper needed for a given print run. That said, counting in this way does not rule out all difficulties. Since the books which have come down to us are not always complete, we are not always able to calculate the exact volume of paper they necessitated. Consequently, we are again obliged to underline the indicative rather than absolute nature of the data obtained in the course of this bibliometric inquiry.

---

34 On the Flemish army, see Geoffrey Parker, *The Army of Flanders and the Spanish Road, 1567–1659: The Logistics of Spanish Victory and Defeat in the Low Countries' Wars* (Cambridge: Cambridge University Press, 2004); Charles-J.A. Leestmans, *Soldats de l'armée des Flandres. Essai sur la vie quotidienne des armées aux Pays-Bas espagnols de 1621 à 1715* ([Bothey]: Par quatre chemins; Brussels: [Ch.-J. Leestmans], 2013).

35 Not included in the USTC, this catalogue is reproduced in facsimile, accompanied by an historical and codicological study, in Pierre Delsaerdt, Yann Sordet (eds), *Lectures princières et commerce du livre. La bibliothèque de Charles III de Croÿ et sa mise en vente* (2 vols., Paris: Édition des Cendres, 2017).

36 On the different methods of measuring print production, see Jean-François Gilmont, 'Prendre les mesures du livre', in Gilmont, *Le livre & ses secrets* (Louvain-la-Neuve: Université catholique de Louvain. Faculté de philosophie et lettres; Geneva: Droz, 2003), pp. 281–295.

This being, the following graph clearly illustrates how counting by sheets offers a very different picture of Brussels book production than counting by titles:

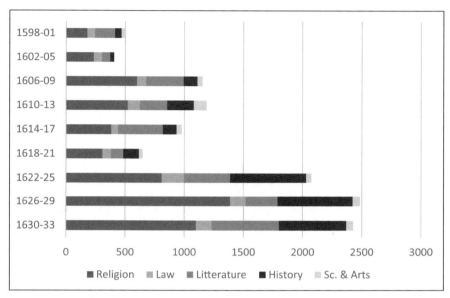

FIGURE 3.4 Book production in Brussels, 1598–1633: paper requirements of the different literary categories

Though the curves of production remain close, a distinct difference can be observed in the respective importance of the various types of publications. The difference between legal and religious works is particularly flagrant. The former suddenly appears almost trivial: 450 titles required only 900 sheets, while 310 religious works necessitated 5,500. This difference is of course easily explained: with a few exceptions, legal publications consisted entirely of edicts and regulatory texts issued by the various Brussels authorities and even the most important of these were relatively concise. The 1616 edict issued by the archducal couple to regulate the printing industry, for example, was printed on a single sheet of paper. The French version of Justus Lipsius's account of the miracle of Our Lady of Halle, printed by Rutger Velpius in 1606, on the other hand, required 20 sheets.[37] To take stock of publishing output at this time, it thus seems that we need to combine at least two methods of counting.

In terms of language, Dutch was the most used, as the following graph illustrates:

---

37   USTC 1506272.

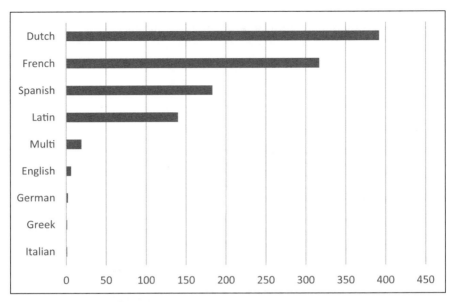

FIGURE 3.5   Book production in Brussels, 1598–1633: breakdown by language

Almost 40 per cent of the works published before 1633 were in Dutch. French books counted for just under 30 per cent. The reign of Albert and Isabella saw a considerable boom of Spanish books, which, after having occupied a very small percentage of the market throughout the sixteenth century, rose progressively to third place at 17.2 per cent: the court, largely composed of Spanish speakers, was clearly avid for texts written in this language.[38] Latin arrived in

---

38   On the Spanish faction of the court and the market of Spanish books in Brussels, see Sébastien Afonso, 'Diffusion de la foi catholique et impression de livres religieux en espagnol à Bruxelles, 1585–1660', in Isabelle Parmentier (ed.), *Livres, éducation et religion dans l'espace franco-belge, XVe–XIXe siècles* (Namur: Presses universitaires de Namur, 2009), pp. 99–113; Cesar Manrique Figueroa, *Cultural Trade between the Southern Netherlands and New Spain: A History of Transatlantic Book Circuits and Book Consumption in the Early Modern Age* (2 vols., unpublished PhD, KU Leuven, 2011–2012); Cesar Manrique Figueroa, 'Los impresores bruselenses y su producción dirigida al mercado hispano, siglos XVI–XVII. El caso de la imprenta del Águila de Oro de Rutger Velpius, Hubert Anthoine-Velpius y la imprenta de los Mommaert', *Erebea. Revista de Humanidades y Ciencias Sociales*, 2 (2012), pp. 205–226; Thomas Werner, 'The "Spanish Faction" at the court of the Archdukes Albert and Isabella', in René Vermeir, Dries Raeymaekers and José Eloy Hortal Muñoz (eds), *A Constellation of Courts: The Courts and Households of Habsburg Europe, 1555–1665* (Louvain: Leuven University press, 2014), pp. 167–221; Renaud Adam, 'Spanish Books in Michiel van Hamont's Bookshop (1569): a Case Study of the Distribution of Spanish Books in Sixteenth-Century Brussels', *Quarendo*, 48:4 (2018), pp. 300–316.

fourth place (13.2 per cent). The number of works printed in other languages was minor, though not entirely negligible: as far as we have been able to count, 19 books were printed in a combination of languages, six in English and two in German; Italian and Greek seem to have been rare, with only one in each language.[39] These figures reflect both the political situation in Brussels and the multilingualism which reigned there at the time. Pierre Bergeron, in his travel journal of 1619, evoked the linguistic customs of Brussels in the following manner:

> The town of Brussels is very large in size, containing a good number of gardens, prairies, woods, parks, promenades and other vast places [...], there is the chancellery, where [convenes] the Council, composed of a president and sixteen councillors. The chancellor acts as lieutenant of the prince in matters of justice. There is also the Council of the Prince, composed of all officers and advisors, for councils of state and war. All the requests presented in these councils are in Flemish, French or Spanish, these three languages being common in Brussels, particularly French, since Spanish is only for the court. In both Antwerp and Brussels, there are schools for learning the French language, etc.[40]

2   Religious Books

Religious works represent about a third of the total number of works printed in Brussels during the reign of the archducal couple; the volume of paper they required represents over half that required for the total number of published works (see graphs 3 and 4). The Brussels presses thus clearly

---

39   On the diffusion of Italian books in Brussels, see Renaud Adam, 'Le livre italien à Bruxelles (1500–1650)', in Renaud Adam, Chiara Lastraioli, Giulia Ventrella (eds), *Itinéraires du livre italien à la Renaissance: regards sur la Suisse romande, les anciens Pays-Bas et la Principauté de Liège* (Paris: Classiques Garnier, 2019), pp. 127–158.

40   "La ville de Brusselles est fort grande de circuit, contenant plusieurs jardins, prez, bois, parcs, pourmenoirs et autres lieux vastes [...], il y a la chancellerie du païs, où le Conseil, composé d'un président et de seize conseillers. Le chancelier est comme lieutenant du prince en la Justice ; mais il y a encore le Conseil des princes avec tous officiers et conseillers pour les Conseils d'Estat et de guerre. Toutes les requestes présentées en ces Conseils sont en flamand, françois ou espaignol, ces trois langues estans communes à Brusselles, mais plus encores le françois, car l'espaignol n'est que pour la court; et mesmes à Anvers et Brusselles, y a escoles pour apprendre la langue françoise, etc.", in Henry Michelant (ed.), *Voyage de Pierre Bergeron ès Ardennes, Liège & Pays-Bas en 1619* (Liège: Société des bibliophiles liégeois, 1875), p. 326.

represented an important means of communication for the spokesmen of the Counter-Reformation. While none of the printers seem to have specialised in any one field of religious literature, all seem to have been keen to publish devotional, hagiographic and spiritual texts. Naturally enough, too, they all avoided publishing liturgical books, this sector of the market being at the time the preserve of the Antwerpian presses and notably that of the Plantin-Moretus family, who benefitted from highly profitable privileges in this field.[41]

As far as devotional texts and miraculous literature were concerned, the widespread appeal of the Marian cult, the Eucharistic cult and cult of the saints was notably strengthened by the publication of numerous minor works – generally in octavo format – destined to assist Catholics in the daily practice of their faith.[42] Philip Numan's description of the miracles ascribed to the Virgin of Scherpenheuvel, published in French, Dutch and Spanish, were notable best-sellers, totalling 19 editions between 1604 and 1618.[43] This success was certainly not unrelated to the archducal couple's strong attachment to this place of worship. Similarly popular was the Spanish version of Giles of Orval's account of the martyr of the twelfth-century Prince-Bishop of Liège, Albert of Louvain, published by the Anthoine-Velpiuses.[44] Publications relating to local cults made up a significant part of the catalogue of the Brussels printers as a whole, ranging from descriptions of the celebration of the town's Eucharistic miracle to texts intended to heighten devotional fervour for the Virgin of the Seven Sorrows and Our Lady of the Rosary.[45] The Brussels printers also contributed to promote the cults of saints linked to various monastic orders that took an active role in the Counter-Reformation movement by publishing accounts of the exemplary lives or martyrdom of their founders or members. In 1633, for example, Lucas van Meerbeeck printed Antonius Sanderus's works

---

41   Léon Voet, *The Golden Compasses: A History and Evaluation of the Printing and Publishing Activities of the 'Officina Plantiniana' at Antwerp* (2 vols., Amsterdam: Vangendt – London: Routledge & Kegan Paul – New York: Abner Schram, 1969–1972); Benito Rial Costas, 'International Publishing and Local Needs: The Breviaries and Missals Printed by Plantin for the Spanish Crown', in Matthew McLean and Sara Barker (eds), *International Exchange in the Early Modern Book World* (Leiden: Brill, 2016), pp. 15–30.

42   On the Marian cult in the Netherlands under the Archduke Albert and the Archduchess Isabella, see Luc Duerloo, 'Archducal Piety and Habsburg Power', in Thomas Duerloo (eds), *Albert & Isabella*, pp. 271–276; Annick Delfosse, '*La Protectrice du Païs-Bas'. Stratégies politiques et figures de la Vierge dans les Pays-Bas espagnols* (Turnhout: Brepols, 2009).

43   The USTC lists 16; the other three were detected through our own research (USTC 5041817, 1001556, 1002607, 1001559, 1002606, 5009514, 1506265, 1002282, 1002605, 1506306, 1005023, 1002285, 1002222, 1002221, 1002604, 1001558).

44   The original text was written in Latin in the 13th century (USTC 1115783).

45   On the Eucharistic cult in Brussels, see *infra* p. [40–44].

THE PRINTING INDUSTRY AND THE COUNTER-REFORMATION   39

on the lives of Saint Angelus of Jerusalem and Andrea Corsini – both venerated by the Carmelites.[46] Six years earlier, Jan van Meerbeeck (Lucas's father?) had published the bull issued by Gregory XV decreeing the canonisation of Philip Neri.[47] Let us also note Gaspar Maximilien Van Habbeke's account of the celebrations organised in honour of Saint Ignatius of Loyola and Saint Francis Xavier, published by Jan Pepermans in 1622.[48]

In the field of spiritual literature, Spanish influence was strong in Brussels, as elsewhere in Europe.[49] The ideas of Teresa of Ávila and figures like Thomas of Jesus found particularly fertile ground in Brussels, where their works were readily published.[50] Within this milieu, it was however Saint Teresa's spiritual advisor, Jerónimo Gracián de la Madre Dios who met with the greatest success. He began publishing in Brussels shortly after his arrival in 1606, in the suite of the Marquis of Guadalest, the newly appointed Spanish Ambassador.[51] Gracián's first Brussels publication issued from the press of Jan Mommaert I in 1608; twenty-five others followed between then and his death in 1614, and a final post-mortem work appeared in 1617.[52] Jerónimo Gracián de la Madre Dios was in fact the most published author in Brussels during the reign of the archducal couple. Let us note in passing that his works were only published in their original language. That said, the Spanish were clearly more intent on imposing their particular form of spirituality than their language. Demonstrating this, the writings of Archduchess Isabella's confessor, Andreas de Soto, also highly

---

46   USTC 1004154, 1004153.

47   This document, not included in the USTC, was unearthed through our own research: *Bulla canonizationis S. Philippi Nerii congregationis oratorii fundatoris, quem Gregorius XV. una cum Beatis Isidoro, Ignatio, Francisco & Teresia, Sanctorum numero adscripsit, a S.mo D.N. Urbano VIII. expedita ... iuxta exemplar Romae* (Brussels: L. van Meerbeeck, 1626) [Brussels, Royal Library of Belgium, II 16.566 A 8].

48   USTC 1005135. On these ceremonies, see Annick Delfosse, 'From Rome to the Southern Netherlands: Spectacular Sceneries to Celebrate the Canonization of Ignatius of Loyola and Francis Xavier', in Jennifer Mara DeSilva (ed.), *The Sacralization of Space and Behavior in the Early Modern World* (Burlington: Ashgate, 2015), pp. 141–159.

49   On France, see: Henri-Jean Martin, *Livre, pouvoirs et société à Paris au XVIIe siècle (1598–1701)* (2 vols., Geneva: Droz, 1969), I. 132–135.

50   References for Teresa of Ávila: USTC 1002967, 1506350, 1002283, 5013063, 5009464, 5016379, 5040342, 1002286. References for Thomas of Jesus: USTC 5040481, 5040323, 5026216, 5035001, 1009623, 1009624.

51   Werner Thomas, 'Jerónimo Gracián de la Madre Dios, la corte de Bruselas y la política religiosa en los Países Bajos meridionales, 1609–1614', in René Vermeir, Maurits Ebben and Raymond Fagel (eds), *Agentes e identidades en movimiento. España y los Países Bajos Siglos XVI–XVIII* (Madrid: Sílex Ediciones, 2011), pp. 289–312.

52   USTC 5040337, 5007070, 5040723, 5009343, 5026566, 5006603, 5003961, 5007071, 5006605, 5042007, 5029816, 5029797, 5040338, 5040339, 5007069, 5014543, 1004461, 5021809, 5029841, 5042047, 5033880, 5040322, 1507156, 5040343, 1003637, 5032287, 5007073.

appreciated in Brussels, were published in French and Dutch as well as Spanish. Twenty of his works (including some re-editions) were printed in Brussels in the first third of the seventeenth century.[53] It is also interesting to note that when Francis de Sales's *Introduction à la vie dévote* was came out in Brussels, it was in Sebastian Fernandez de Eyzaguirre's Spanish translation rather than the original French.[54] Presumably, Hubert Anthoine I, who printed it, reckoned that anyone wishing to read it in French could easily acquire it from the French presses, just as Dutch-speaking readers could have easily turned to the presses of Antwerp or Ghent for the Dutch translation. Amongst the local authors whose works were published directly in Dutch translation, a notable example is the great fifteenth-century mystic Denis Ryckel (also known as Denis the Carthusian), whose works, originally penned in Latin, had an important influence on the spirituality of the fifteenth and sixteenth centuries. Between 1626 and 1628, three texts were printed by three different Brussels printers: Hubert Anthoine I, Govaert Schoevaerdts and François Vivien.[55]

Finally, it is worth underlining the considerable success of the Jesuit Lodewijk Makeblijde's catechism, four editions of which issued from the Mommaert press between 1609 and 1621: three in Dutch and one in Spanish, translated by Claudio Christoval Scheyfve.[56] Written at the request of the Provincial Council of Mechelen (26 June–20 July 1607), this work came to replace Peter Canisius's catechism and remained in use for many years.[57] In 1620, Mommaert also printed Makeblijde's commentary on his own catechism.[58]

3   Etienne Ydens's *Histoire du Saint Sacrement de Miracle*

To finish this account of the Brussels printing industry in the first third of the seventeenth century, it is useful to examine one particular work: the *Histoire du saint Sacrement de Miracle* by Etienne Ydens, canon of St Gudula. Though only a relatively minor author, Ydens played a role in the war waged by the

---

53   The USTC includes eighteen: 440410, 1506090, 5040335, 5040336, 5005898, 5016911, 5029783, 5027462, 1005025, 1507204, 1507189, 1002544, 5025892, 5040326, 3011548, 1002585, 5033388, 5036336. On de Soto's relationship with Isabella, see: Pirlet, *Le confesseur du Prince*, pp. 129–146.

54   USTC 5023651.

55   USTC 1005335, 1024557, 1002521.

56   USTC 1002505, 1002498, 1002588, 5040346.

57   Victor Vander Haeghen, 'Makeblyde (Louis)', in *Biographie nationale [de Belgique]* (44 vols., Brussels: Bruylant, 1866–1986), XIII. 187–190.

58   USTC 1002401.

THE PRINTING INDUSTRY AND THE COUNTER-REFORMATION 41

archducal couple against heresy and his work provides an eloquent illustration of how the religious book market catered to this end during their reign.

The *Histoire du saint Sacrement de Miracle* relates a local legend involving the theft and desecration of hosts by Jews from the Brabant region in the late fourteenth century, the hosts' miraculous reaction and the Jews' punishment.[59] In the dedication to the Archduchess, Ydens explains how he was motivated to take up his pen by the desire to provide pilgrims who spoke neither Dutch nor Latin with a French version of the story. This claim made clear his personal engagement in the fight against Protestantism: the story of the Brabant host desecration was at the time considered as a prefiguration of the wrongdoings of the Reformed Christians who repudiated the dogma of transubstantiation.

The work was printed in 1605 by Rutger Velpius. The colophon and the title page only indicate the year, however a number of chronological indications contained within its pages allow us to narrow down the date: Ydens received permission to publish his work from the official censor, Pierre Vinck (dean of his chapter), on 25 February 1605; the exclusive privilege to print the book for a duration of six years was obtained by Velpius from the Council of Brabant the following month; the dedicatory epistle was signed and dated by the author in Brussels on 14 July. Since it was customary to print the introductory passages of a book last, it is probable that the *Histoire du saint Sacrement de Miracle* issued from the press shortly after this date, particularly as it seems likely that all involved would have been keen to bring it out in time for the annual pilgrimage to the Blessed Sacrament which took place, that year, on the Sunday 17 July. Thus, the whole process – from the authorisation to publish the book to its being put on the market – appears to have taken a total of five months.

The financial conditions surrounding the printing of the book are known to us through the written response, dated 1607, to Ydens's application to the archducal couple for help covering the costs involved. In his application, Ydens had complained of not having received due recompense for his book and of having been obliged to spend over the annual income of his living to have it printed[60]:

---

59 USTC 1003120. On what follows, see Renaud Adam, 'L'*Histoire de Saint sacrement de Miracle* d'Étienne Ydens (1605), œuvre de dévotion ou œuvre polémique?', *Revue Belge de Philologie et d'Histoire*, 92 (2014), pp. 413–433; Id., 'Ydens, Etienne ou Steven', in *Nouvelle biographie nationale* (14 vols., Brussels: Académie royale de Belgique, 1988–2018), XIII. 345–346.

60 'Le chanoine Ydens, auteur de l'Histoire du Saint-Sacrement-de-Miracle de Bruxelles, obtient un subside de 400 livres', *Analectes pour servir à l'histoire ecclésiastique de la Belgique*, 9 (1874), p. 374; Jules Finot, 'Les subventions accordées aux Littérateurs, aux Savants et aux Artistes par les Gouverneurs des Pays-Bas au XVIIe siècle relevées dans les comptes de la recette générales des finances', *Annales du Comité flamand de France*, 9 (1891), p. 175.

HISTOIRE DV S. SACREMENT DE MIRACLE.

REPOSANT A BRVXELLES, en l'Eglise Collegiale de S. Goudele, & des Miracles faictz par iceluy.

Par M. ESTIENNE YDENS *Bruxellois, Prestre Licēt. en la S. Theol. & Chanoine dicelle Eglise.*

L'autre page mōstrera ce qui est adjouté a ceste Histoire.

A BRVXELLES,
Par Rutger Velpius, Imprimeur juré de la Cour, a l'Aigle d'Or, l'an 1605.

FIGURE 3.6 Etienne Ydens, *Histoire du saint Sacrement de Miracle* (Brussels: Rutger Velpius, 1605): title-page
©ROYAL LIBRARY OF BELGIUM, BRUSSELS, LP 9547 A

THE PRINTING INDUSTRY AND THE COUNTER-REFORMATION   43

published with a print run of 850 copies, the total cost came to 500 guilders; 300 for the text and 200 for the 18 engravings.[61] Ydens omitted to mention it, but he had already received funding amounting to 72 guilders from the chapter of St Gudula for the fabrication of the copper plates used for the engravings.[62] Whether or not the archducal couple were aware of this, they saw fit to recompense Ydens with an extra 400 *livres*, which he received on 7 December 1607.

In 1608, three years after the publication of the *Histoire du saint Sacrement de Miracle*, Ydens produced a Dutch translation of his work. This was published by Rutger Velpius in octavo format under the title *Historie van het Heilige Sacrament van Mirakelen* and comprised 352 pages.[63] The only indication of the chronological sequence of this new enterprise is given by the dedicatory epistle, written in Brussels and dated 27 June 1608. Ydens had already announced in the original French version his intention to translate the work into both Dutch and Latin. In anticipation of this, Rutger Velpius had included the Dutch version in his original request for permission to print the work, introduced in 1605. The approbation accorded by Pierre Vinck that same year duly included this projected translation. The long lapse of time before its actual publication is probably explained by Ydens's numerous occupations, as well as reoccurring financial difficulties – notably suggested by the fact that its appearance in 1608 followed closely on the reception of the archducal remittance, on 7 December 1607.

In the new introduction to the translated work, Ydens relates his personal experience in the presence of the profaned hosts, claiming that their miraculous qualities freed him from the spell of a witch. His intent, it would thus seem, was not only to diffuse as widely as possible story of the hosts, but, additionally to alert the masses to the danger represented by witches – veritable instruments of the devil in his eyes, as, indeed, those of the reigning authorities, who viewed witchcraft as one of the most heinous forms of heresy. Ydens's miraculous liberation thus reads as proof of the triumph of the Catholic faith over this ignominy. Legislation in these matters was notably at its most repressive at this time, as attested by the severity of the edict issued against witchcraft by the archducal couple in 1606, which built on that issued by Philip II in

---

61   The engravings are attributed to Adriaen Collaert (ca 1565/1566–1618), member of an illustrious family of Antwerpian engravers. See Ann Diels and Marjolein Leesberg, *The Collaert Dynasty* (8 vols., Rotterdam: Sound & Vision Publishers, 2005), VII. 88–95 (*The New Hollstein: Dutch & Flemish Etchings, Engravings and Woodcuts 1450–1700*).

62   Placide Lefèvre, 'Offrandes princières faites en l'honneur d'une relique eucharistique à Bruxelles au XVIIᵉ et au XVIIIᵉ siècle', *Revue belge d'archéologie et d'histoire de l'art*, 41 (1972), p. 81, n. 8.

63   USTC 1001625.

1592.[64] However, if efforts to suppress sorcery reached their peak under Albert and Isabella, they were very much a feature of the wider Counter-Reformation movement and the crusade against all forms of heterodoxy. Ydens's work is thus far more than a simple example of hagiographic literature: it took an active part in the Counter-Reformation war against all forms of dissidence.

4   Conclusion

This short foray into Brussels book production in the first third of the seventeenth century has allowed us to review the publishing strategies of the printers active at the time, the legislation regulating their activity, and the expansion of the industry in the 1620s. We have seen that religious works constituted a major sector of the book market and that printers tended to concentrate on texts of a devotional, hagiographic or spiritual nature. Alongside this, we have been able to observe the important impact of Spanish spiritual trends and the growth of the Spanish book market. In terms of the latter, it is interesting to note the parallel with the sixteenth-century Parisian publishing milieu, marked by an unprecedented multiplication of books in Italian following the arrival of a member of the Medici family at the French court.[65] Turning back to the question of spiritual trends in Brussels, it also interesting to note the frequent references to local elements (people, places, events ...) contained in religious works, in particular those of a devotional and hagiographic nature. A clearer picture of this could be gained by undertaking a systematic study of preserved works in order to map the geographical area of diffusion of Brussels publications.

As a final word, we feel bound to admit a certain frustration. While the evident willingness of early seventeenth-century Brussels printers to publish texts like Etienne Ydens's *Histoire du saint Sacrement de Miracle* is certainly eloquent

---

64   The literature on this subject is extensive; significant publications concerning the reign of the archducal couple include: Joseph Bernard Cannaert, *Procès de sorcières en Belgique sous Philippe II et le gouvernement des Archiducs tirés d'actes judiciaires et de documents inédits* (Gand: C. Annoot-Braeckman, 1847); Pasture, *La restauration religieuse*, pp. 45–55; Edouard de Moreau, *Histoire de l'Église en Belgique* (5 vols., Brussels: L'Édition Universelle, 1940–1952), v. 363–370; Marie-Sylvie Dupont-Bouchat, Willem Frijhoff, Robert Muchembled (eds), *Prophètes et sorciers dans les Pays-Bas XVIᵉ–XVIIIᵉ siècle* (Paris: Hachette, 1976); Fernand Vanhemelryck, *Heksenprocessen in de Nederlanden* (Louvain: Davidsfonds, 1982); Jos Monballyu, *Van hekserij beschuldigd. Heksenprocessen in Vlaanderen tijdens de 16ᵈᵉ en de 17ᵈᵉ eeuw* (Heule: UGA, 1996).

65   Jean Balsamo, '*L'amorevolezza verso le cose Italiche'. Le livre italien à Paris au XVIᵉ siècle* (Geneva: Droz, 2015).

THE PRINTING INDUSTRY AND THE COUNTER-REFORMATION 45

in its way, we have not been able to unearth any sources revealing these print-ers' inner convictions with respect to the Counter-Reformation movement.[66] Who is to say though that archival research may not yet prove fruitful? This vast and fascinating field of inquiry needs further investigation.

66 On the involvement of Douaisian printers in the Counter-Reformation movement see Olivia Sauvage, 'L'âge d'or des libraires douaisiens sous les Archiducs', in Claude Bruneel, etc. (eds), *Les 'trentes glorieuses' (circa 1600–circa 1630). Pays-Bas méridionaux et France septentrionale. Aspects économiques, sociaux et religieux au temps des archiducs Albert et Isabelle* (Brussels: Archives et bibliothèques de Belgique, 2010), pp. 249–258.

CHAPTER 4

Successful Strategies for Creating a Devotional Best Seller: Canisius's *Manuale Catholicorum* Published by the Plantin Press

Dirk Imhof

Once the city of Antwerp had surrendered to the troops of Alexander Farnese in August 1585, Christopher Plantin decided to leave Leiden and return to Antwerp, arriving in October of that year.[1] As he had done several times previously, Plantin adjusted very quickly to the new situation and the re-instatement of the Roman Catholic faith in Antwerp. In particular, he immediately began to publish several works by Jesuits who had similarly returned to Antwerp to organise the Counter-reformation.[2] Various editions of Franciscus Costerus's successful works, such as the *Libellus sodalitatis* and his meditations on the Passion, are well known. Plantin simultaneously printed various editions of the *Manuale catholicorum* by the Jesuit Petrus Canisius (1521–1597). This work turned out to be even more successful than Costerus's if one considers how often the Plantin Press printed it. Balthasar Moretus II, Plantin's great-grandson, even printed a French translation of it as late as 1662. In this text, I will discuss this work and how Plantin and his successors published it in distinct forms in Latin, Dutch, and French in order to appeal to as great and diverse a public as possible. In addition, I will also demonstrate how the illustration of this work reflected Plantin's and his successors, the Moretuses's, economical but effective approach to illustrating popular religious texts.

Why precisely Plantin decided to print this work by Canisius is unknown. At that time, Canisius was living in a Jesuit College in Freiburg and was a well-known author of catechisms and devotional books.[3] From the beginning of his career in the 1550s, Plantin, like many other European publishers, had

---

1 Leon Voet, *The Golden Compasses. A History and Evaluation of the Printing and Publishing Activities of the Officina Plantiniana at Antwerp* (2 vols., Amsterdam: Vangendt – London: Routledge & Kegan Paul – New York: Abner Schram, 1969–1972). On Plantin's return from Leiden and, in particular, his final years in Antwerp see I. 112–122.

2 For a list of Plantin's editions published between 1585 and 1589 see: *PP* 2508–2518.

3 On Petrus Canisius see, e.g., James Brodrick, *Saint Petrus Canisius, S.J. 1521–1597* (Baltimore: Carroll Press, 1950); Paul Begheyn, 'The catechism (1555) of Peter Canisius, the most published book by a Dutch author in history', *Quaerendo*, 36 (2006), pp. 51–84. For a bibliographic

---

© KONINKLIJKE BRILL NV, LEIDEN, 2023 | DOI:10.1163/9789004510159_005

SUCCESSFUL STRATEGIES FOR CREATING A DEVOTIONAL BEST SELLER   47

published many editions of Canisius's works without any specific agreements or contact with Canisius. This was also the case with the *Manuale catholicorum*, which Canisius wrote to provide good Catholics with prayers for various occasions. It was first published in 1587, both in Ingolstadt by David Sartorius, and in Freiburg by Abraham Gemperlin (but then without Canisius's name).[4] Maybe, one of the Antwerp Jesuits told Plantin about Canisius's new work and may have suggested that Plantin print an Antwerp edition. At the Frankfurt Fair in the autumn of 1587, Plantin purchased six copies of this text from the Augsburg book dealer Georg Willer, perhaps with the intention of using them to prepare his own edition.[5] A letter written by Plantin's son-in-law, Jan Moretus, in March 1588, to Simon Verepaeus also indicates that this priest from 's Hertogenbosch was involved in the preparation (or even may have taken the initiative) for this new edition of Canisius's text.[6] Plantin knew Verepaeus very well through his publication of Verepaeus's Latin grammar, which was used in schools up until the eighteenth century. But, Verepaeus was also the author of a very successful prayer book, the *Precationum piarum enchiridion*.[7] As its content was highly similar to Canisius's *Manuale*, it is not surprisingly that Plantin was in contact with Verepaeus when this text was printed. However, what his role was precisely is not known.

---

overview until 1990 see: László Polgár, *Bibliographie sur l'histoire de la Compagnie de Jésus 1901–1980* (3 vols., Rome: Institutum historicum, 1981–1990), III. nos. 3938–4412.

4   VD16 C 707 (the edition by David Sartorius) and VD16 M 607 (the edition by Abraham Gemperlin) (not in USTC).

5   Antwerp, Plantin-Moretus Museum, Archival document no. 964, *Cahier de Francfort Septembre 1587*, fol. 2r. Henceforth, references to documents from the Plantin-Moretus Museum are referred to as 'MPM Arch.' followed by the number of the document. The titles of the documents are taken from Jan Denucé, *Inventaire des archives Plantiniennes* (Antwerp: De Sikkel, 1926).

6   "Significo igitur nos Manuale nobis a te missum accepisse quod prima oportunitate excudetur. Interea figuras preparabimus necessarias eo ordine quo designatas misisti" (I inform you that we have received the *Manuale* that you have sent us and that it will be printed at the first opportunity. In the meantime, we will prepare the necessary illustrations in the designated order as you have sent); MPM Arch. 10, *Copie de lettres de Plantin 1579–1589*, fol. 189v. Published in: Max Rooses & Jan Denucé (ed.), *Correspondance de Christophe Plantin* (9 vols., Antwerp: J.E. Buschman – Ghent: A. Hoste, 1883 [I]; Ghent: A. Hoste – The Hague: M. Nijhoff, 1885 [II]; Antwerp: De Nederlandsche Boekhandel – The Hague: M. Nijhoff, 1911–1920 [III–IX]), VIII–IX. 365–366 (no. 1352).

7   This work was published by Joannes Bellerus in Antwerp. See: Marcel A. Nauwelaerts, 'Bijdrage tot de bibliographie van Simon Verepaeus', *De Gulden Passer*, 25 (1947), pp. 61–66; Gilbert Tournoy, 'Bouwstenen voor een nieuwe Verepaeusbibliografie', in Marcus de Schepper and Francine de Nave (eds), *Ex officina Plantiniana Moretorum. Studies over het drukkersgeslacht Moretus* (Antwerp: Vereeniging der Antwerpsche Bibliophielen, 1996), pp. 442–444 (= *De Gulden Passer*, 74).

FIGURE 4.1 Petrus Canisius, *Manuale catholicorum* (Antwerp: Christopher Plantin, 1588): title page
© PLANTIN-MORETUS-MUSEUM, ANTWERP, MPM A 1288

1   Plantin's Editions of 1588 and 1589

Payments for printing Plantin's first edition of the *Manuale*, a 16° edition, are recorded from 23 July till 3 September 1588.[8] Plantin had part of the edition illustrated with woodcuts and part with copper plate images, as he usually did with his standard liturgical editions. This implied that some number of the sheets were printed with blank fillers inserted amid the text, where the copper plates were to be printed. Then, these sheets were transferred to Mynken Liefrinck's atelier, where the majority of copper plates for Plantin's illustrated books were printed. By 15 September 1588, Liefrinck was paid for adding the copper-plate illustrations to 514 copies.[9]

---

8   For a description of this edition see: PP, nos. 890 and 891. For the payments for printing it see MPM Arch. 33, *Livre des ouvriers 1580–1590*, fols. 135 and 139.
9   MPM Arch. 20, *Grand livre 1582–1589*, fol. 308 (right side): "den 15e september Manuale in 16° 12 soorten op elckx 5 hondert & 14 bladers beloopen f° 6168 belopt in gelde tot xx st. fl. 61

SUCCESSFUL STRATEGIES FOR CREATING A DEVOTIONAL BEST SELLER

A comparison of Plantin's edition with David Sartorius's 1587 edition from Ingolstadt is very revealing. Although the text itself appears to be the same, Plantin modified its presentation significantly by giving it a much clearer structure. Specifically, Canisius's text contains 16 so-called exercises, one to start the day devoutly and favourably, one at night before going to sleep, one to meditate on Christ's passion, etc. In Sartorius's edition, these exercises are not numbered, nor is there any hierarchical subdivision between them and other subtitles. By simply numbering each exercise and introducing each one with an illustration, Plantin added a clearly visible structure to Canisius's text that is lacking in the Ingolstadt edition. Moreover, while, at first glance, Plantin appears to have followed Sartorius's example for his general introductory images – the IHS monogram – on the title page and the illustration of the crucifix on the altar, with the text "Adoramus te Christe ...", he surpassed Sartorius by also including several extra textual illustrations, in addition to marking each one of the exercises with an image, instead of highlighting just a few of them, as Sartorius had done. In addition, the compositions chosen for the majority of Plantin's illustrations – all currently attributed to Peeter vander Borcht – differ significantly from those included in the Ingolstadt edition.[10] Compare, for example, the illustration at the beginning of the fourth exercise: in the German edition there is a representation of Christ on the Cross, while Plantin's editions have an image of the Adoration of the Magi; or at the start of the fifth exercise, where the German edition has an image of St Veronica to illustrate the Passion, while in the Antwerp editions there is a representation of the Arma Christi.

But, what inspired Plantin's distinctive conception of Canisius's text? One could argue that Verepaeus's approach to teaching Latin grammar, with its emphasis on a clear structure, is reflected in the new structural form of Plantin's edition. It seems less likely, however, that Verepaeus made significant contributions to the new decorative program begun by Plantin and continued by his successors. On the one hand, when Verepaeus made specific suggestions for additional illustrations a few years later (in 1591 or 1592), Jan Moretus declined

---

st. 14" (Manuale in 16°, 12 sorts of each 514 sheets comes to 6168 sheets, at 20 stuivers [per hundred] amounts to 61 guilders 14 stuivers). The currency used in these records is the Brabant guilder (abbreviated as 'fl.' [florin]) which was divided into 20 stuivers (abbreviated as 'st.').

10 Hans and Ursula Mielke, *The New Hollstein Dutch and Flemish Etchings, Engravings, and Woodcuts, 1450–1700. Peeter Van der Borcht Book Illustrations* (6 vols, Ouderkerk aan den Ijssel: Sound & Vision Publishers, 2005–2007), III. 122–129, nos. 957–979 (with reproductions).

to follow them.[11] For following editions of the *Manuale*, he suggested Moretus use the same illustration on the title page as was used by Joannes Bellerus for Verepaeus's *Precationum enchiridion* and add an extra image of the Crucifixion as Bellerus had used in his book on page 70.[12] On the other hand, Plantin had other logical models for the illustration of this text, namely, his own liturgical editions. For, in his endless discussions with the Spanish clergy about the printing of liturgical books for Spain in the 1570s, he was repeatedly asked to mark each start of a new section of the text with an illustration.[13] Moreover, it was with these editions that Plantin had discovered the advantages of sub-dividing one text edition into two versions: one less costly with woodcut illustrations and one with more finely made engravings or etchings for his wealthier clients.

Having thus perfected this efficient means of diversifying the books he had for sale, it would have been simple to apply it to his editions of Canisius's *Manuale* as well.

Immediately following the completion of his 16° edition, Plantin started the work on a 24° edition.[14] It was set and printed between 1 October and 5 November 1588 and its illustrations appear to have been based upon those in Plantin's previous 16° edition.[15] Once again, the edition was sub-divided into two versions, one with woodcut – and the other with copper plate illustrations. This time, Mynken Liefrinck was paid for illustrating 1,036 copies with copper

---

11   "Aliquid succurrat ad ornandum Manuale. Habet Bellerus in fronte nostri Enchiridii precationum, Bona est oratio, cum Ieiunio et Eleemosyna, quae ibi tribus includuntur circulis. Quid si tu in fronte Manualis ita includas tribus circulis haec 3a verba ... quod fecit Bellerus pag. 46 Enchiridii, qui crassius sunt depicti quam sunt qui in fronte eius libri. Praeterea posses curare depingendum virum illum ante Crucifixi imaginem, quam habet Bellerus pagina 70, sed una cum uxore et liberis" (Something occurred to me for the embellishment of the *Manuale*. On the title page of my *Enchiridion precationum* Bellerus printed the words "Bona est oratio", "Cum ieiunio" and "Eleemosyna", within three circles. Would it be possible to do something similar on the title page of the *Manuale*?.... In addition, on p. 70 of the Bellerus edition, there is an image of the Crucifixion. Could you add an illustration [to the Manuale] of a man before this image, but then with his wife and children? MPM, Arch. 94, *Recueils de lettres Am. Tavernier-Litterae incognitae*, p. 295; published in: Marcel A. Nauwelaerts, 'De correspondentie van Simon Verepaeus met de Officina Plantiniana te Antwerpen', *De Gulden Passer*, 36 (1958), pp. 53–55, no. 10).

12   BT, no. 4698 (not in USTC).

13   See Karen L. Bowen, 'Christopher Plantin, Philip II, and the Vatican. Negotiating between personal preferences and pragmatic considerations when designing the Antwerp editions of the new Tridentine missale', *De Gulden Passer*, 92:1 (2014), pp. 31–52.

14   *PP*, nos. 892–893.

15   For payments for typesetting and printing see: MPM Arch. 33, *Livre des ouvriers 1580–1590*, fols. 140 and 144. For the illustrations see: Mielke, *The New Hollstein*, p. 124.

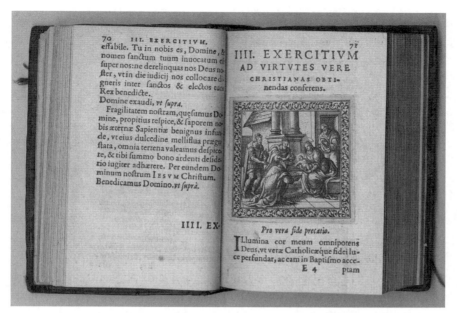

FIGURE 4.2 Petrus Canisius, *Manuale catholicorum*, Antwerp, Christopher Plantin, 1588: pp. 70–71 (beginning of the 4th Exercice)
© PLANTIN-MORETUS-MUSEUM, ANTWERP, A 1288

plate illustrations, twice as many as before.[16] Unfortunately, the total number of copies printed of both editions and, consequently, the number illustrated with woodcuts, remain unknown.

Then, at the beginning of 1589, Plantin also published a Dutch and a French translation of the *Manuale*, both duodecimos.[17] Consequently, within a year, Plantin had published four distinct editions of this text, each of which consisted of one version with woodcuts and one with intaglios (or copper plate illustrations).

The majority of the sales records of these books were noted to booksellers in the Southern Netherlands, including such cities as Douai or Cambrai in present Northern France. Usually, these sales were only for a limited number of copies. The purchase of 100 copies illustrated with woodcuts and 12 with etchings by Joannes Bogardus from Douai on 3 September 1588 was exceptionally large.[18]

16 MPM Arch. 20, *Grand livre 1582–1589*, fol. 308 (right side): "manuale in 24° 6 sorten op elckx 1036 maken te samen 6216 bladeren tot 36 st. t'hondert beloopt fl. 111 st. 14" (Manuale in 24°, 6 sorts of each 1036 comes together to 6216 sheets, at 36 stuivers per hundred amounts to 111 guilders 14 stuivers).
17 *PP*, nos. 894, 895, and 896.
18 MPM Arch. 65, *Journal 1588*, fol. 117r.

TABLE 4.1 Plantin editions of Canisius's *Manuale* in Latin, Dutch and French and their basis selling price

Plantin press no.	Year	Language	Format	Selling price version with woodcuts	Selling price version with etchings
PP 890–891	1588	Latin	16°	5 stuivers	10 stuivers
PP 892–893	1589	Latin	24°	3 stuivers	6 stuivers
PP 894	1589	Dutch	12°	3½ stuivers	8 stuivers
PP 895–896	1589	French	12°	4½ stuivers	9 stuivers

In addition to these local sales, many copies went to Paris and Frankfurt. The Parisian bookseller Michel Sonnius I bought 300 copies of the 16° edition on 23 September 1588: 200 copies illustrated with woodcuts and 100 with etchings.[19] On 4 November 1588 he bought 50 copies of the 24° edition, illustrated with woodcuts, and on 27 April 1589 100 copies of the French edition with woodcuts and 25 of the same with etchings.[20] Similar quantities were sent to the fairs in Frankfurt. Specifically, as of October 1588 Plantin sent several shipments for the coming Lent Fair of 1589: 200 copies in total of the 16° edition with woodcuts and 50 with etchings, in addition to another 200 copies of the 24° edition with woodcuts and 50 with etchings.[21] Jan Dresseler, who took care of Plantin's affairs at the Fair, also sold books, including Plantin editions, for his own profit. Apparently, he preferred the 24° edition: for the Lent Fair of 1589 he himself took an additional 500 copies (350 copies with woodcuts and 150 with etchings).[22] Typical for Dresseler is that he only wished to sell editions that he knew would be popular at the Fair. The fact that he bought 500 copies in total is the best indication that the *Manuale* was likely to be a bestseller.

The small 24° edition with woodcuts was inexpensive, selling for only 3 stuivers without a binding, while the larger 12° editions with etchings were sold for 8 or 9 stuivers per copy, without a binding.[23] When individual clients choose a fine binding for their book, the price rose significantly to 20 stuivers

---

19   MPM Arch. 65, *Journal 1588*, fol. 128r.
20   MPM Arch. 65, *Journal 1588*, fol. 151v and MPM Arch. 66, *Journal 1589*, fol. 56r.
21   MPM Arch. 65, *Journal 1588*, fol. 144v (21 October 1588) and fol. 173r (2 December 1588), and MPM Arch. 66, *Journal 1589*, fol. 3r (5 January 1589).
22   MPM Arch. 66, *Journal 1589*, fols. 24v and 28r.
23   For the currency used in these records see note 9.

SUCCESSFUL STRATEGIES FOR CREATING A DEVOTIONAL BEST SELLER 53

or more. For example, on 9 July 1589, the Jesuit Joannes Melander had to pay 24 stuivers for his bound and gilded copy of a French *Manuel* with etchings, eight times the inexpensive 3 stuivers of a 24° copy with woodcuts.[24]

2   Editions by Jan Moretus I

After Plantin's death on 1 July 1589, his son-in-law Jan Moretus I continued the Press. According to inventories made in the spring of 1590 to estimate the value of all of Plantin's possessions, including his stock of books and all the printing equipment of his Press, there were 24 woodblocks available for the *Manuale*, in addition to four sets of 23 etched plates.[25] One disadvantage of etched plates is that they may wear out very easily because the lines are not always cut deeply

FIGURE 4.3   Petrus Canisius, *Handt-boeck der catholijcken*, Antwerp, Jan Moretus I, 1604, pp. 170–171 (beginning of the 7th exercice)
© PLANTIN-MORETUS-MUSEUM, ANTWERP, A 889

---

24   MPM Arch. 66, *Journal 1589*, fol. 90r.
25   MPM Arch. 98, *Pièces de famille 1549–1589*, p. 514 (for the copper plates) and p. 523 (for the woodblocks).

enough in the plates. In the late 1580s Plantin seems to have preferred etchings above engravings in general. Etchings are far easier and faster to produce because the designer draws the desired image directly into the plate, after which it can be etched into it immediately.[26] This experiment with etchings was not continued by the Plantin Press after 1590, probably because the plates wore out too easily and, if reworking was no longer possible, new plates had to be made anyway. The scarcity of preserved copies of these first editions of Canisius's *Manuale* unfortunately prevents a proper comparison of the impressions which might clarify the use of different plates.

During the 20 years that he was in charge of the Press, Jan Moretus published fourteen new editions of the *Manuale*, in the same variety of languages and formats as Plantin had produced, and, once again, each edition was subdivided into two versions, one with woodcuts and one with intaglios.[27] Around 1600, all of the copper plates were apparently so worn out that reworking was useless, and the decision was made to replace them with engravings. Moreover, a selection of the copperplates made for the *Manuale* were also used for three editions of another prayer book, the *Modus orandi Deum* by the Antwerp priest Henricus Costerius.[28] Jan Moretus made use of his plates as much as possible. In 1604, when Jan Moretus was preparing new 12° and 24° editions of the *Manuale* in French and Dutch, Theodore Galle, Jan Moretus's son-in-law, saw to the production of two new sets of engravings for each format.[29] The plate for the title vignette had to be redone because the first one was made too large.[30] Everyone can make a mistake.

Another error that sometimes occurred was due to the difficulty in predicting how many copies should be printed with woodcuts and how many with etchings or engravings. When it is already difficult for a publisher to predict how many copies he should print in total of an edition, it was all the more so when deciding how many should be printed with woodcuts and how many with engravings. When there appeared a greater demand for copies with

---

26   Karen L. Bowen and Dirk Imhof, *Christopher Plantin and Engraved Book Illustrations in Sixteenth-Century Europe* (Cambridge: Cambridge University Press, 2008), pp. 221–247.

27   Dirk Imhof, *Jan Moretus and the Continuation of the Plantin Press. A Bibliography of the Works published and printed by Jan Moretus I in Antwerp (1589–1610)* (2 vol., Leiden: Brill, 2014), nos. C-6–C-19, I, pp. 156–170 (USTC 74474, 75219, 407084, 430314, 441191, 452708, 1002167 and 1007919; not listed in USTC are the Latin edition of 1606, the Dutch editions of 1596, 1597 and 1604 in 24° and the French editions of 1599 and 1604).

28   Imhof, *Jan Moretus*, nos. C-66–C-68, pp. 201–203 (not in USTC).

29   MPM Arch. 123, *Graveurs I. Galle. 1600–1692*, fols. 11v–12v.

30   MPM Arch. 123, *Graveurs I. Galle. 1600–1692*, fol. 12v: "noch een tytelken voor den hantboeck Canysii in 24 wat kleijnder want het voorgaende te groot was 3 gul." (another small title for Canisius's manual in 24°, somewhat smaller as the previous one was to large: 3 fl.).

engravings than expected, extra impressions from the engravings were printed on white paper and then pasted on top of the woodcuts. This happened with the Dutch edition of the 12° *Manuale*. In 1612, 150 extra impressions were made to paste on top of the woodcuts.[31]

Under Jan Moretus I, there had been a shift of his sales that also had its implication for the sale of Canisius's *Manuale*. Due to the war in France and a dispute with Michel Sonnius II concerning payments for several deliveries of paper, the export of books to France had diminished significantly.[32] Consequently, during his tenure as manager of the Press, the Frankfurt Fair had come to be even more important for the distribution of his editions than it had been under Plantin. Not surprisingly, the Latin editions of Canisius's *Manuale* in particular were sent to Frankfurt. For example, of the 1599 edition, 1,215 copies were sent between 1599 and 1606, representing the majority of the copies printed. Although far fewer in number, Jan Moretus also sent many copies of the Dutch and French editions: as many as 50 copies of each Dutch edition and 100 or 125 copies of the French ones.[33] For, not only booksellers from German speaking regions were present in Frankfurt, but ones from France and the Netherlands as well.

The cost of a copy of Canisius's *Manuale* varied astoundingly depending whether or not a book was bound or decorated, and if so, how. While the cost for an unbound copy of the 1604 12° French edition, illustrated with woodcuts, was only 10 stuivers, the engraver Philips Galle paid 2 guilders (or 40 stuivers) on 20 October 1605 for a bound copy of a Dutch 12° *Manuale* bound "pleyn dor soye".[34] But this was far below the price that the Antwerp merchant Jan Losson paid when he bought a copy for his son Antoine in December 1607. This copy, in which the illustrations were decorated with gold and silver and the book was bound in velour, was sold for 8 guilders and 10 stuivers (or 170 stuivers).[35]

---

31   MPM Arch. 123, *Graveurs I. Galle. 1600–1692*, fol. 22r: "gedruckdt om te placken Canisius in 12° duydts 150 figuren tot 10 sts. thondert – gul. 15 sts." (printed to paste in Canisius in 12° in Dutch 150 images at 10 stuivers per hundred amounts to 15 stuivers).

32   Denis Pallier, 'La firme plantinienne et le marché français pendant la Ligue: les voyages du libraire Théodore Rinsart en France (1591–1596)', in Francine de Nave (ed.), *Liber amicorum Leon Voet* (Antwerp: Vereeniging der Antwerpsche Bibliophielen), 1985, pp. 117–135 [= *De Gulden Passer*, 61–63 (1983–1985)].

33   For example, the shipment for the Frankfurt Fair in the spring of 1605 included 40 copies of the French *Manuel des catholiques in* 12°, 20 of the Dutch *Handt-boeck der catholijcken in* 12°, and another 20 of the Dutch edition in 24° (MPM Arch. 177, *Journal 1605*, fols. 5r and 18r).

34   MPM Arch. 177, *Journal 1605*, fol. 168r.

35   MPM Arch. 179, *Journal 1607*, fol. 215v, noted on 5 December 1607: "1 Manuel de Canisius les figures avec or et argent relie de velour fl. 8 st. 10" (1 Manuale by Canisius, the images with gold and silver, bound in velvet: 8 guilder and 10 stuivers).

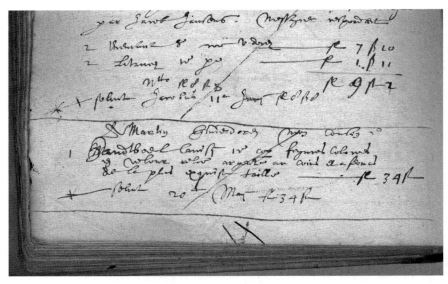

FIGURE 4.4 Sale of a colored copy to Martin Ginderhoven on 18 May 1605
© PLANTIN-MORETUS-MUSEUM, ANTWERP, ARCH. 177, JOURNAL 1605, FOL. 78V

Coloring alone increased the price by 4 to 5 guilders at least. The most expensive copy that I have found thus far is a copy of the Dutch 1604 12° edition, purchased in May 1605 by Jan Moretus's relative Martin van Ginderhoven. This copy was illustrated with the best impressions of the engravings, colored and bound in velour with silver on the corners.[36] It was sold for 34 guilders (or 680 stuivers), more than the cost for a voluminous atlas by Abraham Ortelius. Thus, copies of Canisius's *Manuale* could vary between a simple, relative inexpensive prayer book and an exquisite luxury item for a wealthy collector.

---

36 MPM Arch. 177, *Journal* 1605, fol. 78v, recorded on 18 May 1605: "Martin Ginderhoven mon cousin 1 Handtboeck Canisii 12° coper figures colories en velour relie argente au coins et a fermans de la plus exquise taille fl. 34" (For my nephew Martin van Ginderhoven 1 Handtboeck by Canisius in 12° with colored engravings, bound in velvet with silver on the corners and the clasps, of the most exquisite execution: 34 guilder).

SUCCESSFUL STRATEGIES FOR CREATING A DEVOTIONAL BEST SELLER

3   Editions Published by Jan II and Balthasar Moretus I, and by
     Balthasar Moretus II

When Jan II and Balthasar Moretus I continued the Plantin Press after the
death of their father in 1610, Canisius's *Manuale catholicorum* remained one of
their best sellers, as is clear from the table 4.2.

Theodore Galle's atelier had become proficient in reworking copperplates
so that they could be used as long as possible. Consequently, the plates for
the various editions of the *Manuale* were reworked thoroughly on several
occasions. Specifically, in 1610, 1626, and 1629 all of the plates for the 24° edition were reworked[37]; in 1628 some and in 1630 all of the plates for the larger
12° edition were reworked as well.[38] When preparing a new 24° edition in

TABLE 4.2   Balthasar I and Jan Moretus II editions of Canisius's *Manuale* in Latin,
             Dutch and French and their basis selling price

Year	Language	Format	Selling price version with woodcuts	Selling price version with engravings
1610	French	24°	5 stuivers	12 stuivers
1613	Latin	24°	5 stuivers	12 stuivers
1614	Dutch	12°	10 stuivers	20 stuivers
1615	Latin	12°	10 stuivers	20 stuivers
1620	Latin	24°	5 stuivers	13 stuivers
1620	Dutch	24°	6 stuivers	13 stuivers
1626	Dutch	24°	6 stuivers	14 stuivers
1628	French	12°	13 stuivers	24 stuivers
1629	French	24°	7 stuivers	15 stuivers
1629	Latin	24°	7 stuivers	15 stuivers
1630	Dutch	12°	18 stuivers	30 stuivers
1631	Dutch	24°	8 stuivers	16 stuivers
1634	Dutch	24°	8 stuivers	16 stuivers

37   MPM Arch. 123, *Graveurs I. Galle. 1600–1692*, fols. 20r (1610 French edition), 62v (1626
      Dutch edition) and 76r (1629 Latin edition).
38   MPM Arch. 123, *Graveurs I. Galle. 1600–1692*, fols. 64v (1628 French edition) and 76r (1630
      Dutch edition).

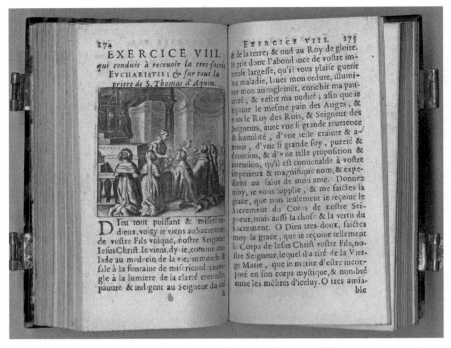

FIGURE 4.5 Petrus Canisius, *Le manuel des catholiques*, Antwerp, Balthasar Moretus II, 1662, pp. 174–175 (beginning of the 8th exercice)
© PLANTIN-MORETUS-MUSEUM, ANTWERP, O.B 1.4

1641 – the printing was begun in August, a month after Balthasar I's death – Balthasar Moretus II finally decided that new plates had to be engraved. On 11 October 1641, Erasmus Quellinus II was paid for designing 21 illustrations for the 24° *Manuale* at a cost of 30 stuivers per drawing.[39] Made more than 50 years later than the original designs, the figures in the illustrations were updated to suit contemporary, mid-seventeenth-century norms. Soon after Quellinus was paid, Cornelis Galle II received 240 stuivers per plate for making new engravings.[40] These new plates were only used for three new editions: one in French in 1642, one in Dutch in 1646, and finally, the last time, for a French 32° edition in 1662.

Generally, the managers of the Plantin Press tended to increase the use of engravings during the first half of the seventeenth century. While the ratio of copies with woodcuts or engravings was, roughly speaking, about 2 to 1 at the end of Plantin's life, it then evened out towards the end of Jan Moretus I's

---

39 MPM Arch. 167, *Dépenses spéciales 1637–1678*, fol. 39r.
40 MPM Arch. 167, *Dépenses spéciales 1637–1678*, fols. 39v and 40v.

SUCCESSFUL STRATEGIES FOR CREATING A DEVOTIONAL BEST SELLER   59

life and shifted even further to a 1 to 2 ratio when Balthasar Moretus I was head of the Press. Later, from the 1640s onwards, woodcuts were only rarely used for inexpensive books. The same evolution can be seen in the case of Canisius's *Manuale catholicorum*. While the total number of copies Plantin printed is not known, among Jan Moretus's first editions, the number of copies illustrated with woodcuts always far exceed the number with engravings. For example, in 1592, the Dutch and French 16° editions in comprised 1,000 copies with woodcuts and 500 with engravings.[41] As of the 1610s this ratio balanced out. For example, in 1613 and 1620, the Latin 24° editions had 2,000 copies, split evenly between those with woodcuts and those with engravings.[42] In the 1620s the majority of the copies printed were illustrated with engravings, for example, the 1630 Dutch 12° edition consisted of 500 copies illustrated with woodcuts and 1,025 with engravings.[43] After 1640, there are no more records of how many copies were illustrated with woodblocks. It remains noteworthy that even when the number of copies printed with woodcuts was declining that in 1628 the Moretuses decided to ask Christoffel Jeghers to make them a new set and replace the old woodcuts that Plantin had commissioned decades before.[44]

Looking at the sales of Canisius's prayer book during the 1630s and 1640s, it appears that the importance of the Frankfurt Fair gradually faded away, and the Press's activities were increasingly focused on their export of liturgical books to Spain.[45] Local booksellers from Antwerp and the Southern Netherlands then became the most regular clients for Canisius's prayer book. Nevertheless, the Plantin Press kept selling a large number of these books in

---

41   Imhof, *Moretus*, note 1 of both nos. C-9 and C-15.

42   MPM M 39, *Catalogue des éditions plantiniennes 1590–1651*, list of editions from 1613, nos. 25 and 26: "1000 [exemplaria] Manuale Catholicorum P. Canisii in 24° fin carrè f[olia] 7 st. 5. 1000 [ex.] Idem figuris aeneis 23 in 24° st. 12" (1000 [copies] of Canisius's *Manuale catholicorum* in 24° on "fin carré" [paper], 7 sheets: 5 stuivers; 1000 [copies] of the same with 23 engravings, in 24°: 12 stuivers), and list of editions from 1620, nos. 62 and 63: "1000 [exemplaria] Manuale Catholicorum Pet. Canisii Soc. Iesu in 24° f[olia] 7 cum fig. ligneis st. 5. 1000 [ex.] Idem in 24° cum figuris aeneis st. 13" (1000 [copies] of the *Manuale catholicorum* by Petrus Canisius S.J. in 24°, 7 sheets, with woodcuts: 5 stuivers; 1000 [copies] of the same in 24° with engravings: 13 stuivers).

43   MPM M 39, *Catalogue des éditions plantiniennes 1590–1651*, list of editions from 1630 nos. 31 and 32: "500 [exemplaria] Handtboeck Canisii in 12° f[olia] 23 st. 18. 1025 [exemplaria] Idem in 12° fig. aeneis st. 30" (500 [copies] of Canisius's *Handtboeck* in 12°, 23 sheets: 18 stuivers; 1025 [copies] of the same in 12° with engravings: 30 stuivers).

44   MPM Arch. 780, *Ouvriers 1622–1629*, fol. 86.

45   On the decline of the Frankfurt Fair in the beginning of the seventeenth century see: Ian Maclean, *Scholarship, Commerce, Religion: the Learned Book in the Age of Confessions, 1560–1630* (Cambridge, Mass.: Harvard University Press, 2012), pp. 211–234.

Cologne and even in Poland, where Christophorus Schedelius in Krakow and Gaspar Forster in Danzig regularly bought dozens of copies of the *Manuale* for further distribution.[46]

4   Conclusion

In 1588, Christopher Plantin made a brilliant decision to publish his own edition of a new prayer book by the Jesuit Petrus Canisius. Using an existing German edition, he made an appealing publication by simply adding structure to the text and enhancing its illustration. Publishing editions in Latin, Dutch and French, in various formats, with either woodcuts or copper plate illustrations, he was able to attract as diverse a range of clients as possible. For the next 70 years, Plantin's successors kept printing new editions, making the most of this prayer book. It is reminiscent of other successful editions by the Press, such as the *Variae litaniae sacrae*. Begun as a prayer book for the Spanish army in 1593 it became a prayer book for Catholics in general and was reprinted throughout the entire seventeenth century.[47] Like Canisius's *Manuale* it had its own set of engravings that was regularly reworked and renewed. As the Moretuses routinely invested in their illustrations by reworking and renewing the copperplates, they must have recognised the importance of the illustrations for the success of their editions. These texts, together with other bestselling prayer books published by the Press during the seventeenth century, made a lasting impression upon their readers and the image they formed of the practice of their faith and devotion.

---

46   See, for example, a record of a shipment of 20 copies to Schedelius on 7 March, or 16 copies sent to Forster on 7 July 1642 (MPM Arch. 250, *Journal 1642*, fols. 37r and 111r, respectively).

47   Dirk Imhof, 'An Author's Wishes versus a Publisher's Possibilities: The Illustration of Thomas Sailly's Prayer Books Printed by the Plantin Press in Antwerp c. 1600', in Feike Dietz, Adam Morton, Lien Roggen, e.a. (eds), *Illustrated Religious Texts in the North of Europe, 1500–1800* (Farnham: Ashgate, 2014), pp. 205–220.

CHAPTER 5

International Sales of Tridentine Emblems Books by the Antwerp *Officina Plantiniana*: The Case of Father Joannes David at the Beginning of the Seventeenth Century

Renaud Milazzo

Among the illustrated books used as tools of reconquest by the Roman Catholic Church, emblems books were one of the favoured media used by Jesuits to promote the Tridentine precepts and concepts from the end of the sixteenth century, when Antwerp was one of the main centres of the Counter-Reformation's dissemination.[1] Indeed, since Alexander Farnese's recapture of the city in 1585, the Low Countries became a stronghold of the Tridentine Reformation and remained under the direct authority of Spain until 1597. The Catholic religion was then the only confession allowed.[2] During the reign of Isabella Clara Eugenia of Austria and her husband Albert of Austria, the development of trade in religious books and prints increased and 49.15 per cent of these works were produced in the city's most important printing workshop, the *Officina Plantiniana*, run since the death of Christophe Plantin in 1589 by his son-in-law Jan Moretus I.[3]

Since the shipment to Leiden in 1584 of engraved woodcuts used as illustrations for the emblematic collections of Sambucus, Junius and Alciato, the *Officina Plantiniana* no longer bore the direct financial risk of making a new

---

1   On the sales of Tridentine emblem books see Renaud Milazzo, *Le marché des livres d'emblèmes en Europe (1531–1750)*, (2 vols., Université Paris-Saclay – University of Versailles Saint-Quentin-en-Yvelines, unpublished PhD thesis, 2017). In the process of publication: Renaud Milazzo, *Le marché des livres d'emblèmes en Europe (1531–1750)*, (Turnhout: Brepols (bibliologia), forthcoming).

2   On the topic of the Low Countries revolt, an excellent synthesis based on a recent and updated bibliography is provided in the following book: Thierry Allain, Andreas Nijenhuis-Bescher, Romain Thomas, *Les Provinces-Unies à l'Époque Moderne* (Paris: Armand Colin, 2019), pp. 16–30.

3   Dirk Imhof, *Jan Moretus and the Continuation of the Plantin Press. A Bibliography of the Works Published and Printed by Jan Moretus I in Antwerp (1589–1610)* (Leiden: Brill, 2014), I. XLIII.

© KONINKLIJKE BRILL NV, LEIDEN, 2023 | DOI:10.1163/9789004510159_006

emblem book.[4] It is true that Plantin's death abruptly interrupted the collaboration between the typographic workshop and the Jesuits with regard to the printing of the *editio princeps* of Hieronymus Natalis's *Adnotationes et Meditationes in Evangelia*,[5] which finally fell into the hands of Martin Nutius in the early 1590s.[6] It was not until 1601 that Jan Moretus I, in collaboration with his brother-in-law, the engraver Theodoor Galle, published the first collection of Joannes David's emblems, the *Veridicus Christianus*. A clergyman, David was an important figure in the struggle against heresy. He worked as a priest for more than twelve years before entering the Jesuit Order in 1582 and became rector of the Jesuit College of Kortrijk and later Ypres in 1586.[7] In his dedication to Petrus Simons, Bishop of Ypres, Joannes David sheds an interesting light on the commercial outlets of the book immediately envisaged at a European level by its publishers.[8] Initially, David wanted to have his text printed in Dutch. Theodoor and Philipp Galle agreed to publish the *Veridicus Christianus* in Antwerp, provided that it should be published in Latin, thus favouring an international rather than a solely local distribution:

> But when everything was ready, and I discussed the printing of the book with the engravers in Antwerp, they only wanted to commit themselves to this venture at their own risk if it was published in Latin....[9]

---

4   The financial difficulties facing Plantin at the end of his life changed his editorial policy. In order to limit new investments, he acquired an important stock of the Laurentius Haechtanus emblem book, *Microcosmus Parvus mundus*, in 1579 and registered the book as part of the list of his own editions and prints with the Dutch version of this same book for Gérard de Jode though his name did not appear on the title page. On this subject, see Karen L. Bowen and Dirk Imhof, *Christopher Plantin and Engraved Book illustrations in the Sixteenth-Century Europe* (Cambridge: Cambridge University Press, 2010), p. 305 and p. 421.

5   Jerónimo Nadal, *Adnotationes et meditationes in evangelia quae in sacrosancto missae sacrificio toto anno leguntur* (Antwerp: Martinus Nutius, 1595) (USTC 413154). On this topic see the introductory study by Walter Melion, in Jerome Nadal, *Annotations and Meditations on the Gospels* (3 vols., Philadelphia: Saint Joseph's University Press, 2003), I, 1–96.

6   Ralph Dekoninck, '*Ad Imaginem*'. *Statuts, fonctions et usages de l'image dans la littérature spirituelle jésuite du XVIIe siècle* (Geneva: Droz, 2005), p. 233.

7   For bibliographic data on David's emblem books see Dirk Imhof, *Jan Moretus and the Continuation of the Plantin Press*, I. 220; Peter Maurice Daly, G. Richard Dimler, *The Jesuit Series, Part One (A–D)* (Montreal, 1991), pp. 147–162. More recently, very brief information on the life of Joannes David can be found in the following study: Peter Maurice Daly, G. Richard Dimler, *The Jesuit Emblem in the European Context* (Philadelphia: Saint Joseph's University Press, 2016), pp. 255–258.

8   Joannes David, *Veridicus christianus* (Antwerp, Jan Moretus I, 1601), p. 3 (USTC 1009429).

9   "*At deum, omnibus ad rem comparatis, cum typorum incisoribus Antverpiae de libro quoque ipso imprimendo transigerem; ea demun lege illi tantum onus suo periculo suscipere voluerunt, si etiam Latine sermone vulgaretur ...*", in David, *Veridicus christianus*, p. 3.

INTERNATIONAL SALES OF TRIDENTINE EMBLEMS BOOKS 63

It was, therefore, an initiative of the engravers, as Dirk Imhof has rightly pointed out,[10] and not Jan I Moretus, as Werner Waterschoot argues.[11]

This trade policy of publishers is significant. Already Christophe Plantin in the years 1565–1570 relied heavily on the sales of emblem books made in his Paris office where he hoped to sell 28 per cent of his stock and 29 per cent during the Frankfurt book fairs to increase his profits.[12] This was even truer for Moretus: the spring and autumn fairs, held on the banks of the Main, in the heart of the Empire, were the cornerstone of the *Officina* because 49 per cent of the emblem books printed by the latter left the shores of the Escaut for the banks of the Main.[13]

For this reason, we have chosen for the purposes of this chapter to only focus our attention on the sales transactions of emblem books carried out during Frankfurt trade fairs, as they account for most of the sales made abroad. Although there were transactions made directly between the Officina and booksellers in Antwerp, or French, Italian or English private individuals, for instance, these remained of secondary importance, and apart from German fairs, the market for the Tridentine emblems books for the *Officina plantiniana* was above all a local market in the Southern and Northern Low Countries.[14]

The chronological framework chosen for this study ranges from 1606 to 1610 is by no means arbitrary. We have privileged an interval of five years during which four of the six emblem books published by Moretus and his son were printed and launched on the international book market. To find out about these sales, we surveyed the archives in the Plantin-Moretus Museum and, in particular, the biannual Frankfurt notebooks rarely used from the standpoint of emblem books.[15] Thus it is possible to follow the sales not only of the main

---

10   Imhof, *Jan Moretus and the Continuation of the Plantin Press*, I. 231.

11   Werner Waterschoot, 'Veridicus Christianus and Christeliicken Waersggher by Joannes David', in Ralph Dekoninck and Agnès Guiderdoni-Bruslé (eds), *Emblemata sacra: rhétorique et herméneutique du discours sacré dans la littérature en images. Emblemata sacra: the Rhetoric and Hermeneutics of Illustrated Sacred discourse* (Turnhout: Brepols, 2007), p. 528.

12   Renaud Milazzo, 'Les ventes de livres d'emblèmes par l'officine Plantinienne de 1566 à 1570', *De Gulden Passer. Journal for Book History*, 93 (2015), pp. 27–29.

13   Based on sales reported in journals and carried out directly at the *Officina*.

14   Milazzo, *Le marché des livres*, forthcoming.

15   References to documents from the Plantin-Moretus Museum are indicated as 'MPM Arch.', followed by the number of the document. The titles of the documents are taken from Jan Denucé, *Inventaire des archives Plantiniennes* (Antwerp: Rob. Bracke, Van Geert, 1926). We consulted the following archives: MPM archive 1001: Cahier de Francfort, lente 1606. MPM archive 1002: Cahier de Francfort, herfst 1606 MPM archive 1003: Cahier de Francfort, lente 1607. MPM archive 1004: Cahier de Francfort, herfst 1607 MPM archive 1005: Cahier de Francfort, lente 1608. MPM archive 1006: Cahier de Francfort, herfst 1608. MPM archive 1007: Cahier de Francfort, lente 1609. MPM archive 1008(1): Cahier de Francfort, herfst

emblem books written by David – the last remaining copies of the original *editio* of the 1601 *Veridicus* and the launch of the 1606 second edition, the sale of the *Occasio arrepta* in 1605, the *Paradisius Sponsi and Sponsae* in 1607, and the *Duodecim Specula* in 1610 –, but also those of a new edition of the *Adnotationes et Meditationes* by Hieronymus Natalis in 1607 following the purchase and transfer of the privilege directly obtained from the rector of the Jesuits of Antwerp, Carolus Scribani in 1605 by Jan Moretus II and his brother-in-law Theodoor Galle.[16] We will first present the main sales results, then focus on the specific acquisitions of works containing a large number of engravings, and then discuss the issue of their distribution.

1   Main Results

More systematically than Christophe Plantin used to do, Moretus and his sons relied on the Frankfurt fairs for the launch of the latest titles released from the press and took advantage of catalogues to make their new releases known. Paris, which accounted for an important market share for the Sambucus, Junius and Alciato emblem books between 1566 and 1570, accounted for only 4 per cent of Jan I Moretus's turnover at the beginning of the seventeenth century. It is true that the *Officina Plantiniana* no longer had a Paris branch after Michel Sonnius bought it on 22 August 1577, when Plantin, needing to ease his cash-flow in

---

1609. MPM archive 1008(2): Cahier de Francfort, lente 1610. MPM archive 1009: Cahier de Francfort, herfst 1610. The 91 volumes of the Frankfurt notebooks are invaluable sources because they are highly detailed. In most of the copies preserved, the first sheets consist of an alphabetical index of the booksellers with whom Plantin or his representatives traded. The main section of the notebooks is made up of invoices detailing by title the quantity of books sold and purchased for each bookseller or printer. The last part of the sheets is devoted to various invoices for books sent from Frankfurt to other cities, travel expenses (travel, accommodation and catering expenses), details of payments in different European currencies and, in most cases, inventories of books left in Frankfurt at the end of the fair. As for the sales journals of the Officina, the notebooks are multi-handed written in French, Dutch and more rarely in German. These are the main sources of sales and purchases of emblem books through the Frankfurt trade fairs until 1586. Unfortunately, they are incomplete. The first documents preserved are those of the Lenten Fair of 1579, then of autumn 1586. The archives then preserve all the notebooks for the years 1587 to 1631.

16   "Theodore Galle mon Beaufrere me doibt pour la moitié des 153 planches des figures de Hieronimus Natalis les quelles ad Ier X^{bre} 1605 avons achapte du R.P. Carolus Scribani par ensemble; et mon beaufrere les a toutes entre les mains, pour voir de les renouveller par commodite ...", in: MPM archive 101 fol. 6v.

Antwerp, decided to sell it.[17] As a result, a large number of volumes were sent to Frankfurt and the Tridentine emblem books did not deviate from this rule. In 1606, for example, 220 texts of the *Veridicus* and 100 *Icones* were sent to the Empire between 31 August and 2 September, suggesting that the text sold without engravings had a greater commercial potential.[18] Following the repurchase of the privilege, the new frontispieces and other engraved elements of the *Adnotationes* do not seem to have been ready in time for the autumn fair, since only seven complete copies, for which the hand that inscribed the orders in the journals took care to indicate that this was the edition of 1599, were sent in a first barrel and five others, without precise date, in another.[19] These ware Natalis's first copies for public sale. Before that, on 30 March, only a "conseillé de Monsieur Morentorf [Moretus]" (advisor to Mr Morentorf) was given a first copy of the illustrations, certainly to test the condition of the copper plates purchased from the Jesuits, which he negotiated a price of 14 guilders instead of 15 guilders.[20] Compared to the shop in Antwerp, where the book was on sale since May 1610, the release of the *Duodecim Specula* in Frankfurt was planned for the autumn fair, since on 29 July a first shipment of 50 copies was sent to the Empire.[21] It was completed on 23 August by a second shipment of 200 copies.[22]

The addition of the various sales of all emblem books made at the Frankfurt book fairs between 1606 and 1610 shows that 1455 copies were acquired either by fellow printers who bought books in bulk or by private individuals who bought a few rare copies.

---

17   Max Rooses, *Le Musée Plantin-Moretus*, (Antwerp: G. Lazzarini, 1919), p. 149. For several reasons, Jan Moretus I had lost this market since the early 1590s and, as Dirk Himhof stressed, "Export to Spain was also very limited until it resumed in the second decade of the seventeenth century. Trade with German cities had therefore become essential for the distribution of his editions ...", in: Dirk Imhof, 'Three future Cologne publishers as apprentices in Antwerp: Bernhard Wolters, Johann Kinckius and Cornelis van Egmont', *The Library*, 7th s., 17:1 (2016), pp. 3–27, see especially, p. 4.

18   A first barrel comprising "50 imagines Veridicus" was sent to the banks of the Main on 31 August (MPM archive 178 fol. 142v). On 2 September, barrel number 3 contained "50 Veridicus Icones" and barrel number 4 "112 Christianus Veridicus" and "20 Occasio arrepta" (MPM archive 178 fol. 144r). A further bale of books contained "108 Veridicus Christianus" (MPM 178 fol. 145r).

19   31 August, "7 Natalis complet (1599)" in barrel no. 2 (MPM archive 178 fol. 142v). On 2 September "5 Natalis complet" in barrel no. 4 (MPM archive 178 fol. 145r).

20   "1 imagines Natalis f[olio] ... 15 fl. a payer pour accord 14 fl" (MPM archive 178 fol. 47r). "Unless noted otherwise, all of the sums of money in the cited records from Christopher Plantin's business were noted in florins, which is another name for Carolus or Brabant guilder", quoted by Bowen and Imhof, *Christopher Plantin and Engraved Book illustrations*, p. XIII [1 guilder = 20 patars (or stuivers)].

21   MPM archive 217 fol. 139r.

22   MPM archive 217 fol. 156r.

Market share of emblem books at Frankfurt trade fairs from 1606 to 1610

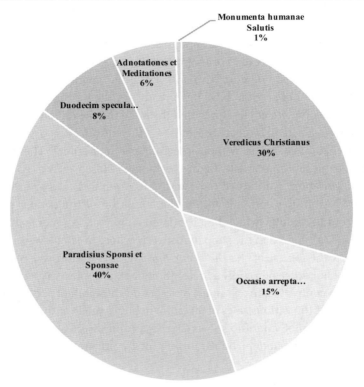

FIGURE 5.1 Market share of the various David's emblem books at the Frankfurt Fairs from 1606 to 1610 according to the Cahiers de Francfort kept at the Plantin-Moretus Museum in Antwerp

The graph above shows the market share of the various works. For the entire period under study, the *Paradisius Sponsi* (586 copies) sold better than the second edition of the *Veridicus* (429 copies). Less popular, the *Occasio Arrepta* sold half as well as the two previous books (224 copies). The *Duodecim Specula* made the worst start for a new emblem book. Only 120 of the 250 copies sent to Frankfurt were sold, compared with 255 for the launch of the *Paradisius*. However, as we have just mentioned, unlike previous books, the *Mirrors* of David had been on sale since May at the *Officina Plantiniana*. Natalis's *Folio* seems to have sold with great difficulty and only represented 6 per cent of the market share in Frankfurt (88 copies). A unique case in the consulted archives, the selling prices of the book in Frankfurt were different from those of Antwerp: when the book was sold with the mention "compl[et]" (complete) it was priced 28 guilders in Frankfurt but only 24 in the *Officina*. The lack of precision in

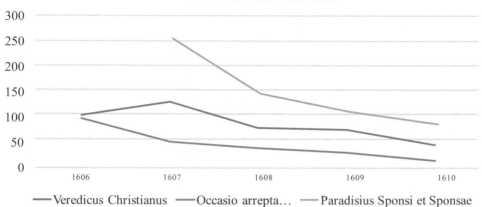

FIGURE 5.2 Sales of Joannes David's emblem books at the Frankfurt fairs between 1606 and 1610

the recording of notebook data raises more difficulties in interpreting some results. However, it seems that a version of the book with the frontispiece from 1599 and bearing Martin Nutius's address (hence the inscription of the date in brackets when the barrels were sent for the fair) was also sold for only 18 guilders. The *Evangelicae historiae imagines*, with 153 illustrations accompanying the author's text, were sold at a price of 14 guilders. The booksellers and publishers present at the fair chose, unsurprisingly, to invest in the cheapest version since 28 copies of the 1599 edition (full version, text plus image) were sold throughout this period, compared to only 9 for the 1606–1607 edition. A few rare exemplars still in stock of the *Monumenta humanae Salutis*[23] by Arias Montano were sold (8 specimens, 2 of which are in in-octavo format and 6 in in-quarto format) and were mainly acquired by private individuals, unfortunately anonymous, whose transactions are recorded at the end of the Frankfurt notebooks under the heading, 'ventes à menu' (meaning sales made directly at the bookstore).

As far as sales techniques are concerned, the results obtained stress that the autumn fair seems to be favoured by the Moretus for launching new products. The three books, that we can track for sale were all presented at this fair and the graph below confirms the importance of the launch fair, which concentrates most of the sales.

---

23   We imitate here Christopher Plantin who always indicated the work in this form in the various account books. The exact title is Arias Benito Montano, *Humanae salutis monumenta* (Antwerp: Christophe Plantin, 1571) (USTC 411594).

68   MILAZZO

The following years witnessed a sharp decrease in sales and there was a dramatic drop at the next fair. The variations are less significant for the *Veridicus* because it was a second edition. At the time of its release on the market the modest demand allowed for sales to resume and increase in 1607 before decreasing again but less dramatically than David's other emblem books.

2   Characteristics of *Veridicus, Paradisius* and *Adnotationes sales*

The search for a rapid return on investment convinced printers to propose several versions of works that had a large number of engraved plates and, therefore high manufacturing costs. David's *Veridicus christianus* and *Paradisius Sponsi* as well as Nadal's *Adnotationes* were sold in three versions. The most affordable solely contained the text (1 guilder and 15 patars for the *Veridicus*, 5 guilders for the *Adnotationes*), whilst the most expensive was a combination of text and images (6 guilders and 15 patars for David, 24 florins for Natalis). When the number of illustrations justified a separate edition, Theodoor Galle offered copies under the title *Icones* that were comprised the engravings but no text.[24] These were published under his own name, that of David disappeared (5 guilders for the *editio princeps* of the *Veridicus*, 15 guilders for the *Icones* of Natalis). As these prices suggest, Jesuit works were only available to an affluent readership. Compared to basic necessities, collections of Tridentine emblems books remained relatively expensive to buy.[25] The Jesuit adoption of the emblematic form was thus paradoxical: they sought to reach a young and literate public through texts and the illiterate with the images (as Jesuit authors

---

24   This was an agreement between Theodoor Galle and Jan Moretus I. The engraver who owned the copperplates sold in his name the printing of the images only. The printer was in charge of distribution directly in Antwerp or at Frankfurt fairs. See Imhof, *Jan Moretus and the Continuation of the Plantin Press*, I. 220.

25   At the beginning of the seventeenth century, the acquisition of a complete copy of the *Adnotationes* and *Meditationes* of Nadal (i.e. printed text and engravings) represented the equivalent of 47 working days for a worker, the complete edition of the *Veridicus Christianus*, 10 working days. The acquisition of the Nadal book was equivalent to the purchase of about 924 dried herrings, while David's *Veridicus* was equivalent to 125 kg of rye or 8 kg of candles – according to our calculations based on the figures given by Léon Voet in the chapter 'The purchasing power of the guilder', in *The Golden Compasses. A History and Evaluation of the Printing and Publishing Activities of the Officina Plantiniana at Antwerp* (2 vols., Amsterdam: Vangendt – London: Rutledge & Kegan Paul – New York: Schram, 1969–1972), I. 442–443.

FIGURE 5.3 Montage of two separate sheets of the Veridicus Christianus, emphasising the relationship between image and text. Jan David, *Veridicus christianus* (Antwerp: ex officina Plantiniana, 1601)

mention in many prefaces), which in the latter case seems incompatible with the pricing of the works. It is likely that these emblem books at the time of their conception were primarily kept for internal use. This is particularly true for Nadal's volumes. However, the 'price' factor alone does not justify the sale of these works in three versions.

Figure 5.3 shows the two-page montage of the *Veridicus Christianus*, which provides a better understanding of the relationship between image and text. The engraving is the emblem. Indeed, we find the three constituent elements of the emblematic form, the title, the image and the epigram in three languages: Latin, Dutch and French. The long texts by Joannes David, which stretch over several pages, are assimilated to the comments of the emblem. If you look closely at the engravings, you will notice that several scenes are identified by capital letters engraved in the illustration. As shown by the arrows on the montage, they refer to the commentary that allowed readers to switch from image to text. The image thus plays an essential role and seems inseparable from the text and the book was conceived in this way by the author. In fact, he first thought of illustrating his text, which he wished to make available to young people to facilitate the learning of catechism, and the engravings were clearly intended for people who could not read:

> It seemed appropriate to illustrate it with annotations and 100 engraved images so that understanding readers could grasp the text with their eyes, while the incompetent and toughest spirits, in any case, could look at it by sight.[26]

However, the three graphs below show that the image in the Tridentine emblems books only played a secondary function for readers. Indeed, a significant proportion of sales only involved the printed text. Thus 61.1 per cent of the volumes of *Paradisius Sponsi and sponsae* and 52 per cent of the volumes of Natalis *Adnotationes* purchased contained only the text. The difference is less marked for the *Veridicus* where sales of text alone, 157 volumes, were very slightly lower than sales of the book with text and image, 163 volumes. *Icones* alone remained stable with an average of 24 per cent of sales.

As regards the distribution between volumes sold with or without images, these results are identical to those of the Antwerp *Officina*. For David's two collections, it is possible to know from sales journals the exact number of copies that could be sold with a combination of text and images. We know that Moretus and his sons bought lots of engraved images directly from Theodoor Galle and that he could buy copies of the text from the *Officina* if he wanted to sell complete copies.[27] In both cases, the journals keep records of these acquisitions. Between 1606 and 1610, the *Officina Plantiniana* purchased 488 lots of images of *Veridicus* and 447 of *Paradisius* from the engraver. Galle, meanwhile, obtained 96 copies of the text of the first title and 86 copies of the second title over the same period. This means a total of 584 *Veridicus Christianus* or 46 per cent of the total print run and 533 *Paradisius* or 35 per cent of the total print run that could be sold in their full form.[28]

A significant number of Catholic readers attached more importance to the text than to the image and did not perceive the book of emblems as forming a whole. However, as Walter S. Melion points out, the absence of the image

---

26   "*Ea Ipsa deinde scholiis quibusdam, atque adeo centum in aes incisis iconibus illustrare visul est; ut, qui lecta intelligerent, eadem quasi subiecta oculis viderent: & rudiores, quae alias non possent, ipso saltem intuiti legerent*", in: David, *Veridicus christianus*, p. 3.

27   Jan Moretus I had to pay Theodoor Galle for each sets of prints of the 100 engravings he wished to combine with the text.

28   Cumulative figures for all journals consulted for the reference period: For 1606–1608, MPM archives 178–180. For the years 1609 to 1610, MPM archive 216 and MPM archive 217.

considerably reduces the scope and message of the text.[29] Moreover, the sales were in total contradiction with Joannes David's initial approach, which, it should be remembered, sought to facilitate the learning of the catechism for young people with the illustrations of the *Veridicus*, among other things. So how do we explain these results? The answer, it seems to us, was given by Jan Moretus I and Theodoor Galle. Their knowledge of the book and print market, respectively, should not be underestimated. At the very moment of manufacturing David's books, they agreed on the terms of sale and planned to present their products in three forms, and from the outset a sale's price was determined for the text alone.[30]

The fact that the *Icones* sold better than the combined versions was not surprising in Antwerp, where the print market developed strongly, even though it slowed down somewhat after 1585, when Spain's reconquest of the Southern Low Countries led to the immigration of great engravers to Paris.[31]

In spite of everything, at the beginning of the seventeenth century the print market was structured and the number of amateurs and collectors steadily increased until the beginning of the eighteenth century. It is this market that the lots of engravings sold separately clearly targeted. Theodoor Galle's name replaced the printer's name in the frontispiece of the title page, and if the printer wanted to sell them, he had to buy them.

---

29   Walter S. Melion's approach follows the presentation of our first results concerning the international sales of Joannes David's books at the conference held in Liege in February 2017. I would like to thank him warmly for our many rich and fascinating exchanges which, although they did not provide a definitive answer to the question, allowed me to enrich my thinking.

30   At the same conference, Dirk Imhof, curator at the Plantin-Moretus Museum in Antwerp, pointed out that it is technically more complicated for printers to insert the image directly on the back of the text as Plantin himself wrote it: "We add to this that these figures must be printed in books in that all of the cited figures printed separately on white paper will be given at a much lower price than when they are printed in the named books. It is always more difficult to print the figures in the books themselves and, what makes more of a difference, it frequently happens that something is erroneously printed, and then the sheet is lost and the entire book is unusable as a result", in Bowen and Imhof, *Christopher Plantin and Engraved Book*, p. 363. This is not the case here. While it is true that some customers certainly combined text and image themselves, the distribution of volumes of text-only and *Icones* in Frankfurt confirms the primacy of text over image.

31   Hélène Duccini, 'Traditions iconographiques et partage des modèles en Europe (première moitié du XVIIᵉ siècle)', *Le Temps des médias*, 11:2 (2008), pp. 10–24 (esp. 16–18). On this topic, the reference study remains to this day that of Jan Van Der Stock, *Printing Images in Antwerp. The Introduction of Printmaking in a City: Fifteenth Century to 1585* (Rotterdam: Sound & Vision Interactive Rotterdam, 1998).

72   MILAZZO

The importance of sales of texts-only editions targets, in our opinion, a clientele with fewer resources than the more wealthy who could acquire the whole book (text + image). We know that until an advanced date, readers preferred text over image. The absent image, as Michel Pastoureau expressed it, has more enriching virtues on the reader's imagination than the image presented and the sales of David's emblem books confirm this trend.[32] It is not necessary to have the engraving in front of your eyes, in this way, the reader who wishes to fulfil his meditation duty adopts the Ignatian method, where mental image occupies an important place in spiritual exercises.[33] This practice persists well after the publication of Joannes David's books. The *Imago primi saeculi Societatis Jesu*, published by Balthasar Moretus in 1640, is an emblematic in-folio work commemorating the first century of the Jesuit Company's existence. A notebook containing the sales made at the Frankfurt fairs between 1644 and 1647 shows that the Jesuit festive book is sold in a version combining text and image, 17 guilders, the *Icones* cost 14 guilders and the text alone is sold for 3 guilders.[34]

3   Geography of Sales

The below map shows that sales are concentrated around the two major demographic regions of the Rhine/Palatinate (Cologne, Mainz, Strasburg and Basel for the Rhine, Heidelberg on the Neckar), Saxony and along the Main (Frankfurt, Würzburg and Nuremberg). Unsurprisingly for the Tridentine emblem books, we notice the predominance of the Catholic cities of the Holy Empire (Cologne, Mainz, Trier, Worms, Ingolstadt and its Catholic university) as well as in the Habsburg states of Austria (Graz).

For the book fair cities, Frankfurt is well represented and as is Leipzig. As the latter's fair became increasingly important, it is logical that many volumes were sent to Saxony.[35] The first effects of the Counter-Reformation can also be

---

32   Michel Pastoureau, 'L'illustration du livre : comprendre ou rêver ?', in Roger Chartier and Henri-Jean Martin (eds), *Histoire de l'édition française* (4 vols., Paris: Cercle de la Librairie, 1989–1991), I. 605–606.

33   On the Ignatian method and the role of the mental image in spiritual exercises see: Pierre-Antoine Fabre, *Ignace de Loyola. Le lieu et l'image* (Paris: Vrin, 1992), which devotes many chapters to this issue.

34   MPM archive 187 fol. 24v.

35   Sales in Frankfurt began to decline sharply in favour of Leipzig after Sweden's siege of the city in 1631. Major companies such as the Willer or Zetzner companies were forced to reduce their respective activities. See John L. Flood, '*Omnium totius orbis emporiorum compendium*: The Frankfurt Fair in the Early Modern Period', in Robin Myers, Michael

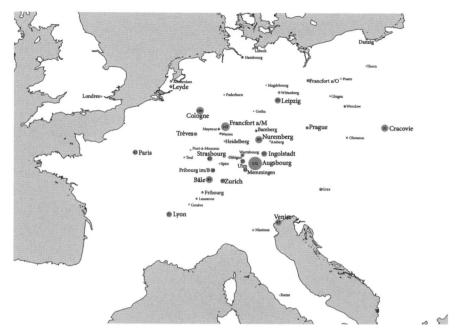

FIGURE 5.4 Sales by cities of emblem books published by the Officina plantiniana at the Frankfurt fairs (spring and autumn) between 1606 and 1610 according to the Cahiers de Francfort kept at the Plantin-Moretus Museum in Antwerp

seen with the presence on the map of cities where Jesuit colleges were established (Pont-à-Mousson, Würzburg, Olomouc). The progress of the Roman Church is particularly visible in cities such as Freiburg and Basel.

In fact, Freiburg gradually became a great centre of Tridentine spirituality and many Marian Confraternities and Congregations blossomed in German-speaking Switzerland.[36] In contrast, the map suggests two further observations: the first is the significant presence of cities that had converted to Lutheranism or Calvinism where Jesuit structures were absent at this period; the second is the importance of the volumes that were transported to Augsburg, which remains the largest distribution centre in terms of the quantity of volumes purchased.

The importance of David's volumes, which fill the barrels of the booksellers of Nuremberg (95 volumes), Basel (85 volumes) and Zurich (33 volumes)

Harris and Giles Mandelbrote (eds), *Fairs, Markets & the Itinerant Book Trade* (London: Oak Knoll Press, 2007), p. 25.

36 Bernard Vogler, *Le Monde germanique et helvétique. À l'époque des réformes. 1515–1618* (2 vols., Paris: Société d'édition d'enseignement supérieur, 1981), II. 462–463.

between 1606 and 1610, may come as a surprise because of the confessional position of these cities, which adhered to Protestantism very early on. An analysis of the orders placed by booksellers and printers reveals the two-way trade in Tridentine emblem books in Europe. The main bookseller in Nuremberg who was supplied by the Moretus is Balthasar Caymox or Caimox. The *Dictionnaire des artistes dont nous avons des Estampes* of Karl-Heinrich von Heinecken – we consulted the 1789 edition published in Leipzig – indicates the existence of a "Balthasar Caimox. Marchand d'estampes à Nuremberg"[37] Because he was present at every fair, we conducted a survey of his purchases of *Veridicus Christianus*. The result shows that all the copies that reached Nuremberg contained the illustrations or were the *Icones* with Galle's address. The analysis of Basel and Zurich sales confirms this trend. It is therefore for the print markets (and not book markets) that these purchases are made each year at fairs.

On the contrary, in the Swabian city of Augsburg, Catholics and Protestants had always lived together. The city's economic power was greatly undermined by the rise of political-religious conflicts in the second half of the sixteenth century. At the beginning of the seventeenth century, no city symbolised more the hardening of identity and the stakes of ideological normalisation.[38] The heirs of Georg Willer had preserved one of the largest bookstores in Southern Germany. The large number of volumes that they systematically bought at each fair and the success of their Viennese branch demonstrates that they had a sufficiently large distribution network to sell stocks and meet specific demands. If one observes the purchases of the *Paradisius* made by Georg Willer's heirs in Augsburg at the fairs during the reference period, out of 82 volumes acquired, 56 contain only the text alone, 6 the text and the illustration, 20 the engravings alone.[39]

For this period, the example of volumes leaving Frankfurt for Krakow is particularly interesting.[40] In the Polish-Lithuanian confederation, united in a

---

37   Karl-Heinrich von Heinecken, *Dictionnaire des artistes, dont nous avons des estampes, avec une notice détaillée de leurs ouvrages gravés*, Volume 3, (Leipzig, 1789), p. 488.

38   See on this topic see Etienne François, *Protestant et Catholique en Allemagne. Identités et pluralisme. Augsbourg, 1648–1806*, (Paris: Albin Michel, 1993).

39   Accumulation carried out on all Frankfurt notebooks, including the springs and autumns fairs according to the chronological framework (see note 15).

40   Laurent Tatarenko, 'Pluriconfessionnalité et politique de tolérance: le cas de la Pologne', in Wolfgang Kaiser (ed.), *L'Europe en conflits. Les affrontements religieux et la genèse de l'Europe moderne vers 1500-vers 1650* (Rennes: Presses universitaires de Rennes, 2009), pp. 239–266.

single state in July 1566, the political and religious context was marked by a balance between a predominantly Protestant nobility and two models of traditional Christianity, Catholic and Orthodox.[41] This nobility, which played an increasingly important political role, was thwarted in its ambitions when the Counter-Reformation movement tried to reverse the principles of tolerance under the reign of the very Catholic Sigismund Wasa III. Many conversions weakened the Protestants, Sigismund III hoping that the strengthening of Catholicism would reinforce the monarchy. His policy obliged him to confront a major revolt in 1606–1607.[42] It was during these years of instability and crystallisation of the positions of Catholics and Protestants that Father Joannes David's 91 books were purchased by booksellers residing in Krakow. It is unlikely that these books were intended for students at the University, where enrolments were significantly reduced during this period.[43] Irina Kaniewska, in her study on the students of Krakow, tells us that as soon as they settled in Poland, the Jesuits intended to found a school there, which they only achieved after 1611.[44] In our opinion, it was as a tool for conversion, as a weapon of the Counter-Reformation, that we should consider the presence of David's emblems in Krakow rather than as a teaching tool for teachers and students of the colleges, even if these two elements are not contradictory.

On the subject of David's collections, our study confirms the conclusions of Éva Knapp and Gábor Tüskés on emblematics in Hungary. Indeed, it is more than likely that, through Augsburg, a number of works had been delivered to Vienna, thus allowing direct access to the Hungarian market. Their analysis of 37 libraries catalogues of Jesuit institutions shows that the author of the *Veridicus Christianus*, although present in some libraries, was not among the most represented Jesuit authors. The emblematic works most often used by Jesuit fathers to support their courses were published later. Among the

---

41   See on this topic see Tatarenko, 'Pluriconfessionnalité et politique de tolérance: le cas de la Pologne', pp. 256–257.

42   Tatarenko, 'Pluriconfessionnalité et politique de tolérance: le cas de la Pologne', p. 257.

43   Irina Kaniewska, 'La conjoncture étudiante de l'Université de Cracovie aux XVIIᵉ et XVIIᵉ siècles', in Dominique Julia, Jacques Revel and Roger Chartier, (eds), *Histoire sociale des populations étudiantes* (2 vol., Paris: Éditions de l'Ecole des hautes études en sciences sociales, 1986–1989), I. 136.

44   The Jesuits founded a boarding house for novices in 1611 and opened a theological school in the autumn of 1623. Grammar courses for lay students began in 1625. Kaniewska, 'La conjoncture étudiante de l'Université de Cracovie aux XVIIᵉ et XVIIIᵉ siècles', see in particular footnote 5, page 151.

authors most in demand, works by Jeremias Drexel (224 volumes in 25 libraries), Henricus Engelgrave (187 volumes in 23 libraries) and Herman Hugo (98 volumes in 12 libraries) ranked far ahead of David's works (fewer than 20 volumes in all libraries consulted).[45]

Sales to Venice appear to be a duel market. They occurred at a time when Catholic missionaries needed tools to reconquer the populations converted to the Protestant faith who had taken refuge in the valleys of North-Western Piedmont to flee the persecutions of Catholics.[46] Venice was also an important centre of the printmaking trade.

4   Conclusion

Jan Moretus I fully understood the changes that took place in the Antwerp book market after the Calvinist episode, which saw the emergence of an industry dedicated to the Tridentine book market. Moreover, according to Maurice Sabbe, one of the curators of the Plantin-Moretus Museum, an analysis of the editions printed on all the city's presses gives a faithful picture of the religious and intellectual currents 'modifiés' (modified).[47] Not only did printers serve the Counter-Reformation, but they also adapted to the artistic tastes of the moment by producing impressive luxurious editions.[48] The taste of the affluent customer for fine illustrations led to an increase in the number of copper plate engravings.

---

45   Éva Knapp and Gábor Tüskés, 'Teaching of Emblematics in Jesuit Colleges', in Marc Van Vaeck, John Manning (eds), *The Jesuits and the Emblem Tradition. Selected Papers of the Leuven International Emblem Conference, 18–23 August, 1996* (Turnhout: Brepols, 1999), pp. 115–159. See table of most represented Jesuit authors page 136. Consult also: Éva Knapp and Gábor Tüskés, *Emblematics in Hungary. A Study of the History of Symbolic Representation in Renaissance and Baroque Literature* (Tübingen: Max Niemeyer Verlag, 2003).

46   Chiara Povero, 'Controverses entre catholiques et réformés : duels verbaux avec les armes pointues de la rhétorique', in Martin Dumont (ed.), *Coexistences confessionnelles en Europe à l'époque moderne*, (Paris: Les Éditions du Cerf, 2016), pp. 65–84.

47   Maurice Sabbe, *La vie des livres à Anvers aux XVIe, XVIIe et XVIIIe siècle*, (Brussels: Éditions du Musée du livre, 1926), p. 99.

48   As Stijn Van Rossem points out, at the beginning of the sixteenth century, the city of Antwerp experienced a relative economic and cultural boom and printers were oriented towards the luxury trade and the spread of the precepts and concepts of the Council of Trent. See for instance Stijn Van Rossem, 'The Bookshop of the Counter-Reformation Revisited. The Verdussen Company and the Trade in Catholic Publications, Antwerp, 1585–1648', *Quaerendo* 38 (2008), pp. 306–321 (esp. 306–307).

This evolution modified the status of the image in David and Natalis's Tridentine emblem books. The engraving captured the emblematic form that included three of the fundamental elements that composed the emblem (Text, image and epigram). The long texts that accompanied the image can be compared to the extensive commentaries on Andrea Alciato's emblems that appeared after the 1550s and which transformed the original small book into an encyclopaedic work of thousand pages, a practice increasingly imitated by the authors of emblem books and more particularly by Jesuits. Consequently, with Joannes David, the image became independent of the text. Larger in size, it was considered a work of art in its own right. The coppers, with their high manufacturing costs, were produced directly by the great Antwerp merchants and engravers. A double market was thus created, opposing readers for whom the text was more important than the image to collectors and print enthusiasts.

As Walter Melion perfectly pointed out, in all the prefaces of his emblem books, Joannes David 'propounds a general *doctrina imaginis* that construes sacred images as key instruments of spiritual reflection, instruction, and renewal'.[49] His long explanatory text, as we have seen, played a fundamental role: without the text, the image lost a lot of meaning. In this sense, sales reflected a real paradox between the author's intentions and the use of the book by readers. Amputated from the image or text, the general meaning of the message that Joannes David wished to communicate is diminished. From the acquirer's point of view, a first explanation was certainly the high price of the complete book. Without the images, the Jesuit's text was more affordable and, as a result, reached a wider customer base. When the images were collected and sold separately, the sales at the Frankfurt trade fairs speak for themselves: the main centres of the print trade were clearly mainly interested in the David and Natalis *Icones* market. This market was reserved for a more discerning and wealthy audience. On the other hand, it is regrettable that, because of the lack of further documentation, it is only possible to analyse the first sales circle for emblem books.

---

49 Walter S. Melion, 'Figured Personification and Parabolic Embodiment in Jan David's Occasio Arrepta, Neglecta' in Walter S. Melion and Bart Ramakers (eds), *Personification. Embodying Meaning and Emotion* (Leiden, Boston: Brill, 2016) p. 371.

PART 2

Publishing Enterprises

∴

CHAPTER 6

A French Book in the Low Countries: Matthieu de Launoy's *Déclaration et Réfutation* and Its Reissues in Douai, Cambrai and Antwerp (1578–1579)

Alexander Soetaert

In the past decades, historians have frequently juxtaposed the long conflicts that paralysed both France and the Spanish Habsburg-ruled Low Countries during the late sixteenth century, respectively known as the Wars of Religion and the Dutch Revolt. Starting in the 1560s, both conflicts were provoked by the increasing number of Calvinist faithful, dividing a formerly unified *corpus christianum* and provoking civil war. Both countries experienced traumatising periods of iconoclasm and military and religious violence. Yet, remarkable differences have been noticed too. While Catholics in the Low Countries generally refrained from the use of violence, their French counterparts were involved in the large-scale killing of religious opponents, most notably during the St Bartholomew's Day massacre in 1572.[1] The outcomes of the conflicts were also very different. By the mid-1580s the Low Countries became divided between the emerging Dutch Republic in the north, where Calvinism became the established religion, and the southern provinces, again controlled by Spanish-Habsburg authorities, who exclusively accepted the profession of the Roman Catholic faith. By contrast, following the defeat of the radical Catholic League, the French monarchy finally succeeded in pacifying the conflict with the Edict of Nantes (1598), granting limited and temporal freedom of worship to the Huguenots.

Moving beyond mere comparison, several scholars have demonstrated that both conflicts were intensely interrelated, especially on the level of diplomatic negotiations,[2] and that developments and events in France resonated and

---

1 Judith Pollmann, 'Countering the Reformation in France and the Netherlands: Clerical Leadership and Catholic Violence 1560–1585', *Past & Present*, 190 (2006), pp. 83–120. On the same topic, see also Juliaan J. Woltjer, 'Violence During the Wars of Religion in France and the Netherlands: a Comparison', *Nederlands Archief voor Kerkgeschiedenis*, 76 (1996), pp. 26–45.
2 See for instance, Nicola M. Sutherland, *The Massacre of St. Bartholomew and the European Conflict 1559–1572* (London: MacMillan, 1973), esp. chapters III, VIII, IX, XIII, XV, XVI; Jean-François

influenced those in the Low Countries. The development of Reformed doctrine and churches in the Low Countries, for instance, was closely modelled after the French example.[3] In the sphere of printed communication, Andrew Pettegree has discussed the transfer of Catholic texts across the French border, pointing to the many (news) texts of French origin reprinted in Antwerp and Louvain from the 1560s onwards.[4] However, much more research is needed to map such connections, especially between the Catholic parties in the conflicts. It is also striking that the role of the French-speaking or Walloon provinces, located in the south of the Low Countries, has hitherto received but little attention. The dialects of Artesia, Hainaut, Namur and the extreme south of Flanders certainly differed from those spoken in Paris and elsewhere in France, but (as I have argued elsewhere) booksellers in towns such as Arras, Douai, Mons, and Saint-Omer had to rely on the French book market to meet the demands of their largely French-speaking clientele.[5] In this respect, the contribution of the French-speaking provinces to the transfer of Catholic texts between France and the Low Countries appears more important than has hitherto been acknowledged.

Offering a first glance at the place of the French-speaking Low Countries in the textual exchange with France, the following pages are devoted to one particular book, entitled *La déclaration et réfutation des fausses suppositions et perverses applications d'aucunes sentences des saintes Écritures, desquelles les Ministres se sont servis en ce dernier temps à diviser la Chrétienté*. Written by Matthieu de Launoy and Henri Pennetier, it was first printed in Paris in late

---

Labourdette, *Charles IX et la puissance espagnole: diplomatie et guerres civiles (1563–1574)* (Paris: H. Champion, 2013), esp. pp. 87–102, 153–168, 518–527.

3 Nicolaas H. Gootjes, *The Belgic Confession: its History and Sources* (Grand Rapids: Baker Academic, 2007), esp. pp. 62–67; Gérard Moreau, *Histoire du protestantisme à Tournai jusqu'à la veille de la révolution des Pays-Bas* (Paris: Belles Lettres 1962).

4 Andrew Pettegree, 'France and the Netherlands: the Interlocking of Two Religious Cultures in Print During the Era of Religious Wars', *Nederlands Archief voor Kerkgeschiedenis*, 84 (2004), pp. 318–337. On news networks, see also the more extensive study by Rosanne Baars, *Rumours of Revolt. Civil War and the Emergence of a Transnational News Culture in France and the Netherlands, 1561–1598* (Leiden: Brill, 2021).

5 Alexander Soetaert, 'Printing at the Frontier. The Emergence of a Transregional Book Production in the Ecclesiastical Province of Cambrai', *De Gulden Passer*, 94 (2016), pp. 137–163, esp. pp. 141–142. For instance, over 50 percent of the titles mentioned in the 1569 bookshop inventory of Alard Alexandre in Saint-Omer, were printed in France. The inventory of the bookshops in Mons, drawn up in the same year, shows that more than 40 percent of the Latin books were printed in France, as well as three quarters of the French-language books. See Sébastien Afonso, *Imprimeurs, société et réseaux dans les villes de langue romane des Pays-Bas méridionaux (1580–ca 1677)* (Université Libre de Bruxelles, unpublished PhD thesis, 2015–2016), pp. 18–19.

A FRENCH BOOK IN THE LOW COUNTRIES   83

1577.[6] In the two years following the *editio princeps*, the book was not only regularly reissued in Paris, but also reprinted, rearranged and translated into Dutch in Douai and Cambrai, just north of the French border.[7] Unlike the pamphlets analysed by Andrew Pettegree, the *Déclaration et réfutation* was an elaborate controversial treatise covering over two hundred folios. It was not the kind of text that a printer would hastily put on his press. Before investing a considerable amount of time, labour and money in the production of yet another edition, publishers must have been convinced of its commercial potential. Why did they decide to reprint the book anew themselves, rather than importing copies from Paris, as they usually did? Why did they select this particular book, among the many hundreds of editions that yearly came from Parisian presses? What or who incited them to do so? How can the remarkable appeal of this particular French book in the Low Countries be explained, and what does this tell us about interaction between Catholics on both sides of the border?

1   Paris, Geneva and Dordt

First of all, it might be helpful to cast an eye on the motivations of the original French authors, Matthieu de Launoy and Henri Pennetier. Launoy is possibly best known as one of the leaders of the Parisian section of the Catholic League that contested the legitimacy of Henry of Navarre-Bourbon as the successor of King Henry III.[8] Following the collapse of the Parisian League in March 1594, Launoy's firm ideological conviction, combined with his overtly anti-royalist and subversive opinions, drove him into exile in the Spanish-Habsburg Low

---

6   Matthieu de Launoy and Henri Pennetier, *La declaration et refutation des fausses suppositions, et perverses applications d'aucunes sentences des sainctes Escritures* (Paris: Jean du Carroy, 1577) (USTC 763).

7   Matthieu de Launoy and Henri Pennetier, *La refutation des fausses suppositions, et perverses applications d'aucunes sentences des sainctes Escritures …* (Douai: Jean Bogart, 1578) (USTC 13153); Id., *Petit bouclier de la foy catholique* (Douai: Jacques Boscard, 1578) (USTC 13154); Id., *La declaration et refutation des fausses suppositions, et perverses applications d'aucunes sentences des sainctes Ecritures, desquelles les Ministres se sont servis en ce dernier temps, à diviser la Chrétienté* (Cambrai: Victor Robat, 1579) (USTC 7636); Id., *Die verclaringhe ende verworpinghe van het valsch verstant en[de] tquaet mis bruycke[n] van sommige sententie[n] der heyliger schrifture[n] / de welcke die ministers misbruyckt hebben in dese laetste tyde[n] om te scheyden en[de] te beroeren de Christenheyt* (Douai: Jean Bogart, 1578) (USTC 13153).

8   Some biographical details about Launoy can be found in D. Masson, 'Launoy (Matthieu de)', in *Dictionnaire de biographie française* (21 vols., Paris: Letouzey & Ané, 1933–), XIX, col. 1356–1357.

Countries, along with many more so-called *ligueurs de l'exil*.[9] But two decades earlier, while completing the *Déclaration et réfutation*, Launoy appears to have still been expecting a solution from the French monarchy. In the dedicatory letter to King Henry III, Launoy praised the continuous efforts made by the king, as well as by his mother Catherine de' Medici and his brother François, Duke of Anjou, in surmounting and pacifying the conflicts dividing the kingdom. It was his profound hope that his native country would finally find a longstanding period of peace.[10] However, it is hardly coincidental that he expressed these hopes only twelve days after the signing of the Treaty of Bergerac (14 September 1577). Although this new religious compromise limited the free profession of Reformed doctrine to one place per district, it had still not been forbidden altogether, much to the regret of radical Catholics such as Launoy.[11] As he phrased it, a durable pacification would not even be thinkable if the "ruses of Satan" and Huguenot falsities were not fully uncovered.[12] In this regard, Launoy's eulogy for the monarchy conceals a fundamental critique of its willingness to pacify with the Huguenots and tolerate Calvinist worship in the kingdom.

Surprisingly, in the years preceding the writing of the *Déclaration et réfutation*, Launoy had made quite a U-turn himself. He first served as a Catholic priest, but started professing the Reformed doctrine around 1560. After his conversion in Geneva, he worked as a minister and preacher in Champagne and later in Tournai and Valenciennes, the most important Calvinist strongholds in the French-speaking Low Countries. By the time of the St Bartholomew Day's massacre, Launoy was back in Paris. Around 1576 he reconverted to Catholicism and again travelled to the Low Countries, this time to Dordt in Holland. Only early in 1577 did he return to the French capital.[13] Considering his confessional wanderings, one can hardly think of a person better placed than Launoy to

---

9   Roger Descimon and José Javier Ruiz Ibáñez, *Les ligueurs de l'exil. Le refuge catholique français après 1594* (Seyssel: Champ Vallon, 2005), esp. p. 264.

10   Launoy and Pennetier, *La refutation des fausses suppositions*, fols. *v v–*vi r. In the same months, also a shorter book by the same authors came off the presses at Paris, in which they defended themselves against the accusations of some Reformed ministers: Matthieu de Launoy and Henri Pennetier, *Defense ... contre les fausses accusations & perverses calomnies des Ministres, de Paris, Sedan & autres êpars és Provinces adiacentes* (Paris: Jean Du Carroy, 1577) (USTC 12178).

11   Mack P. Holt, *The French Wars of Religion* (Cambridge: Cambridge University Press, 2005), pp. 111–112. The dedicatory letter was signed on 29 September.

12   Launoy and Pennetier, *La refutation des fausses suppositions*, fol. *vi v.

13   Lina Taha Akkache, *Mathieu de Launoy et son 'Discours chrestien': édition critique – annotations – commentaire* (Université de Tours, Centre d'études supérieures de la Renaissance, unpublished PhD thesis, 1990), pp. 21–34.

A FRENCH BOOK IN THE LOW COUNTRIES

uncover the so-called Huguenot falsities as detailed and systematically as it was attempted in the *Déclaration et réfutation*. A former Huguenot minister, Launoy could draw from a perfect knowledge of the Reformed doctrine. He could also dispose of a considerable number of compromising anecdotes and details about the fundamental doctrinal disagreements that divided Reformed theologians. He could now exploit this inside information in favour of the Catholic cause.

Next to Launoy's name, the title-page of the book also mentions that of Henri Pennetier, but no details are known about his life, except that he was likewise a former Huguenot minister who had recently converted to Catholicism. Some passages in the book indicate that Pennetier had taken refuge in England for some time, before meeting with Launoy in Guînes, a small town near Calais. There are no specifications as to which parts had been written by him or if maybe the whole book was a collaborative work. Yet, it is striking that he is always referred to by his last name and mostly in relation to recent developments in England.[14] When anecdotes from Dordt are recalled, on the other hand, these are consistently told in the first person singular.[15] Launoy most probably only relied on Pennetier for very specific sections of the book. Therefore, I will use only Launoy's name hereafter.

After the completion of his book, Launoy turned to the Parisian printer Jean Du Carroy, who printed it in early October 1577. As mentioned before, this first edition was swiftly followed by several reissues. A second, revised and enlarged edition, including an entirely new chapter on transubstantiation, appeared in April of the following year. A third edition was published in May 1579 and a last one appeared in 1582. Although the printing privilege had been granted to Du Carroy in July 1577, it was shared with another Parisian publisher, Guillaume de La Noue, early in 1578. As such, several copies of the second, third and fourth editions bear the name of the latter publisher in their imprints.[16] In addition to these Parisian editions, the Angoulême printer Jean de Minières reissued the book in 1579.[17] This swift succession of editions suggests that the book appealed to the French readership.

---

14   Launoy and Pennetier, *La refutation des fausses suppositions*, fols. 32v, 135v–136r.

15   *Ibidem*, fols. 109r, 112v–113r, 129v.

16   See, USTC 763 (Jean Du Carroy, 1577 – 1st edition), 2601 (Jean Du Carroy, 1578 – 2nd edition), 7285 (Guillaume de La Noue, 1578 – 2nd edition), 1941 (Jean Du Carroy, 1579 – 3rd edition), 21774 (Jean Du Carroy and Guillaume de La Noue, 1579 – 3rd edition) and 75022 (Guillaume de La Noue, 1582 – 4th edition).

17   Matthieu de Launoy and Henri Pennetier, *La déclaration et réfutation des fausses suppositions & perverses applications d'aucunes sentences des Sainctes escritures* (Angoulême: Jean de Minières, 1579) (USTC 62023/62114). I have not been able to consult this edition

Launoy subdivided his voluminous book in three parts. A first one was entirely devoted to the defence of Catholic doctrine. He especially focused on the points that had been questioned and rejected by the Reformed faith, such as the importance of good works, the celebration of Mass and the veneration of saints and images. The second book elaborated on the legitimacy of the Catholic Church, which – according to Launoy – was firmly rooted in apostolic tradition. He argued that the Calvinists should be considered mere sectaries lacking any legitimate claim and that this was amply illustrated by specific aspects of their doctrine. In a final part, the author took a seemingly more conciliatory tone, exhorting Huguenots to follow his example and return to the Catholic Church.[18] Here, Launoy substantiated the call he had already made in the 'Avertissement', urging those who had left the Church "not solely to depend on the opinion of their Doctors, and leaders of their sects", but to "think and consider carefully the doctrine of the Roman Church and the reasons put forward here".[19] So, after having defended Catholic and refuted Calvinist doctrine, thereby also justifying his own conversion, Launoy ultimately aimed at convincing his former brethren to follow in his footsteps.

The *Déclaration et réfutation* was indeed picked up on the other side of the confessional divide, yet it was not met with approval. The book even provoked a detailed reaction from Geneva, composed by the theologian Lambert Daneau (ca 1635–ca 1590). This *Réponse chrétienne*, published in 1578, meticulously refuted the accusations issued by Launoy in the first part of his book.[20] According to the foreword, sequel editions were to rebut the positions expressed in the second and third book, but these apparently never materialised.[21] However, since the book was not only proving Calvinist doc-

---

     and to determine whether it uses the sheets of one of the previous Paris editions or is a complete or partial reprint of one of these.

18   For a detailed description, see Taha Akkache, *Mathieu de Launoy et son 'Discours chrestien'*, pp. 65–73.

19   "… [de] ne se point tant arrester à leur opinion & ne pas tellement iurer, *In verba Magistri*, c'est à dire, ne dependre pas tellement de la seule opinion de leurs Docteurs, & chefs de leurs sectes, qu'ils ne pensent & considerent diligemment la doctrine de l'Eglise Romaine & les raisons que nous leur mettons icy en avant, pour mieux & plus prudemment aviser à eux.", in Launoy and Pennetier, *La refutation des fausses suppositions*, ** iij v.

20   [Lambert Daneau], *Response chrestiene, au premier liure des calomnies & renouvelees faussetez de deux Apostats, Matthieu de Launoy … & Henry Pennetier* ([Geneva: Claude Juge], 1578) (USTC 2602).

21   In 1580 a second edition of Daneau's *Response* was issued, but it still includes only the reaction to the eight chapters of the first book of the *Déclaration et réfutation*: [Lambert Daneau], *Response chrestienne aux calomnies et renouveles faussetez de deux Apostats, Matthieu de Launoy … & Henry Pennetier* ([Geneva: Jean de Laon], 1580) (USTC 2917).

A FRENCH BOOK IN THE LOW COUNTRIES

trine wrong, but also reaffirming the most important Catholic principles, it may have been directed just as much to a Catholic readership. The *Déclaration et réfutation* also contained a very strong, although more implicit message for the French Catholics: if they really longed for a durable peace, they should first and foremost remain true to the old faith.

To support his reasoning, Launoy often referred to his time in the Low Countries, and Dordt in particular.[22] Still, the book neither offered a systematic description or analysis of the Dutch Revolt, nor a thorough comparison with simultaneous developments in France. He actually also referred to England, Scotland and Germany.[23] He may have conceived the plan for the *Déclaration et réfutation* already in the Low Countries, and the developments there certainly influenced his thinking. However, it was published in Paris and was presented as a reaction against the recently concluded Treaty of Bergerac, rather than to the Pacification of Ghent of 1576. Launoy had previously preached in the Low Countries as a Calvinist minister and would find himself there again as a *ligueur de l'exil* after 1594, but there is no evidence that he was in contact with Catholic circles in Habsburg territories during the late 1570s. So, the question remains why particularly this book aroused the interest of printers and readers in the Low Countries. To solve this problem, the remainder of this chapter will more carefully discuss the successive editions issued there, asking how they were adapted to local circumstances and who may have initiated their publication.

2 Tournai

The first edition of Launoy's book printed outside France was that edited by Jan de Mouronval, priest of the cathedral church of Tournai. He dedicated his version, retitled *Petit bouclier de la foi catholique*, to the inhabitants of Tournai on the occasion of the new year 1578. Since no printer operated in Tournai in these years, the book was printed by Jacques Boscard in the university town of Douai. Unlike for the Paris editions there is no colophon indicating an exact date of printing, but it probably came off the press early in 1578, a few months following the *editio princeps*.[24] In his dedicatory letter Mouronval explained that he highly valued Launoy's book, but also realised that it was

---

22   Launoy and Pennetier, *La refutation des fausses suppositions*, fols. 71r–v, 72v, 108v–109r, 112v–113r, 129v, 174r–v.

23   *Ibidem*, fols. 16r, 20r, 32v, 71r–v, 72v, 102r–103r, 135v–136r, 164r, 174r.

24   On Mouronval (sometimes also spelled Moronval), see: Paul Bergmans, 'Mouronval (Jean de)', in *Biographie nationale [de Belgique]* (43 vols, Brussels: Bruylant, 1866–1986), XV, col. 274–275.

prolix and interwoven with discourses and narrations that delay the reader from being able to take in promptly the doctrine it included and that it is of such a high price that not everyone can afford to have it.[25]

The Tournai priest thus abandoned the idea of a complete reissue. Instead, he selected the sections that appeared most important to him and rewrote these as dialogues between Launoy and the frequently mentioned Huguenot minister Capel, reducing a book of several hundred pages to no more than ninety. In the margins, he consistently referred to the exact location of the subjects discussed in the original Parisian version.

Mouronval's selection unveils a lot about his appreciation of the original book and the readership he had in mind. Over two thirds of the text came from the first part of Launoy's text, explaining the key points of Catholic doctrine. So, the *Petit bouclier* mainly elaborated on justification, images, the Holy Sacrament, praying to the saints and, most notably, the Mass. By contrast, large sections of the second and third books, refuting Reformed doctrine and convincing Calvinists to return to the Catholic Church, were left out. The pleas for pacification prominent in Launoy's dedicatory letter almost completely disappeared. As the title of this new version aptly indicated, this was a "little shield of the Catholic faith": a book first and foremost intended to defend Catholic doctrine, rather than decisively to refute Calvinism or to gain converts. Consequently, it was aimed at a Catholic readership far more explicitly than the original. Mouronval himself highlighted this reorientation in the dedicatory letter: in the first place, he wanted to make sure that the readers were able to extract the essentials of Catholic doctrine from the book in order to prevent more Catholics from leaving the Church. So, in contrast to its original author, the priest judged the book especially appropriate to remedy the ignorance of the Catholic faithful, much more than to convince stubborn Calvinists.

Although the *Petit bouclier* came off a press located in Douai, it should be considered as a reaction to recent developments in Tournai. The bishop's town, one of the major Calvinist strongholds of the Low Countries, was harshly treated by royal forces in the aftermath of the iconoclastic riots of 1566. The Duke of Alba dismissed the town magistrate and started a thorough repression, arresting, imprisoning, banishing and executing hundreds of inhabitants. Many more sought refuge in England or elsewhere, while Habsburg authorities

---

25 "prolixe & entremeslé de discours & narrations, lesquelles retardant le lecteur d'en pouuoir tirer promptement la doctrine y contenue, ioinct qu'il est de tel pris, que chascun n'a moien de l'auoir", in: Launoy and Pennetier, *Petit bouclier*, A2r–v.

A FRENCH BOOK IN THE LOW COUNTRIES

started a re-catholicisation policy in Tournai.[26] Following the Pacification of Ghent (1576), however, large groups of refugees returned and, by the summer of 1578, they called upon this agreement to demand the free profession of their faith, which was promptly forbidden by the town's governor.[27] By that moment, Mouronval had apparently already left Tournai, heading for Amiens in France. The reasons for his departure remain unknown, but it seems that he maintained contacts in France for some years already. This possibly explains why he was among the first to notice Launoy's book.[28] Notwithstanding his departure, his version was clearly conceived as an answer to the renewed Calvinist threat in Tournai, and the Low Countries more generally.

3   Douai

In the same year as Mouronval's anthology, a complete reissue of Launoy's treatise was printed by Jan Bogart, a Leuven native who had moved to Douai a few years before and was now becoming the town's most prolific printer. This edition included all chapters and preliminaries of the original edition. The only addition was an undated ecclesiastical approbation, given by the English Catholic theologian Thomas Stapleton, then Regius Professor of Theology of the University of Douai. It can only be guessed who was the driving force behind this edition, but again there is a clear link to the local political situation. In March 1578, the lord of Escobecques, governor of the province of Lille-Douai-Orchies, enforced an exceptional renewal of the town magistrate, an outright violation of Douai's privileges. The newly-established magistrate was exclusively composed of adherents of the rebellious States-General and William of Orange, although its members were not overtly Calvinist. Almost immediately they decided to expulse the English College, a seminary for the training of English missionary priests founded a decade earlier by the later

---

26   Adolphe Hocquet, *Tournai et le Tournaisis au XVIe siècle, au point de vue politique et social* (Brussels: Académie royale de Belgique, 1906), pp. 152–182; Charlie R. Steen, *A Chronicle of Conflict: Tournai 1559–1567* (Utrecht: HES, 1985).

27   Hocquet, *Tournai et le Tournaisis au XVIe siècle*, pp. 213–114, 228. According to Hocquet some 6000 Protestants returned to Tournai. The contemporary Barthélémy Liétart, delegate for the Tournaisis at the States-General in Antwerp in 1578, estimated the number demanding freedom of belief to 700 or 800 (see his account published in the *Bulletin de la Commission royale d'histoire*, 3rd series, 11 (1870), pp. 371–424, on p. 421).

28   Bergmans, 'Mouronval (Jean de)', col. 274. According to several biographical dictionaries cited by Bergmans, another book by Mouronval (of which I have not found any copies) was published in Paris in 1574. If this information is correct, this may explain how Launoy's book came to his attention.

Cardinal William Allen. In October, the magistrate went even further by expelling the Jesuits, a decision justified as a measure to prevent armed uproar. Shortly thereafter, the royalist party regained control of the town hall. The renewal of the administration was revoked and those who had participated to the *coup d'état municipal*, as Frédéric Duquenne has described it, were to be excluded from all future appointments.[29] In early January 1579, the Union of Arras reconciled the Province of Walloon Flanders, to which Douai belonged, with King Philip II.

The events of 1578 must have deeply shocked the university town's staunchly Catholic academic and political elites. Douai had remained a predominantly Catholic town since its university, founded by the king in 1559, was conceived as a "bulwark against heresy" on the French frontier. Unlike Tournai and Valenciennes, the town was unaffected by the iconoclastic riots of 1566 and, consequently, had not faced royal siege or large-scale repression.[30] But during the summer of 1578 local Calvinists equally demanded freedom of worship which was, just like in Tournai, immediately refused. Although the old order was restored by the end of the year, these events probably explain the complete reissue of the *Déclaration et réfutation*. Its printing was probably initiated and was doubtlessly acclaimed by Douai's traditionally Catholic elites. In any case, it received support of Thomas Stapleton, who was allowed to stay in Douai because of his appointment at the university. Yet, possible commercial motives must also be taken into account. As indicated above, in order to serve local readerships Douai booksellers strongly depended on the French book market. It is plausible that, as a result of the intense commercial contacts with Paris, some copies of the *Déclaration et réfutation* swiftly reached Douai and that Bogart, informed about the book's editorial success across the border, decided to undertake a full reprint.

---

29   Frédéric Duquenne, *Un tout petit monde. Les notables de la ville de Douai du règne de Philippe II à la conquête française (milieu du XVIe siècle – 1667). Pouvoir, réseaux et reproduction sociale* (Université Charles de Gaulle – Lille 3, unpublished PhD Thesis 2011), pp. 335–343. See also his 'Des "républiques calvinistes" avortées? La contestation des échevinages à Douai et Arras en 1577 et 1578', in Monique Weis (ed.), *Des villes en révolte: les républiques urbaines aux Pays-Bas et en France pendant la deuxième moitié du XVIe siècle* (Turnhout: Brepols, 2010), pp. 53–63.

30   Duquenne, *Un tout petit monde*, pp. 315–320.

4 Cambrai

A third edition of the *Déclaration et réfutation* in the Low Countries appeared in 1579. Both 1578 editions were based on the first version of Launoy's book, printed in early October 1577. As early as April 1578, however, Launoy revised his text and augmented it with a new chapter on another key point in Catholic doctrine, transubstantiation. The Douai reprints may thus have been outdated by the very moment of their publication. This may have been the reason why Victor Robat, a bookseller in nearby Cambrai, decided to publish yet another edition in 1579, now including the new chapter on transubstantiation.[31] Cambrai, a town located even closer to the French border, also went through turbulent times in these years. Officially, the town and its immediate surroundings, the Cambrésis, were a prince-bishopric belonging to the Holy Roman Empire. Since the 1520s, however, the town experienced increasing Habsburg influence. This evolution was interrupted in 1576 when Baudouin de Gavre, baron d'Inchy, took possession of the citadel built by Emperor Charles V. The archbishop, who also held the title of Duke of Cambrai, was forced to take refuge in Mons, the capital of the neighbouring County of Hainaut. The Baron d'Inchy initially sided with the rebellious States-General of the Low Countries, but later sought support from the Duke of Anjou, the brother of the French king Henry III to whom Launoy had dedicated his book.[32]

---

31   Launoy and Pennetier, *La declaration et refutation des fausses suppositions* (Cambrai, 1579). Some copies of this print run were reissued in 1604 with a distinct title page, abbreviating the author's names as "M. de L." and "H.P.", changing the title in *Le tout-scavoir des sages docteurs de la bande sathanique* and with the imprint of Balthazar Bellère, Bogart's son-in-law (USTC 1116659). Such copies are preserved in the Bibiothèque municipale de Douai, the Národní knihovna in Prague, the Bodleian Library in Oxford, the Middle Temple Library in London and the Österreichische Nationalbibliothek in Vienna. In order to fully anonymise this reissue, also parts of the preliminaries were reprinted. As a result, sig. Av and sig. A2r are both numbered '2'. A small strip in between these two pages made it possible to bind the newly-printed preliminaries with the rest of the book, printed in 1579. It remains unclear who was behind this reissue, but the anonymisation may be explained by the fact that, by 1604, Launoy had been completely compromised by his involvement in the Catholic League.

32   Inchy was put aside in 1581 and replaced by the French Sieur de Balagny, a supporter of the Catholic League. Only in 1595 did Cambrai finally return to Habsburg influence, with its inhabitants choosing King Philip II as their sovereign. See José Javier Ruiz Ibáñez, 'Théories et pratiques de la souveraineté dans la Monarchie hispanique: un conflit de juridictions à Cambrai', *Annales. Histoire, Sciences Sociales*, 55 (2000), pp. 623–44, esp. p. 626; Frédéric Duquenne, *L'entreprise du duc d'Anjou aux Pays-Bas de 1580 à 1584: les responsabilités d'un échec à partager* (Villeneuve d'Ascq: Presses universitaires du Septentrion 1998), pp. 86–87; Cyrille Thelliez, 'Contribution à l'histoire de Cambrai et du

In spite of the growing French influence in the border town, there is no evidence that Robat's edition of the *Déclaration et réfutation* resulted from direct cross-border contacts. Several elements again point to Catholic circles in Douai. First, Robat did not operate a press himself and judging from the typographic ornaments used in his edition, it was also produced by Bogart in Douai.[33] Furthermore, the approbation delivered by Thomas Stapleton for Bogart's 1578 edition was copied. Additionally, the French translation of a sermon by the German preacher Martin Eisengrein (1535–1578) that was added to Robat's edition, places it in a Douai context. Eisengrein's sermon was first issued in Ingolstadt in 1562 and thereafter reprinted and translated into Latin by the Carthusian writer Laurentius Surius in Cologne. Already in 1564 a French translation by the Benedictine controversialist René des Freuz appeared in Paris.[34] The translation added to the 1579 Cambrai edition, however, was a totally new one, based on Surius's Latin translation and composed by Jacques Bourgeois (d. 1600), provincial of the Order of the Most Holy Trinity.[35] He dedicated his translation to Anna Roelofs, spouse of the Douai law professor and later Bishop of Tournai Jean Vendeville (1527–92), recently characterised as a member of the so-called 'loyal opposition' to King Philip II, a group opposing his most repressive approach to the revolt but principally remaining loyal to the Spanish crown.[36]

Cambrésis: comment, en 1595, la France et le maréchal de Balagny perdirent Cambrai?', *Anciens pays et assemblées d'états*, 47 (1968), pp. 148–169, esp. pp. 151–153.

33 In addition to the *Déclaration et réfutation* only one more edition bearing Robat's imprint is known. According to the account books of the *Officina Plantiniana* at Antwerp, Robat was active as a bookseller between 1565 and 1609, when he was succeeded by his son Guillaume. See, Antwerp, Museum Plantin-Moretus, *Archief*, no. 17 (fols. 78, 149, 215, 326 & 480), no. 40 (fols. 132), no. 110 (fols. 38) and no. 111 (fols. 7). The ornaments and initials used are identical to those in Petrus Bacherius, *Tabula sacrorum carminum, piarumqve precum enchiridion* (Douai: Jean Bogart, 1579) (USTC 11095).

34 Martin Eisengrein, *Ein Christenliche predig aus was ursachen so viel leut in vilen landen vom pabstum zum Lutertumb fallen und wie wir zu disen schweren leuffen widerstand thun sollen* (Ingolstadt: Weißenhorn, 1562) (VD 16 E 781, USTC 642676). For the Cologne reprint, see VD 16 ZV 4942 (USTC 642661). For the Latin translation, see VD 16 E 783 (USTC 624064). For the French translation printed at Paris for Nicolas Chesneau, see USTC 593. On Surius's translation, see Hildegard Hebenstreit-Wilfert, *Wunder und Legende. Studien zu Leben und Werk von Laurentius Surius (1522–1578), insbesondere zu zeiner Sammlung 'De probatis Sanctorum historiis'* (Eberhard-Karls-Universität Tübingen, Unpublished PhD thesis, 1975), pp. 33–34.

35 Jean François Foppens, *Bibliotheca Belgica, sive Virorum in Belgio vitâ, scriptisque illustrium catalogus*, (2 vols., Brussels: Pierre Foppens, 1739), I. 504.

36 Violet Soen, 'The Loyal Opposition of Jean Vendeville (1527–1592): Contributions to a Contextualized Biography', in Dries Vanysacker etc. (eds), *The Quintessence of Lives.*

That the *Déclaration et réfutation* was jointly issued with Eisengrein's older sermon is no coincidence. First of all, the biographies of both authors bear striking resemblances. While Launoy was a Huguenot preacher until the mid-1570s, Eisengrein had been a Lutheran minister prior to his conversion in the late 1550s. In addition to his duties as a parish priest and professor in Ingolstadt, Eisengrein was an enthusiastic preacher maintaining close relationships with the Duke of Bavaria, Albert V. His sermons strongly defended Catholicism and he deliberately delivered them in towns where Lutheranism had been tolerated before. They also dealt with the Eucharist, transubstantiation and the veneration of saints, exactly the same issues that had occupied Launoy in the first part of his treatise.[37] The sermon added to the 1579 edition not only explained why so many had converted to Lutheranism, but also indicated how one could resist the "temptation of Satan". According to Jacques Bourgeois his translation was ordered by the printer, but he clearly agreed with the intentions of the Bavarian author. In fact, he had noticed the sermon earlier on and always found it particularly helpful in keeping the faithful in the Church in a region that, to his regret, was daily subject to the "tricks, deceptions and intriguing of the heretics".[38] The translator did not dare to question the Vendeville's orthodoxy, but he vividly hoped that the sermon would guide his dedicatee while her husband was busy with public affairs.

Local clergy and printers in the French-speaking provinces of the Low Countries, it has become clear, were not satisfied with simple reprints of Launoy's book. Both Mouronval's anthology and Bourgeois's translation point to a much more creative approach. While rearranging the text into dialogues or adding a carefully selected sermon by an influential German preacher, local actors reinforced the message for a Catholic readership, which had remained rather implicit in the original version. Launoy was primarily driven by his own experience as a convert and aimed to expose the falsities of Reformed faith and subsequently urge his former brethren to follow his example. Catholics in the French-speaking parts of the Low Countries were likewise confronted with an increasing Calvinist threat, yet judging from the successive editions of

---

Intellectual Biographies in the Low Countries, presented to Jan Roegiers (Turnhout-Leuven: Brepols 2010), pp. 43–62.

37 Philip M. Soergel, *Wondrous in his Saints: Counter-Reformation Propaganda in Bavaria* (Berkeley: University of California Press, 1993), pp. 105–109.

38 Martin Eisengrein, *Sermon excellent et catholique, monstrant pourqvoy tant de gents se rendent pour le iourd'huy de party des lvtheriens & commen en ce temps calamiteux, il fault resister aux tentations de Satan par lesquels il oppugne la foy* (issued with the edition cited in n. 31). The two pages including the dedicatory letter lack both page numbers and signatures. These pages precede page Aa r.

the *Déclaration et réfutation*, conversion was not their first concern. By means of Launoy's book they were primarily aiming at a Catholic readership, valuing the text not so much for its controversial merits, as for its potential to prevent more Catholics from being seduced by Reformed doctrine.

5   Douai (bis)

The remarkable combination of Launoy's originally French book and Eisengrein's originally German sermon illustrates how the French-speaking provinces took an intermediary position between France, the Holy Roman Empire and the Low Countries. This potential is confirmed by the surprisingly fast Dutch-language translation of the *Déclaration et réfutation*, also printed by Bogart in 1578.[39] The translation was most likely based on Bogart's French-language edition of the same year, as it lacks the chapter on transubstantiation, which first appeared in the Parisian edition of April 1578. The title-page of this Dutch-language version states that the book had "shortly been translated into our Netherlandish [i.e. Dutch] language", but did not mention the translator's name. However, the ecclesiastical approbation on the back side of the title-page, reveals his initials as F.I.V.S.T.D.[40] I was not able to decipher these letters, but the latter three of them most probably refer to the translator's theology doctorate, as the Latin name of such a degree, *Sacrae Theologiae Doctor*, was commonly abbreviated as S.T.D. The fact that Dutch-language editions were extremely rare in French-speaking Douai further stresses the significance of this swift translation. Some twenty royal placards and ordonnances in Dutch were printed in the town shortly after 1580, but these were ordered by royal governor Alexander Farnese and were not followed by any more Dutch editions until the mid-1610s.[41] Even Bogart, who was a native Dutch speaker and had printed dozens of Dutch-language books during his earlier activity in

---

39   Launoy and Pennetier, *Die verclaringhe ende verworpinghe*.

40   In the ecclesiastical approbation Arnould le Massy, dean of the Chapter of Saint-Amé in Douai, mentions that he had carefully compared the Dutch translation with the Paris edition of Jean Du Carroy, printed at the end of April 1578. So, the translation was certainly issued later than April 1578.

41   Albert Labarre, 'Impressions en flamand à Arras, Douai, Lille et Saint-Omer XVIe–XVIIIe siècle', *Les Pays-Bas français*, 4 (1979), pp. 30–42.

A FRENCH BOOK IN THE LOW COUNTRIES 95

Louvain, stopped publishing in Dutch following his arrival in the university town in the mid-1570s.[42]

If Douai's leading printer showed scarce interest in Dutch-language editions, why then did he issue a Dutch-language translation? Much like with the editions discussed before, an answer to this question may be found in the succession of events during the year 1578. Following the Pacification of Ghent two years before, town magistrates in the largely Dutch-speaking County of Flanders and Duchy of Brabant started to experiment with forms of religious toleration, or at least co-existence. Instead of appeasing the situation, this policy further strengthened the Calvinist party, which finally was able to install Calvinist town magistrates (often referred to as Calvinist republics) in towns such as Antwerp, Bruges, Brussels and Ghent during the late 1570s.[43] The new leaders initially only turned against the most vocal supporters of royal power, but in the longer run the Catholic clergy and laity were asked to swear loyalty, or otherwise leave the town. As Geert Janssen has described, this caused an exodus of several thousand of Catholics, most of them temporarily settling on the borders of the Low Countries.[44] From late August 1578, groups of Dutch-speaking refugees sought refuge in Douai.[45] Tension had risen there too, even leading to an illegitimate renewal of the town magistrate. Yet, local Calvinists were never granted the free profession of their faith, let alone given political power. Unlike in many Flemish and Brabant towns, where Calvinist control would only end in the mid-1580s, in Douai the old order was restored before the end of the year.

Even if the translator's name remains unknown, it is very plausible that he belonged to this recently arrived group of refugees. Indeed, Launoy's book

---

42 Violet Soen, Alexander Soetaert and Johan Verberckmoes, 'Verborgen meertaligheid. De katholieke drukpers in de kerkprovincie Kamerijk (1560–1600)', *Queeste: tijdschrift voor middeleeuwse letterkunde in de Nederlanden*, 22 (2015), pp. 62–81, esp. pp. 69–71.

43 For a recent account on the Calvinist republics in the Low Countries, see Monique Weis (ed.), *Des villes en révolte*. See also the classic studies on Ghent and Antwerp: Guido Marnef, *Antwerp in the Age of Reformation. Underground Protestantism in a commercial metropolis 1550–1577* (Baltimore: Johns Hopkins University Press, 1996); Johan Decavele (ed.), *Het eind van een rebelse droom: opstellen over het calvinistisch bewind te Gent (1577–1584) en de terugkeer van de stad onder de gehoorzaamheid van de koning van Spanje (17 september 1584)* (Gent: Stadsbestuur, 1984).

44 Geert Janssen, *The Dutch Revolt and Catholic Exile in Reformation Europe* (Cambridge: Cambridge University Press, 2014), pp. 44–47, 64.

45 Antoon Viaene, 'Vlaamse vluchtelingen te Douai: hun verweer tegen Marnix' Biënkorf, 1578–1584', *Handelingen van het Genootschap voor Geschiedenis te Brugge*, 93 (1956), pp. 5–37.

fitted their cause very well. While Douai's elites merely had to fear Calvinist demands, their fellow-faithful from Flanders and Brabant had actually witnessed a Calvinist turnover and were ousted from their home towns by the new magistrates. For these groups, the *Déclaration et réfutation* may have been primarily attractive for its initial controversial value. The book proved a very welcome point-by-point refutation of the most important aspects of Reformed doctrine, which helped to question the legitimacy of the newly-installed Calvinist republics. Simultaneously, the book proved that their own Catholic doctrines were correct and explained its most essential points, including transubstantiation and the veneration of saints and images. This made it a very useful tool for the development of the more militant kind of Catholicism that, as Geert Janssen has argued, resulted from this experience of dislocation.[46] On a more practical level, with Bogart the refugees immediately encountered a printer who not only stood firm in his Catholic convictions, but also had experience in printing Dutch-language texts and disposed of the gothic characters in which these texts were usually composed. Once again, Launoy's book, originally responding to French events, was appropriated by Catholics in the Low Countries and used to strengthen their own position.

6   Antwerp

Possibly through the contacts the refugees maintained with their home region, the translation of the *Déclaration et réfutation* reached Antwerp in 1578, where it was swiftly reprinted by Hendrik Wouters.[47] During the years of the Calvinist republic in Antwerp (1577–1585), Wouters was one of the printers who continued to issue Catholic devotional and controversial material. At first sight, his reissue of the Dutch translation closely resembles the Bogart edition. On closer scrutiny, however, the type was entirely recomposed.[48] The Antwerp printer

---

46   Janssen, *The Dutch Revolt and Catholic Exile*, esp. Chapter 4: The Counter-Reformation of the Refugee, pp. 82–103. See also his earlier article: 'The Counter-Reformation of the Refugee. Exile and the Shaping of Catholic Militancy in the Dutch Revolt', *Journal of Ecclesiastical History*, 63 (2012), pp. 671–692.

47   Matthieu de Launoy and Henri Pennetier, *Die verclaringhe ende verworpinghe van het valsch verstant ende tquaet misbruycke[n] van sommige sententie[n] der heyligher schrifture[n]* (Antwerpen: Hendrik Wouters, 1578) (USTC 414962/414963).

48   This edition included 166 numbered folios, instead of 144 in Bogart's edition. The Antwerp edition preserved the dedicatory letter to Henry III, but this section was moved to the end of the book.

A FRENCH BOOK IN THE LOW COUNTRIES   97

also added an extract of a printing privilege granted to him on 3 December 1578 regarding both the French and the Dutch versions of the book and applying to the entire Low Countries.[49] On the title-page of the 1578 edition Bogart already claimed the possession of such a privilege, yet he did not include an abstract of it. Printing privileges were frequently subject to malversation and it should be considered that Bogart merely pretended being granted the monopoly to print, sell and distribute Launoy's book in the Low Countries.[50] In any case, the sheer fact that two printers claimed the possession of a privilege for the same book, reflects its commercial importance.

The popularity of the *Déclaration et réfutation* can also be deduced from the Dutch-language translation of the *Réponse chrétienne*. As mentioned earlier, this equally voluminous book, composed by the Reformed theologian Lambert Daneau, provided a detailed rebuttal of the positions expressed by Launoy. The original French version was published as early as 1578, but the Dutch-language translation was only printed in Antwerp in 1583. It had been translated into

---

49   "The Royal Majesty has allowed and allowes Hendrik Wouters, sworn bookseller, to make print and sell in all His Majesty's lands of *par deça* a book in French and Dutch, named *Die verclaringhe ende verworpinghe* ..., Made in French by Matthieu de Launoy and Henri Pennetier, sometime ministers of the aforesaid Reformed religion. &c. Prohibiting all other printers and booksellers to reprint the same, or to sell copies printed elsewhere, within the time of the following four years under the penalty and seizure included in the Privilege. Given at Antwerp on the third of December. Anno 1578. Signed Mesdach. The same Privilege is also granted in the Council of Brabant. Signed Mesdach." The exact wording of the privilege is as follows: "De Coninclijcke Magisteyt heeft toeghelate[n] ende laet toe He[n]ricken VVouters gesvvore[n] boeck vercooper te moge[n] doen drucken, en[de] vercoope[n] in alle sijne Mag. lande[n] va[n] hervvaerts ouer eene[n] boeck in Franchois ende nederduyts, genoempt. *De verclaringe ende vervvorpinge va[n] het valsch verstant ende tquaet misbruyck van sommige sente[n]tien der heyliger shcrifture[n] de vvelcke de ministers vande religie (die me[n] noempt de gereformeerde) misbruyckt heb-be[n] in dese leste tijden om te scheyden ende te beroere[n] de Christe[n]heyt.* Ghemaeckt int Franchois door Mattheeus va[n] Launoy en[de] He[n]rick Pennetier, eertijts ministers der voorschreue[n] gereformeerder religie[n]. &c. Verbiedende alle andere druckers ende boeckvercoopers de selue nae te moghen drucken, oft elders ghedruckt te vercoopen, bin-nen den tijdt van vier Iaren naestcomende op de pene ende verbeurte in de Priuilegie begrepen. Ghegeuen Thantvverpen den derden Decembris. Anno. 1578. Onderteekent Mesdach. Ghelijcke Priuilegie is oock verleent inden Raede van Brabant. Onderteeckent Mesdach."

50   Notably, in 1588 Bogart was forced to apologize to the Privy Council in Brussels for hav-ing printed the text "Cum privilegio" on the title-page of a book for which he had not previously obtained a printing privilege. See, Michel Baelde, 'De toekenning van druk-kersoctrooien door de Geheime Raad in de zestiende eeuw', *De Gulden Passer*, 40 (1962), pp. 19–58, on p. 34.

Dutch by the Calvinist minister Johannes Florianus (1522–1585), then living in Brussels, but the dedicatory letter was signed by Thomas Tilius (ca 1534–1590), a former abbot of the Cistercian Abbey of St Bernard in Antwerp, who converted to Calvinism in the mid-1560s.[51] Tilius claimed the initiative for the translation, admitting that Launoy's book had strengthened many "unstable people ... in their blind idolatry and superstition and opened the mouth of the libellers". He admitted that the book had been used many times to make doctrinal accusations against himself and his fellow-ministers and that it was still in use for that purpose as he wrote. Therefore, he finally deemed necessary a Dutch-language translation, which he hoped could serve as a "medicine against the strong poison" Launoy's book had spread and further discourage his Catholic adversaries.[52] Tilius's comments not only confirm the enduring popularity of the *Déclaration et réfutation*. They once again also prove the book's durable effectiveness and the double function it continued to play for Catholics in the Low Countries, simultaneously helping them to attack their opponents and to deepen their own faith.

---

51   Guido Marnef, 'Thomas van Thielt ca 1534–1590', in Henri Installé etc. (eds)., *Luister en rampspoed van Mechelen ten tijde van Rembert Dodoens 1585–1985* (Brussel: Ministerie van de Vlaamse Gemeenschap, 1985), pp. 108–110. A biographical sketch by the same author can be accessed through www.dutchrevolt.leiden.edu (accessed 19 July 2017).

52   [Lambert Daneau], *Christelycke antwoorde*, * ij r°: "With which [book] they have kept many unstable people upright / many wilfully strengthened in their blind idolatry and superstition / and opened the mouth of the libellers: so that their booklets since a long time and as of today are raised as a sign of triumph against the Reformed Religion and have many times been used to reproach us ... so that I have been caused to provide / that the aforesaid reply would be as a medicine against the strong poison transmitted into our Dutch language / so that it would break the haughtiness of the papists / and be of service to all lovers of the truth." The exact wording reads as follows: "Met welcken [boek] sy vele wanckelmoedighe mensche[n] te ruggen gehouden / veele moetwilling in hare verblinde afgoderije en[de] superstitie gesterct / en[de] den lasteraers den mondt openghedaen hebben: so dat hare boecxkens ouer lange en[de] noch hedendaechs als een triumpht-eecken tegen de gereformeerde Religie worden opgericht en[de] ons menichmael voor geworpe[n] ... so ben ic geoorsaect gheweest te besorgen / dat de voorschruen beant-woordinge als eene medecijne tege[n] het sware vergift soude in onse duytsche sprake ouerghestelt worden / op dat sy den hooghen moet der pausghesinden souden brecken / ende allen liefhebberen der waerheyt dienstelijck wesen."

A FRENCH BOOK IN THE LOW COUNTRIES

7   Conclusion

The case of *Déclaration et réfutation* is exceptional. The discussion of its successive editions in Douai, Cambrai and Antwerp in the years 1578 and 1579 does not permit us to draw definitive conclusions about the transfer of Catholic texts between France and the Low Countries during the later decades of the sixteenth century or the intermediary role the French-speaking provinces played in this process. Yet two observations can be made. First, it should be indicated that the several editions of Launoy's book foreshadow an even larger interest in French texts in the following decades. During the late 1580s and early 1590s, many French news pamphlets, especially those sympathetic to the cause of the Catholic League, were reprinted in the border towns of the Low Countries. From the early 1590s on, the interest increasingly widened to devotional and spiritual books. Printers in the border region started massively and almost systematically to reprint the works of France's most acknowledged and innovative religious writers, including the Jesuits Louis Richeome and Étienne Binet and the bishops François de Sales and Jean-Pierre Camus.[53] In this perspective, the case of the *Déclaration et réfutation* can be seen as the forerunner of a still more intensive transfer of Catholic texts from France to the Low Countries through the presses of French-speaking border towns such as Arras, Douai and Cambrai.

Second, the editorial history of the *Déclaration et réfutation* also offers further insight into the development of Catholic print culture and communication strategies during the Dutch Revolt.[54] Already in the late 1570s, Catholic elites faced with a Calvinist threat clearly recognised the potential of the printing press, not only to attack their religious and political adversaries, but also to instruct their fellow-faithful in the right doctrine. To this purpose, a book written by two French converts was judged particularly useful. Yet, not only did they reprint the originally French book, it was also abridged by a Tournai priest, supplemented with a translation of a German sermon by a Trinitarian and translated into Dutch, most probably by someone from Flanders or Brabant who had sought refuge in the French-speaking provinces. While Launoy's first

---

53   I give a more detailed analysis of this evolution in: Soetaert, 'Printing at the frontier', pp. 148–152.

54   Some recent studies on this topic include: Judith Pollmann, *Catholic identity and the Revolt of the Netherlands* (Oxford: Oxford University Press, 2011); Monica Stensland, *Habsburg Communication in the Dutch Revolt* (Amsterdam: Amsterdam University Press, 2012); Id., 'Not as Bad as All That: The Strategies and Effectiveness of Loyalist Propaganda in the Early Years of Alexander Farnese's Governorship', *Dutch Crossing*, 31 (2007), pp. 91–112.

intention was to convince his former brethren of the truth of the Catholic faith, in the Low Countries his book was clearly redirected towards a Catholic audience. The book continued to prove its value in religious debates, as the comment of Thomas Tilius has showed, but those who favoured its successive reissues in the Low Countries also acknowledged its potential for catechising the faithful. As such, rather than merely a tool to persuade hardened Calvinists, the *Déclaration et réfutation* became part of the attempt to win back the hearts of Catholic believers, to remedy their ignorance of orthodox doctrine and to prevent still more of them leaving the old church.

CHAPTER 7

'Per Modum Compendii a Leonardo Damerio Leodiensi in Lucem Editum': Odo van Maelcote, Léonard Damery, the *Astrolabium Aequinotiale*, and the Parallactic Print between Italy and the Southern Netherlands in the Age of Galileo

Ruth Sargent Noyes

1   The *Astrolabium AEquinoctiale*

In 1601, German-born Jesuit mathematician Christopher Clavius[1] (Bamberg 1538–Rome 1612), professor and head of the reformed Mathematics Academy at the Collegio Romano,[2] wrote to Odo van Maelcote (Brussels 1572–Rome 1615) in Liège to invite the twenty-nine year old to join him in the *urbe* to

---

1   Rome, APUG [=Archivio della Pontificia Università Gregoriana, Rome], 530 c. 37r–v. See Ugo Baldini (ed.), *Christophorus Clavius. Corrispondenza* (7 vols. in 14 fasc., Pisa: Università di Pisa, Dipartimento di matematica, 1992), IV, 1, no. 170, pp. 124–125. For Clavius see James Lattis, *Between Copernicus and Galileo: Christoph Clavius and the Collapse of Ptolemaic Cosmology* (Chicago: University of Chicago Press, 1994); 'Clavius, Christoph', in *Complete Dictionary of Scientific Biography*. 2008. <http://www.encyclopedia.com> (accessed 18 March 2015); Ugo Baldini, including 'Christoph Clavius and the Scientific Scene in Rome', in George V. Coyne, etc. (eds), *Gregorian Reform of the Calendar* (Vatican City: Specola Vaticana, 1983), pp. 137–170; *Legem impone subactis: Studi su filosofia e scienza dei Gesuiti in Italia, 1540–1632* (Rome: Bulzoni, 1992); Idem (ed.), *Christoph Clavius e l'attività scientifica dei Gesuiti nell'età di Galileo* (Rome: Bulzoni, 1995); Idem, 'The Academy of Mathematics of the Collegio Romano from 1553–1612', in Mordechai Feingold (ed.), *Jesuit Science and the Republic of Letters* (Cambridge, Massachusetts: MIT Press, 2003), pp. 47–98. Research for this essay was supported by the Novo Nordisk Fonden Mads Øvlisen postdoctoral fellowship in art history, grant no. NNF18OC0032062.

2   For intersections of Jesuit culture and science in this period see Michele Camerota, *Galileo Galilei e la cultura scientifica nell'età della Controriforma* (Rome: Salerno, 2004); Rivka Feldhay, 'Religion', in Katherine Park and Lorraine Daston (eds), *The Cambridge History of Modern Science* (7 vols., Cambridge: Cambridge University Press, 2006), III. 727–55; Sheila Rabin, 'Early Modern Jesuit Science. A Historiographical Essay', *Journal of Jesuit Studies* 1:1 (2014), pp. 88–104; Udías Vallina, *Jesuit Contribution to Science: A History* (Cham: Springer, 2015); Mark Waddell, *Jesuit Science and the End of Nature's Secrets* (Farnham: Ashgate, 2015).

© KONINKLIJKE BRILL NV, LEIDEN, 2023 | DOI:10.1163/9789004510159_008

pursue advanced mathematical study and research.[3] The invitation constituted Clavius's reply to a gift Maelcote had dispatched as a transalpine *nuncius*[4] the previous year on 19 October 1600: a variation on the planispheric astrolabe of the Brabantine Jesuit's own design, the *astrolabium aequinoctiale*, or equinoctial astrolabe.[5] A notional device of paradoxical simplicity and complexity, Maelcote's invention presented a self-sufficient heuristic apparatus of self-professed truthfulness for the accurate generation of cosmological knowledge constituted by astronomical measurements of parallax – the different perception of the apparent position of a single celestial target observed from disparate viewpoints (i.e., how something seen from point A appears differently seen from point B) – performed over long distances, theoretically on an unprecedented global scale. While attempting to extend and resolve as never before the frontiers of terrestrial perception, the equinoctial astrolabe also

---

3   Bibliography on Maelcote is tantamount to needles in a haystack: for a biographical overview see August Ziggelaar, *François De Aguilón, S.J. (1567–1617)*, *Scientist and Architect* (Rome: Institutum Historicum S.I., 1983), pp. 45–47. For his correspondence with contemporaries see Biblioteca Angelica, Rome, MS. 1773, cc. 74v–75r; Baldini (ed.), *Corrispondenza*, II.i.68–9; Antonio Favaro (ed.), *Carteggio inedito di Ticone Brahe: Giovanni Keplero e di altri celebri astronomi e matematici dei secoli XVI. e XVII.* (Bologna: N. Zanichelli, 1886), pp. 147–150, 372–374; Max Casper and Franz Hammer (eds), *Johannes Kepler. Gesammelte Werke* (20 vols., Munich: C.H. Beck, 1937), XVII. 63–65; Antonio Favaro (ed.), *Le Opere di Galileo Galilei* (20 vols., Florence: G. Barbèra, 1968), XI. 87–88, 92–93, 445, 536–537; Luce Giard and Antonella Romano, 'L'usage jésuite de la correspondance. Sa mise en pratique par le mathématicien Christoph Clavius (1570–1611)', in Antonella Romano (ed.), *Rome et la science moderne. Entre Renaissance et Lumières* (Rome: École française de Rome, 2008), pp. 65–119. Maelcote's attributable works are exceedingly rare. Besides the two astrolabic publications (1607 and 1610) and astronomical orations (1604 and 1611) discussed here, see the unpublished *In libros Aristotelis de Caelo Adnotationes et Quaestiones*, prepared for the Collegio Romano course in Natural Philosophy of 1611–12, noted by Corado Dollo: Biblioteche Civica e Recupero Ursino, Catania, Mss. Civ. E 94, cc. 488–529. See further mention of Maelcote's work in geometry and astrolaby in, respectively, Christoph Clavius, *Christophori Clavii ... Geometria practica....* (Munich: Johannes Albini, 1606), pp. 313–314 (USTC 2040263); François de Aguilon, *Francisci Aquilonii e Societate Iesu Opticorum Libri Sex: Philosophis Iuxta ac Mathematicis Utiles* (Antwerp: widow Christophe Plantin and Jan Moretus, 1613), p. 624.
4   For the term 'nuncius' in this period see Nick Wilding, *Galileo's Idol: Gianfrancesco Sagredo and the Politics of Knowledge* (Chicago: University of Chicago Press, 2014), pp. 89–92.
5   For Maelcote's equinoctial astrolabe see below and Ernst Zinner, *Deutsche Und Niederländische Astronomische Instrumente Des 11.-18. Jahrhunderts* (Munich: Beck, 1956), pp. 149, 236, 435; Henri Michel, *Traité de l'Astrolabe* (Paris: Alain Brieux, 1976), pp. 71–72, 174; A.J. Turner, *The Time Museum. Catalogue of the Collections. Volume 1: Time Measuring Instruments, Pt. 1: Astrolabes and Astrolabe Related Instruments* (Rockford, IL: The Time Museum, 1985), p. 83, no. 233, p. 164, fig. 142 and p. 165, fig. 143; Raymond d' Hollander, *L'astrolabe: histoire, théorie et pratique* (Paris: Institut océanographique, 1999), p. 163; James E. Morrison, *The Astrolabe* (Rehoboth Beach, DE: Janus Publishing, 2007), pp. 281–286.

thematised (indeed, reified) the limits of human vision and its reconciliation. Issue of the technologically and intellectually renowned and confessionally fraught cradle of instrument design in the Low Countries, Maelcote's contraption not only materialised in its ipseity and bodied forth in its production, propagation, and praxis, the labile quiddity of transalpine confessionalisation and authorial personification pervading its inventor's geopolitical biography, institutional identity, and broader cultural-intellectual milieu, but also engendered a species of mathematical-astronomical knowledge, to borrow Mario Biagioli's description of Galileo Galilei's concurrent telescopic self-fashionings, "constituted through a range of distance-based partial perceptions."[6] Put differently: the *astrolabium aequinoctiale* ontologised not "how a knowledge claim travels from A to B, but at how the transactions made possible by the fact that A and B are distant from each other allow for the production of such a knowledge claim."[7]

Over the course of the following decade Maelcote – spurred on by exchanges with astronomer-mathematicians within and outside the Society (and, for that matter, the orthodox boundaries of Ptolomaic cosmology and Catholic doctrine), the multiple advents of celestial novelties both astral and mechanical (new stars and the telescope), and the thriven, riven, competitive, vituperative discourse their septentrional-meridional conjunction fomented – would perform upon his own authorial persona and his originary notional astrolabe a punctuated, ateleological sequence of reformative, transformative evolutions by means of corporeal, material, graphical, and textual imprinting technologies, resulting not in a single author and instrument so much as an 'author-instrument clade' (i.e., a non-linear grouping that includes a common ancestor and all living and extinct offshoots). At the same time, however, achieving a sort of ontological syzygy with his instrument's selfsame parallactic thing-ness, Maelcote realised a rhetorical strategy of 'parallactic self-fashioning' whereby these consecutive transmutations were narrativised as a self-evident succession of systematically deferred re-presentations of variously partial but implicitly progressively more complete and correct glimpses of a common target (the notional *astrolabium aequinoctiale*, object-avatar for

---

6 Mario Biagioli, *Galileo's Instruments of Credit: Telescopes, Images, Secrecy* (Chicago: University of Chicago Press, 2006), p. 26. For Galileo's relations with the Jesuits see especially the work of Rivka Feldhay, William Wallace, and (with caution) Pietro Redondi; for the social constitution of scientific truth in this period see the work of Steven Shapin, including (with Simon Schaffer), *Leviathan and the Air-pump: Hobbes, Boyle, and the Experimental Life* (Princeton: Princeton University Press, 1985) and *A Social History of Truth: Civility and Science in Seventeenth-century England* (Chicago: University of Chicago Press, 1994).

7 Biagioli, *Galileo's Instruments*, p. 26.

its inventor) to a geographically far-flung but ideologically coterminous community of hypothesised observers – all the while partly obscuring his authorial selfhood with an array of inscribed and artisanal personifications.[8] My direct and indirect gestures here to Galileo are not gratuitous. Taken together, several striking aspects of the form, fabrication, and transalpine promulgation of the *astrolabium aequinoctiale* present the Brabantine Jesuit and his invention as suggestive analogues to the Tuscan and his monopolised machines, the geometric compass and telescope, at an historical moment when the instrument culture of astronomical and natural-philosophical reformation (but what might be termed today 'scientific innovation') was shifting from astrolaby (and mechanical instruments more broadly) to telescopy (and optical-dioptrical instruments).[9] What follows plots against the complex matrix of cultural exchange – mediating things, persons, places, practices, institutions, distance, and time – that collectively engendered the *astrolabium aequinoctiale* how Maelcote reconceived and represented his instrument as a practical and ideological parallactic machine analogous to the telescope, with which answers to the period's thorniest mathematical-astronomical problems and most incendiary cosmological controversies might be sought collaboratively, and divergent and potentially heterodox viewpoints across confessions on a common target quantified and reconciled. In so doing this essay proposes a microhistory of the instable period of confessionalisation c. 1600, and its fluctuating networks

---

8 See Michel Foucault, 'What is an Author?' in Josué Harari (ed.), *Textual Strategies: Perspectives in Post-Structuralist Criticism* (Ithaca, N.Y.: Cornell University Press, 1979), pp. 141–60; Stephen Greenblatt, *Renaissance Self-fashioning: From More to Shakespeare* (Chicago: University of Chicago Press, 1980); Ian Hunter, 'The history of philosophy and the persona of the philosopher', *Modern Intellectual History*, 4.3 (2007), pp. 571–600; for these issues in early modern science see Bruce Moran, 'Courts and academies', and Steven Shapin, 'The Man of Science', in Katherine Park and Lorraine Daston (eds), *The Cambridge History of Science, Volume 3: Early Modern Science* (Cambridge: Cambridge University Press, 2006), pp. 251–71 and 179–91; for the Jesuit scientific context see Michael John Gorman, 'Mathematics and Modesty in the Society of Jesus: The Problems of Christoph Grienberger (1564–1636)', in Mordechai Feingold (ed.) *The New Science and Jesuit Science: Seventeenth Century Perspectives* (Dordrecht: Kluwer, 2003), pp. 1–120; for the Galilean see Wilding, *Galileo's Idol*, and Mario Biagioli, *Galileo, Courtier: The Practice of Science in the Culture of Absolutism* (Chicago: University of Chicago Press, 1993).

9 Bibliography on the topic of Galilean telescopy is vast: for a helpful overview of recent Galilean bibliography see Nick Wilding, 'Galileo and the Stain of Time', *California Italian Studies*, 2.1 (2011). <http://www.escholarship.org/uc/item/8453362b> (accessed 20 October 2017). Informative studies taking up the question of how Galileo associated himself with the compass and telescope include Biagioli, *Galileo's Instruments* and Wilding, *Galileo's Idol*; see also Eileen Reeves, *Galileo's Glassworks: the Telescope and the Mirror* (Cambridge: Harvard University Press, 2008).

THE ASTROLABIUM AEQUINOTIALE, AND THE PARALLACTIC PRINT 105

wherein and whereby ductile objects and personae operated as mutable intermediaries across and among confessional and institutional prerogatives within and between the Southern Netherlands and Italy.[10] It also undertakes to problematise narrativising teleologies positing the exceptionality of Galilei and teloscopy on one hand, and the inevitability of the former's clash with the Order and resultant fall and the latter's ascendancy hand in hand with Copernicanism on the other. I begin by way of a tandem biography of Maelcote and his astrolabe.

2 Odo van Maelcote

Odo van Maelcote was born 28 July 1572 in Brussels to Jean van Maelcote (Louvain c.1536–Brussels 1616); the elder Maelcote, doctor of law, was appointed by Philip II to the council of Brabant (1571), and subsequently elevated to the rank of vice-chancellor.[11] Forced by the crisis in Brussels to flee with the Spanish (1576), Jean and his family had returned (1578), later intervening in the reconciliation of the city with Philip II (1585), and obtaining pardon for Lierre (1582).[12] Against this backdrop unfolded the formation of Odo, positioned historically amongst the initial confessionalised generations born in fraught *oltralpe* territories.[13] After two years studying philosophy in Douai, he attained the degree

---

10   For cultural exchange and cultural transfer see the work of Peter Burke and also Bernd Roeck, 'Introduction', in Herman Roodenburg (ed.), *Forging European Identities, 1400–1700* (Cambridge: Cambridge University Press, 2007), pp. 1–29. For objects as agents of cultural exchange see Sven Dupré and Christoph Lüthy (eds), *Silent Messengers: The Circulation of Material Objects of Knowledge in the Early Modern Low Countries* (Münster: Lit, 2011).

11   *Biographie nationale [de Belgique]* (43 vols, Brussels: Bruylant, 1866–1986), XIII. 43–44. The elder Maelcote's volume on civil law was published in Louvain in 1652 and Liège in 1699: *Joannis Malcoti Lovaniensis J.U.D. In suprema Brabantiae curia consiliarii, ad Tit. XVIII. Lib. I. Cod. de juris et facti …* (Louvain: Joannes Vryenborch, 1652) and (Liège: Lambert Thonon, 1699).

12   See the work of Geoffrey Parker, beginning with his *The Dutch Revolt* (Ithaca, N.Y.: Cornell University Press, 1977); for mathematical practitioners in this context see that of Ad Meskens including *Practical Mathematics in a Commercial Metropolis: Mathematical Life in Late 16th Century Antwerp* (Dordrecht: Springer, 2013) and *Joannes Della Faille S.J.: Mathematics, Modesty and Missed Opportunities* (Brussels: Belgisch Historisch Instituut te Rome, 2005).

13   For early modern confessionalism see Ute Lotz-Heumann, 'Confessionalization', and Keith P. Luria, 'Religious coexistence', both in Alexandra Bamji et al. (eds), *The Ashgate Research Companion to the Counter-Reformation* (Burlington: Ashgate, 2013), pp. 33–53 and 55–72, respectively.

of *magister artium* before joining the Society in Tournai (1590).[14] After theological studies in Louvain (1592–1596) he taught Greek (1597) at the college in Liège, then the next highest class of the Latin school in Antwerp (1598); on 10 April 1599 he was ordained in Antwerp, returning that year to Liège to teach Greek and moral theology.[15] On 19 October 1600, leveraging an institutionalised homosocial culture of epistolary and gift exchange, he sent the aforementioned specimen of his *astrolabium aequinoctiale* to Clavius, a potential protector renowned for his 'instrument-philia'.[16] Clavius possessed (and likely produced) a multimedia collection of contraptions that attest to the central role instruments played in his mathematical ways of knowing across domains, not merely recording but actively reforming knowledge and the didactic methods to engender it.[17] Maelcote's astrolabic nuncius inaugurated an oscillatory Italo-Roman – Flandro-Belgian transalpine pilgrimage that would last the rest of his relatively short life. At the turn of the seventeenth century, thanks largely to Clavius's monumental talents and efforts to reform Society mathematics pedagogy and research, coupled with 'his' Academy's institutional configuration and near-global reach, not only made it unique in the scientific history of Europe at the time,[18] but also developed the mathematical sciences into something of a stalking horse to convert protestants.[19] Like others of his background such as Johannes Faber and Joannes Della Faille working at the intersection of natural philosophy and mathematics, regardless of precise confessional origins, Maelcote's physical person, intellectual-authorial persona(e),

---

14   For an overview see Gerrit Vanden Bosch, 'Jesuits in the Low Countries (1542–1773): A Historiographical Essay', *Jesuit Historiography Online*. <http://dx.doi.org/10.1163/2468 -7723_jho_COM_192551> (accessed 30 November 2017).

15   ARSI [=Archivum Romanum Societatis Iesu, Rome], Flandro-Belgica 9, ff. 140v–141r, 203, 261r; Flandro-Bel. 43, ff. l, 7, 15, 25, 37v, 50r, 56r, 102.

16   For approaches to this sphere of cultural exchange see Mario Biagioli, 'Knowledge, Freedom, and Brotherly Love: Homosociality and the Accademia Dei Lincei', *Configurations* 3.2 (1995), pp. 139–66; Gorman, 'Mathematics and Modesty ...'; Alexander Marr, *Between Raphael and Galileo: Mutio Oddi and the Mathematical Culture of Late Renaissance Italy* (Chicago: University of Chicago Press, 2011).

17   Valentina Nicolucci (ed.), *Magistri Astronomiae dal XVI al XIX Secolo: Cristoforo Clavio, Galileo Galilei e Angelo Secchi: Testimonianze Documentarie e Strumenti Scientifici* (Roma: De Luca Editori D'arte, 2014). For early modern instruments see the work of Jim Bennett, including 'The Mechanical Arts', in Park and Daston (eds), *The Cambridge History of Science*, pp. 673–695.

18   Baldini, 'The Academy of Mathematics', p. 54.

19   Peter Dear, *Discipline and Experience: The Mathematical Way in the Scientific Revolution* (Chicago: University of Chicago Press, 1995), p. 7.

THE ASTROLABIUM AEQUINOTIALE, AND THE PARALLACTIC PRINT 107

and epistemic and material output would negotiate confessional schisms and be mobilised in the service of inter- (and intra-) confessional polemics.[20]

By 1600, planispheric astrolabes evinced a series of theoretical, practical, and material limitations for early modern European users, which gave rise to various innovative variations on the basic object-type, of which Maelcote's was one (indeed the last one to be fabricated).[21] His entailed several translations of conventional design impinging on the stereographic projections on the rete and tympanum, resulting in a device that on one level presented as relatively streamlined and globally self-sufficient, readily workable with less physical-material encumbrance for both northern and southern latitudes (especially with regard to tympanum plate usage), and on another level promised enhanced astronomical accuracy for a given instrument size.[22] Formally, the circle defining the circumference of the tympanum plate represents the equator (thus the appellation equinoctial), with the smaller interior circle representing either the Tropic of Cancer, for positive declinations, or the Tropic of Capricorn, for negative declinations. Given that the equinoctial tympanum's entire perimeter – rather than the mid-sized engraved circle on the plate, as was conventionally the case – figured the equator, this accommodated more scales than on a conventional astrolabe of equal dimensions, creating sufficient space on an ample-sized latitude plate, worked by the hand of an expert engraver, for an exceptional resolution of one single degree, and thus the potential for increased accuracy in computations.[23] Furthermore, the *astrolabium æquinoctiale* was usable for any declination, given that inverting a tympanum for a northern hemisphere astrolabe converted it into a tympanum for a southern astrolabe, and transmuted it from a northern to southern projection, with

---

20   See Meskens, *Joannes Della Faille S.J.*; Silivia De Renzi, 'Courts and Conversions: Intellectual Battles and Natural Knowledge in Counter-Reformation Rome', *Studies in History and Philosophy of Science*, 27.4 (1996), pp. 429–449; Sabina Brevaglieri, 'Science, Books and Censorship in the Academy of the Lincei. Johannes Faber as cultural mediator', in Maria Pia Donato and Jill Kraye (eds), *Conflicting Duties. Science, Medicine and Religion in Rome (1550–1750)* (London-Turin: Warburg Institute Colloquia, 2009), pp. 109–133.

21   Michel, *Traité de l'Astrolabe*; James E. Morrison, *The Astrolabe*. For an instructive overview with concise bibliography see also Silke Ackermann, 'Astrolabe': <https://www.mhs.ox.ac.uk/epact/article.php?ArticleID=2> (Accessed 29 November 2017). For astrolabes as cosmological models see Adam Mosley, *Bearing the Heavens: Tycho Brahe and the Astronomical Community of the Late Sixteenth Century* (Cambridge: Cambridge University Press, 2007), esp. 'Instruments', pp. 209–288; Jim Bennett, 'Geometry in Context in the Sixteenth Century: The View From the Museum', *Early Science and Medicine*, 7.3 (2002), pp. 214–30.

22   See Morrison, *The Astrolabe*, pp. 280–283.

23   Allan Chapman, 'The design and accuracy of some observatory instruments of the seventeenth century', *Annals of Science*, 40.5 (1983), pp. 457–471.

their respective calculations: thus, negative altitudes for northern declinations became positive altitudes for the southern declinations. The rete as well participated in these translations, folding together northern (boreal) and southern (austral) stars.[24] The *astrolabium aequinoctiale* at once firmly situated Maelcote within and distinguished him as a go-between from two overlapping septentrional domains to the Roman ambit: that of the Jesuit "school" of mathematics in the Spanish Netherlands,[25] and that of Flemish-born astrolabists.[26] The *oltralpe* pedigree likely appealed to period perceptions that superior raw materials like metal ores, as well as instruments and instrument makers, printer's ink, and engravers were of northern provenance – perceptions likewise cultivated regarding the telescope.[27] In designating his equinocatial machine and using it to appeal to his Jesuit superior, Maelcote was doubtless aware that others, including Christoph Grienberger, had transmitted from a distance "unsolicited solutions to celebrated problems or instruments" in hopes of obtaining just such an invitation, and that Clavius himself had designed a universal equinoctial dial.[28]

3 Parallax

To Clavius the device's arrival must have appeared particularly well-timed in 1600, coming on the heels of the professor's efforts to establish officially the Mathematics Academy and enhance the status of the discipline – hitherto distinctly subordinate to philosophy and theology – for cultivating advanced knowledge in the Order, recruiting noble patronage, and suppressing

---

24 Michel, *Traité de l'Astrolabe*, pp. 71–72; Morrison, *The Astrolabe*, pp. 283–284.

25 A school was in fact not founded until 1617, by St Vincent. See Ziggelaar, *François De Aguilón*; O. Van de Vyver, 'L'école de mathématiques des Jésuites de la province flandro-belge au XVIIᵉ siècle', *Archivum Historicum Societatis Iesu*, 49 (1980), pp. 265–278; G.H.W. Vanpaemal, 'Jesuit Science in the Spanish Netherlands', in Mordechai Feingold (ed.), *Jesuit Science and the Republic of Letters*, pp. 389–432.

26 See Zinner, *Deutsche und Niederländische Astronomische Instrumente*; Meskens, *Practical Mathematics*. See also the work especially of Henri Michel and Koenraad Van Cleempoel, including, respectively: 'Un astrolabe de Lambert Damery', *Ciel et Terre*, 55 (1939), 86–93 and *A Catalogue Raisonné of Scientific Instruments from the Louvain School, 1530 to 1600* (Turnhout: Brepols, 2002). For the sixteenth century see Steven Vanden Broecke, *The Limits of Influence: Pico, Louvain, and the Crisis of Renaissance Astrology* (Leiden: Brill, 2003), pp. 113–136.

27 Silvio Bedini, *Science and Instruments in Seventeenth-Century Italy* (Aldershot: Variorum, 1994), pp. 256–292, 89–115. See also Wilding, *Galileo's Idol*; Reeves, *Galileo's Glassworks*.

28 Gorman, 'Mathematics and Modesty ...', pp. 12–13.

heresies.[29] Maelcote's austral-boreal astrolabe also came on the Roman scene just at a time when, as Nick Wilding indicates, the papacy, above all through the global Inquisition and the Society's missionary activities, "began to realize something approaching a global temporal order".[30] The inclusion of the austral constellations surely imbued it theoretically and ideologically in an era when European powers and the Jesuits were exploring the southern hemisphere to a wide range of political, epistemic, and spiritual ends.[31] Indeed, the *astrolabium aequinoctiale* would seem, proleptically, to have anticipated extra-Societal and -confessional theorising later in the century on the Order's potential "to function as an enormously powerful scientific instrument" in both hemispheres, for the worldwide advancement of knowledge across diverse domains, in the pursuit of resolving global conundrums such as the quest for longitude.[32] Shortly after 1600, following more than a half-dozen comets appearing during the last quarter of the sixteenth century, a confluence of terrestrial and celestial innovations demanded accelerated observational activity among the Jesuits, which in turn necessitated more precise instrument culture to produce trustworthy astronomical calculations with unprecedentedly high stakes: on one hand, the advent and dissemination of Tycho Brahe's new observations and newly exact observational standards, driven by innovative instrumentation.[33] On the other, a pseudo-nova in Cygnus (1600),[34] a

---

29   Michael John Gorman, 'From "The Eyes of All" to "Usefull Quarries in philosophy and good literature": Consuming Jesuit Science, 1600–1665', in John W. O'Malley et al. (eds), *The Jesuits: Cultures, Sciences, and the Arts, 1540–1773* (Toronto: Toronto University Press, 1999), pp. 170–89. See also Baldini, 'The Academy of Mathematics', pp. 51–52; Lattis, *Between Copernicus and Galileo*; Antonella Romano, *La Contre-Réforme Mathématique: Constitution et Diffusion d'une Culture Mathématique Jésuite à la Renaissance (1540–1640)* (Rome: École française de Rome, 1999); Dennis Smolarski, 'The Jesuit *Ratio Studiorum*, Christopher Clavius, and the Study of Mathematical Sciences in Universities', *Science in Context*, 15.3 (2002), pp. 447–457; Romano Gatto, 'Christoph Clavius' 'Ordo Servandus in Addiscendis Disciplinis Mathematicis' and the Teaching of Mathematics in Jesuit Colleges at the Beginning of the Modern Era', *Science & Education*, 15 (2006), pp. 235–258.

30   Wilding, 'Galileo and the Stain of Time'.

31   Michel, *Traité de l'astrolabe*, pp. 71–72; Morrison, *The Astrolabe*, p. 286.

32   Gorman, 'From "The Eyes of All"', p. 173.

33   Mosley, *Bearing the Heavens*.

34   Mosely, *Bearing the Heavens*; Jean-Pierre Luminet, 'Blaeu, Willem Janszoon', in Thomas Hockey et al. (eds), *Biographical Encyclopedia of Astronomers* (New York: Springer, 2014), pp. 242–244.

supernova in Sagittarius-Serpentarius (1604),[35] and Haley's comet (1607),[36] appeared in the heavens in rapid succession,[37] inflecting the Copernican threat through Protestant and Galilean prerogatives.[38] Hence, before and during the rise of telescopy, members of the Academy innovated diverse devices, such that according to Ugo Baldini, two groups of specialists emerged among the members *c.1600*: the first, pure mathematicians who occasionally participated in astronomical observations; the second, individuals such as Maelcote with solid mathematical foundation and special competence in the construction of instruments and observational astronomy.[39] In fact, given the timing of the pseudo-nova in Cygnus in 1600, first observed in early August of that year, it is possible that this celestial novelty prompted the young Maelcote to expedite his astrolabe to Rome, proffered as a means whereby the Jesuits under Clavius's guidance might mount an cosmological counteroffensive, or approach a détente: against schismatic divides in the sciences and religion in this period should also be plotted cross-confessional exchanges and rapprochements made possible by instruments and instrument makers, and the proficiencies and knowledge their intersection engendered; Clavius, for his part in turn-of-the-*seicento* novae debates, already by 1585 in regard to the nova in Cassiopeia (1572) wrote in support of the phenomenon as superlunary – i.e. situated in the firmament of the fixed stars – and therefor accepted the possibility of mutability in the furthermost eighth celestial orb, which (like Brahe and Kepler) he attributed to Divine miraculous portent.[40] Regardless of confessional and doctrinal differences, all parties theorising novelties made recourse to precise replicable astronomical observations, and to the 'rule of truth' provided by the 'doctrine of parallax'.[41] Parallax, the dissimilar perception of a single target from disparate viewpoints, was also variously termed *diversitas*

---

35 Patrick Boner, *Change and Continuity in Early Modern Cosmology* (Dordrecht: Springer, 2011), esp. pp. 67–92; Miguel Granada, 'After the Nova of 1604: Roeslin and Kepler's Discussion on the Significance of the Celestial Novelties (1607–1613)', *Journal for the History of Astronomy*, 42.3 (2011), pp. 353–390.

36 Tofigh Heidarzadeh, *A History of Physical Theories of Comets, from Aristotle to Whipple* (Dordrecht: Springer, 2008).

37 Dario Tessicini and Patrick Boner (eds), *Celestial Novelties on the Eve of the Scientific Revolution, 1540–1630* (Florence: L.S. Olschki, 2013).

38 For the potential Copernican implications of the 1604 nova, for example, in Keplerian and Galilean theorising, see further discussion below.

39 Baldini, 'The Academy of Mathematics', p. 57.

40 Lattis, *Between Copernicus and Galileo*, pp. 147–53; Miguel Granada, 'Michael Maestlin and His Unpublished Treatise on the Nova of 1604', *Journal for the History of Astronomy*, 45.1 (2014), pp. 91–122.

41 Granada, 'Michael Maestlin', pp. 98–99.

aspectus (Maelcote), *differentia* (Kepler), and *diversità* (Galileo); in astronomy, parallax could be used to determine the relative and actual positions of heavenly bodies, and hence adduced cosmological ramifications.[42] The epistemic and discursive potential of the issue of the questions of parallax was central in the mathematical, astronomical, and cosmological culture of the turn of the century, to the extent that when rumours circulated upon publication of the Tuscan astronomer's *Sidereus nuncius* (1609), some contemporaries presumed the decisive discoveries therein were stellar parallactic revelations (partly true but today largely overlooked). Parallax was polemically theorised to disparate ends by not only Maelcote (as will be seen shortly), but also Brahe, Kepler, Clavius, Grienberger, Galileo, and others.[43] Although stellar parallax would not be detected until the nineteenth century, it was thought in Maelcote's lifetime by among others Galileo that discovering proof of parallax in the case of astral bodies could confirm the earth's movement, and thereby Copernicanism; on the other hand, geocentric cosmologists like Clavius posited that a celestial target's lack of discernible parallax would instead firmly locate it to the farthest stellar regions of the cosmos.[44] Prior to telescopy as a means for investigating parallax, a geometrical operation termed trigonometric parallax – for all intents and purposes triangulation – performed with mechanical instruments was the basic method used to measure parallactic phenomena, and it was best performed by two simultaneous observers, located at two vantage points as far apart as possible, concurrently observing the same target.[45] Subsequent computations combining the target's perceived positions from the two widely separated points, together with the relation between the two points, resulted in the actual distance to the target (from the earth's centre).[46]

---

42   Lattis, *Between Copernicus and Galileo*, pp. 58–60.

43   Harald Siebert claims Galileo's *Dialogo* (1632) "makes it clear that the question of annual [stellar] parallax is the critical issue in the cosmological controversy." Harald Siebert, 'The Early Search for Stellar Parallax: Galileo, Castelli, and Ramponi', *Journal for the History of Astronomy*, 36 (2005), pp. 251–271.

44   For early modern stellar parallax see the work of Christopher M. Graney. See also Lattis, *Between Copernicus and Galileo*, pp. 58–60, 147–156; Mosley, *Bearing the Heavens*, esp. pp. 62–63, 66–67, 70–73, 160–62.

45   For a helpful overview of parallactic triangulation and instructive diagrams see Kaj Aa. Strand, 'Parallax', *Encyclopædia Britannica*. <https://www.britannica.com/science/parallax> (accessed 1 December 2017); Lattis, *Between Copernicus and Galileo*, pp. 58–60.

46   For Jesuit correspondence networks see Feingold (ed.), *Jesuit science and the republic of letters* and Steven J. Harris, 'Confession-Building, Long-Distance Networks, and the Organization of Jesuit Science', *Early Science and Medicine*, 1.3 (1996), pp. 287–318. For analogous studies see Wilding, *Galileo's Idol*; Mosely, *Bearing the Heavens*.

The equinoctial astrolabe's austral-boreal tympanum configuration would have made it seemingly ideal for staging collaborative measurement-making on a truly global scale, bootstrapping Jesuit networks for the purposes of performing parallax computations.[47] Let us imagine that two separate observers were first given identical copies of the equinoctial astrolabe, which given copperplate engraving and printing technology on paper would be theoretically possible. Then, the two observers were dispatched along pre-determined longitudinal routes – one to the far reaches of the northern hemisphere, one to the southern – which given the Society's global reach was theoretically possible after 1600. They would then use the invertible tympanum to position themselves along mirror-image lines of latitude, from where they might simultaneously record observations around a common celestial target.[48] The resulting data, bearing also in mind the one degree accuracy afforded by the device, would have presented itself as optimally choreographed according to a performance of credibility, whereby on the one hand a trustworthy scientific community was built by the virtue of the astrolabe's design and deployment, which required extensive, visible collaborative networks. On the other the same design and deployment were such that the observational process executed by that geographically transcendent community was essentially automated, divesting astronomical praxis of the creep-in of human error (or at least minimising that error), for more truthfully determining parallax by rendering its source – the selfsame scientific community – into a "a passive conductor of information, a disinterested mediator of knowledge,"[49] while also making all the world their parallactic stage for the performance of Society mathematical-astronomical identity (of course, the operations speculatively described above could also involve participants external to the order). Hypothesising the rise of the representation in Maelcote's oeuvre of his instrument as an automated-automating device for prosecuting parallax, we might then look for instances after 1600 where the Jesuit demonstrated more general parallactic knowledge both individual and institutional by graphic, textual, or and/or ceremonial means, and where he did so in clear connection to the *astrolabium aequinoctiale*.

---

47   Lattis, *Between Copernicus and Galileo*, pp. 147–56.

48   Favaro (ed.), *Le Opere di Galileo*, X. 69–71; Siebert, 'The Early Search for Stellar Parallax', p. 253.

49   Gorman, 'From "The Eyes of All"', p. 171.

THE ASTROLABIUM AEQUINOTIALE, AND THE PARALLACTIC PRINT

4 Parallactic and Astrolabic Collaborations

We find, in fact, just such instances, which, significantly, also coincided with three types of events: first, the advent of celestial novelties, in the form of novae and comets, newly-discovered heavenly bodies, or features of those bodies; second, the advent of mechanical, visual, or textual apparati (instruments and images, epistles and publications) advancing the discovery and delineation of such novelties; and third, the advent of the Order's mathematics Academy into elite courtly circles, or vice versa, that of the courtly milieu into the Collegio Romano. From early 1602, Maelcote was in Rome as a special student of mathematics in Clavius's Academy; the following year he was professor of mathematics at the Collegio together with Grienberger, then in 1604 extraordinary professor of mathematics.[50] That same year, following the detection on 9 October of a supernova at the foot of Serpentarius (Ophiuchus), Maelcote delivered on 23 December a widely-attended discourse at the Collegio, *Problema de Stellis novis in quo impressiones aereae ab aethereis discernuntur.*[51] The soft target and absentee audience of this public oration was Galileo,[52] who by early December had delivered in Padua a series of three lectures on the nova, wherein he used parallax to locate the new star in the outermost firmament, and hypothesised the phenomenon as terrestrial vapour ascended into the celestial sphere.[53] A manuscript copy of *Problema de Stellis novis* surviving in the Biblioteca Nazionale Centrale, Rome, conserves four tipped-in diminutive printed images executed in a combination of etching and burin engraving, suggestive of the ambitions of the Jesuit text, which may have been considered for publication.[54] On the other hand, gestures to the images in the text suggest that the small-scale prints were instead distributed to those in the audience (widening the scope of the oration through subsequent scrutiny and dissemination), perhaps in combination with identical larger-scale pictures displayed for the occasion; the prints would have supplanted the speech

---

50 Ziggelaar, *François De Aguilón*, pp. 45–47.

51 *Problema de Stellis novis in quo impressiones aereae ab aethereis discernuntur*, 23 December 1604, BNCR [= Biblioteca Nazionale Centrale, Rome], Fondo Gesuitico 1186, ff. 108r–114v. Published in Baldini, *Legem impone subactis*, pp. 158–167; See also Baldini, 'La nova del 1604'.

52 *Problema de Stellis novis*, f. 110v; Baldini, 'La nova del 1604', p. 72.

53 William Shea, 'Galileo and the Supernova of 1604', in Massimo Turatto et al. (eds), *1604–2004: Supernovae as Cosmological Lighthouses*, ASP Conference Series, 342 (2005), pp. 13–20.

54 The dimensions of each do not exceed a few centimeters.

after the fact, becoming functional avatars for the ephemeral performance.[55] Whereas Baldini attributes authorship of *Problema de Stellis novis* to Maelcote, Gorman makes a convincing case based for an attribution to Grienberger, with Maelcote acting as personifying-performative mouthpiece; collaborative authorship is not out of the question.[56] *Problema de Stellis novis* invited listeners to ascend with him to the heavenly realm to behold the celestial phenomenon which is the target of his discourse – alluding to the upper 'observatory' in the Collegio, one of the institutional spaces where Clavius and his collaborators made observations – and, should they refrain, offered to proceed with a chosen legate.[57] This special nuncius to accompany the young mathematician was none other than the parallactic *problemata* that followed. The parallactic technique employed in the eulogy, trigonometric parallax, i.e. triangulation, carried out according to the double-observer method, concluded a lack of stellar parallax for the astral novelty, which in turn located it in the firmament among the fixed stars.[58] Yet *Problema de Stellis novis* refrained from pronouncing on the nature of the substance of the stellar corpus (for example, with regards to its [in]corruptibility), rhetorically deferring such judgments to philosophers. But trigonometric parallax – instrumentalised, theorised, and performatively publicised by Clavius's academicians – was hereby installed with fanfare as the potential means to capture, quantify, and render discernible for a community of authenticating witnesses otherwise unintelligible astronomical truths (prior to telescopy), and the mechanism by which various cosmologies (Copernican, Aristotelian, or otherwise) might be collaboratively tested and, potentially, reformed. By early 1607, Maelcote was at the College in Brussels as teacher of the cadets of the archduke.[59] His courtly instructional duties coincided that year with taking the solemn vows on 25 July in Ghent, and the appearance of Haley's Comet, observed in early autumn. Apparently before this convergence of events, in the spring of 1607 Maelcote had published in Brussels under the aegis of a local family of instrument makers the first instructive exposition of the theory, fabrication, and use of the equinoctial astrolabe, *Astrolabium aequinoctiale, Odonis Malcotij Bruxellensis e Societate Iesu. Per modum compendij a*

---

55 For analogous distribution of prints in promotion of Jesuit hagiographical agendas see Ruth S. Noyes, *Peter Paul Rubens and the Counter-Reformation Crisis of the Beati Moderni* (New York: Routledge, 2017), pp. 149–154.

56 Gorman, 'Mathematics and Modesty', pp. 87–91.

57 In fact, not formalised as such until the next century. Baldini, 'La nova del 1604', pp. 81, 87.

58 Baldini, 'La nova del 1604', p. 84.

59 ARSI, Flandro-Bel. 43, fol. 200v.

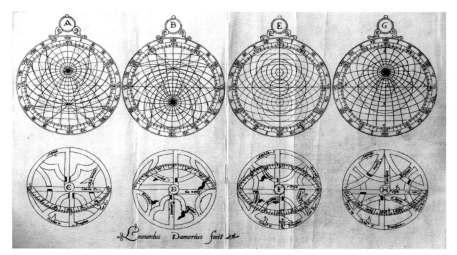

FIGURE 7.1 Léonard Damery after Odo van Maelcote, *Equinoctial astrolabe*, in *Astrolabium aequinoctiale, Odonis Malcotij Bruxellensis e Societate Iesu. Per modum compendij a Leunardo Damerio Leodiensi in lucem editum* (Brussels: Rutger Velpius, 1607). Burin engraving
© ROYAL LIBRARY OF BELGIUM, BRUSSELS, VH 8.416 A 1

Leunardo Damerio Leodiensi in lucem editum (hereafter '*Astrolabium* [1607]').[60] Prefacing the sixteen-page page octavo booklet, a tipped-in plate (20 × 12 cm) burin-engraved by Léonard Damery illustrated six miniature iterations of the *astrolabium aequinoctiale* expounded in the concise text, including austral, boreal, and two 'universal' austral-boreal configurations for tympanum and rete.

The publisher, chief loyalist printer Rutger Velpius, played a significant if problematic role in the 'paper war' attending reconciliation in the Low Countries.[61] Monica Stensland argues on the basis of the vernacular languages typically printed on Velpius's presses, that the already reconciled population, and not the rebel one, was his main loyalist target audience.[62] The choice of Latin, however, for the work in question may belie similar claims for this text which, while published through the person of Damery, was most certainly

---

60   Odo van Maelcote [Léonard Damery], *Astrolabium aequinoctiale, Odonis Malcotij Bruxellensis e Societate Iesu. Per modum compendij a Leunardo Damerio Leodiensi in lucem editum* (Brussels: Rutger Velpius, 1607), A1v. (USTC 1506309).
61   *Biographie nationale [de Belgique]* (43 vols, Brussels: Bruylant, 1866–1986), XII. 799–807.
62   Monica Stensland, *Habsburg Communication in the Dutch Revolt* (Amsterdam: Amsterdam University Press, 2012), pp. 110–13. See also Paul Arblaster, *From Ghent to Aix: How They Brought the News in the Habsburg Netherlands, 1550–1700* (Leiden: Brill, 2014), p. 54.

penned by the Jesuit himself.[63] The equinoctial astrolabe was herein framed as heir to the Ptolemaic astronomical instrument tradition and the latest iteration of modern-day astrolabic innovation after Frisius, de Rojas, and Stöffler.[64] *Astrolabium* [1607] fashioned for the device a tripartite origin story sanctified by the institutional apparati of Counter-Reformation Catholic orthodoxy, from Leonard's prefatory epistle to Maelcote, which aligned its author, addressee, and object (the astrolabe) along a Jesuitic Roman axis, through the concluding *approbatio* of Petrus Vinck of Brussels, censor for the Council of Brabant.[65] Damery's dedicatory letter established simultaneously the conjoined ingenuity and trustworthiness of Maelcote, his astrolabe, and the imbrication of septentrional-meridional socio-cultural and religious-institutional networks that engendered and ratified both.[66] However, relocating the site of publication from the Collegio Romano to the north and displacing the authorial persona from Maelcote to Damery had made possible the bypassing of Roman and Society mechanisms and networks of censure; Maelcote would approximate this tactic for a second time in 1610 in the *urbe*. This may have been for the sake of adherence to Jesuit conventions of modest self-abnegation and authorial absconding, like Maelcote's mathematical peers Grienberger and Christoph Scheiner.[67] But it cannot be ruled out that there was something potentially problematic about the essence of the equinoctial astrolabe and its functions that made publishing on it in Rome at the Collegio at mid-decade too delicate an undertaking. The brief text outlining the seventeen basic operations of the equinoctial astrolabe made no mention of parallax; what is more, neither the text nor Damery's engraved plate seem sufficient to fully understand and operate Maelcote's complicated device and the complex operations it could be used to prosecute. The booklet was thus intended to supplement, rather than supplant, the *astrolabium aequinoctiale* and the expertise of its creator and fabricator(s), and could only fully benefit readers when complemented by a large-scale specimen (by Damery) and private tuition (by Maelcote). Taken

---

63 In Italy Galileo and members of the Accademia dei Lincei contemporaneously debated regarding whether to publish the astronomer's discoveries in Italian or Latin for related reasons. See Ruth Noyes, 'Mattheus Greuter's sunspot etchings for Galileo Galilei's *Macchie Solari* (1613)', *The Art Bulletin*, 98.4 (2016), pp. 464–485.

64 Maelcote [Damery], *Astrolabium aequinoctiale*, A2r.

65 Astrid Stilma, 'Justifying War: Dutch Translations of Scottish Books around 1600', in Andrew Hiscock (ed.), *Mighty Europe 1400–1700: Writing an Early Modern Continent* (Bern: Peter Lang, 2007), pp. 55–70, at 58. See also Dirk Imhoff, *Jan Moretus and the Continuation of the Plantin Press: A Bibliography of the Works Published and Printed by Jan Moretus I in Antwerp (1589–1610)* (2 vols., Leiden: Brill, 2014), II. 225, 261, 622, 631, 644, 732.

66 Maelcote [Damery], *Astrolabium aequinoctiale*, A1v.

67 Gorman, 'Mathematics and Modesty'; Noyes, 'Mattheus Greuter's sunspot etchings'.

THE ASTROLABIUM AEQUINOTIALE, AND THE PARALLACTIC PRINT 117

together, the instrument, its inventor and manufacturer, and its promotion constitute a case strikingly similar to that of Galileo and the geometric compass, for which the Tuscan mathematician had published in-house a description in 1606 (though without illustrations) as part of evolving marketing tactics to maintain his commercial-intellectual monopoly on the contraption.[68]

Damery's prefatory epistle addressed to Maelcote specified that some years previous Lambert Damery (father to Léonard) had engraved copperplates after Maelcote's invention and printed numerous paper specimens (none survive to my knowledge), suggesting that the young Jesuit had first dispatched a printed paper exemplar across the alps to Clavius in Rome (given the rather large instrument size this would have been a much more practical alternative to one of solid brass).[69] The Musée de la Vie Wallonne in Liège preserves a unique astrolabe made by Lambert Damery, a variant of Maelcote's equinoctial invention on the other for the latitude of Brussels (51°) with a double rete with a combination of Flemish, French, and Latin inscriptions engraved on its various components that taken together suggest the instrument may have been adapted for pedagogical use.[70]

Another variant attributed to Lambert Damery formerly in the collection of the Royal Observatory of Belgium incorporates a tympanum of Maelcote's *aequinoctial* type on the front, again for a 51° latitude, with a comparable equinoctial double rete.[71] The Musée des Arts et Métiers Paris conserves two copperplates for printing paper equinoctial tympanum plates engraved by Ferdinand Arsenius (possible son of Gualterus Arsenius,[72] nephew of Gemma Frisius) and incised "Odo Malcot [sic] invenit Ferd[inand] Arssenius [sic] Sculp[sit]," which I would date to *c*.1610.[73]

Additional Arsenius-engraved paper exempla – unsigned, but identical in style and dimensions to the Paris printing plates – of tympanum and rete design variations on the *astrolabium aequinoctial* survive bound in a copy of

---

68   Wilding, *Galileo's Idol*, pp. 40–49; Biagioli, *Instruments of credit*, pp. 7–13. For a comparable case see Marr, *Between Raphael and Galileo*.

69   Maelcote [Damery], *Astrolabium aequinoctiale*, A1v.

70   Henri Michel, *Catalogue des Cadrans Solaires du Musée de la Via Wallonne*, 2nd ed. (Liège: Éditions du Musée Wallon, 1974), pp. 66–67.

71   Royal Observatory of Belgium, conserved at the Royal Museums of Art and History, Brussels, Inv. G 1911 bis. Henri Van Boxmeer, *Instruments anciens de l'Observatoire Royal de Belgique* (Brussels: Royal Observatory of Belgium, 1996), pp. 12–13.

72   For Gualterus Arsenius see Zinner, *Deutsche und Niederländische astronomische Instrumente*, pp. 236–238, 679; Victor A. Rasquin, *Dictionnaire des Constructeurs Belges d'Instruments Scientifiques* (Brussels: Comité National de Logique, d'Histoire et de Philosophie des Sciences,1996), pp. 2–4; Van Cleempoel, *Catalogue Raisonné*.

73   Musée des Arts et Métiers, Inv. 00913-0000 and 00914-0000.

FIGURE 7.2 Lambert Damery after Odo van Maelcote, stereographic astrolabe, c.1600–1610. Engraved brass
© MUSÉE DE LA VIE WALLONNE, LIÈGE, MVW 4000035

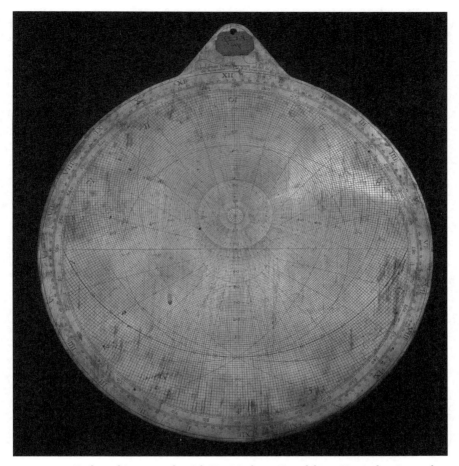

FIGURE 7.3   Ferdinand Arsenius after Odo Van Maelcote, "Astrolabium Hemisphaericum ad lat. 66 ½ / Odo Malcot invenit Ferd. Arssenius Sculp" (Aequinoctial austral-boreal tympanum printing plate, latitude 66 ½ [=arctic circle]), c.1610 (terminus post quem). Copper, burin-engraved
© MUSÉE DES ARTS ET MÉTIERS-CNAM, PARIS, 00914-0000

the 1610 Roman edition on Maelcote's invention, on which more shortly. All of these surviving examples, all of which present idiosyncratic characteristics, prompted Michel to suggest that the Jesuit collaborated with the extended family of manufacturers as a sort of mathematical-theoretical advisor for novel astrolabe designs, with the Damerys and Arsenius engraving.[74] Taken together, all these surviving pieces testify to the fact that Maelcote was, in collaboration

---

74   Michel, 'Un astrolabe de Lambert Damery'; Zinner, *Deutsche und Niederländische Astronomische Instrumente*, pp. 149, 236, 435.

with his skilled fashioners in the north, and likely his theoreticians and fellow instrumentalists in the Collegio Romano too, rapidly modifying his original *c.*1600 innovation, to the extent that by 1610 within the short span of a decade the *astrolabium aequinoctial* represented not so much a fixed, stable instrument type, but rather a labile, epistemic clade, constantly adapting according to evolving sociocultural conditions and theoretical demands, spinning off of itself new sub-species.

By 1608 or 1609, the Jesuit was once again in Rome, where he served as Mathematics professor at the Collegio Romano from 1609–1610. By 1610 (possibly even the previous year), Maelcote had received a gift of a 'Dutch spyglass' from just such a potential private student, the Antwerp-based Peter Scholier, whom he had likely first met in Antwerp or Louvain, where the latter was student of Law.[75] Academicians in Clavius's circle employed the new device during hundreds of nocturnal observations, and claimed for them priority over Galileo in observing Saturn's phases, thereby hinting at Maelcote's telescopic superiority.[76] In spring 1610 Maelcote published in Rome a second pseudonymic exposé of his equinoctial invention, *Astrolabiorum seu Vtriusque planispherij vniuersalis, et particularis vsus. Per modum compendij traditus à Valeriano Regnartio Belga* (hereafter '*Astrolabiorum* [1610]').[77] Virtually identical passages found in this more extensive 57-page quarto volume and that published in Brussels in 1607 confirm Maelcote's common authorship.[78] The revised astrolabic *opusculum* comprised seven chapters revealing the astrolabe's trigonometric parallactic potentiality.[79] This included demonstrations of triangulation that may signal Maelcote's fixation, analogous to Galileo's (eventually telescopic) approach, on measuring double stars to discover annual parallax and thereby

---

75 Georges Monchamp, *Galilée et la Belgique: Essai historique sur les vicissitudes du système de Copernic en Belgique* (Saint-Trond: G. Moreau-Schouberechts, 1892), pp. 23–5; Georges Monchamp, 'Les correspondances belges du grand Huygens', *Bulletins de l'Académie royale des sciences, des lettres et des beaux-arts de Belgique*, 3rd series, 27 (1894), pp. 255–308, 270–275.

76 *Œuvres complètes de Christiaan Huygens*, 22 vols. (The Hague: M. Nijhoff, 1888–1950), II: 489–491.

77 Odo van Maelcote [Valerian Regnard], *Astrolabiorum seu Vtriusque planispherij vniuersalis, et particularis vsus. Per modum compendij traditus à Valeriano Regnartio Belga....* (Rome: Bartholomaeus Zannettus, 1610), A1, A2. The approbation of the Vatican Master of the Sacred Palace bears the date 8 February 1610; the dedicatory epistle is dated March 1610.

78 Compare the 1607 passage in Maelcote [Damery], *Astrolabium*, A2, to that from 1610 in Maelcote [Regnard], *Astrolabiorum*, p. 44. See also Leuven, KADOC Documentation and Research Center on Religion Culture and Society, Bosm. IIa, 11.

79 The treatment of trigonometric parallax at p. 27; terrestrial triangulation pp. 52–53.

THE ASTROLABIUM AEQUINOTIALE, AND THE PARALLACTIC PRINT

confirm or deny terrestrial rotation.[80] The dedicatee, 15-year-old Roman-born Prince Francesco Peretti Damasceni (1595–1655), likely a current (or hoped-for) private pupil of Maelcote, hailed from the ranks of nobility whence Clavius already for decades had been recruiting (to Grienberger's dismay) tutees from outside the Order for ad hoc mathematical instruction (some ten such individuals for the period 1594–1596 alone), in hopes of weaponising mathematics and noble youths against heresies, recruiting new members and patronage for his Academy while also socio-culturally legitimising their endeavours.[81] A copy of *Astrolabiorum* [1610] in the Biblioteca Angelica, Rome, bearing a unique burin-engraved title page with the prince's coat of arms, was likely a presentation copy.[82] The prefatory epistle eulogising the teenage Prince of Venafri promised as forthcoming large-scale prints of the instruments outlined in the text; in fact, a few surviving copies, including the Angelica dedication copy, preserve as many as fifteen such additional etched and burin-engraved printed cut-and-reassemble sheets, which could be reconfigured into manipulatable specimens of astrolabes of Frisius, Rojas, Stöffler, and Maelcote (the latter designed for the latitude of Rome, i.e. approximately 41°).[83] I specify 'manipulatable' and not 'usable' because the scale and accuracy of manufacture (or, rather, lack thereof) of these supplementary plates would have most certainly rendered the resulting do-it-yourself specimens unsuitable – indeed, untrustworthy – for performing anything other than the most basic of astrolabic operations: these prints constituted preliminary pedagogical teaching-aids,

---

80 Christopher Graney and Henry Sipes, 'Regarding the Potential Impact of Double Star Observations on Conceptions of the Universe of Stars in the Early 17th Century', *Baltic Astronomy*, 18 (2009), pp. 93–108.

81 Stefano Boero, 'Peretti Damasceni, Francesco', *Dizionario biografico degli Italiani*. <http://www.treccani.it/enciclopedia/francesco-peretti-damasceni_(Dizionario_Biografico)/>(accessed 1 December 2017). See also Gorman, 'From "The Eyes of All"' and 'Mathematics and Modesty'.

82 Bound in skin; w/cover 16 × 20.5 cm; w/out 15.5 × 20.560; 57 pp. including end tables, + 15 added end engraved diagrams/templates, and 3 engraved fold-out diagrams, pp. 7, 44 [detached], 47.

83 Maelcote [Regnard], *Astrolabiorum*, 2A. Copies in the Biblioteca Angelica, Rome: h.5.16 (15 supplementary plates); Rome, Biblioteca Nazionale Centrale: 14. 12.C.23, MISC. B.155.10 (missing supplementary plates]); 34. 7.C.10.3 (15 supplementary plates), 55. 4.C.28.1 (7 supplementary plates; bound with Galileo Galilei, *La operazione del compasso ... di Galileo Galilei* ... (Padua: Paolo Frambotto, 1640)); Bibliothèque de l'Université, Liège: Section B (R04261B) (missing supplementary plates); Brussels, Royal Library of Belgium: VB 4.973 A 4 RP (missing supplementary plates); ETH-Bibliothek, Zürich: Rar 4336 (missing supplementary plates); Zentralbibliothek, Zürich: NE 1951 (18 supplementary plates of different facture, see below).

not reliable machines for prosecuting the parallactic machinations described in the text, a ductus leading prospective users to an expert source (object and person) rather than an instrumental avatar supplanting both.[84] For this consumers would have had to procure for themselves a larger and more exactingly produced device from Maelcote himself; his publication and all its paratextual graphic and material apparati effectively re-situated the expertise inhering in the slim volume's astrolabic corpus, to the corpus of the Jesuit mathematician. Maelcote's tactic of deferring the ultimately imprecise supplementary prints presents as strikingly similar to that attributed by Biagioli to Galileo and the telescope around this same time; the Tuscan astronomer-mathematician supposedly delayed information and withheld superior telescopic technology to maintain priority and monopolise knowledge.[85] At the time of publication *Astrolabiorum* [1610] included four tipped-in plates modelled after Damery's print in *Astrolabium* [1607]: on one plate, the inventions of Frisius, Rojas, Stöffler, and Maelcote.[86] On a second, the *astrolabium aequinoctiale* (traced and engraved from Damery's 1607 print).[87] And on a third, a modified variant of Maelcote's contraption, newly presented and described in 1610, a so-called *Hemisphaeria Aequinoctialia* – actually a hybrid bihemispherical universal-equinoctial compendium-contraption merging Maelcote's design, as well as those of Frisius, Rojas, and Stöffler, in addition to boreal and austral terrestrial and celestial maps rendered from their respective poles – an astrolabic chimera totally over eighteen components, not including the mater or throne (eight stereographic plates, four retia, two terrestrial and two celestial plates, rule, and other bits and pieces).[88]

---

84   This was confirmed by printing out scale digital photos of the supplementary prints, cutting and assembling the respective pieces, which resulted in rather clumsy and poorly calibrated instruments.

85   The inexactitude of the *Astrolabiorum* supplementary plates is confounding: Grienberger himself was a skilled draftsman and possibly engraver. See Gorman, 'Mathematics and Modesty'.

86   Actual pagination varies across surviving copies. 'ASTROLABIA Universalia & Particularia. 1a Figurarum tabula compendij Astrolabiorum Valer Regnartij pro folio 6'.

87   'Odonis Malcotij Astrolabia Aequinoctialia Hemisphaerica edita a Val. Regnartio. 2a Figurarum tabula Compendij Astrolabiorum Valer. Regnartii pro fol. 43'. The plate dimensions of the engraving adapted from Damery's 1607 print measure 20.3 × 12.2 cm.

88   "Hemisphaeria Aequinoctialia. 3a Figurarum tabula compendij Astrolabiorum Valeriani Regnartij pro folio 47. In hac tabula 3a ultra octo hemispheria Borealia et Australia A.B.C.D.E.F.G.H. adiecimus est Astrolabia supraposita, ut omnia simul una eademque opera hic ab oculos ponere."

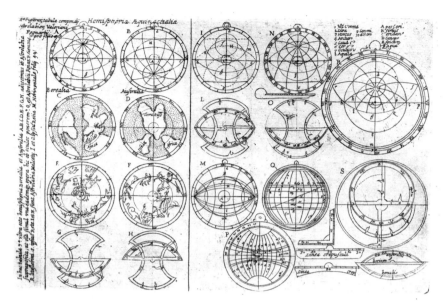

FIGURE 7.4 Valerian Regnard after Odo van Maelcote, *Hemisphaeria AEquinoctialia*, in *Astrolabiorum seu Vtriusque planispherij vniuersalis, et particularis vsus. Per modum compendij traditus à Valeriano Regnartio Belga* [...] (Rome: Bartholomaeus Zannettus, 1610). Burin engraving
© BIBLIOTECA ANGELICA, ROME, H.5.16

In addition to the two equinoctial copperplates for printing paper astrolabe tympanums in Paris engraved by Ferdinand Arsenius mentioned above,[89] a copy of *Astrolabiorum* (1610) in the Zentralbibliothek Zürich includes eighteen large supplementary printed sheets of a different facture from the fifteen additional sheets surviving in certain Roman copies; the Zürich prints, though unsigned, evince dimensions and facture identical to the Arsenius Paris copperplates, with 1610 as *terminus post quem*.[90]

Moreover, the Zürich prints correspond to the components of the newly reconfigured *Hemisphaeria Aequinoctialia* represented (albeit in miniature) and described in the 1610 *opusculum*. The Paris tympanum plates, incised *Astrolabium Hemisphaericum*, belong to the same set of new astrolabic metamorphoses. It would thus appear that around 1610 Maelcote, while publishing

---

89 Musée des Arts et Métiers, Inv. 00913-0000 and 00914-0000.
90 NE 1951. Latitude plate diameter = 27.20 cm. For full volume including all supplementary plates see <http://www.e-rara.ch/zuz/content/titleinfo/15059336> (accessed 1 December 2017).

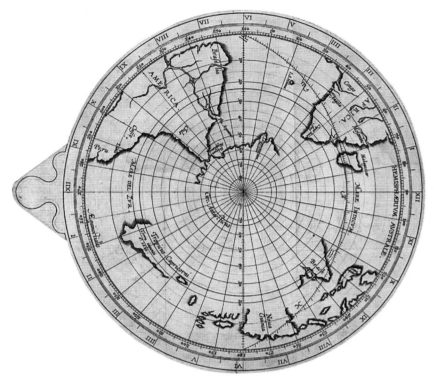

FIGURE 7.5   Ferdinand Arsenius after Odo Van Maelcote, *Hemisphaeria AEquinoctialia* terrestrial austral hemisphere plate, in *Astrolabiorum seu Vtriusque planispherij vniuersalis, et particularis vsus* [...], c.1610 (terminus post quem). Burin engraving
© ZENTRALBIBLIOTHEK ZÜRICH, ZÜRICH, NE 1951

in Rome his radically evolving invention and issuing small-size astrolabic imprints with no true practical astronomical purpose, also had Arsenius in the Southern Netherlands produce large-scale imprints with a superior degree of exactitude that could serve observational and computational ends in the field. This field, furthermore, was expanding: the Paris copperplates are configured for latitudes of 66.5° and 75°, siting their postulated users at and beyond the arctic circle, respectively. These most extreme of austral and boreal coordinates only make sense when considered in light of the principles governing trigonometric two-point parallax: the more distant the two points, the better the resulting measurements. Maelcote had pushed his device to its theoretical limit and beyond the geospatial limitations of its potential operators; rather than an appeal to actual practice and mathematical utility, we might then comprehend the *Hemisphaeria Aequinoctialia* as a hypothetical intellectual fantasy for how the parallactic space race might be won.

THE ASTROLABIUM AEQUINOTIALE, AND THE PARALLACTIC PRINT   125

5   Valerianus Regnartius, *belga*

Astrolabiorum [1610] also signalled the personificative advent on the Roman scene – or indeed anywhere in documented records – of the person (or persona) of Valerian Regnard (Valerianus Regnartius), *belga*.[91] He may have started as a nameless artisan in the instrument workshops in Leuven, Brussels, or Liège, before traveling with Maelcote to Rome.[92] The name appears on Roman engravings until the 1650s, including, notably, early Jesuit devotional hagiography from the first quarter of the *seicento*, and together with that of German-born engraver Mattheus Greuter on a legal document in 1635.[93] Complicating the fact that printed images signed with the *Regnartius* moniker continued to appear well after Maelcote's death in 1615, by mid-century it was common knowledge in Jesuit circles that *Valerianus Regnartius* was indeed a pseudonymic authorial mask assumed by Maelcote.[94] It is tempting to ponder whether Maelcote may have himself (as Gorman argues for Grienberger) engraved instruments and devotional figural images under an assumed identity (taken up after his death by others in the Society), or he impersonated his own innovations by means of collaborators like Damery and Regnard external to the Order.[95] *Astrolabiorum* [1610] evolved the pseudonymic-collaborative strategy that had engendered *Astrolabium* [1607], and interpolated both into a discursive chain of polemical personifying parallactical publications taking up

---

91   Antonio Bertolotti, *Artisti francesi in Roma nei secoli XI, XVI e XVII: ricerche e studi negli archivi romani* (Mantua: G. Mondovi, 1886), p. 105; Bertolotti, *Artisti Belgi ed Orlandesi a Roma nei Secoli XVI e XVII; Notizie e Documenti raccolti negli Archivi Romani* (Bologna: Arnaldo Forni Editore, 1974), p. 226. For a bibliographic overview of Regnard see Peter Fuhring, 'Valérien Regnart and the representation of architecture in early seventeenth-century Rome', in Eckhard Leuschner et al. (eds), *Ein privilegiertes Medium und die Bildkulturen Europas: Deutsche, Französische und Niederländische Kupferstecher und Graphikverleger in Rom von 1590 bis 1630* (Munich: Hirmer Verlag, 2012), pp. 257–277.

92   For a comparable case see Giuseppe Gabrieli (ed.), *Il Carteggio Linceo della Vecchia Accademia di Federico Cesi (1603–1630)*. Atti della Reale Accademia Nazionale dei Lincei, 6.7 (Rome: Tipografo della Reale Accademia Nazionale dei Lincei, 1938), pp. 474–476.

93   See for example the earliest joint illustrated *Lives* of Ignatius of Loyola and Francis Xavier: Valerian Regnard, *S. Ignatii Loyolæ Soc: Iesv fvndatori: qvædã miracvla ... a Valeriano Regnartio delineata, et sculpta* (Rome: [s.n., s.d.]) The only joint surviving copy, to my knowledge, is in the Boston College Burns Library, BX4700.L7 R44 1600 JESUITANA. See Juan Iturriaga Elorza, 'Hechos prodigiosos atribuidos a San Francisco Javier en grabados del siglo XVII', *Príncipe de Viana*, 55.203 (1994), pp. 467–514.

94   KADOC (see note 79), Bosmans IIa, 25–30; Pedro de Ribadeneira and Philippe Alegambe, *Bibliotheca scriptorum Societatis Jesu* (Antwerp: apud Johannem Meursium, 1643), p. 360. (USTC 1003302).

95   Something similar has been argued by Michael John Gorman for the contemporary case of Grienberger. See Gorman, 'Mathematics and Modesty in the Society of Jesus'.

questions of controversial celestial novelties and the varying degrees to which parallactic analyses of these novelties could adequately and truthfully philosophise them.[96] This chain began with Galileo's dialogue on the 1604 nova and continued with the Tuscan astronomer's 1612–1613 and 1618–1619 debates with Jesuits Christoph Scheiner and Orazio Grassi about, respectively, sunspots and new comets.[97] Meanwhile Maelcote himself investigated the heavens telescopically, observing the Jovian satellites from the beginning of 1611 and sunspots in the company of Galileo and later writing to Kepler (11 December 1612) about these experiences.[98] The following year in Rome Maelcote again acted as go-between for the Collegio and Galileo: together with Clavius and Grienberger he responded to a letter from Cardinal Roberto Bellarmino (1542–1621) of April 1611 addressed to "mathematicians of the Collegio Romano" requesting comment on the ramifications for Aristotelian cosmologies of Galileo's telescopic observations – especially those recently published in his *Sidereus nuncius* (Venice: 1610).[99] On 18 May 1611 a festival was held in Galileo's honour at the Collegio and Maelcote delivered an oration similar to that in 1604, *Nuntius*

---

96   Maelcote [Regnard], *Astrolabiorum*, 1A. Neither the specific phrase *sub nomine* nor the larger tactic were new or unique to Maelcote's project in 1610. See Hunter, 'The persona of the philosopher'; Franklin Williams, 'Renaissance Names in Masquerade', *PMLA*, 69 (1954), pp. 314–323.

97   Christoph Scheiner, *Rosa Vrsina, Sive, Sol ex Admirando Facvlarvm & Macularum Suarum Phoenomeno Varivs* ... (Bracciano: Apud Andream Phaeum Typographum Ducalem, 1626–1630), p. 7; *Johannes Kepler. Gesammelte Werke*, XVII.362. For the nova see Galileo Galilei, *Dialogo de Cecco di Ronchitti da Bruzene in perpuosito de la stella nuova* (Padua: Tozzi, 1605) and Stillman Drake (ed.), *Galileo against the Philosophers in His Dialogue of Cecco Di Ronchitti (1605) and Considerations of Alimberto Mauri (1606): In English Translations* (Los Angeles: Zeitlin & Ver Brugge, 1976); for the sunspots see Reeves and van Helden (eds), *Galileo and Scheiner on Sunspots 1611–1613* (Chicago: University of Chicago Press, 2010); Noyes, 'Mattheus Greuter's etchings'; for the 1618 comets see Stillman Drake (ed.), *The Controversy on the Comets of 1618: Galileo Galilei, Horatio Grassi, Mario Guiducci, Johann Kepler* (Philadelphia: University of Pennsylvania Press, 1960).

98   Eileen Reeves and Albert van Helden, 'Verifying Galileo's Discoveries: Telescope Making at the Collegio Romano', in Rolf Riekher et al. (eds), *Meister und die Fernrohre: das Wechselspiel zwischen Astronomie und Optik in der Geschichte* (Frankfurt: Verlag Harri Deutsch, 2007), pp. 127–141.

99   For Bellarmino's exchange with the four Jesuits see Favaro (ed.), *Le Opere di Galileo*, XI. 87–88, 92–93; Lattis, *Between Copernicus and Galileo*, pp. 190–192. For Bellarmino's cosmological theories see Ugo Baldini and George V. Coyne (eds), *The Louvain lectures (Lectiones Lovanienses) of Bellarmine and the autograph copy of his 1616 declaration to Galileo* (Vatican City: Specola Vaticana, 1984); Barry Brundell, 'Bellarmine to Foscarini on Copernicanism: A Theologian's Response', in Guy Freeland and Anthony Corones (eds), *1543 and All That: Image and Word, Change and Continuity in the Proto-Scientific Revolution* (Dordrecht: Kluwer Academic Publishers, 2000), pp. 375–393.

THE ASTROLABIUM AEQUINOTIALE, AND THE PARALLACTIC PRINT 127

sidereus Collegii Romani, with the notable difference that in this second case the addressee was physically present.[100] Similar to his earlier performance, however, the 1611 eulogy implied Jesuit priority in celestial discoveries and inflectively employed parallax to allude indirectly to provocative cosmologies; parallax, moreover, figured as a node of discursive detente bringing together Galileo's text, wherein the only feature of the telescope discussed in detail was its utility for determining trigonometric parallax, and Jesuit prerogatives.[101] Based on parallactic computations, *Nuntius sidereus Collegii Romani* posited the sun as a centre of planetary motion, and gestured – to the scandal of the Collegio philosophers – to the contradiction of Aristotelian-Ptolemaic cosmologies.[102] When sunspots began to be observed in Rome in September that year, Maelcote may have played a part, with Swiss-born Catholic convert Paul Guldin (St Gall 1577–Graz 1643; Collegio student and member of the Mathematics Academy from 1609), in notifying Scheiner in Ingolstadt, thereby setting off the solar debates between the Bavarian Jesuit (pseudonymically) and the Tuscan that would unfold 1612–1613.[103] During these few years after 1610 Maelcote must have overseen Ferdinand Arsenius's engravings for the nearly twenty printing plates for paper iterations of the *Haemisphaeria equinoctialia*, witnessed the unfolding sunspots polemic, and assisted Grienberger with publication of the 1612 celestial catalogue *Catalogus veteres affixarum longitudines, ac latitudines conferens cum novis*.[104] The full title of this latter

---

100   *Nuntius Sidereus Colegii Romani*, 18 May 1611(Biblioteca Apostolica Vaticana, Rome: Bar. Lat. 231 ff. 177r–182r.) published in Favaro (ed.), *Le Opere di Galileo*, III. 291–298.

101   Galileo Galilei, *Sidereus nuncius magna, longeque admiralia spectacula pandens, suspiciendaque proponens vnicuique, praesertim verò philosophis, atque astronomis, quae à Galileo Galileo patritio Florentino* ... (Venice: apud Thomam Baglionum, 1610), pp. 38–39 (USTC 4021754); Biagioli, *Instruments*, p. 105.

102   James Lattis, *Between Copernicus and Galileo*, pp. 194–195.

103   Reeves and van Helden, *On sunspots*, pp. 46–48. For Guldin including his confessional background see Georg Schuppener, 'Kepler's relation to the Jesuits – A study of his correspondence with Paul Guldin', *NTM Zeitschrift für Geschichte der Wissenschaften, Technik und Medizin*, 5.1 (1997), pp. 236–244. For his mathematical contributions see Rivka Feldhay, 'The Cultural Field of Jesuit Science', in John W. O'Malley et al. (eds), *The Jesuits*, pp. 107–130.

     Ruth Noyes, 'Mattheus Greuter's sunspot etchings for Galileo Galilei's *Macchie Solari* (1613)', *The Art Bulletin*, 98.4 (2016), pp. 464–485.

104   Christoph Grienberger, *Catalogus veteres affixarum longitudines, ac latitudines conferens cum nouis. Imaginum Caelestium prospectiua duplex. Altera rara Ex Polis mundi, in duobus Hemisphaerijs Aequinoctialibua, per Tabulas Ascensionem Rectarum et Declinationum. Aletra Nova Ex mundi Centro, in diversis planis Globum Caelestem tangentibus, per tabulas Particulares. Utraque Caelo et accuratioribus Tychonis observationibus quam simillima. Christophori Griembergeri Oeni Halensis, e Societatis Iesi, Calculo ac Delineatione,*

work (... *Altera rara Ex Polis mundi, in duobus Hemisphaerijs Aequinoctialibus, per Tabulas Ascensionem Rectarum et Declinationum*), and the tipped-in plates likely engraved by Grienberger with Regnard and/or Maelcote figuring the austral and boreal constellations and nearly identical to two of the Arsenius-engraved plates, bespeak a connection to Maelcote's *Hemisphaeria Aequinoctialia*: the astrolabe, the 1610 treatise, and the 1612 catalogue were to be used in concert.[105] In early 1612 van Maelcote returned to the Spanish Netherlands, stopping on the way to visit first Galileo and then German Jesuit communities, pursuing telescopic structural modifications and celestial observations in both cases. A few months later Clavius died. After a time in Brussels first, then Antwerp (1613), given complaints about his health Maelcote was allowed to return to the papal city, where together with Grienberger he succeeded Clavius in leading the Academy of Mathematics, but died himself two years later on 14 May 1615, in the papal city, just as attacks there on heliocentrism were gaining momentum within and without the Order, on the eve of the examination of the Copernican doctrine by the Congregation of the Index and the Holy Office.[106]

6 Parallactic Self-Fashioning

Parallel to the process of transformative fragmenting multiplication undergone by Maelcote's authorial persona[e], the *astrolabium* and *aequinoctiale* adhering to Maelcote's ingenuity in 1600 and 1607 had in a few short years riven, multiplied, and morphed by 1610 into *astrolabiorum* and *aequinoctialia*.[107] But this progression of fractures and divisions, maskings and personifications, transmutations and multiplication, was represented by Maelcote instead as a series of successively clarifying parallactic relocations. Each subsequent reiteration of Maelcote's ingenuity reified in a reissue of his instrument, while grafted onto the previous, was presented as a more complete, less obstructed view of that which came before, as if social, intellectual, and temporal distance had allowed for a change in viewpoint re-sited for his audience, which

---

      elaborata. (Rome: apud Bartholomaeum Zannettum, 1612 [*Approbatio* 15 July 1611]). (USTC 4028375).

105   A single volume currently in the collection of the Bibliothèque de l'Université de Liège from the Jesuit College, Douai, preserves the *Catalogus* bound together with *Astrolabiorum* (Bibliothèque de l'Université de Liège: R019095B).

106   Ziggelaar, *François De Aguilón*, pp. 45–47; Baldini, 'The Academy of Mathematics', p. 84 n. 45.

107   Maelcote [Regnard], *Astrolabiorum*, p. 45.

THE ASTROLABIUM AEQUINOTIALE, AND THE PARALLACTIC PRINT   129

in turn afforded a clearer vision of a pre-existing target, over time re-viewed as it should have been perceived (and notionally always had been) – but was, in fact, a perpetually metamorphising target in a process of becoming. Maelcote had been leveraging parallax as a discursive strategy for the self-fashioning of his instrument[s] and himself as inventor and author. Availing himself of resources and tactics strikingly similar to those of Galileo, from 1600 until the end of his life Maelcote realised parallax as a rhetorical strategy, and in turn the *astrolabium aequinoctiale* as a parallactic machine, over time discursively fashioning it as an instrument for credibly prosecuting parallactic operations, and re-forming tutees (Society or otherwise) into a homogeneous culturally, geographically and institutionally transcendent network of parallactic practitioners.[108] It is a striking historical coincidence (striking enough, in fact, to exceed the realm of mere coincidence) that during the years following the 1604 nova – for which the best usable data measurements came not from Rome or Italy but Germany – both Galileo and Maelcote 1) delivered public lectures on the phenomenon and its computational and cosmological implications (Maelcote in Rome, Galileo in Padua); 2) made their pseudonymic and co-authorial debut in print publishing with and as another graphic and textual records of their mathematical prosecution of the nova; 3) employed this discursive production to variously intervene in priority disputes and philosophical debates surrounding the nova's initial detection and ultimate interpretation; 4) recoursed to parallax and parallactic performances in these dealings as the precise and trustworthy technology of the future for eventually reaching conclusive answers; 5) reformed (even retrofitted) and re-presented pre-existing instruments for truthfully and effectively pursuing trigonometric parallactic operations; 5) regularly modified their respective instruments in collaboration with diverse manufacturers to maintain their effect of expertise and thereby intellectual monopoly on parallax; 6) offered their modified devices to potential noble patrons according to the currency of contemporary socio-epistemological gift economies; 7) shifted to the telescope by 1610 while not fully abandoning their earlier enterprises.[109] The equinoctial astrolabe in a sense delimited the final frontier (or, death rattle) of astrolaby, issued from a body at once individual and institutional that concurrently investigated (albeit sceptically and cautiously) the incipient field of telescopy.[110] In hindsight,

---

108 Wilding, *Galileo's Idol*, Harris, 'Confession-Building'.
109 For Galileo's part see Biagioli, *Instruments of credit*, pp. 7–13; Wilding, *Galileo's Idol*, pp. 38–49.
110 For Jesuit attitudes in Rome towards the telescope in the early years see the work of Reeves and van Helden.

Maelcote's and the Order's sustained investment in astrolabic innovation at the dawn of the telescopic age might seem outmoded at best. Yet during the first decade-and-a-half of the *seicento* that the Brabantine Jesuit would live, the telescope's eventual primacy was far from obvious, and the possibility to conduct astronomical research utilising the two technologies in tandem surely appeared promising, as Maelcote in his person and practice likely attempted to reconcile them as complimentary, not inimical: after all, the same year he received in a telescope from Antwerp, he also published on his astrolabe in Rome.

CHAPTER 8

An Imperial Crusade? Public Opinion in Antwerp and the Response to the Bohemian Crisis

Paul Arblaster

The Habsburg response to the Bohemian crisis of 1618–1620 led to two quite distinct epiphenomena in the city of Antwerp: the licensing of the city's first newspaper, and the establishment of a confraternity of concerned citizens willing to pray for, and pledge support to, the maintenance of the legitimate authority of Catholic princes. Both these initiatives made limited use of the rhetoric and imagery of crusading, a very specific field of reference within the broader context of warfare against enemies of the Church. Such rhetoric and imagery was deployed sparingly, and in light of the institutional and fiscal implications that 'crusading' still bore within the Habsburg monarchy more broadly may to some extent have been counter-productive.

1   Newspapers

The starting-point for this enquiry was the front page of a seventeenth-century newspaper, published in Antwerp by a man called Abraham Verhoeven.[1] In 1605 Verhoeven acquired a monopoly throughout the Habsburg Netherlands on printing pictures of the news from woodcuts or copperplates. From that time on he specialised in the production of engravings and pamphlets about current affairs, although not to the exclusion of almanacs, prayer cards, and other staples of the printing trade. His rate of issue of news pamphlets attained a frequency that begins to suggest the term 'periodical press' in the years 1617–1619, but it was not until the beginning of 1620 that he presented his news pamphlets as a single series. In February 1620 he adopted consecutive signatures on each issue. From the beginning of 1621, issues were consecutively numbered on

---

1   Paul Arblaster, *From Ghent to Aix: How They Brought the News in the Habsburg Netherlands, 1550–1700* (Leiden: Brill, 2014), pp. 1–6, 74–171; see also Alphonse Goovaerts, *Abraham Verhoeven d'Anvers le premier gazetier de l'Europe. Etude Bio-Bibliographique* (Antwerp: P. Kockx, 1880); Franz Jozef Van den Branden, *Ontstaan van het nieuwsblad te Antwerpen: Abraham Verhoeven, zijn leven, 1575–1652* (Antwerp: Drukkerij Buschmann, 1902); Marcel Stijns, 'Abraham Verhoeven en de pers', *Vlaamse Gids*, 42:3 (1958), pp. 143–149.

© KONINKLIJKE BRILL NV, LEIDEN, 2023 | DOI:10.1163/9789004510159_009

132 ARBLASTER

the front page. This was true even of issues dedicated entirely to satirical commentaries written in verse, that might more properly be thought of as special issues. The series had no running title, but is known to historians as the *Nieuwe Tijdinghen*. By then, weekly newspapers were already well established in several cities in the German language area, and had made their first appearance in Amsterdam and London.[2]

Verhoeven was, however, in one respect ahead of his time. While the first newspapers followed the genre conventions of manuscript *avvisi*, Verhoeven combined these with the conventions of the occasional news pamphlet to produce an entirely new form of news publication. This was the first newspaper to adopt an eight-page newsbook format, and the first to privilege particular news items by drawing attention to them on the front page, illustrating them with relevant woodcuts, and commenting on them on the inside pages with editorial introductions and asides.[3] Some other seventeenth-century newspapers were illustrated, but on a regular basis this never went further than a globe or a winged Mercury on the masthead.[4]

Among the woodcuts that adorn Verhoeven's front pages are some slightly unusual images. What is unsurprising about a wartime newspaper is that there was a preponderance of images of battle. Some of the woodcuts Verhoeven most often reused show squares of pike and musket, cavalrymen skirmishing with pistols, or the deployment of light artillery, or again the throwing up of siege works. Occasionally, though, news of on-going wars was accompanied by strangely anachronistic pictures. In one such, reused in different contexts, a force of knights on horseback armed with swords and lances, one with a cross prominent on his shield, charge across the plain before an exotic city to drive off a force of turbaned, scimitar-wielding enemies whose standard is the crescent moon. Devoid as it is of documentary value, nevertheless the symbolic appropriateness of this image is clear when it appears on the front

---

2 See Else Bogel and Elger Blühm, *Die deutschen Zeitungen des 17. Jahrhunderts: Ein Bestandsverzeichnis mit historischen und bibliographischen Angaben*, 3 vols. (Bremen: Schünemann Universitätsverlag, 1971); Folke Dahl, *Dutch Corantos, 1618–1650* (The Hague: Koninklijke Bibliotheek, 1946); Folke Dahl, *Bibliography of English Corantos and Periodical Newsbooks, 1620–1642* (London: Bibliographical Society, 1952); Arthur der Weduwen, *Dutch and Flemish Newspapers of the Seventeenth Century, 1618–1700* (2 vols., Leiden: Brill, 2017).

3 The sorts of stories given this treatment are discussed in Kristin Van Damme and Jeroen Deploige, 'Slecht nieuws geen nieuws. Abraham Verhoeven (1575–1652) en de "Nieuwe Tijdinghen": periodieke pers en propaganda in de Zuidelijke Nederlanden tijdens de vroege zeventiende eeuw', *Bijdragen en mededelingen betreffende de geschiedenis der Nederlanden*, 113:1 (1998), pp. 1–22.

4 For instance, on the Parisian *Gazette* and *Nouvelles ordinaires*, or Munich's *Mercurij Ordinari Zeitung*.

AN IMPERIAL CRUSADE?   133

page of an issue reporting skirmishes between Poles and Turks on the frontiers of Christendom[5] – especially as the war in question was precipitated by Osman II's decision in 1620 to depose Gaspar Gratiani, a member of the Order of Knights of the Christian Militia, as vaivoda of Moldavia.[6] But the very same image was also used to represent the Battle of Fleurus.[7] A different image of pre-firearm cavalrymen fighting below pennants of the cross and the crescent represents victorious cavalrymen in Habsburg service in the Rhineland in the spring of 1622.[8]

There is little sign in the text that readers were being encouraged to think of the Habsburgs' military opponents in Germany and the Low Countries as in some way equivalent to the paynim of crusader romance, but the re-use of these two images to illustrate news of the war in the Low Countries and the Rhineland surely indicates that this was the case. A picture of a Roman soldier with a crucifix emblazoned on his shield (suggestive of Constantine or Heraclius) appears to have been used only once, to stand for the struggles in Italy and Switzerland for control of the Alpine passes.[9] Such images show a clear awareness of the history of crusading as it was understood by crusaders.[10]

However, the surviving reports and editorials in the *Nieuwe Tijdinghen* contain no direct verbal invocation of crusading ideals. The closest they come are at second hand, most strikingly in coverage of the general muster of the Army of Flanders in July 1621, when a Carmelite preacher addressed the assembled soldiery in Spanish and French, telling them that just as they carried swords to defeat their enemies, so he carried the Cross of Christ as the rapier with

---

5   *Nieuwe Tijdinghe* (henceforth *NT*) 1622 no. 95 (Antwerp: Abraham Verhoeven, 1 July 1622), 'Nieuwe Tijdinge wt Duytslant vanden Hongherschen Landtdach ende hunne Tractatie. Met Tijdinghen wt Turckijen, ende Polen' (USTC 1114441).

6   See Vernon J. Parry, 'The Ottoman Empire 1617–48', in George R. Potter et al. (eds), *New Cambridge Modern History* (14 vols., Cambridge: Cambridge University Press, 1957–1979), IV. 636; Manfred Stoy, 'Das wirken Gaspar Gracianis (Gratianis) bis zu Ernennung zum Fürsten der Moldau am 4. Februar 1619', *Südost-Forschungen*, 43 (1984), pp. 49–122.

7   *NT* 1622 no. 135 (2 September): 'Waerachtighe Nieuwe Tijdinghe van de groote ende miraculeuse Victorie vercreghen in Brabant teghen Mansfelt ende den Dollen in Halberstadt' (USTC 1114490).

8   *NT* 1622 no. 61 (29 April), 'Nieuwe Tijdinghe hoe dat de Staeten van Hollandt eenighe Compagnien Ruyters hebben gesonden tot secours van den Dollen Halberstadt, ende sijn onder weghen gheslaghen ghewerden' (USTC 1114335).

9   *NT* 1625 no. 30 (18 April), 'Nieuwe Tijdinghen van de Oorloghe in Italien' (USTC 1114889). On the strife in the Grisons, see Andreas Wendland, *Der Nutzen der Pässe und die Gefährdung der Seelen: Spanien, Mailand und der Kampf ums Veltlin, 1620–1641* (Zürich: Chronos, 1995).

10   Barbara Baert, *A Heritage of Holy Wood: The Legend of the True Cross in Text and Image*, translated by Lee Preedy (Leiden: Brill, 2004), pp. 164–193, 216–238.

134 ARBLASTER

which he had defeated the Enemy, and that they should not doubt but that God would grant them victory, since they would be fighting in a just cause and for the Holy Catholic Apostolic Roman Faith[11]:

> Alsoo ghy daer draecht een Rappier oft zweerdt aen u zyde om den Vyant te verwinnen, so drage ick dit Cruys Christi aen mijn syde, d'welck ick hier in mijn handt hebbe, ende mijn Rappier is, daer ick mijnen Vyandt mede hebbe verwonnen, ende en twijffelt daer niet aen Godt sal u de Victorie verleenen, want ghy sult vechten voor een Rechtveerdighe sae-cke, ende het H. Catholijck Apostolijc Roomsche Gheloove.

But even without direct talk of crusading, Verhoeven's editorial interventions use standard pious phrases of providentialism, imprecation, and thanksgiving, which leave the reader in no doubt that reports of Habsburg victories were reports of the furthering of God's cause. Possibly the most explicit visual image in this regard is one not reused for other news reports but surely not cut especially for the occasion: an image of the effects of bad weather on a Dutch expeditionary force, shown as an angel of wrath pouring out the waters of the storm on sinking ships and drowning seamen.[12]

Nobody could accuse the Habsburgs' Protestant enemies of being behindhand when it came to providentialism and religious motivations for warfare. In the United Provinces, prayer and fasting were encouraged as a way for non-combatants to support the war effort, and during a number of the campaigns and sieges of the 1620s, as well as in years of plague or dearth, Wednesday was decreed a weekly day of public prayer for victory or deliverance.[13] Thomas Scott, an English propagandist for the Calvinist international, in a lengthy pamphlet entitled *The Belgick Soldier. Or, Warre was a blessing* looked back nostalgically to the halcyon days of Queen Elizabeth, when England strained every muscle to battle with the popish Antichrist in Scotland, Ireland, Flanders, France, on the High Seas and in the West Indies.[14]

One of the specially made woodcuts that Verhoeven printed represented coins struck by Christian of Brunswick bearing the inscription 'Flagellum

---

11   *NT* 1621 no. 107 (29 July), pp. 7–8, 'Tijdinghe wt Brussel, ende oock den legher in Vlaenderen wat daer ghepasseert is' (USTC 1114236).

12   *NT* 1622 no. 173 (20 Dec.), 'Nieuwe Tijdinge vanden gefaeilleerden Aenslach die den Vyandt gehadt heeft met allen zijn Schepen' (USTC 1114515).

13   Nicolaas Christiaan Kist, *Neêrland's Bededagen en Biddagsbrieven: Een bijdrage ter opbouwing der geschiedenis van Staat en Kerk in Nederland* (2 vols., Leiden: S. and J. Luchtmans, 1848–1849), I. 179–192, II.116–138.

14   Printed in London, 1624 (USTC 3011632).

AN IMPERIAL CRUSADE? 135

sacerdotum. Ich wil der pfaffen straffen'.[15] It shows the duke's self-image as an instrument of divine justice, but in this context also the ironies of the providential dispensation. Thousands of these coins were captured from his baggage train after his defeat at Kirchhausen in May 1622. At least some of these coins had been struck from silver looted from the shrine of St Liborius of Paderborn, and a satirical broadsheet produced in Holland had celebrated the 'transformation' of St Liborius into thalers in the style of a miracle story to promote a pilgrimage shrine.[16] Verhoeven's riposte was to credit St Liborius with Brunswick's next setback, near Frankfurt.[17]

Another saint to get special mention – and the only saint to get his picture in the papers – was St Norbert, the twelfth-century founder of the Premonstratensian Order. In 1627 St Norbert's relics were translated from Magdeburg to Prague, in a ceremony that coincided with the highpoint of the identification of the imperial Habsburg cause with crusader ideology.[18] Verhoeven's illustrator portrays Norbert trampling both the devil and the heretic Tanchelm, whose preaching in early twelfth-century Antwerp had led many astray.[19] Norbert was the founder of the Premonstratensian Abbey of St Michael in Antwerp, which in the course of time had become a member of the First Estate in the States of Brabant, and this historic connection ensured local interest in the story, which Verhoeven covered in a sixteen-page double issue, including a potted life of the saint. There was even a suggestion that Antwerp should imitate Brussels's veneration of St Gudula, Mechelen's of St Rombout, Lier's of St Gummarus and Ghent's of St Bavo, by instituting an extra annual holiday in honour of the city's 'apostle'. That Antwerp's apostle, unlike those of Brussels, Mechelen, Lier or Ghent, was often shown trampling a heretic may

---

15 *NT* 1622 no. 75 (31 May), 'Waerachtich ende gheheel pertinent relaes van den grouwelijcken ende bloedigen slach gheschiet int'Pfaltz-Graven Landt boven Heydelbergh' (USTC N4-498). See also Andreas Wang, *Der 'Miles Christianus' im 16. und 17. Jahrhundert und seine mittelalterliche Tradition. Ein Beitrag zum Verhältenis von sprachlicher und graphischer Bildlichkeit* (Bern: H. Lang, 1975), pp. 177–194.

16 *Westphaelsche transformatie, alwaer S. Liborius verandert in Rijxdaelders* ([Amsterdam: Claes Jansz. Visscher II], 1622) (USTC 1116032). A copy can be consulted at <http://www.rijksmuseum.nl/nl/collectie/RP-P-OB-2501>.

17 *NT* 1622 no. 97 (1 July), 'Verhael van die groote Victorie, die Godt almachtich door den H. Liborius Bisschop ende Patroon van Paderborne, aen ons volck verleent heeft, over den Dollen Halberstadt' (USTC 1114443).

18 *NT* 1627 no. 77 (3 July), 'De Heerlycke Translatie vanden Heyligen Norbertus' (USTC 1115205).

19 Aubertus Miraeus, *Ordinis Praemonstratensis Chronicon* (Cologne: Bernhard Wolter, 1613), pp. 27–45 (USTC 2029364); Joannes Chrysostomus van der Sterre, *Het leven van den H. Norbertus, sticht-vader der Ordre van Praemonstreyt ende apostel van Antwerpen* (Antwerp: Geeraerdt van Wolsschaten, 1623), pp. 202–229 (USTC 1435855).

itself not be without some unspoken significance, and it is perhaps not too fanciful to see it as visually aligning Norbert with Santiago Matamoros.[20]

A combination of factors that included a providentialist outlook, military-political confessional conflict, a new interest in the historical study of sanctity, and the importance of religious institutions as social actors, mean that seventeenth-century newspapers should be expected to engage with religious themes and images in a wide variety of ways. The far more numerous images of warfare are also to be expected. But the combination of religious and martial imagery in patently anachronistic woodcuts of crusaders is an exceptional curiosity. The deployment of such images coincides in time with another unusual development in Antwerp that might be rather more significant than mere coincidence.

2 Pledges

In February 1620, the month that the *Nieuwe Tijdinghen* made its appearance as a serial publication, the painter Peter Paul Rubens declined to provide private financial assistance to the military treasury of the Habsburg forces being sent from Flanders to Bohemia. In itself this may not sound terribly surprising. Armies are not usually maintained by voluntary subscription. But several of those in Rubens's social circle in Antwerp did precisely what he had declined to do, pledging individual contributions to maintain soldiers from the Low Countries in Habsburg service in Bohemia. Those who did so included Joannes Woverius, who sits beside Justus Lipsius in Rubens's famous *Four Philosophers*. An alderman of Antwerp, he had been a university friend of the painter's deceased brother Philip (also in the group portrait). In the 1620s, Woverius, Rubens, and the printer Baltasar Moretus (head of the Plantin Office) corresponded about current affairs and exchanged newsletters.[21] Woverius and Moretus each pledged one year's pay for three infantry soldiers. So did Woverius's father-in-law, the financier Rogier Clarisse. His brother-in-law (his sister's husband), Jean della Faille, another alderman of Antwerp, pledged for two.

---

20   On the iconography of St Norbert see Trudo J. Gerits, *Sint-Norbertus in de Brabantse kunst*, exhibition catalogue (Averbode: Abdij Averbode, 1971).

21   Max Rooses and Charles Ruelens (eds) *Correspondance de Rubens et documents épistolaires concernant sa vie et ses oeuvres*, (6 vols., Antwerp: Veuve De Backer, 1887 [vol. I]; J. Maes, 1898 [vol. II]; J.-E. Buschmann & J. Maes, 1900 [vol. III]; J.-E. Buschmann, 1904–1909 [vols. IV–VI]), III. 110–112 (esp.).

AN IMPERIAL CRUSADE? 137

In total, in the first few weeks of 1620, a hundred and fifty-eight pledges were received from individuals, families, and business partnerships in Antwerp, to a total of 46,200 guilders, calculated as the equivalent of one year's pay for 308 infantry soldiers.[22] As far as army finances go, even if one takes the attitude that every little helps, this is not an overwhelming sum, even though it shows a considerable outlay by the individuals concerned. The most significant effect that the pledges must have had was that before the year was out over a hundred prominent citizens of Antwerp, and several dozen resident foreigners (mostly Portuguese and Italians), could pride themselves on having personally contributed, in however small a way, to the resounding Habsburg victory in the Battle of the White Mountain.

The ledger of their pledges shows a targeted approach to fund-raising. First the clergy were approached. The bishop of Antwerp pledged to support 15 soldiers, the dean of Antwerp cathedral 10, the archdeacon 2, but despite these fine examples few other ecclesiastical office-holders could be drawn. Nor could the secular officials appointed to exercise royal jurisdiction in the city. The city council was more forthcoming. Both mayors, seventeen of the twenty aldermen, all three pensionaries, all five secretaries, one of the four clerks of the council, and both the overseers of the cloth hall pledged to support at least one man apiece, in a few cases two or even more. Nicholas Rockocx, knight, signed up for six. Lesser officials were less generous, declining to contribute, or pledging a third or a half of a year's pay for an infantryman. The fund-raisers then turned to foreign merchants, and natives with substantial foreign connections. Here the response was rather more impressive. The Portuguese merchants clubbed together to pledge for forty soldiers. A few individuals stand out for their generosity: Willem van Immerseel pledged to support ten soldiers, Martin della Faille eight, the Van der Goes brothers ten between them; but these were the heads of major merchant houses.[23] More frequent was a pledge for one or two soldiers. Finally, ordinary citizens were approached, a few of whom were found willing to subscribe for a year's pay, or a fraction of a year's pay.

---

22   Antwerp, Stadsarchief, Privilegiekamer 1588, 'Guerre de Bohême. 1620. Souscription pour l'entretien de l'armée'.

23   On Van Immerseel, see Eddy Stols, *De Spaanse Brabanders of de Handelsbetrekkingen der Zuidelijke Nederlanden met de Iberische wereld 1598–1648* (2 vols., Brussels: Koninklijke Vlaamse Academie, 1971); on the della Failles, see Wilfrid Brulez, *De Firma della Faille en de internationale handel van Vlaamse firma's in de 16e eeuw* (Brussels: Paleis der Academiën, 1959); on the Van der Goes, see Erik Duverger, 'De moeilijkheden van Jan Baptist van der Goes met Willem van Can en Jacques de Moor: Een bijdrage tot de geschiedenis van de tapijtkunst en de tapijthandel in het begin van de XVIIe eeuw', *Bijdragen tot de Geschiedenis*, 51 (1968), pp. 69–90.

The scheme was such a success in Antwerp that there was talk of trying other cities throughout the Habsburg Netherlands, but somehow this promising start was also the end of the affair. There are vague mentions of obstacles, difficulties, opponents, but no clear statement of who opposed the scheme or why. All we know is that nothing more was heard of it. Antwerp remained unique in having seen this unusual experiment in army funding. Or perhaps it should be seen as an experiment in tying the urban elite to the military projects of the dynasty in a way that gave them an unusually personal stake in faraway victories.

In order to understand just what was so important about Antwerp, that such an experiment should take place there at all, we should consider the usual methods of army funding. The financing of Habsburg forces in the Low Countries had two sources: local taxes, and remittances from Spain (known as *asientos*). At any one time, between a quarter and a sixth of military income might derive from local taxes, making them a secondary but not inconsiderable source of supply.[24] The more substantial Spanish funds were the most striking operation of the new global economy: silver mined in Mexico and Peru secured loans from Genoese (and later Portuguese) banks, paid out at the New Exchange in Antwerp.[25] Antwerp was not only the northern point of the Monarchy's financial triangle, where bullion from Seville and letters of credit from Genoa were converted into ready money. It was also the main market for the various commodities required by the Army of Flanders, most importantly grain, cloth, and armaments. From 1601 the military authorities dealt with only two individuals – the *asentista* for pay and the *proveedor general* for provisions – but each of these had to draw on a wider network of financiers and suppliers to meet their contractual obligations.

This gave the wealthy inhabitants of Antwerp a double function in the mercantile-military complex of the Spanish Monarchy: they contributed as the payers of taxes, both direct and indirect, but in many cases also as the contractual providers of cash and provisions.[26] These were not people whose opinions

---

24 Geoffrey Parker, *The Army of Flanders and the Spanish Road, 1567–1659: The Logistics of Spanish Victory and Defeat in the Low Countries' Wars* (Cambridge: Cambridge University Press, 1972), pp. 139–145, 287; Miguel Ángel Echevarría Bacigalupe, 'Recursos fiscales y guerra en Europa: Flandes, 1615–1622', *Manuscrits*, 13 (1995), pp. 273–307; also the figures and tables appended to René Vermeir, *In staat van oorlog: Filips IV en de Zuidelijke Nederlanden, 1629–1648* (Maastricht: Shaker Publishing, 2001).

25 Parker, *Army of Flanders*, pp. 146–156.

26 Hans Pohl, 'Zur Bedeutung Antwerpens als Kreditplatz im beginnenden 17. Jahrhundert', in *Die Stadt in der europäischen Geschichte: Festschrift Edith Ennen*, edited by Werner Besch et al. (Bonn: Ludwig Röhrscheid, 1972), pp. 667–686; Etienne Rooms, 'Organisatie van de bevoorrading en de bezoldiging der troepen in dienst van de Spaanse monarchie in

could be dismissed out of hand, as a crisis of confidence in Antwerp would be bound to have profound repercussions on military funding and supply – as events in 1629–32 and 1640–43 were to show all too clearly. In the run-up to the Bohemian campaign the government would have been keen to convince the civic elite of Antwerp that their future well-being depended on the outcome of a quarrel in a far-away country about which they knew very little. The same group of people was presumably the primary intended readership of Abraham Verhoeven's *Nieuwe Tijdinghen*, and precisely those targeted by the fund-raising campaign of early 1620.

The organisers of the fund-raising were the secular priest Aubertus Miraeus, the Jesuit Carolus Scribani, and the layman Jan de Gaverelle. A fourth man, a shadowy presence who can be linked to the scheme only tenuously, was the resident foreigner Emanuel Sueyro. Each one of these four is a figure of interest in his own right. Emanuel Sueyro (1587–1629), Knight of Christ, was a Portuguese New Christian, and head of Spain's secret intelligence operations in the Low Countries.[27] As such he reported to the Spanish ambassador in Brussels, rather than to the Archdukes Albert and Isabella, the local Habsburg sovereigns. He was also an antiquary, a Spanish translator of Sallust and Tacitus, and had been a merchant until his 1617 knighthood in an order that prohibited its members from engaging in trade. Whether his involvement went beyond reporting on what was happening, and encouraging the generous response of the Portuguese merchants, is unclear.[28]

Jan de Gaverelle (1579–1645) was one of the pensionaries to the city of Antwerp, a lawyer kept on permanent retainer to advise the magistrates and represent the city to external jurisdictions, but he was soon to enter the king's service – first in Spain as a member of the Supreme Council of Flanders, and then back in the Low Countries as a Privy Councillor and as Commissioner General of the Flemish fleet.[29] While in Spain, he too became a Knight of Christ. He was lay head of Antwerp's Sodality of the Scapular of Our Lady, and after his

---

de Zuidelijke Nederlanden (1567–1713)', in *Liber Alumnorum Karel van Isacker S.J.*, special issue of *Bijdragen tot de Geschiedenis*, 63/1–4 (1980), pp. 121–147. See also Maurits A. Ebben, *Zilver, brood en kogels voor de koning: Kredietverlening door Portugese bankiers aan de Spaanse kroon, 1621–1665* (Leiden: Rijksuniversiteit, 1996).

27   On Sueyro see Miguel Ángel Echevarría Bacigalupe, *La diplomacia secreta en Flandes, 1598–1643* (Bilbao: Universidad del País Vasco, 1984), pp. 157–192.

28   Echevarría Bacigalupe, *La diplomacia secreta*, p. 159.

29   Floris Prims, *Jan de Gaverelles (1579–1645): Een figuur uit de katholieke renaissance* (Antwerp and Utrecht: Standaard, 1946); also the laudatory *Exploits de la Flotte Royale de Dunkerke, soub la sage conduite de Gaverelle Chevalier de l'ordre de Christus* (Brussels, Widow of Hubert Anthoon-Velpius I, 1635) (USTC 1435551).

return from Spain founded a new sodality for the ransoming of Christian slaves in North Africa. Besides his career as a civic and royal official, he can thus be seen to have been heavily engaged in the prayer-groups that were so important a part of civil society in seventeenth-century Catholic Europe.[30]

Aubertus Miraeus (1573–1640) came from a family of merchants and minor royal officials in Brussels, and one of his uncles had been a bishop of Antwerp. He had studied in Leuven and Douai, and made a name for himself as an antiquary. He was friendly to the Jesuits, and had at one time been prefect of their Latin Sodality in Antwerp. He held a canonry of Antwerp cathedral, as well as being one of the chaplains to the court of the Archdukes Albert and Isabella in Brussels. Linked by blood to the loyalist middle classes in Brussels, by profession to the clerical establishment in Antwerp and to the court, and by scholarship to intellectual circles throughout the Low Countries, Miraeus was a perfect opinion broker, and as we shall see he fulfilled that role in more ways than one.

Opinion was a key political concept. One of the foremost theorists of 'opinion' or 'reputation' in the political philosophy of the time was none other than Carolus Scribani (1561–1629), author of the anti-Machiavellian treatise *Politico-Christianus*.[31] Scribani was the son of an Italian doctor, Hector Scribani, a cadet nobleman who became court physician to Margaret of Parma, and of a Flemish patrician woman, Maria Vander Beke, whose armigerous forebears were among the magistrates of Ghent. Like Miraeus, he was the nephew of a former bishop of Antwerp. He joined the Society of Jesus in 1582. In 1620 he had recently served a term as provincial of the Flemish Province of the Society and been appointed rector of the Jesuit college in Brussels; from 1598 to 1614 he had been rector of the Jesuit college in Antwerp. Many of those from whom Scribani solicited pledges in 1620 would have been former students or their parents.

These were the individual fund-raisers. Their activity took place not in a vacuum, but through yet another prayer group: the Sodality for the Defence of the Faith, whose members were expected to pray daily for the preservation

---

30 Louis Châtellier, *L'Europe des dévots* (Paris: Flammarion, 1987). On earlier French examples of the mobilisation of religious associations of laymen in religious conflict, see Robert R. Harding, 'The Mobilization of Confraternities against the Reformation in France', *Sixteenth Century Journal*, 11:2 (1980), pp. 85–107.

31 Printed at Antwerp by Martin Nutius in 1624 (USTC 1003511). On Scribani's political views, see Robert Bireley, *The Counter-Reformation Prince: Anti-Machiavellianism or Catholic Statecraft in Early Modern Europe* (Chapel Hill: University of North Carolina Press, 1990), esp. pp. 171–177.

AN IMPERIAL CRUSADE?

and mutual concord of Christian princes and magistrates, and to contribute according to their ability towards the costs of defence against enemies of the Church. The ultimate brains behind the organisation were Ferdinand II's ambassador in Rome, Maximilian von Trautmansdorf, and the imperial councillor and secretary of finances, Matthias Arnoldin von Klarenstein.[32] The logic was that it would in the long term be more cost effective to pay in advance for the defence of existing churches than to hold collections for the building of replacements at a later date. It was an argument that convinced Paul v to make over Italian tithes to Ferdinand II in January 1620.

Sueyro, Gaverelle, Miraeus and Scribani were all individuals with a background in the urban classes of patricians, merchants and professionals, all operating on the fringes of the courtly aristocracy and royal office-holding. They were well placed to mediate between court and city, and to find ways to express a community of interests between the two. That they should have chosen to do so by emphasising the religious aspect of the Bohemian conflict is perhaps surprising, but they did so in a very particular way: they portrayed it as a defensive campaign to preserve legitimate authority, and as part of a much broader defensive struggle. Nor were they indiscriminate in their religious animosities. There is no suggestion that Protestantism as such was the enemy. On the contrary, in Miraeus's writings (as in the reports in the *Nieuwe Tijdinghen*) a clear distinction is apparent between 'civil' Protestants (Lutherans, Anglicans, Arminians), and the seditious Calvinists (Gueux, Huguenots, Puritans, etc.) who were in league with Turks and Tatars.[33]

3   Prayers

Monetary contributions were only part of the purpose of the Sodality for Defence of the Faith, and in the event proved to be a one-off part. The on-going commitment of the membership was to pray for the defence of legitimate authority. Christian prayer for those in authority is as old as Christianity itself, with Paul instructing Timothy that:

---

32   Victor Brants, 'La Société de Défense de la Foi sous Albert et Isabelle', *Analectes pour servir à l'histoire ecclésiastique de la Belgique*, 36 (1910), pp. 169–186.

33   For this element in the *Nieuwe Tijdinghen*, see Paul Arblaster, 'Posts, Newsletters, Newspapers: England in a European System of Communications', in Joad Raymond (ed.), *News Networks in Seventeenth-century Britain and Europe*, special issue of *Media History*, 11:1 + 2 (2005), p. 31.

I desire therefore first of all things that obsecrations, prayers, postulations, thanksgivings be made for all men, for kings and all that are in pre-eminence, that we may lead a quiet and a peaceable life in all piety and chastity.[34]

Prayers for deliverance from enemies have also been common. In the sixteenth-century Low Countries such prayers were given topical and local colouring in a number of prayer books. The most influential of these was Simon Verrept's *Enchiridion precationum piarum*, first published in 1565, on the eve of the Dutch Revolt. By 1605 the Latin text had gone through forty editions.[35] It was translated into French, Dutch and German, and inspired similar efforts in English.[36] As the title page to the revised French edition indicates, it was a collection of prayers drawn from the writings and prayer books of holy fathers and illustrious doctors, both ancient and modern ('des escrits & livres des prieres des saints peres, & docteurs illustres, tant anciens que modernes'): the oldest items were attributed to David and Solomon; the most recent were drawn from the writings of contemporaries such as the Dutch Jesuit Peter Canisius, the bishop of Roermond, Willem Lindanus, and Pope Pius v.[37]

In amongst the typical prayers for morning and evening, before confession, after communion, for the sick, for the dying, and so forth, there are a number of prayers for times of war and conflict. These include an 'Oraison necessaire au temps present contre les erreurs de la Foy' (a prayer against doctrinal errors made necessary by the present times), taken from the work of the German Dominican Johann Faber of Heilbronn, which focuses on asking that the person praying not be led astray[38]; 'Trois Oraisons pour lire au temps de guerre, ou de persecution, ou de sedition' (Three Prayers to be read in times of war, or persecution, or sedition), the first drawn from Judith 9 ('O Seigneur Dieu de noz peres, regarde maintenant le camp des Assiriens, comme lors il t'a pleu

---

34 1 Timothy 2:1–2, after *The New Testament of Jesus Christ* (Rheims: Jean de Foigny, 1582) (USTC 156842); spelling modernised.

35 Stanley Morison, *English Prayer Books: An Introduction to the Literature of Christian Public Worship* (Cambridge: Cambridge University Press, 1949), p. 111.

36 Eamon Duffy, 'Praying the Counter-Reformation', in James E. Kelly and Susan Royal (eds), *Early Modern English Catholicism: Identity, Memory and Counter-Reformation* (Leiden: Brill, 2017), pp. 206–225, esp. pp. 217–219.

37 Simon Verepaeus, *Recueil ou manuel des devotes oraisons*, revised edition (Antwerp: Jean Bellerus, 1572) (USTC 13121).

38 Verepaeus, *Recueil*, pp. 150–151; Johann Fabri, *Precationes Christiana devotione et pietate plenae, ex sacris literis et D. Augustino singulari studio concinnatae et selectae* (Dillingen: Sebald Mayer, 1556) (USTC 685774).

AN IMPERIAL CRUSADE? 143

regarder le camp des Egiptiens' – Lord God of our fathers, look upon the camp of the Assyrians now, as thou didst vouchsafe to see the camp of the Egyptians, etc.), the second from Esther 13, and the third, again, from Johann Faber[39]; and an 'Oraison des Catholiques pour l'Eglise miserablement affligée des here-tiques' (a Prayer of Catholics for the Church miserably afflicted by heretics, drawing on Franciscus Titelmans's paraphrase of Psalm 78) calling on God to remember his promises and deliver his people from the hands of their ene-mies, the gentiles, barbarian nations and infidels, with neither the Faith nor knowledge of God's name, that have surprised and vanquished his people by force of arms and occupied their cities, polluting the Temple dedicated to his honour and service with horrible abominations, soiling the vessels that had been consecrated to the service of the Temple[40]:

> O Dieu, les Gentils, & les nations Barbares, & infideles, qui n'ont point de Foy, ne cognoissance de ton Nom, sont entrez en ton heritage, ilz ont surprins ton peuple par forces d'armes, & comme vaincueurs ont occupé noz citez. Ilz ont pollu ton Temple dedié à ton honneur & service par leur horribles abominations. Ilz ont souillé tous les vaisseaux qui estoyent consacrez au service du Temple ...

To the general litany of saints was added a prayer by Peter Canisius that included the petition 'delivre les Chrestiens affligez de toute angoisse & trib-ulation dechasse le grand Turc ennemy des Chrestiens, & tous les ennemis de l'Eglise' (deliver the Christians afflicted with all anguish and tribulation),[41] and at the very end of chapter 9, in some editions, was an 'Oraison pour la tranquillite de l'Eglise, contre la cruaute des brigans Heretiques du temps present' (Prayer for the tranquility of the Church, against the cruelty of the brigand Heretics of the present time), drawn from Pius v's reformed Little Office of the Blessed Virgin: 'regarde tes temples profanez par les mains des infidelles ... la vigne plantée par ta dextre, laquelle le cruel sanglier s'efforce d'exterminer ...' (look upon the temples prophaned by the hands of infidels ...

---

39   Verepaeus, *Recueil*, pp. 151–156.

40   Verepaeus, *Recueil*, pp. 207–211; Franciscus Titelmans, *Psalterium Davidicum paraphrasi-bus* (Antwerp: Joannes Steels, 1553) (USTC 403017).

41   Verepaeus, *Recueil*, p. 347; the source reference given is 'Pet. Canisius li. Cathol. prec.', but the precise source has not been identified. On Canisius see Hilmar M. Pabel, 'Peter Canisius and the Protestants: A Model of Ecumenical Dialogue?', *Journal of Jesuit Studies*, 1 (2014), pp. 373–399.

the vineyard planted by thy right hand, which the wild boar endeavours to root out).[42]

All of these prayers were suitable to times of religious conflict, but none was really what one might call militant. In the following generation of prayer books this was to change. While Simon Verepaeus had been a schoolmaster and a confessor to nuns, the Jesuit Thomas Sailly was a military chaplain.[43] He went further than Verepaeus in adding to his prayer books a specific litany of saints to call on in time of war, for the most part saints who had themselves been soldiers, kings or emperors.[44] This was so novel that Sailly provided historical notes justifying the inclusion of certain figures.[45] To give the litanies even more topical relevance, Sailly also added one of the patron saints of the Low Countries ('ad proprios Sanctos ac Sanctas Belgii'), which strikingly included the petition 'Ut totum Belgium omnesque populos Aquilonares ad studium pacis ac unitatis revoces': that all the Low Countries including all the people of the North should be recalled to the study of peace and unity.[46]

Both the litany of soldier saints and the litany of Belgian saints were adapted in the French prayer book of one of Sailly's brothers in religion, Antoine d'Averoult, specifically as prayers for 'the present calamities'.[47] The litany of soldier saints – now also including emperors, kings, dukes, counts,

---

42 Verepaeus, *Recueil*, pp. 348–349. English translation adapted from *The Primer or Office of the Blessed Virgin Marie*, [translated by Richard Verstegan] (Antwerp, Arnout Conincx, 1599), p. 280 (USTC 415589).

43 On Sailly's understanding of his military mission see Silvia Mostaccio, 'Spiritual Exercises: Obedience, Conscience, Conquest', in Ines G. Županov (ed.), *The Oxford Handbook of Jesuits* (New York: Oxford University Press, 2019), pp. 75–104, esp. pp. 89–91; id., 'Dieu à la guerre. Les émotions de Dieu et la guerre des Quatre-Vingt Ans aux Pays-Bas espagnols', in Chrystel Bernat and Frédéric Gabriel (eds), *Émotions de Dieu. Attributions et appropriations chrétiennes (XVIᵉ–XVIIIᵉ siècle)*, (Bibliothèque des Hautes Études, 184; Turnhout: Brepols, 2019), pp. 205–229, esp. pp. 207–218.

44 Thomas Sailly, *Thesaurus litaniarum ac orationum sacer* (Brussels: Rutger Velpius, 1598), pp. 163–167 (USTC 402450).

45 The Blessed Virgin Mary through the shrine at Mariazell, where Louis of Hungary had built a church after a victory against the Turks; Abraham who led 318 men to rescue Lot from a royal army (Genesis 14); Moses who prayed for Joshua's victory over Amalek (Exodus 17); Isaiah who foretold the Assyrian retreat from Jerusalem (2 Kings 19); John the Baptist the patron saint of the Knights of Malta, and so forth. Sailly, *Thesaurus*, pp. 167–172.

46 Sailly, *Thesaurus*, pp. 193–199, esp. p. 198.

47 Antoine d'Averoult, *Pieux gemissemens des catholiques a jetter es presentes calamitez* (Douai: Jean Bogard, 1610) (USTC 1117205).

AN IMPERIAL CRUSADE?   145

etc. as 'Letanies des saincts soldats, empereurs, roys, ducqs, comtes, &c.' – lost its historical notes, and some of its less obvious intercessors.[48] It was followed immediately by the litany of Belgian saints, 'Letanies des saincts, principalement du Pays-bas, que doibvent souvent reciter au temps present ceux du pays' (Litany of the saints, principally of the Low Countries, that those of the country should often recite at the present time).[49] 'Ora pro nobis' became 'Priez pour ceux du Pays-bas'. The petitions, tailored to the local context, followed Sailly's Latin example. Those to which the response was 'Delivrez nous Seigneur' (Deliver us, Lord) included petitions to be saved from the profanation of churches and all sacrilege; from seditions, divisions, war and all rebellion; from pestilence, famine, war and the destruction of the land; from the tyranny and cruelty of heretics; and from the yoke of Turks and the power of pagans:

> De la prophanation des Eglises & de tout sacrilege.
> Des seditions, divisions, guerre & de toute rebellion.
> De la peste, famine, guerre, & destruction du pays.
> De la tyrannie & cruauté des heretiques.
> Du joug des Turcs & de la puissance des payens.

Those to which the response was 'Nous vous prions escoutez ceux du Pays-bas Seigneur' (We ask you to hear those of the Low Countries, Lord) included petitions that the pope and all the clergy should pacify and reform the Church; that emperor, king, governor, and all princes should be true Catholics and defenders of the Church; that all should be maintained in unity of faith and obedience to the Church; that those in error should submit to the Church; that all new sects and errors should be abolished; that the people of the Low Countries should be delivered from all scandals and loose living; that the enemies of the Church be humbled and converted to the truth; that all of the Low Countries should be recalled to a love of peace and unity; and that the unique and eternal sacrifice of the Church should be retained in the Low Countries with the grace to celebrate it well:

> Que vous excitez & adressez nostre sainct Pere le Pape & toute le Clergé
> às pacifier & reformer l'Eglise.

---

48   d'Averoult, *Pieux gemissemens*, pp. 255–262.
49   d'Averoult, *Pieux gemissemens*, pp. 263–282.

Que faites vrayement Catholiques & defenseurs de la foy Catholique l'Empereur N. le Roy Philippes, nostre Gouverneur N. avec tous les Princes.

Que les maintenez tous en l'union de la foy & obeyssance de l'Eglise.

Que reduisez ceux qui errerent à l'obeyssance de l'Eglise.

Que vueillez abolir toutes nouvelles sectes & erreurs en la foy.

Que delivrez les gens d'Eglise du Pays-bas de scandales & de toute liberté & saleté de vie.

Qu'il vous plaise humilier les ennemis de l'Eglise, & les convertir à la voye de verité.

Que revoquez tout le Pays bas à l'amour de paix & union.

Que retenez l'unique & perpetuel sacrifice de l'Eglise en ce Pays-bas, & donnez la grace de la bien celebrer.

Although d'Averoult had dropped Sailly's historical notes from the litany of soldier saints, he made up for it by adding geographical notes on the locations of relics in the Low Countries after the litany of Belgian saints.[50] There is little evidence that d'Averoult's work was widely known, but Sailly's was printed in Brussels, Cologne, Antwerp and Paris, with the Brussels edition going into several printings. His prayers would have been a perfect model for anyone planning to pray for the emperor and for the defence of the Faith.

4 Crusaders

If the urban middle classes could share in the war effort through a sodality for prayer, those of a higher social status could do the same through a more elevated body, the Ordo Equitum Militiae Christianae, or the Order of the Knights of the Christian Militia, founded in 1616. This was intended as a crusading organisation under the leadership of Charles Gonzaga, duke of Nevers, a descendant of the last imperial house of Constantinople, and as a conduit for co-operation against the Turks of forces from France, Poland and Italy as well as from the Austrian Habsburg territories of Central Europe.[51] The Capuchin

---

50   d'Averoult, *Pieux gemissemens*, pp. 283–204.

51   Emile Baudson, *Charles de Gonzague, Duc de Nevers, de Rethel et de Mantoue, 1580–1637* (Paris: Librairie Académique Perrin, 1947), pp. 103–133, 172–194, 210–226 (referring particularly to Paris, BnF Mss. F. Fr. 4723 and 1054 Nouv. Acq., the latter being 'Registre de l'Ordre de la Milicia Chrestienne'); David Parrott, 'A "prince souverain" and the French Crown: Charles de Nevers, 1580–1637', in Robert Oresko, G.C. Gibbs and H.M. Scott (eds), *Royal*

AN IMPERIAL CRUSADE?   147

Father Joseph, Richelieu's 'grey eminence', was a keen early supporter. The Christian Militia was consciously modelled on the crusader orders of the Middle Ages, and described and discussed as such in the second edition of Aubertus Miraeus's *Origines equestrium, sive Militarium ordinum libri duo*.[52] Miraeus's first reference to the order in print had been in a pamphlet published in 1621.[53] That Emanuel Sueyro was a member of a medieval military order (the Knights of Christ, founded in Portugal in 1319 as a successor order to the suppressed Templars), while Jan de Gaverelle was soon to become one, may also indicate some deeper commitment to crusading ideals, for all that the habit of a Knight of Christ was becoming more a royal reward for loyal service than a sign of active membership in a group committed to crusading.[54]

As an antiquary who had studied the crusading orders of knighthood, Miraeus would have been well aware that non-combatants could also 'take the cross' by supporting an expedition with prayers and almsgiving. When the Spanish ambassador to Brussels, the Marquis of Bedmar, wrote to Philip III

---

and Republican Sovereignty in Early Modern Europe: Essays in Memory of Ragnhild Hatton (Cambridge: Cambridge University Press, 1997), pp. 161–164. See too Andrei Pippidi, *Tradiția politică bizantină în țările române în secolele XVI–XVIII* (2nd edition, Bucharest: Corint, 2001), pp. 289–290; Parry, 'The Ottoman Empire', p. 637. The first chapter of the order was held at Vienna in March 1619; its constitutions were approved by Gregory XV on 10 May 1621, and confirmed by Urban VIII on 6 February 1624.

52   Printed in Cologne by Johann Kinckius, 1638, pp. 84–87 (USTC 2022882). The first edition (Antwerp: David Mertens, 1609, USTC 1003308), culminated with a description of the founding of the Order of Knights of the Redeemer by Vincent Gonzaga, Duke of Mantua and Montferrat, in 1608, and the Order of St Stephen in Tuscany in 1561. Miraeus had earlier issued an eight-page pamphlet on the Knights of the Redeemer, *Equitum redemtoris Jesu Christi* (Antwerp: Hieronymus Verdussen I, 1608) (USTC 1003524).

53   Aubertus Miraeus, *De Bello Bohemico Ferdinandi II. Caesaris auspiciis feliciter gesto commentarius. Ex quo seditiosissimum Calviniae secte genium, & praesentem Europae statum licet agnoscere* (Brussels, Johan Pepermans, [1621]), p. 39 (USTC 1508358).

54   Fernanda Olival, 'Structural Changes within the 16th-century Portuguese Military Orders', *Electronic Journal of Portuguese History*, 2:2 (2004), pp. 1–20. Online at http://hdl.handle .net/10316.2/25409. I am grateful to Lee Preedy for drawing my attention to the importance and origins of the order. See also Elena Postigo Castellanos, 'Caballeros del Rei Católico. Diseños de una nobleza confesional', *Hispania*, 55:189 (1995), pp. 169–204; Fernanda Olival, 'Os Áustrias e as reformas das Ordens Militares portuguesas', *Hispania*, 64/1:216 (2004), pp. 95–116; *Definicoens e Estatutos dos cavalleiros e freires da Ordem de Nosso Senhor Iesu Christo com a Historia da Origem e principio della* (Lisbon, Ioam da Costa, 1671): first promulgated 1628. On the continuing symbolic importance of the crusader past in the Spanish military orders, see Lester P. Wright, 'The Military Orders in Sixteenth and Seventeenth Century Spanish Society: The Institutional Embodiment of a Historical Tradition', *Past & Present*, 43 (1969), pp. 34–70.

on 27 February 1620 to inform him of the Antwerp scheme, he described it as being organized 'en forma de Cruzada contra infieles'.[55] This is no rhetorical flourish, but an almost legalistic analogy, for in Spain the link between almsgiving and military endeavour was still strong.

'Cruzada' had a very specific meaning when it came to Spain's war finances: it was one of the three headings under which the Spanish Church contributed to the royal treasury, under the oversight of the Comisaria de Cruzada.[56] The Treasurer General of the Cruzada was a royal financial official with particular influence on the circulation of silver in Spain.[57] It was an appointment that might go to a royal banker.[58] Anybody who supported duly licensed crusades could enjoy the spiritual benefits of being a crusader without having to take up arms themselves, and one of these benefits was a lighter requirement for fasting during Lent: rather than all animal foods, including eggs, cheese and butter, those taking part in a crusade only had to refrain from eating flesh meat.[59] The relevant concessions were not uncontroversial, and had to be renegotiated with each new pope. Paul V, elected in 1605, was initially reluctant to issue a cruzada bull at all, but finally conceded one in 1609, for the standard term of sixteen years.[60] There was concern within Spain that the populace properly understand just what duties and privileges contributing to the cruzada entailed, leading to publications explaining the implications in full.[61]

---

55   Reproduced in Brants, 'Société de Défense de la Foi', p. 186.

56   Sebastián Coll and José Ignacio Fortea, *Guía de fuentes cuantitativas para la historia económica de España*, vol. 2 (Madrid: Banco de España, 2002), pp. 48, 53–54.

57   Antonio Dominguez Ortiz, *Politica y Hacienda de Felipe IV* (Madrid: Editorial de Derecho financiero, 1960), p. 140.

58   Carlos Álvarez, 'The Role of Institutions to Solve Sovereign Debt Problems: The Spanish Monarchy's Credit (1516–1665)', Universidad Carlos III de Madrid Economic History and Institutions Series 04, Working Paper 03–08 (February 2003), p. 32 <https://ideas.repec .org/p/cte/whrepe/who30804.html>; Carlos Álvarez, 'Spanish Monarchy's Monetary Problems in the Seventeenth Century: Small Change and Foreign Credit', Universidad Carlos III de Madrid Economic History and Institutions Series 05, Working Paper 03–09 (February 2003), pp. 18–19 <https://ideas.repec.org/p/cte/whrepe/who30905.html>.

59   Alfonso Pérez de Lara, *Compendio de las tres gracias de la santa cruzada* (Madrid: Imprenta Real, 1610), esp. pp. 32–34 (USTC 5021657). Scans from the Complutense University of Madrid on Google Books as id=2nzaIxi7EEcC.

60   Jose Goñi Gaztambide, *Historia de la Bula de Cruzada en España* (Vitoria: Editorial del Seminario, 1958), p. 629.

61   Hence Pérez de Lara, *Compendio*, cited above, but above all Tomás Rodriguez, *Explicacion de la bulla de la sancta cruzada* (Alcalá de Henares: Juan Íñiguez de Lequerica, 1589) (USTC 341333) and its many updated reprints to 1618.

AN IMPERIAL CRUSADE? 149

While the system of contributing to the defence of Christendom by donating to the cruzada was only in force in Spain, Sardinia, Sicily, and Spanish territories in the Americas and the Philippines, its existence was known to the rest of Europe. In the view of the French geographer Pierre Davity, the extraordinary levy of the cruzada, which had essentially become customary, effectively added an extra kingdom to the Spanish crown's tax base[62]:

> Mais ce n'est rien de ces tributs, au regard de ce qu'il en tire extraordinairement, & mesme l'on peut dire coustumierement pour la plus grande partie, comme de la Croisade qui lui vaut le revenu d'un Royaume, ...

A pamphlet printed in Haarlem in 1598 provided the Spanish original and a Dutch translation of the 1591 proclamation in Madrid of the cruzada conceded by Pope Sixtus V in 1590, asserting in the preface (apparently not having noticed that the proceeds went to the Spanish crown rather than to the pope) that this was yet another example of the papacy's love of filthy lucre.[63]

Nor was Bedmar the only writer to link sodalities and crusades. In 1609 the Dutch historian Emanuel Van Meteren had somewhat luridly described the Sainte-Maison of Tholon, a Savoyard sodality founded in 1598 to proselytise the Calvinists of the Alps, as a crusade under another name.[64] The accusation

---

62   *Les estats, empires, et principautez du monde* (Paris: Pierre Chevalier, 1616), p. 151 (USTC 6001371). Scans from the University of Lausanne on Google Books at id=r9M-AAAAcAAJ.

63   *Bulle ofte aflaets-brief van de heylighe cruysvaert, ghegunt ende bevolen te vercondigen, door den H. Roomschen Vader, Paus Sixtus de vijfde in de Coninckrijcken van Spaignien, ende Eylanden daer onder sorterende, ende in de Coninckrijcken van Sicilien ende Sardaignen, in faveur der gener die behulpich en dienstigh zyn, int oorlogh ende oncosten des selve, aen Philippus Coninck van Spagnien, tegens d'ongheloovighen ende Ketters* ([Haarlem: Gillis Rooman], 1598) (USTC 424068). Copy from the University of Amsterdam, scanned by the National Library of the Netherlands, on Google Books at id=HqhlAAAAcAAJ.

64   'Dit verbont ofte Ligue en wilden sy niet noemen Cruysvaert ofte Cruciata, hoe-wel op de selvighe fondamenten gefondeert, om dat niet hatich te maken by de Ghereformeerden, daer-men noch beter opinie van hadden, dan van Turcken, Saracenen ende Machumetanen.' (They would not call this union or League a Crusade, although it was built on the same foundation, so as not to make it hated of the Reformed, of which they had a better opinion than of Turks, Saracens and Mahomedans). Emanuel Van Meteren, *Belgische ofte Nederlantsche Oorlogen ende Gheshiedenissen* (Schotlandt buyten Danswijck [false address]: Hermes van Loven [pseudonym], 1609), fols. 89v–90r (USTC 1019441). Copy from the University of Amsterdam, scanned by the National Library of the Netherlands, on Google Books at id=8sVkAAAAcAAJ.

was picked up by a Huguenot polemicist,[65] and his work was reported in the *Mercure françois*, which repeated the accusations before shredding them.[66]

Perhaps those who sabotaged the hopes to extend fund-raising from Antwerp to the rest of the Habsburg Netherlands were fearful that the sodality's activities were a back-door attempt to introduce the 'cruzada' in the Low Countries. Such suspicion, and resistance, would be consistent with other examples of attachment to fiscal privileges in the Habsburg Netherlands.[67] Certainly, by the time the archducal government got round to licensing the sodality in May 1620, there was no longer any question of it being a conduit for military funding.[68] It is pure speculation, but perhaps this also accounts for Verhoeven's reluctance to use the word 'crusade', despite his printing pictures of crusaders: such images could bring heroes of a particular type to mind without eliciting the awkward fiscal connotations of the word 'crusade'.

5   Propaganda of the Past

As mentioned before, however, Verhoeven did have other ways of suggesting that this might be a holy war. One of the more striking devices deployed, in January 1621, was the representation of the anti-Habsburg international as the seven-headed Beast of the Apocalypse, with Calvinist preachers crouching to suckle at its teats, and Holland as the Whore of Babylon. This should be taken with a pinch of salt. Calvinists declaiming 'The Pope is the Antichrist!' might

---

65   'Ils ne voulurent point donner le nom de croisade à ceste Ligue, combien qu'elle avoit esté fondee sur les mesmes fondemens.' Théophile Brachet de La Milletière, *Discours des vrayes raisons pour lesquelles ceux de la religion en France peuvent et doivent, en bonne conscience, résister par armes à la persécution ouverte que leur font les ennemis de leur religion et de l'Estat* (s.l.: s.n., 1622) , pp. 10–15, esp. p. 11 (USTC 6010673). Scan from Lyon Public Library on Google Books at id=H8SQQovxf5MC.

66   *Mercure françois, ou Suitte de l'Histoire de nostre temps*, (25 vols., Paris: Jean Richer, 1613 [vol. I]; Estienne Richer, 1615–1619 [vols. II–V]; Jean Richer, 1621–1623 [vols. VI–VIII]; Jean and Etienne Richer, 1624–1628 [vols. IX–XIII]; Etienne Richer, 1630?–1637 [vols. XIV–XX]; Olivier de Varennes, 1639–1647 [vols. XXI–XXIII]; Jean Henault, 1648 [vols. XXIV–XXV]), VIII. 155–164 (USTC 6011097). Scan from the Bavarian State Library on Google Books at id=oVxBAAAAcAAJ.

67   See e.g. Paul Arblaster, 'Dat de boecken vrij sullen wesen: Private Profit, Public Utility and Secrets of State in the Seventeenth-Century Habsburg Netherlands', in Joop Koopmans (ed.), *News and Politics in Early Modern Europe, 1500–1800* (Leuven: Peeters, 2005), pp. 79–95.

68   Victor Brants (ed.), *Recueil des Ordonnances des Pays-Bas: Règne d'Albert et Isabelle, 1597–1621* (2 vols., Brussels: J. Goemaere, 1909–1912), II. 467–468.

AN IMPERIAL CRUSADE?

mean what they said, but here we have a rhetorical exercise meant more to satirise such pronouncements than to appropriate them. Nevertheless, this is not to deny a serious purpose to the tract. In the course of developing his theme the anonymous contributor did set out a view of European affairs that justified the renewal of war with the Dutch while simultaneously diverting Habsburg military resources elsewhere. The Babylonian Whore of Holland, drunk on the blood of the poor persecuted Arminians, was in league with the Huguenots, the Savoyards, the Venetians, Frederick of the Palatinate, the Transylvanians, the Tatars and the Turks. These provided the identification of the seven heads of the beast. But here the biblical parallel merges with a classical model, and the Habsburgs take on something of the look of Hercules battling the Hydra: the Savoyard head had been muzzled, and the Palatine head struck off.[69]

The view of European affairs presented here was to be the guiding principle of Verhoeven's editorials throughout the decade.[70] It was not original. In 1620 Antwerp had never had newspapers before, or a sodality for the defence of the faith, but the language of confessional warfare in which both spoke would have been familiar to anyone over the age of thirty. If generals begin a conflict expecting to fight the previous war, then in this case so too did propagandists. The conceptual framework was one built in the 1580s. English Catholic refugees from the regime of Elizabeth had been instrumental in its creation. An overview of the Bohemian crisis, probably penned for Verhoeven by no less a contributor than Aubertus Miraeus, cites William Reynolds's *Calvino-Turcismus* (printed posthumously in 1597).[71] Another of Verhoeven's writers was the English Catholic exile Richard Verstegan, who in his polemical and martyrological works of the 1580s and 90s had done much to develop the themes that were being redeployed in the 1620s.[72] Of course, not all were Englishmen.

One of those writing in favour of a Christian Militia in the 1620s was Jean Boucher, dean of Tournai, a former propagandist for the French Catholic

---

69   On the persistent reuse of the imagery of Hercules in Habsburg propaganda, see e.g. Marie Tanner, *The Last Descendant of Aeneas: The Hapsburgs and the Mythic Image of the Emperor* (New Haven, CT: Yale University Press, 1992).

70   Paul Arblaster, 'Policy and Publishing in the Habsburg Netherlands, 1585–1690', in Brendan Dooley and Sabrina A. Baron (eds), *The Politics of Information in Early Modern Europe* (London and New York: Routledge, 2001), pp. 183–185.

71   *Belli Bohemici Origo, Progressus, & finis* (Antwerp: Abraham Verhoeven, 1620), p. 4 (USTC 1115660).

72   Paul Arblaster, *Antwerp & the World: Richard Verstegan and the International Culture of Catholic Reformation* (Leuven: Leuven University Press, 2004), pp. 116–118, 198; Christopher Highley, 'Richard Verstegan's Book of Martyrs', in Christopher Highley and John N. King (eds), *John Foxe and His World* (Aldershot and Burlington VT: Ashgate, 2002), pp. 183–197.

League who had first arrived in Flanders as a refugee after Henry IV's taking of Paris.[73] His earlier writings had included *La vie et faits notables de Henry de Valois* (1589), detailing that king's crimes, and *Sermons de la simulée conversion, et nullité de la prétendue absolution de Henry de Bourbon* (1594), explaining why Henry of Navarre was still not a Catholic even after being received into the Church. Both were much reprinted.[74] In 1595 he had even contributed to an *Apologie pour Jehan Chastel*, which did not prove so popular.[75] In 1598 he preached a funeral sermon in Tournai Cathedral for Philip II, 'le meilleur Roy de la terre, le plus mal traicté de tous' (the best King in the world, the most mistreated of all), whose many virtues had made him 'la butte de tous les mescreans de la terre, Idolatres, Mahometans, Juifs, heretiques de toutes sortes, & de leurs confederez les politiques' (the target of all the miscreants of the world, Idolaters, Mahomedans, Jews, heretics of all sorts, and their confederates the *politiques*).[76]

Deceased authors of the 1580s could still be pressed into service in 1620. In April 1620, the Brussels bookseller Jan Mommaert obtained permission to print a work under the title *Avisos y exortationes a los Reyes y Principes toccantes al pesso y conservation de su authoridad y las causas que producen las guerras en Europa*, attributed to the Jesuit Pedro de Ribadeneyra, a propagandist for the Spanish Armada of 1588 who had died in 1611.[77] Another writer

---

73 On Boucher see Bruce Hayes and Paul Scott (eds), *Jean Boucher (1548–1646?): prêtre, prédicateur, polémiste*, special issue of *Œuvres et critiques*, 18 (2013); also Robert Descimon and José Javier Ruiz Ibáñez, *Les Ligueurs de l'exil: Le refuge catholique français après 1594* (Seyssel: Champ Vallon, 2005), *passim*, esp. pp. 252–260. His publication inspired by the Christian Militia was *Couronne mystique ou dessein de chevalerie chrestienne pour exciter les princes chrestiens a rendre le debvoir a la pieté chrestienne contre les ennemis d'icelle* (Tournai, Adrien Quinque, 1623) (USTC 1120812).

74 USTC 3422, 10322, 10916, 13928, 30667, 34646, 47247, 54500, 59861, 65865, 81048 (*La Vie*); 6329, 14062, 34170, 34171, 74468, 79236 (*Sermons*).

75 Published anonymously without indication of place (USTC 6084).

76 *Oraison funebre, sur le trespas de tres hault, tres grand et tres puissant monarque dom Philippe second* (Brussels: Rutger Velpius, 1599), sig. [F3r] (USTC 10407). Reprinted Antwerp: Jan Moretus, 1600 (USTC 13440).

77 Brussels, State Archives of Belgium, Spanish Privy Council, 1277/134. No such title is extant. This was presumably to be a reprint of Ribadeneyra's *Tratado de la religion y virtudes que deue tener el principe christiano, para governar y conservar sus estados* (published at the Plantin Office in Antwerp in 1594 and again in 1597; USTC 441388, 440194), perhaps in combination with his *Tratado de la tribulacion* (first printed Madrid, 1589; USTC 337773). See also Peer Schmidt, *Spanische Universalmonarchie oder "teutsche Libertet": das spanische Imperium in der Propaganda des Dreissigjährigen Krieges* (Stuttgart: F. Steiner, 2001), p. 406.

of the 1580s, Joannes Molanus, a highly influential theologian at Leuven, had placed the Habsburgs' struggles in the sixteenth-century Low Countries, and the fifteenth-century founding of Leuven University itself, in a lineage of Brabantine holy war going back long before the crusades, to victories against Arian Visigoths and pagan Frisians and Danes.[78] He even likened the Duke of Parma to a Hercules battling a many-headed Hydra of heresies.[79]

The Protestant Thomas Scott, in arguing for the blessings of religious war, was not the only writer to take the days of Queen Elizabeth as in some way normative. These had also been the days of Philip II, whose tireless efforts to fight Turks and Calvinists on many fronts produced a justificatory and inspirational rhetoric of confessional combativeness which spoke to those in Antwerp trying to make sense of the Bohemian crisis, because they had heard it in childhood and early youth. This is a point about generational continuity, but perhaps also about historical continuity: the Thirty Years' War, the second phase of the Eighty Years' War, and the seventeenth-century Huguenot Wars were all to some extent about the unfinished business of the sixteenth-century Wars of Religion.

6 Conclusions

However that may be, the main conclusions of this article lie elsewhere. Firstly, the material set out here shows two of the ways in which those in power in the Habsburg Netherlands engaged with public opinion. In preparing their response to the Bohemian crisis, the regime's opinion-brokers sought to convince the crucial constituency of Antwerp's urban elite that this was a defensive war against the enemies of the Church, and a war against one element of an international conspiracy (the words 'axis of evil' come unbidden to mind) that had the Dutch Republic at its heart. So far from being a dynastic distraction from local needs, the commitment of military resources in Bohemia and the German Rhineland really was part of a defensive war against the Dutch, however little it might look like it. This was a multimedia approach that used different means to direct both the thoughts and the prayers of the urban elite to the goals of the dynasty.

---

78   Joannes Molanus, *Militia Sacra Ducum et Principum Brabantiae* (Antwerp: Plantin Office, Widow Plantin and Jan Moretus, 1592) (USTC 402270).

79   Molanus, *Militia Sacra*, p. 132.

Secondly, in order to understand seventeenth-century newspapers, analysis of contents and study of archival remains relating to the press are insufficient. Folke Dahl, whose contributions to the history of the news press are fundamental, took the position that these were the proper limits of newspaper history as such.[80] But without looking at the wider culture of the intended readership, which in this instance includes the associational culture of religious sodalities and knightly orders, as well as prayer books and the writings of historians, controversialists and geographers, it would be impossible to make full sense of Verhoeven's use of pictures of crusaders alongside his eschewing of the word 'crusade'. What at first seemed a rather strained symbolism, comes into focus as part of a very specific set of opinion-forming moves not directly related to the press at all.

80 Folke Dahl, 'Amsterdam – Earliest Newspaper Centre of Western Europe: New Contributions to the History of the First Dutch and French Corantos', *Het Boek*, new series, 25:3 (1939), pp. 161–198.

CHAPTER 9

Printed Christian *hilaritas* under Archdukes Albert and Isabel (1598–1621)

Johan Verberckmoes

Albert of Austria (1559–1621) and Isabel of Spain (1566–1633) were rulers of the Spanish Habsburg Netherlands whose piety was exemplary and touched upon the daily lives of their court and subjects.[1] In particular Albert promoted many new initiatives to steer public opinion in the direction of dynastic bound devotions.[2] Both favoured an overwhelming display of relics, pilgrimage sites, altars, cults, processions as well as a private religiosity to endorse a reinvigorated Catholic religion as a key mobilising societal force of their state. But the impact of their avowed efforts on the daily lives of their subjects and the willingness and autonomy of these to identify a patriotic Catholicism continue to be debated.[3] In this chapter, I explore the pivotal role of religion in these decades through the lens of the management of emotions, in particular the emotion of joy.[4] Recent theories strongly relate individual emotions and their

---

1 Werner Thomas and Luc Duerloo (eds), *Albert and Isabella 1598–1621* (2 vols, Turnhout: Brepols, 1998). I thank Heleen Wyffels for thoughtful comments on an earlier version and the editors of this volume for their accurate corrections.

2 Luc Duerloo, *Dynasty and Piety. Archduke Albert (1598–1621) and Habsburg Political Culture in an Age of Religious Wars* (Farnham: Ashgate, 2012), in particular Chapter 2: Rural Pursuits, pp. 57–102; Idem, 'Pietas Albertina. Dynastieke vroomheid en herbouw van het vorstelijk gezag', *BMGN: Low Countries Historical Review*, 112:1 (1997), pp. 1–18.

3 Margit Thöfner, *A Common Art: Urban Ceremonial in Antwerp and Brussels during and after the Dutch Revolt* (Zwolle: Waanders, 2007) and Tamar Cholcman, *Art on Paper: Ephemeral Art in the Low Countries: The Triumphal Entry of the Archdukes Albert and Isabella into Antwerp, 1599* (Turnhout: Brepols, 2014) emphasise, although each in a different perspective, the mutual interests of the Antwerp citizens and the Archducal court in Brussels during the Joyous Entries. The compliance of practices of devotion of both rulers and subjects in relation to the political significance of the Archducal reign is a topic of ongoing research, see for instance the recent assessments in Cordula van Wyhe (ed.), *Isabel Clara Eugenia: Female Sovereignty in the Courts of Madrid and Brussels* (London: Holberton, 2011); Annick Delfosse, *La "Protectrice du Païs-Bas": stratégies politiques et figures de la Vierge dans les Pays-Bas espagnols* (Turnhout: Brepols, 2009).

4 Darrin M. McMahon, 'Finding Joy in the History of Emotions', in Susan J. Matt and Peter N. Stearns (eds), *Doing Emotions History* (Urbana, Chicago and Springfield: University of Illinois Press, 2014), pp. 103–119; Barbara H. Rosenwein, *Generations of Feeling: A History of*

© KONINKLIJKE BRILL NV, LEIDEN, 2023 | DOI:10.1163/9789004510159_010

bodily expression to social practice.[5] For the early modern period, joy has been equated with the ethical register of happiness, also in a religious sense, as well as endorsed as a primal emotion.[6] The former refers to a social dynamic of structuring mind and body, the latter to intense personal satisfaction.[7]

The contention of this chapter is that during the reign of the Archdukes, printers and religious writers stimulated Catholic reform that expressly included religious joy and laughter. Moreover, the gendered roles of the Archdukes promoted that emphasis on spiritual delight in the religious production. *Hilaritas* and *gaudium spirituale* are adequate descriptions of the combination of ordered and socially controlled emotion on the one hand and deeply spiritual joy on the other.[8] Religious laughter is often misunderstood as separate and even oppositional to profane laughter which would be the only kind of liberating laughter. Yet, when spiritual values are expressed in rituals, performances and earthly material analogies and symbols the frontiers between the sacred and the profane begin to shift. In such a communicative and performative situation, the religious experience transgresses the boundaries between this world and another, numinous one. The performance of holiness paradoxically emphasises unity as well as difference and this has a structural analogy with the force of the comic that also combines exclusiveness and inclusiveness.[9] When spiritual writers in the Archducal Habsburg Netherlands took up *hilaritas* as a guide they subscribed to the shifting boundaries between the normative emphasis on Catholic devotion and the unsettling effects of comic words, for instance in the persistent anti-Protestant mockery that also continued during the times of Albert and Isabel. In theoretical perspective, an analytic separation between a mild spiritual humour and profane mockery is untenable and it moreover does no justice to the religious dynamic

---

    Emotions, 600–1700 (Cambridge: Cambridge University Press 2016), in particular Chapter 8: Despair and Happiness, pp. 248–287.

5   Monique Scheer, 'Are Emotions a Kind of Practice (and is That What Makes Them Have a History)? A Bourdieuian Approach to Understanding Emotion', *History and Theory*, 51 (2012), pp. 193–220.

6   Adam Potkay, *The Story of Joy: From the Bible to Late Romanticism* (Cambridge: Cambridge University Press, 2007).

7   Susan Broomhall (ed.), *Gender and Emotions in Medieval and Early Modern Europe: Destroying Order, Structuring Disorder* (Farnham: Ashgate, 2015).

8   Tobias A. Kemper, *'Iesus Christus risus noster*. Bemerkungen zum Bewertung des Lachens im Mittelalter', in Anja Grebe and Nikolaus Staubach (eds), *Komik und Sakralität. Aspekte einder ästhetischen Paradoxie in Mittelalter und früher Neuzeit* (Frankfurt am Main: Peter Lang, 2005), pp. 16–31 traces the medieval history of *hilaritas*.

9   Katja Gvozdeva and Werner Röcke (eds), *"Risus sacer – sacrum risibile": Interaktionsfelder von Sakralität und Gelächter im kulturellen und historischen Wandel* (Bern: Lang, 2009), pp. 16–18.

PRINTED CHRISTIAN HILARITAS   157

of the period. I will argue an Archducal Christian *hilaritas* on the basis of the printed religious production of the period and analyse to what extent the paradox of holy laughter permeated Archducal Catholicism.

The considerable printed production of devotion manuals and spiritual handbooks for clergy and lay people in the early decades of the seventeenth century suggests a major emphasis on such attitudes and emotions as earnestness, dutiful piety, self-control of the senses, compassion, as well as love of God, mothers, fathers, family, friends and those in need.[10] From various perspectives and with different intonations, a whole range of authors, some local, many ancient and quite a few Southern European, formulated ideas, expectations and practices intent on ordering emotions.[11] For the Spanish Habsburg Netherlands, the link with Mediterranean and French Catholicism was guiding, as a recent survey of the Catholic book production in the ecclesiastical province of Cambrai has demonstrated.[12] Translations from Italian and Spanish, often through prior French translations, made Cambrai from the 1590s into a transmission centre of Tridentine piety and pastoral care. When the Archdukes promoted Catholic religion as a major tool of societal cohesion, the religious book production in Cambrai as well as Antwerp, in Dutch, French and Latin and eventually a few other languages, laid the foundations for this cultural shift.

As a general rule, printed Catholica re-established Late Antique and Medieval Christian notions of contempt of the world materialising in an intense disregard and rejection of the primary impulses of body and mind. Intriguingly, however, even the sternest defenders of a highly restrictive bodily and mental attitude, such as the twelfth-century promoter of the Cistercians Bernard of Clairvaux, had also given humour, cheerfulness, joy and laughter a place as a religious force.[13] In this contribution, I want to analyse if and to what extent *hilaritas*, *eutrapelia* and other Christian formulations of the emotive power of hilariousness were part of the printed offensive of Catholic reform

---

10   *Bibliotheca catholica neerlandica impressa 1500–1727* (The Hague: Martinus Nijhoff, 1954), pp. 122–254 lists about 8800 titles, the large majority of which are devotional, pastoral and exemplary literature intent on shaping practices among religious and lay people. *Impressa Catholica Cameracensia (ICC)* is a recent database on the religious book and its networks in the ecclesiastical province of Cambrai (1559–1659), integrated in the database Odis.be. The database is referenced ICC-ODIS.

11   Susan Broomhall (ed.), *Ordering Emotions in Europe, 1100–1800*, (Leiden: Brill, 2015).

12   Alexander Soetaert, *De katholieke drukpers in de kerkprovincie Kamerijk: contacten, mobiliteit en transfers (1559–1659)*, Verhandelingen van de Koninklijke Vlaamse Academie van België voor Wetenschappen en Kunsten. Nieuwe reeks 34 (Leuven: Peeters, 2019).

13   Laurence Moulinier, 'Quand le malin fait de l'esprit. Le rire au Moyen Age vu depuis l'hagiographie', *Annales. Histoire, Sciences Sociales*, 52:3 (1997), pp. 457–475.

at the time of the Archdukes and what the implications of this were for the Archducal outreach to the population at large. To be sure, *hilaritas* was less a concept than the better known *eutrapelia* that had gained credit with Thomas Aquinas. But, in the seventeenth-century *hilaritas* was more widely used to denote the use of recreation as a way to open the mind to virtue.[14]

Humour is relevant because it pertains to the history of social relations, more particular in this case the avowed intention of court, clergy and commoners to re-establish peace after the exhaustive and long-drawn-out Dutch Revolt. Denigration, ridicule and mockery had been harsh weapons during the religious and political struggles of the sixteenth century.[15] In contrast to this, the new age of reconciliation and prosperity under Archducal protection envisioned convivial relationships. Paintings by Jan Brueghel the Younger of Albert and Isabel attending a peasant wedding banquet and a peasant dance are emblematic of attempts of the political and religious authorities to reconstruct cohesiveness in society.[16] While the interpretations of these paintings vary from conceptions of promoting community and cooperation between rulers and ruled to practices of distinction between an alien court culture and local custom, the imagery at least suggests allegiance to comic Bruegel.[17] Moreover, the many political rituals of the Archducal reign favoured festivities and assorted amusement, and elicited a boisterous cheerfulness as political propaganda. Through Joyous Entries, urban processions, celebrations of the shooting guilds and other types of public display, urban governments and court officials introduced to audiences the political message of a newly found

---

14   To my knowledge the only sustained, yet brief exploration of *hilaritas* in the seventeenth-century Habsburg Netherlands is Karel Porteman, 'De jezuïeten in de Nederlandse letterkunde van de zeventiende eeuw', *De zeventiende eeuw*, 14:1 (1998), pp. 3–13 (pp. 9–10).

15   Anne-Laure Van Bruaene, 'Revolting Beasts: Animal Satire and Animal Trials in the Dutch Revolt', in Walter S. Melion, Bret Rothstein and Michel Weemans (eds), *The Anthropomorphic Lens. Anthropomorphism, Microcosmism and Analogy in Early Modern Thought and Visual Arts* (Leiden: Brill, 2015), pp. 23–42; Luc Racaut, *Hatred in Print: Catholic Propaganda and Protestant Identity during the French Wars of Religion* (Aldershot: Ashgate, 2002).

16   Werner Thomas, 'Isabel Clara Eugenia and the Pacification of the Southern Netherlands', in Cordula van Wyhe (ed.), *Isabel Clara Eugenia: Female Sovereignty*, pp. 180–201; Cordula van Wyhe, 'Archducal Leisure and Peasant Pleasure: New Aspects of Jan Brueghel's Peasant Weddings in the Prado Museum', *Münchner Jahrbuch für Kunstgeschichte* 56 (2005), pp. 83–105; *El arte en la corte de la archiduques Alberto de Austria e Isabela Clara Eugenia 1598–1933 : un reino imaginado* (Madrid: Sociedad estatal para la conmemoración de los centenarios de Felipe II y Carlos V, 1999), pp. 164–167.

17   Thomas and Duerloo, *Albert and Isabella*; Walter S. Gibson, *Pieter Bruegel and the Art of Laughter* (Berkeley: University of California Press, 2006).

PRINTED CHRISTIAN HILARITAS 159

patriotic unity based on productive fun born out of shared interests and the final establishment of peace.

However, the major emphasis on devotion and pacification at the time of the Archdukes hardly conceals that the times were conflictual and political crisis persisted. The Christian trope of the misery of the world was as acute as ever. That is where the Bourdieusian emphasis on habitus as performance and practice is relevant,[18] in this case of a paradoxical spiritual joy that negotiates the unity of religion and the divisiveness of society. In this perspective, I will undertake a qualitative analysis of the idea of *hilaritas* in the printed output of the Catholic Archdukes' reign. I will first identify the promoters of spiritual joy and explain the rediscovery of *gaudium spirituale* in the long-term context of Christian *eutrapelia* and *hilaritas* since Late Antiquity. I will then consider the relationship of this context to the Archdukes as rulers. A contemporary assessment of cheerfulness as not only a state of mind but also a way of knowing crystallised in the figure of the Greek laughing philosopher Democritus. He was in this period restyled a Catholic. Yet, the distrust of the irreverence of humour and laughter was as old as a religiously motivated jollity. This also resurfaced under the Archdukes. A vast majority of religious writers firmly rejected "the inappropriate, rude jests and obscene jokes of which the world is full and that corrupt ethical norms".[19] They countered this with a vast array of spiritual literature founded on the idea that the ultimate joy was with God and moderation in this life therefore the rule. Nevertheless, although binary opposition between modesty and exuberance was part of the inherited cultural system, also in the years of Albert and Isabel the contradictions of uncontrollable laughter and therefore the porous boundaries between the sacred and the profane were not contained. Productive tensions between a laughter situated in heavenly glory and a laughter in the service of the redemption of the world created new forms of Christian humour.[20] Through a short presentation of a book of sayings of the Jesuit Joannes David and the *Pia hilaria* of another Jesuit, Angelinus Gazaeus, I will suggest that new research in this perspective may broaden our understanding of the revitalisation of Catholic religion.

---

18   Scheer, 'Are Emotions a Kind of Practice'.

19   Franciscus Schottus, *Thesaurs Selectorvm Exemplorvm Sententiarumq[ue]* (Antwerp: Martin Nutius, 1607), Epistola dedicatoria, p. [A]v°: 'ineptis illis nugis ac quisquilijs, & iocis scurrilibus, quibus ut plenus mundus est, ita mores corrumpuntur', HPB DE-601. GVK.386070776.

20   Johan Verberckmoes, *Laughter, Jestbooks and Society in the Spanish Netherlands* (Basingstoke: Macmillan, 1999) explored this in a long term perspective of the sixteenth and seventeenth century.

1 Promoting *hilaritas*

As Michel de Certeau contends, the laughter of a saint was not indicative of his (or her) sense of humour, but referred to his (or her) interior disposition.[21] *Gaudium spirituale* was the expression of the resolve of the Christian as well as his triumph to be among the chosen of God. The Latin vocabulary *hilaris/ hilarus* (cheerful), *hilaritas* (cheerfulness) and *hilare* (to be cheerful) had been widespread in Roman Antiquity. Its medieval derivations *hilaramen* (cheerfulness) and *hilarizare* or *hilariter agere* (to act cheerful) signalled a continuing popularity.[22] Roman *hilaritas* had referred to the emotion of gaiety as well as to specific occasions and joyful rituals, whether in late December or during Carnival time. Early Christianity had picked this up in a double sense. One strand, following the advice on the contempt of worldly occupations, practiced Cicero's admonition: "men are not made happy by merriment and wantonness, nor by laughter and jest, on the contrary they are made happy by staunchness and firmness and that often though they are in gloom".[23] This rejection of jollity was the firm basis of a non-laughing Christian piety transmitted through the ages. The other strand recalibrated *hilaritas* as a positive virtue, in Christian terms translating it as *gaudium spirituale*. In the first centuries of Christianity, quite a few saints and martyrs carried the male Latin name Hilarius, meaning joy.[24] A fifth-century example was a monk of the abbey of Lérins (on an island near Cannes) who became bishop of Arles. His fellow monk Eucherius, himself bishop of Lyon, wrote a hagiography of Hilarius that was edited by Heribert Rosweyde in Antwerp in 1621.[25] Ascetic spirituality and the rejection of the flesh were the hallmark of monks like Hilarius and the source of their joy. This conception fitted the emphasis of the Archducal court on an introspective Catholic religion as the basis of their state.

---

21   Michel de Certeau, *La fable mystique. XVIe–XVIIe siècle* (Paris: Gallimard, 1982), p. 63.

22   Charles du Fresne du Cange, *Glossarium ad scriptores mediae et infimae Latinitatis* (3 vols, Frankfurt am Main: Johann David II Zunner for Johann Adam Jung, 1710), II. 840.

23   "Non hilaritate et lascivia, nec risu aut joco, sed saepe etiam tristes firmitate et constantia sunt beati" (*De Finibus bonorum et malorum*, II. 65–66).

24   The *Dictionnaire d'histoire et de géographie ecclésiastiques* (32 vols., Paris: Letouzey et Ané, 1912–2018), XXIV. 447–462 lists 25 male Christians *Hilarius* up to the sixth-century and XXIV. 465–466 3 female martyrs *Hilaria*; col. 467–479 lists 5 *Hilarianus*, 10 *Hilarion* and 4 *Hilarus*. On the carnivalesque inversion of Hilarion of Gaza in early sixteenth-century Castile, see Ryan D. Giles, *The Laughter of the Saints. Parodies of Holiness in Late Medieval and Renaissance Spain* (Toronto: University of Toronto Press, 2009), pp. 42–51.

25   Eucherius Lugdunensis, *De laude eremi ad Hilarium Lerinensem monachum libellus* (Antwerp: Balthasar Moretus, widow Johannes Moretus, and Johannes Meursius, 1621) (USTC 1003715).

PRINTED CHRISTIAN HILARITAS 161

Sternness was a guiding emotion in post-Tridentine Catholic piety and it certainly would benefit from a fresh look from the viewpoint of a history of emotions.[26] I am definitely not defending that the historiography on the Archdukes mistakenly overlooked some more light-hearted approaches to religion. But, as gravity was heavily promoted as a norm, relaxation became an issue. This was particularly the case in a context of education. A fully formed religious person had during contemplation little or no regard for frivolity. For instance, Ignatius of Loyola admonished to avoid laughing and provoking laughter during spiritual exercise.[27] In contrast, the *Ratio Studiorum* of the Jesuits, their educational program introduced since the 1580s, encouraged the regents of the Jesuit colleges to stimulate *hilaritas* and *alacritas* (mirth) among the professors, in particular among those who taught grammar and the arts to young pupils.[28] This was to encourage the professors who trained the youngest pupils in the less attractive subjects (compared to philosophy and theology). The 1580s Jesuit rules for school theatre explored similar means of relaxation (*remissio animi*), stimulating joyfulness (*hilaritas*) among the teachers and cheering (*ex-hilari*) among the pupils and their parents.[29] Yet, from the late 1590s the stimulation of *hilaritas* disappeared from the rules, although the practice was perpetuated.

The second context in which *hilaritas* was promoted were reflections on stimulating conversation among Christians by such people as Francis de Sales. De Sales, like other French clergy of the late sixteenth and early seventeenth century, reached back to Scholastic authors like Albertus Magnus and Thomas Aquinas who had reconfigured *eutrapelia* as a virtue, borrowing the concept from Aristotle. As the Scholastics, de Sales appreciated *eutrapelia* as a moderate

---

26 The assessment of Henri Pirenne, *Histoire de Belgique* (7 vols., Brussels: H. Lamertin, 1909–1932), IV. 381 on "la sombre piété des Espagnols" has loomed large in the historiography. Pirenne is ideologically motivated in his explanation accusing the Spaniards of importing that gravity. The overall emphasis on an interior disposition in spiritual and pastoral writing in the early seventeenth century has in recent historiography been properly contextualised as a political and religious dynamic not per se pertaining to individual emotions; Duerloo, *Dynasty and Piety*, 22–34 emphasises that the grave demeanour of Archduke Albert was a result of the austere regime of his education, but also qualified him as a competent ruler.

27 The 8th explanation in the 1st week of the Spiritual Exercises of Ignatius of Loyola, see Ignatius de Loyola, *Écrits*, Maurice Giuliani (ed.) (Paris: Desclée de Brouwer, 1991), pp. 98–99.

28 Adrien Demoustier and Dominique Julia (eds), *Ratio studiorum. Plan raisonné et institution des études dans la Compagnie de Jésus* (Paris: Belin, 1997), p. 69; I owe this reference to Rosa De Marco, who I also thank for stimulating comments on *eutrapelia* and *hilaritas*.

29 Christel Meier, 'Sakralität und Komik im lateinischen Drama der Frühen Neuzeit', in Gvozdeva and Röcke, *"Risus sacer"*, pp. 163–184, on pp. 164–165 with further literature.

cheerfulness that was appropriate in conversation. The subject of this honest joking was frivolous occasions offered by the imperfections of man. It was a liberating and friendly kind of jollity on the condition that it did not alter into mockery and disapproval and condemnation of a fellow human being. The thirteenth-century devout French king St Louis, for example, had after dinner preferred recreation with some fun and quodlibets rather than high-minded thinking.[30] De Sales and other defenders of *eutrapelia* and *urbanitas* (conviviality), like the French bishop Jean-Pierre Camus, were printed in the Habsburg Netherlands since the 1610s.[31]

Hilaritas was also practiced beyond the context of colleges and companionship. Among the religious orders promoting ascetic life the emotion of spiritual joy was of a specific kind. The life of penitence and self-negation of the religious turned some of these into fools of Christ, as the honed formula was since early Christianity.[32] One of their hallmarks was convulsions of their bodies during spiritual trance resulting in, among others, fits of laughter, as had happened to thirteenth-century Beatrice of Nazareth.[33] Concerns with laughter were not exceptional among post-Tridentine saints. Filippo Neri allegedly practiced humility when reading funny stories of Piovanno Arlotto.[34] The scabrous stories of a down-to-earth parish priest of Fiesole were presumably a rhetoric trick of his hagiographers to enhance the saint's sanctity and praise his good humour. Autobiographies also reveal reflections on impulses to laugh and good cheer. Teresa of Avila repeatedly noted in her *Vida* that she had laughed when remembering that she once had given value to money or when ascertaining how difficult it was to have good thoughts.[35] This was the

---

30 Francis de Sales, *Introduction à la vie dévote*, part III, chapter 27, see Francis de Sales, *Œuvres*, André Ravier (ed.) (Paris: Gallimard, 1969), p. 207; Jacques Le Goff, 'Laughter in the Middle Ages', in Jan Bremmer and Herman Roodenburg (eds), *A Cultural History of Humour. From Antiquity to the Present Day* (Cambridge: Polity Press, 1997), pp. 40–53 (p. 44 on St Louis as *rex facetus* according to his biographer Jean de Joinville).

31 Soetaert, *De katholieke drukpers*; Francis de Sales, *Introduction a la vie devote* (Douai: Balthazar I Bellère, 1611) (USTC 1117278) and six more editions in the 1610s.

32 De Certeau, *La fable mystique*, pp. 48–70; Michael A. Screech, *Ecstasy and the Praise of Folly* (London: Duckworth, 1980).

33 Paul Vanden Broeck, *Hooglied: de beeldwereld van religieuze vrouwen in de Zuidelijke Nederlanden, vanaf de 13de eeuw* (Ghent: Snoeck-Ducaju, 1994), p. 68.

34 Louis Ponnelle and Louis Bordet, *Saint Philippe Néri et la société romaine de son temps (1515–1595)* (Paris: 1958), p. 95; Arlotto Mainardi, *Motti et facetie* (Firenze, per Bernardo Zucchetta ad instantia di Bernardo Pacini, [circa 1515]) (USTC 811019). USTC lists about thirty editions and reprints in the sixteenth century.

35 Jeannine Poitrey, *Vocabulario de Santa Teresa* (Madrid: Universidad pontificia de Salamanca, 1983), p. 598, lemma 'reír'; *Humor y espiritualidad en la escuela teresiana primitiva. Selección de textos de Teresa de Avila, Hieronymus Gracián de la Madre Dei, Ana de*

PRINTED CHRISTIAN HILARITAS   163

laughter of humility of St Benedict and since the late sixteenth century reval-
ued in religious orders such as the Carmelites and Discalced Carmelites, much
promoted by the Archdukes. The spiritual self-inquisition of mystics and converts of these orders in their autobiographies and confessions reveal the ambi-
guities of the bodily expression of laughter. The saints experienced the joy they
advocate as radically different from ordinary humour that always ridicules others and laughs at sinful activities. Mystics allegedly laughed about themselves.
Interestingly, many of these mystics were female, suggesting to some extent a
gendered *hilaritas*.

The model of infectious mirth spread through the many convents in the
Habsburg Netherlands, both male and female, in songs, prayers and exemplary
stories. The Capuchin Lucas van Mechelen, of Jewish-Portuguese descent
and active in both the Dutch and French speaking parts of the Habsburg
Netherlands, formulated in emotional and sensitive terms the popular idea in
all contemplative religious orders that God is the true source of joy and that
the soul only finds joy in God. His spiritual songs thrive on words as joy, happiness, contentment, pleasure, comfort, sweetness and the like.[36] The mystic
rejected the world and her unruly passions and chose the hard road of mortification, but that ended in intense merriment. Lucas van Mechelen labelled
this thinking "the joyful requiem".[37] Moreover, spiritual literature in the vernacular conveyed the sense of Christian joy beyond the boundaries of convents and among a wider population. One title announces a "happy mountain
of spiritual joy mixed with virtue for the young".[38] An English translation of
Francis de Sales sounded even more promising: *Delicious entertainments of the
soule*.[39] The popular devotional handbook for young girls, *The pilgrimage of
Little Dove and My Own Will to their Beloved One*, thrived on the success of the

---

    Jesús, etc. Presentado por Simeón de la Sagrada Familia y Ildefonso de la Visitación (Burgos:
    Monte Carmelo, 1966).

36   Karel Porteman, *De mystieke lyriek van Lucas van Mechelen (1595/6–1652)* (2 vols., Ghent:
    Koninklijke Academie voor Nederlandse taal- en letterkunde, 1977–1978), II. 320–325,
    335, 348.

37   *Den boeck der gheesteliicke sanghen bedeelt in twee deelen Den bliiden requiem [...] het
    welck den rechten wegh is tot het Cloosterken der gheestelijcke verrijsenisse [...] d'welck het
    tweede deel is van desen boeck [...] eenen religieus van d'oorden van sinte Francois ghenaemt
    minder-broederen capucynen* (Antwerp: Hendrick Aertssens – Mechelen: s.n., 1631) (USTC
    1510239, STCV 3147327).

38   *Parnassus, dat is den blijdenbergh der gheestelijcker vreught ghemenght met deught veur
    de jonghe jeught* (Antwerp: Geeraerdt I van Wolsschaten, 1619) (USTC 1508088), reprinted
    in 1623 (USTC 1435865).

39   Francis de Sales, *Delicious entertainments of the soule* (Douai: Gerard Pinchon, 1632)
    (ICC-ODIS 36367, USTC 3016207).

pious girl that kept waiting for the joy to be with Christ in heaven while her quirky girlfriend tried every opportunity of gratifying her senses with fun and games but was each time bitterly deceived.[40]

2 Democritus and the Archdukes

Was there a place for *hilaritas* in the Archducal strategy of sustaining state authority with Catholic religion? At first glance, this seems a paradoxical question, as more austere variants of Catholicism and convent spirituality received their support. Moreover, Archduke Albert was little versed in social conversation and avoided showing his emotions.[41] On the other hand, the court was lively and enjoyed the privileges of aristocratic pastime. The public image of Isabel among peasants and in guild shootings endorsed that aspect of relaxation as a public strategy.[42] Therefore, the boundaries between religious and profane, ordered and relaxed, were constantly shifting. Moreover, and most importantly, the gendered humours of the Archdukes were the direct result of their ideological positioning as devout rulers. Each embodied a different side of the coin. Albert was the living proof that refraining from frivolous activities was the proper attitude of the good Christian ruler. Isabel, according to contemporary opinion as a woman more prone to instability in her emotions,[43] expressed the happy contentment of salvation of the Christian.

The nexus between the emotional impact of piety and the quality of a ruler was a cultural model that existed since Antiquity. In this tradition, the exemplary functions of kings were measured in terms of their emotional management. Early Christianity had adopted this model and duplicated it. Both the saint and the king were expected to disseminate a pleasing appearance as a sign of their spiritual contentment and to encourage similar joy among their people. Fourth-century St Martin had "a kind of joy [*laetitia*] shining in his face", in the words of his contemporary and biographer Sulpicius Severus. According to Einhard Charlemagne had a "joyful and cheerful expression" (*vultu laeti et*

---

40 Boëtius Adamsz à Bolswert, *Duyfkens ende Willemynkens pelgrimagie tot haren beminden binnen Ierusalem* (Antwerpen: Hieronymus Verdussen I, 1627) (USTC 1436226). See Karel Porteman and Mieke Barbara Smits-Veldt, *Een nieuw vaderland voor de muzen: geschiedenis van de Nederlandse literatuur, 1560–1700* (Amsterdam: Bert Bakker,) 2008, pp. 486–488.

41 Duerloo, *Dynasty and Piety*, pp. 30–34.

42 The English envoy in Brussels William Trumbull assessed on 24 April 1614 that Isabel "delighteth much in rurall pastimes, he [Albert] in devotion and managing of affaires", quoted in Duerloo, *Dynasty and Piety*, p. 11.

43 Broomhall, *Gender and Emotions*.

PRINTED CHRISTIAN HILARITAS 165

hilari).[44] The formula applied to martyrs and other exemplary Christians as well as to local lords and kings and their spouses.[45] The women responded with a gentle smile to the courtliness of the troubadours. For the men a smiling appearance signalled their benevolence and religiosity as rulers. On the other hand, the king occasionally and depending on the context, chose not to smile in order to retain his legitimacy as ruler among festive courtiers. St Louis of France did so as did Archduke Albert.[46] Both conformed to the stereotype instigated by Plutarch in his biographies of good rulers. The smile of the king occasionally had a more specific meaning. In the context of feudal relations, the suzerain smiling at his vassal was a sign of tribute and confirmation of their mutual relationship. In other words, such cheerfulness was contractual. A variant of these were smiles with judicial implications. In charters at the end of the eleventh century "the smiling donor" (*hilaris dator*) occurs at a time that donations were less important and less voluntarily made.[47] The expression seems to have been assigned to assess a situation as satisfactory to both parties and thus the result of some form of negotiation followed by the explicit endorsement of the donator. Summarised, and applied to the Archdukes, their smiles and non-smiles were gendered state decisions.

Since early Christianity *hilaritas* communicated approval, both in a religious and in a political sense. In the course of the Middle Ages a cheerful expression (*hilari vultu*) was fully loaded in religious significance. St Francis of Assisi referred to it when encouraging his brethren to withstand tribulations and those who tormented them.[48] Moreover, *hilaritas* was interpreted as a smile rather than a laugh. This was in concordance with a major distrust of combustible laughter since the earliest days of Christianity.[49] Christians were

---

44   Matthew Innes, '*He never even allowed his white teeth to be bared in laughter*: the Politics of Humour in the Carolingian Renaissance', in Guy Halsall (ed.), *Humour, History and Politics in Late Antiquity and the Early Middle Ages* (Cambridge, Cambridge University Press, 2002), pp. 131–156 (quotes on p. 140).

45   Gerd Althoff, 'Vom Lächeln zum Verlachen', in Werner Röcke and Hans Rudolf Velten (eds.), *Lachgemeinschaften. Kulturelle Inszenierungen und soziale Wirkungen von Gelächter im Mittelalter und in der Frühen Neuzeit* (Berlin-New York: Walter de Gruyter, 2005), pp. 3–16 (pp. 6–7).

46   On St Louis see Innes, 'He never even allowed', p. 141; on Albert see Duerloo, *Dynasty and Piety*, p. 32.

47   Le Goff, 'Laughter in the Middle Ages', p. 51, quoting Fernand Vercauteren, "'Avec le sourire ...'", in *Mélanges offerts à Rita Lejeune* (2 vols., Gembloux: Duculot, 1969), I. 45–56.

48   Le Goff, 'Laughter', p. 51.

49   Jacques Le Goff, 'Le rire dans les règles monastiques du Haut Moyen Âge', in Claude Lepelley a.o. (eds), *Haut Moyen-Âge. Culture, éducation et société* (La Garenne-Colombes: Publidix, 1990), pp. 93–103.

commonly advised to be economic with laughter, as this was usually interpreted as the fastest road to sin. Particularly in monastic rules laughter and cheerfulness were seriously restricted and explained as tricks of the devil.[50] In this context, monarchs equally had to be careful when to smile and when not. Following the Bible that sadness is in this world and joy among the pious in heaven was the surest guidance for Christians. Yet, even then, discussions of appropriate cheerfulness of a Christian resurfaced.

Thirteenth-century Scholastic, Thomas Aquinas, and his master, Albertus Magnus, were among the theologians who had tried to resolve the perennial debate among Christians between the pernicious effects of demonstrative joy (encouraging the devil) and the need of the Christian to show relief and pleasure to be among the righteous. To do so, the Scholastics turned to an idea of rational cheerfulness. Thomas Aquinas equated *hilaritas* and *iucunditas* (gladness) and added a string of similar terms to the equation: *exultation, gaudium, laetitia, felicitas* and *delectatio*. These were all different, he argued, from *delectatio animalis* (beastly fun) and *scurrilitas* (farce), that indicated an insane mind. *Hilaritas* was honest recreation steered by the mind, visible on the face and indicative of a secure future among the faithful. For Aquinas intellectual, moral and social imperatives all contributed to distinguish good laughter from bad laughter.[51]

At the time of the Archdukes cheerful mystics, relaxed Jesuit school teachers and honest Christians practicing *eutrapelia* or being mirthful about mortification of the flesh built upon the rich heritage of *hilaritas*. Religiously motivated cheerfulness was always circumscribed and given to a particular context. In a political sense, it was equally sensitive. A good ruler might laugh to outwardly manifest his piety, but his laughter (certainly when more than a smile) might also be suspected to denote sinfulness and such vices as pride or lust. In the end, what mattered was the overall attitude of the sovereigns and their propagation of piety as a state matter. Albert resorted to gravity, Isabel to levity, conforming to gender divisions of hilarious female mystics of Carmelite descent and royal stereotypes of expressly avoided laughter. But, there was no doubt that their common joy was spiritual given their support of the religious orders that stimulated *gaudium spirituale*.

Hilaritas and *eutrapelia* were not uncontested, however. The opposite of cheerfulness was sadness and in post-Tridentine Europe that was equally

---

50   Le Goff, 'Laughter', pp. 44–46.
51   Michel-Marie Dufeil, 'Risus in theologia Sancti Thome', in Thérèse Bouché and Hélène Charpentier (eds), *Le rire au moyen âge dans la littérature et dans les arts* (Bordeaux: Presses universitaires de Bordeaux), 1990, pp. 147–163.

PRINTED CHRISTIAN HILARITAS 167

and arguably more appreciated as a Christian virtue. The strife in the heart between the contradictory emotional reactions of relief and depression had been a staple of humanist culture. The late sixteenth-century Dominican friar and philosopher Giordano Bruno, for instance, gave his comedy *Candelaio* (The Torchbearer, 1582) the motto "joy in sadness, sadness in joy" (*tristitia hilaris/ tristis hilaritas*).[52] Bruno's conception of an inherently tragicomic human experience and following from that fighting emotions was similar to the cultural model of comparing Heraclitus to Democritus.[53] That model gained currency in the seventeenth century.[54] It provided an intellectual tool in the visual and literary arts to frame the working of the passions. Heraclitus of Ephesus and Democritus of Abdera had been philosophers in Classical Greece. Heraclitus was melancholic about the stupidity of man and Democritus cheerful. Already in Classical Antiquity their opposite reactions had been translated into the unstoppable tears of the one and the uncontrollable laughter of the other.[55] In the Renaissance, their effusive reactions resurfaced and since the late sixteenth century the model was paradigmatic.

A particular Christian reading of Heraclitus and Democritus emerged in the early seventeenth century. Pierre de Besse, court preacher to the French king Louis XIII, published in 1615 first a Christian Heraclitus and then a Christian Democritus.[56] In the preface to the latter, he infused the laughter of Democritus with centuries of Christian teaching about the proper boundaries of joking. "When he laughs, do not think that he mocks, because when laughing he tells

---

52 Anna Laura Puliafito Bleuel, *Comica pazzia. Vicissitudine e destini umani nel Candelaio di Giordano Bruno* (Firenze: Olschki, 2007).

53 August Buck, 'Democritus ridens et Heraclitus flens', in Hans Sckommodau and Harri Meier (eds), *Wort und Text. Festschrift für Fritz Schalk* (Frankfurt am Main: Klostermann, 1963), pp. 167–186.

54 Bérénice Vila Baudry, 'In tristitia hilaris, in hilaritate tristis: Lope de Vega y la figura de Demócrito y Heráclito', *Escritura e Imagen*, 6 (2010), pp. 87–112; Loris Petris, 'Rire ou pleurer? L'homme face au monde, de Rabelais à Montaigne', *L'information littéraire*, 58:2 (2006), pp. 12–21; Angel M. García Gómez, *The Legend of the Laughing Philosopher and its Presence in Spanish Literature (1500–1700)* (Córdoba, Universidad de Córdoba, 1984); Albert Blankert, 'Heraclitus und Democritus in het bijzonder in de Nederlandse kunst van de 17de eeuw', *Nederlands Kunsthistorisch Jaarboek*, 18 (1967), pp. 31–124.

55 Thomas Rütten, *Demokrit – lachender Philosoph und sanguinischer Melancholiker. Eine pseudohippokratische Geschichte* (Leiden: Brill, 1992); Cora E. Lutz, 'Democritus and Heraclitus', *The Classical Journal*, 49:7 (1954), pp. 309–314.

56 Pierre de Besse, *L'Héraclite chrestien, c'est à dire les regrets et les larmes du pécheur pénitent* (Paris: Nicolas Du Fossé, 1615) (USTC 6013808); Pierre de Besse, *Le Démocrite chrestien, c'est-à-dire le mespris et mocquerie des vanités du monde* (Paris: Nicolas Du Fossé, 1615) (USTC 6010161).

the truth".[57] Many Christian writers had condemned mockery as the work of the devil and had therefore rejected laughing all together, backed by the theological proof that in the New Testament Christ had been reported weeping but never laughing.[58] But de Besse harked back to the Scholastics and their exhortation that laughter expressed the truth of conviction. Moreover, the French court preacher used a Stoic frame of the passions to defend his Democritus. He argued that the tears of Heraclitus demonstrated that his heart was weak and not up to the strong emotions that were the hallmark of the Christian (who firmly stuck to his convictions). "Laughing and mocking in the midst of the afflictions means standing up against the vanities of the world, demonstrating virtue and showing that one is man", de Besse explained.[59] In France such unequivocal defence of laughter caused a literary flurry and some polemic. The French Jesuits Louis Richeome and Etienne Binet, bishop Jean-Pierre Camus and others explored the market of popular religious printing with a light touch. Some of their work was upon publication reprinted in the archdiocese of Cambrai in the 1620s and 1630s.[60] The Douai born Jesuit Antoine de Balinghem delighted in a similar prose, outpouring devotional recommendations for daily life one after the other in a series of books that delighted in household references such as kitchens and table talk as well as medical and food metaphors.[61] This alliance between other worldly spirituality and grotesque materiality of life on earth was a pedagogic tool of spiritual writers to reassure a wide audience of the pertinence of Catholic religion in daily life.

The Heraclitus and Democritus of Pierre de Besse were not published in the Archducal Netherlands, but it appeared in Latin translations in Cologne, the safe haven of Catholic printing closely connected to the Habsburg Netherlands

---

57   Pierre de Besse, *Le Démocrite chrestien*, preface ; Henri Bremond, *Histoire littéraire du sentiment religieux en France depuis la fin des guerres de religion jusqu'à nos jours* (12 vols., Paris: Bloud et Gay, 1921–1936), I. 308–321; Jean-Loup Charvet, 'Les larmes à l'époque baroque, un paradoxe éloquent', *Mélanges de l'École française de Rome*, 105:2 (1993), pp. 539–566.

58   Joachim Suchomski, *Delectatio und Utilitas: ein Beitrag zum Verständnis mittelalterlicher komischer Literatur* (Bern: Francke, 1975).

59   Pierre de Besse, *Le Démocrite chrestien*, preface.

60   Soetaert, *De katholieke drukpers*; see, for instance, Louis Richeome, *L'adieu de l'ame devote laissant le corps* (Arras: Gilles Bauduyn, 1591) (ICC-ODIS 35792, USTC 74349); Etienne Binet, *Consolation et rejouissance pour les malades, et personnes affligées* (Arras: Guillaume de La Rivière, 1618) (ICC-ODIS 37726, USTC 1119656); Jean-Pierre Camus, *Premieres homelies festives* (Cambrai: Jean de La Rivière, 1619) (ICC-ODIS 37410, USTC 1119751).

61   Antonius Balinghem, *Apresdinees et propos de table contre l'excez au boire et au manger pour viure longuement, sainement et sainctement* (Lille: Pierre de Rache, 1615) (USTC 1119156).

PRINTED CHRISTIAN HILARITAS 169

and a specialised centre of religious Latin printing.[62] Another Heraclitus had been published in 1613 by the Augustinian Hermit Georges Maigret from his convent of Huy in the Archdiocese of Liège.[63] The title emphasises that Maigret, as de Besse, was inspired in invoking Heraclitus to indulge of tears of repentance. These penitential books were aimed at a learned and motivated audience. They applied the Christian trope of contempt of the world to raise an emotional charge that aided the firmness of conviction and belief. "To disdain worldly vanities", as the title runs of a devotional treatise of the sixteenth-century Spanish Franciscan Diego de Estella, translated into Dutch and published in Brussels in 1614.[64] Tears were the channel along which religious truth was conveyed most deeply.[65] This culture of tears permeated Catholic spirituality in the late sixteenth and early seventeenth century. It materialised the sweetness of the heart and the sensitivity of feeling God from the inside out. This proved in the post-Tridentine world an apt formula to discredit the overwhelming emphasis in court and fashionable culture on the five senses and all kinds of worldly and bodily knowledge. Affluent tears were for common believers a proof of piety and endurance.

However, Democritus was not without his supporters in the Archducal Netherlands either. The Leuven Latin humanist Eryicius Puteanus delivered in 1611 a late December oration on Democritus at his University. His printer Johannes Christophorus Flavius printed it in the University city in 1612.[66] This was some years before Pierre de Besse published his Democritus in Paris. Puteanus defended the laughter of Democritus as a proper reaction of the good Christian. Better to laugh than to sin, was his shorthand for respectful Christian hilarity. Puteanus had used the occasion of frivolous disputations in

---

62   Pierre de Besse, *Heraclitus christianus, hoc est peccatoris poenitentis suspiria, lachrimae* (Cologne: Johann Kinckius, 1614) (USTC 2029559), reprinted in 1615 and 1618; Pierre de Besse, *Democritus christianus, id est, contemptus vanitatum mundi* (Cologne: Johann Kinckius, 1616) (USTC 2095380), reprinted in 1618.

63   Georges Maigret, *Les larmes ou gémissement de l'Héraclite chrestien, ressuscité miraculeusement de l'enfer, et baptisé, pour prendre à un chascun l'art de déplorer sa misère, selon l'un et l'autre hommes* (Liège: Christian Ouwerx, 1613) (*Bibliotheca catholica*, 5913).

64   Diego de Estella, *Van des wereldts ydelheden te versmaden* (Antwerp: Hieronymus Verdussen I, 1614) (USTC 1005224).

65   For a pertinent analysis see Joseph Imorde, 'Gustus Mysticus. Zur Geschichte und Metaphorik geistlicher Empfindsamkeit', in Johann Anselm Steiger (ed.), *Passion, Affekt und Leidenschaft in der Frühen Neuzeit* (2 vols., Wiesbaden: Harrassowitz, 2005), II. 1105–1133.

66   Erycius Puteanus, *Democritus, sive De risu dissertatio saturnalis: publicè Lovanii habita* (Louvain: Joannes Christophorus Flavius, 1612) (USTC 1005027); see Johan Verberckmoes, 'Puteanus' Democritus, sive de risu', *Humanistica lovaniensia*, 49 (2000), pp. 399–409.

the winter term to stage an unusual Democritus and his plea was in the form of a round of argumentation and not an instruction. Yet Puteanus was an official historiographer of the Archdukes and his plea for Democritus, as some of his other writings, signalled the emotional power of humour as a balance against one-sided sadness. This alternation followed the bible word: "Blessed are you who weep now, for you will laugh" (Luke 6:21). In theological terms this was often translated as laughing when in heaven with God, but some chose to translate the dynamic in terms of this world. *Triumphus risus de lacrymis*, was the title of a laudatory poem on the occasion of Joannes David taking office as abbot of the Premonstratensian abbey of Ninove in Flanders in 1613.[67] David rebuilt the abbey and its church after destruction during the Dutch Revolt. The laughter on his accession therefore praised a new start while it also confirmed the spiritual goal of participating in the joy of Christ. This evidence about the opposing emotions of sadness and gladness in the early 1610s confirms that the Twelve Years Truce (1609–1621), especially in its initial stage, boosted morale among the population in the Habsburg Netherlands, or at least made them emotionally sensitive to fluctuations between pessimism and optimism.

3   Pious Hilarity

So far, *hilaritas* has mainly been conceived as an instrument of moderate joy promoted by religious orders and an Archducal court keen on pacifying a population and in the process enhancing support for post-Tridentine Catholicism. But, unleashing, however cautious, a sense of humour, is bound to transgress boundaries. Humour makes victims and from a theological viewpoint had therefore been much repressed during the Middle Ages, so to avoid the danger of mocking and offending fellow Christians or, worst of all, God. But, also during the Middle Ages the boundaries of this had been flexible and moving. This was not different in the early seventeenth century. In particular, the polemic between Reformed and Catholics had in the sixteenth century opened the sluices of mocking and smearing. This did not disappear under the Archdukes, although attempts were made by all authorities to quieten the hearts. But, still, in theatre plays, during processions and in pamphlet wars Protestants were

---

67   Joannes David, *Triumphus risus de lacrymis et Sacrae Aedis Norbertinæ Ninivensis post luctum gaudia dum* (Louvain: Joannes Masius, 1613), a copy in KU Leuven Libraries, Maurits Sabbe Library.

PRINTED CHRISTIAN HILARITAS

bedevilled and belittled.[68] The Flemish Jesuit Joannes David, active in Ghent, Ypres and Courtrai was a household name of anti-Protestant mockery. Some fierce, anonymous pamphlets are attributed to him. Most date from the last years of the sixteenth century and the first decade of the seventeenth century and belonged to the period of instability and uncertain recovery prior to the Twelve Year Truce. Some of David's last vehement pamphlets, published in Antwerp in 1610 and 1611, presumably were a warning against a threatening influx of Calvinists in Antwerp under the more relaxed circumstances of the Truce.[69] Also the Antwerp based exiled English polymath and polemicist Richard Verstegen made Protestant bashing his trade mark. Interestingly, however, his production of humorous literature in Dutch filled with the ridiculing of Protestants only started during the last years of the Truce, from 1617 onwards.[70]

Similar to David and some other Jesuits was *Le Rabelais réformé des ministres*, allegedly printed by Christophe Girard in Brussels in 1619 and reissued by the same printer in 1620 and 1621, and other printers in Douai and Lyon in 1620.[71] The Brussels imprint and printer were fictitious to avoid persecution in Paris. In this virulent pamphlet, the Poitiers based French Jesuit François Garasse satirically denounced Protestant pastors in debasing and grotesque imagery and accused the famous Calvinist preacher of Charenton, Pierre du Moulin, of being a reborn Rabelais and spreading obscenities among his flock.[72] Catholics combatively accusing Protestants of debauchery had been very much part of the French wars of religion.[73] These mocking pamphlets testify of the frontiers of the comic. The sharpest laughter brought to large audiences continued to fuel the politics and the religion of the period.

Quite a few spiritual authors demonstrated to be well aware of the porousness of the boundaries between proper humour and the degrading kind when invoking the trope of replacing with their own ascetic work worldly books

---

68   Anna E.C. Simoni, 'The Mockers Mocked: the Brussels Play of Saint Ignatius, 1610, and its Dutch Counter Attack', *Archief- en bibliotheekwezen in België*, 47 (1976), pp. 644–649; Maurits Sabbe, *Brabant in 't verweer: bijdrage tot de studie der Zuid-Nederlandsche strijdliteratuur in de eerste helft der 17ᵉ eeuw* (Antwerp: Resseler, 1933).

69   J. Andriessen, 'Joannes David', *Nationaal Biografisch Woordenboek*, (23 vol., Brussels: KVAB, 1964), I. 377–383.

70   Paul Arblaster, *Antwerp and the World: Richard Verstegan and the International Culture of Catholic Reformation* (Leuven: Leuven University Press, 2004), pp. 105–128.

71   USTC 1003678, 1004448, 1117812, 1508411.

72   On the polemic and the opposition against the mocking method of Garasse, see Marc Fumaroli, *L'âge de l'éloquence* (Geneva: Droz, 2002), pp. 326–333.

73   Denis Crouzet, *Les guerriers de Dieu : la violence au temps des troubles de religion (vers 1525–vers 1610)*, 2 vols (Seyssel: Champ Vallon, 1990); Luc Racaut, *Hatred in Print*.

filled with improper stories generating much laughter and greatly appreciated among the public. A Dutch language devotional work, based on the medieval scholastic Albertus Magnus, pleaded to consider mockery and blasphemy as worth nothing and gave as a remedy to compare it to mosquitos flying before a man's eyes.[74] This was the real change for authors who promoted *hilaritas* as Christian joy. How to replace powerful, grotesque comic images and words that swarmed before the eyes and ears of the faithful with proper humour? Or, in other words, how did clerical authors deal with the ever shifting boundaries between profane and religious humour? In this last section, I will give some indications on how this challenge was defined in the period of the Archdukes.

The already mentioned Flemish Jesuit Joannes David was a case in point. He not only indulged in ridiculing the religious enemy, but was also a prolific ascetic writer and well versed in Latin and in Dutch, seeking different audiences. He also explicitly turned to popular culture. In 1606, he published at the Plantinian printing house a Dutch language collection of proverbs.[75] In the preface he hoped that his readers would abandon jest-books that shot much dishonesty in the hearts of the reader. Instead he proposed a little game. The book was to be used by a man reading the first page and a woman the second. This framed the book as a parlour game for presumably a young couple. The lottery aspect of his title was translated as an encouragement to open the book at random and profit from its contents.

Reading David's selection of proverbs in the prescribed way yields some interesting perspectives on contemporary views on virtuous hilarity. Conforming to contemporary gender divisions, most sayings with prescriptions on how to laugh are on the female side of the book. The admonitions on laughter reprimand those who laugh while tickling themselves (they are self-satisfied, but that is mere vanity), those who laugh easily and enjoy foolish tricks, those who believe that being laughed at equals friendship (some person's laughter "does not go beneath the chin or throat" and are therefore not real friends), those who cherish cheerfulness in the house (because sadness waits before the door), and praises those who laugh silently and subdued "in their fist" as a sign of a joyful heart (and not laugh with those who have misery).[76] This reads like a catalogue of situations for young women to train their laughter in social situations and commit to restraint. On the other hand, the saying on laughing

---

74   Albertus Magnus, *Een seer devote contemplatie* (Antwerp: widow Jacob Mesens, 1630), pp. [C1=25]v°-[C2=26]r° (USTC 1436290).

75   Donaes Idinav [=Joannes David], *Lot van vviisheyd ende goed gelvck: op drije hondert ghemeyne sprek-vvoorden* (Antwerp: Jan Moretus I, 1606) (STCV 3112733, USTC 1001604). See Porteman and Smits-Veldt, *Een nieuw vaderland*, pp. 295–296.

76   Donaes Idinav, *Lot van wiisheyd*, pp. 39, 51, 83, 153, 241.

PRINTED CHRISTIAN HILARITAS   173

easily also acknowledges that these people also easily weep tears and that is seen as a sign of "sweet nature". That connection between laughter and tears suggests that spiritual joy is the ideal. The male side of the book of proverbs has more sayings on fools and foolish behaviour. These pages warn in a series of sayings on fools and fool's caps not too behave like fools, talk like fools, look out for the company of fools, and mock others as fools do.[77] That reads like another catalogue, in this case of socially undesirable situations and friendships of a boisterous male culture. One saying on laughter on the male pages therefore alerts to avoid laughing "like rented horses" when they are being bridled, cautionary adding that where the gallows are missing there are still trees. This seems a straightforward defence of clerics that reprieve young boys of indulging in cheerfulness just for the fun of it. In all, David defended in these proverbs a gendered and corrective laughter, but also one that promoted joyful companionship, in stark contrast to his anti-Protestant prose.[78]

An educational attempt of defining Christian hilarity was in the aptly titled *Pia hilaria*.[79] This collection of Latin verse anecdotes was first printed in Douai in 1617 and in the seventeenth century reprinted in ten different cities. The author was Angelin Gazet, a Jesuit of the Gallo-Belgian province and member of a family of clergy and writers. Gazet was rector of the Jesuit colleges of Arras, Valenciennes and Cambrai. His *Pia hilaria* recycled dozens of stories about saints from medieval hagiography. Some focused on the grotesque tricks of the devil. From Vincent of Beauvais, Gazet borrowed the story of a painter (localised as Belgian) who painted such ugly devils on a fresco in a church that the devil himself shook his scaffolding to make the painter fall down.[80] The *hilaritas* was in these stories no less than the ridiculing of devils and a variety of monstrous figures, such as a Peruvian servant living in Brazil who ate nothing but figs and symbolised global stupidity. A large subset of the stories demonstrated how saints lived in harmony with animals, St Francis being a prime example and the subject of the first story in the collection. In that case, *hilaritas* denoted a pacified natural environment in accordance with Gods plan.

---

77 Donaes Idinav, *Lot van wiisheyd*, pp. 20, 52, 170.
78 For a new evaluation of mild humour as a response to contemporary polemic see Lieke J. Stelling, "'Leaving their Humours to the Word Mongers of Mallice": Mocking Polemic in Tarltons Newes Out of Purgatorie (1590) and Two Contemporary Responses', *Shakespeare Jahrbuch*, 154 (2018), pp. 140–154. In such perspective the humour of Joannes David deserves a fresh reading.
79 Angelin Gazet, *Pia hilaria variaque carmina* (Douai: Balthazar Bellère, 1617) (ICC-ODIS 39022, USTC 1117542).
80 Angelinus Gazaeus, *Pia hilaria* (Antwerp: Balthasar Moretus, 1629), pp. 36–41 (STCV 6649386, USTC 1003874).

The many reprints and several reeditions in the course of the seventeenth century suggest that the *Pia hilaria* touched a sensitive string. The stories were presumably used for educational purposes, for teaching the young Latin in school or on the stage. Jesuit colleges might have been the primary context. A copy of the 1631 version published in Cologne mentions in handwriting that a Joann Christoph Geydert had donated the book to a Joannes Christophorus Schleidorn on 18 August 1637 in the context of a Jesuit college. This brings *hilaritas* to the classrooms, but also in a secure context of teaching salvation through example. In a short exhortation to reader (*lector*) and listener (*auditor*), Gazet emphasises the virtue of his humorous stories. These are qualified as joyful and salty, but not hurtful and unbridled.[81]

4 Conclusion

During the reign of the Archdukes, *hilaritas* was a significant cultural model for the promotion of Catholic religion. Clerical authors built on the immemorial Christian tradition of conceptions, ideas and practices of spiritual joy and transformed it into a tool of the revitalisation of religion. Religious authors emphasised the plenary joy of the true Christian. Laurentius Beyerlinck, canon of the Antwerp Cathedral of Our Lady and influential book censor, documented in his collection of Christian sayings a lemma on laughter (*risus*) with the firmness of the third-century martyrs Pionius and Sabina, who were mocked and insulted by their opponents yet stuck to their Christian religion. Even when tortured and threatened with death, Pionius encouraged with laughter the newly converted runaway slave girl Sabina. When she asked him why, he answered: "this is what God likes, for we are Christians; and those who stand firm in their belief in Christ shall laugh forever".[82]

Constancy of the faith was an approved recipe of post-Tridentine Catholicism. Religious authors turned to different strategies to enter this message of truth in the heads, hearts and souls of their flock. Promoting *hilaritas* was a strategy based on the emotional impact of examples that brought the profane bodily need for relaxation and play in accordance with elevated and disembodied spiritual goals. Saints were in that respect not different from any ordinary Christian. Each had to fight the same combat against the temptations

---

81 *Ibid.*, p. [**pages**] : "hilara, non molesta, non effrenia […], plena candidi salis".

82 "Ita Deo placet, Christiani enim sumus: et qui fide firmâ in Christum sunt, risu ridebunt perpetuo", in: Laurentius Beyerlinck, *Apophthegmata christianorum* (Antwerp: Jan Moretus, 1608), p. 526 (STCV 6623226, USTC 1003491).

of the devil and foolish amusement testifying that the devil represented only a void. *Hilaritas* and *eutrapelia* were, therefore, a state of mind that could be taught. In the Jesuit colleges, the young were given encouragement through funny stories about grotesque tricks of the devil and speaking animals, as well as the relaxed approach of their professors. Those who matured as Christians learned in the exemplary lives of saints that mortification of the flesh was a good basis of infectious mirth and convulsive laughter. Most striking in this survey of the printed production of *hilaritas* of the early seventeenth-century Habsburg Netherlands are the global Christian sources of the *gaudium spirituale*. Spanish mystics, French Catholic clergy and exemplary stories from Christian Antiquity up to contemporary missionary activity in Asia, Africa and America are the backbone of religious humour. Devotional books printed in the archdiocese of Cambrai were in this as important as the production in the Dutch and Latin printing centres Antwerp, Leuven and Cologne.

The Archdukes conformed to the models of a Christian ruler that had been circulating since late Antiquity. This model had gained new pertinence after the destructive mocking and divisiveness that was the legacy of the sixteenth century. Christian religion had been torn apart and, in the process, reciprocal insulting between Catholics and Protestants had gained currency as a proper mechanism of defence and even of conversion. This also persisted during the Archducal reign, as the pamphlets of Joannes David and Garasse's *Rabelais réformé* demonstrated. In promoting piety as the pillar of their politics, the Archdukes steered a clear course away from the arms of ridicule. Relying on the legacies of spiritual joy, the stern Albert and the responsive Isabel represented as a couple the duality of giving in to cheerfulness as an emotion and refraining from it as a safeguard of their legitimacy. This strategy of the Archducal court was explicitly gendered and a further hypothesis is that the production as well as the reception of *hilaritas* recipes may equally have been gendered. Democritus was the exponent of the male variant of *hilaritas* and represented a more foolish laughter among boisterous men that when wisely directed to spiritual affairs was justified. As canon Beyerlinck phrased it: "a wise man laughs if there is a reason" (as opposed to fools who laugh without reason).[83] Isabella and Carmelite nuns were less inhibited in showing spiritual joy as a profane manifestation of genuine hilarity.[84] *Hilaritas* was in that sense an ordered as well as gendered emotion that structured the religious culture

---

83 "ridet fatuus nulla dum causa subest, [...], at prudens causa dum subest, ridet", in: Beyerlinck, *Apophthegmata christianorum*, p. 526.

84 Frances E. Dolan, 'Why Are Nuns Funny?', *Huntington Library Quarterly*, 70:4 (2007), pp. 509–535.

of the early seventeenth-century Habsburg Netherlands. As a manifestation of Baroque Catholicism, spiritual joy was presumably more female than male and more convent-style than worldly.[85] On the other hand, *hilaritas* also crossed Christian confessions. Take the Geneva trained Calvinist minister Nicolas Vedelius, who from late March 1630 was working in the famous Latin school in Deventer. He pleaded for optimism as a Christian duty in *Sanctus Hilarius, sive antidotum contra tristitiam pro sancta hilaritate* (1632).[86] Translations in other languages appeared throughout the seventeenth century. For a Calvinist theologian and, moreover, a man endorsing cheerfulness was not a straightforward road.

In the Spanish Habsburg Netherlands *hilaritas* had a long future. To give just one example: references to joy (*hilaritas*) and cheerfulness (*iucunditas*) in the first two volumes of the monumental *Acta Sanctorum*, on the month of January and published in 1643. The two volumes contain twenty-four textual references to *hilaritas* and twenty to *iucunditas* as descriptors of the beneficial condition of the saints. The *Acta* contain, for instance, the dialogue of Gregory the Great on monk Merulus of Rome's Benedictine abbey of St Andrew who was wonderfully given to tears and who died with great quiet and joy of mind.[87] The Neapolitan martyr Potitus was comforted by the Holy Spirit and this made his face radiate with cheerfulness.[88] In short, for learned audiences as well as for the silent religious majority, *hilaritas* was a cultural tool of careful emotional management. It strengthened the bonds among Christians and brought relaxation to the heart of the pious state and its citizens.

---

85   Nathalie Grande, 'Humour et mystique chez Agnès de Langeac', *La Vie spirituelle*, 160 (2006), pp. 21–37.

86   Nicolaus Vedelius, *S. Hilarius seu Antidotum contra tristitiam pro sancta hilaritate* (Leiden, [Willem Chrisiaensz vander Boxe] for Franciscus Hegerus, 1632) (USTC 1019131).

87   "cum magna securitate animi atque hilaritate defunctus est", in: *Acta Sanctorum quotquot toto orbe coluntur, vel a Catholicis Scriptoribus celebrantur, quae ex antiquis monumentis Latinis, Graecis, aliarumque gentium collegit, digessit, notis illustravit Ioannes Bollandus Societatis Iesu Theologus, Servata primigenia Scriptorum phrasi. Operam et studium contulit Godefridus Henschenius eiusdem Societatis Theologus. Ianuarii Tomus II. XVI. posteriores dies complectens* (2 vols., Antwerp: Joannes Meursius 1643), II. dies 17 (USTC 1512073).

88   "vt confortante Spiritu sancto facies eius sumeret iucunditatis splendorem", in: *Acta Sanctorum*: I. dies 13.

PART 3

Prints and Iconography

∵

CHAPTER 10

Militant Printers' Marks across the Southern Low Countries (1561–1640): A Survey at the Heart of the *Emblematic Era*

Rosa De Marco

1   The Printer's Mark in the *Aetas Emblematica*

Among the *imprese* (devices) that the Italian Jesuit Silvestro Pietrasanta (1590–1647) presented in his work *De symbolis heroicis libri IX*, he included a printer's mark, that of Christopher Plantin, based in Antwerp, 'at the Golden Compass' (fig. 10.1 and table 10.1, nr.1).[1]

FIGURE 10.1   Cornelis I Galle after Paul Peter Rubens, Plantin's Mark in Silvestro Pietrasanta, *De symbolis heroicis libri IX* (Antwerp: Balthasar Moretus)
© UNIVERSITY LIBRARY OF LIEGE, LIÈGE, 374B

---

1 Silvestro Pietrasanta, *De symbolis heroicis libri IX* (Antwerp: Balthasar Moretus, 1634), pp. 382–383. On this work, see Peter M. Daly, G. Richard Dimler, *The Jesuit Emblem in the European*

180 DE MARCO

Plantin's mark respectively show a hand using a compass, point held firm, the other mobile to trace a circle, figure of perfection bearing the motto 'Labore et Constantia'. The printer explained the meaning of the mark in the preface of his polyglot Bible (1573), saying that the fixed limb of the compass represents the constancy, and the movable one is the work.[2]

The *De symbolis heroicis* is dedicated to Pier Luigi Carafa (1581–1655), Apostolic Nuncio at Cologne, and whom Pietrasanta, as his confessor, accompanied on a pastoral visit to Liege between 1627 and 1634.[3] It was during this visit that he finished his book, which was published in 1634 by the grandson of Christopher Plantin, Balthasar Moretus I. In opening of the *præmium*, Pietrasanta declares his desire to make known "the force and nature" of *imprese* in those regions (i.e. the Spanish Low Countries) where, he claimed, they were still little known.[4] In reality, this was merely a rhetorical expedient enabling him

---

Context (Philadelphia, Saint Joseph's University Press, 2016), pp. 62–65. On its influence and, notably, its use as a source for the *Imago Primi Saeculi*, see Lydia Salviucci Insolera, *L'Imago primi saeculi (1640) e il significato dell'immagine allegorica nella Compagnia di Gesù. Genesi e fortuna del libro* (Rome: Pontificia Università Gregoriana, 2004), pp. 165–167. For a useful description of the engravings in *De symbolis heroicis libri IX*, see Max Rooses, *Catalogue du Musée Plantin-Moretus* (Antwerp: J. Buschmann, 1887), p. 92, n. 44.

2 On Plantin's mark, see in particular: Leon Voet, *The Golden Compasses. A History and Evaluation of the Printing and Publishing Activities of the Officina Plantiniana at Antwerp* (2 vols., Amsterdam: Vangendt – London: Routledge & Kegan Paul – New York: Abner Schram, 1969–1972); Hugh William Davies, *Devices of the Early Printers 1457–1560. Their History and Development* (London: Grafton, 1935), pp. 678–679.

3 See Uberto Limentani, "In Germania e nel Belgio con un viaggiatore del Seicento", in *Studi secenteschi*, 2 (1961), pp. 119–144.

4 "Expositurus vim et naturam rei, in his regionibus, quad artem et præcepta saltem, non adeo notæ ...", in Pietrasanta, *De symbolis heroicis libri IX*, p. 1. The Jesuit Claude François Ménestrier recalled Pietrasanta's purpose: "Le Père Silvestre Petrasancta, Jesuite Romain, ayant esté plusieurs années dans les Païs-Bas avec Pierre Loüis Carrafe Nonce Apostolique du S. Siege, & depuis Cardinal, trouva l'usage des Devises introduit en la plûpart des Colleges de ces païs là, sans qu'on en sçeut bien les regles. Cela l'obligea d'en composer un traité durant son sejour à Liege. Ce traité imprimé à Anvers l'an 1634 a pour titre de *Symbolis Heroicis Libri IV* [*sic*] *authore Silvestro Petrasancta Romano e Societate Iesu*" ("Father Silvestre Petrasancta, Roman Jesuit, having been in the Netherlands for several years with Pierre Louis Carrafe, Apostolic Nuncio of the Holy Siege, and since Cardinal, found the use of the devices introduced in most of the Colleges of these countries without the rules being well understood. This forced him to write a treatise on it during his stay in Liege. This treatise printed in Antwerp in 1634 is entitled *Symbolis Heroicis Libri IV* [*sic*] *authore Silvestro Petrasancta Romano e Societate Iesu*"): Claude François Ménestrier, *La philosophie des images, composée d'un ample recueil de devises et du jugement de tous les ouvrages qui ont été faits sur cette matiere* (Paris: Robert J.B. de la Caille, 1682), pp. 43–44.

A SURVEY AT THE HEART OF THE *EMBLEMATIC ERA* 181

to enter into the debate concerning *imprese*[5] – notably, their exact definition and the norms of their composition – which had been gaining interest since the mid-sixteenth century.[6] That the genre was already well-known and appreciated in the Low Countries is clearly attested by the numerous works already published there at the time.[7] There is little doubt too that Pietrasanta was not aware of the fact, since he chose to translate the Italian word *impresa* by the Latin *symbolum heroicum* – a direct reference to the title of one of the first books of *imprese* printed in the Low Countries: Claude Paradin and Gabriele Simeoni's *Symbola heroica*.[8]

Arguing against many of his predecessors, in particular Girolamo Bargagli (1537–1586), Pietrasanta postulated that the essential principle of the *impresa* was the articulation between image and text and that this relationship largely prevailed over the separate importance of either the image or the text. He considered Plantin's mark to exemplify perfectly this indivisible solidarity between image and text. The golden compass appears in book VIII, chapter VIII: *An lemma Symboli Heroici possit esse translatum, seu metaphoricum*, where, as the title indicates, he discussed a particular type of articulation between image (*figura*) and motto (*lemma*) that Pietrasanta defined as "translational or metaphorical".

---

5 Guido Arbizzoni believes this declaration indicated Pietrasanta's intention to promote himself as a pioneer of the *impresa* genre beyond Italy. See Guido Arbizzoni, '*Imprese* as Emblems: the European Reputation of an Italian Genre', in Donato Mansueto etc. (eds), *The Italian Emblem: A Collection of Essays* (Glasgow: University of Glasgow 2007), pp. 1–31 (esp. pp. 20–21).

6 The principal theorists engaged in this debate included Scipione Ammirato (1531–1601), Agostino Tasso (1451–1510), Paolo Giovio (1483–1552), Emanuele Tesauro (1592–1675), and Saavedra Fajardo (1584–1648).

7 See Alison Adams and Marleen van der Weij (eds), *Emblems of the Low Countries: A Book Historical Perspective* (Glasgow: University of Glasgow, 2003); John Landwehr, *Emblem and Fable Books Printed in the Low Countries, 1542–1813: A Bibliography* (Utrecht, Hes Publishers, 1988).

8 Claude Paradin, Gabriele Simeoni, *Symbola heroica* (Antwerp: Christophe Plantin, 1562) (USTC 440779). This work is the Latin version of Claude Paradin, Gabriele Simeoni's *Les devises heroiques* (Antwerp: Christophe Plantin, 1561) (USTC 9805) (1st ed.: Lyon, 1551, USTC 9862), which was the first book of emblems published by Plantin. Several editions of both the French and Latin versions of this work were produced in Antwerp by Plantin and by the widow Joannes Steelsius (USTC 13070). The French version was also printed in Douai, Leuven and Leiden. See Alison Adams, Stephen Rawles, Alison Saunders, *A Bibliography of French Emblem Books* (Geneva: Droz, 2002), pp. 249–267. See also Landwehr, *Emblem and Fable Books*.

182   DE MARCO

As he explained, in Plantin's mark the *lemma* imbued the *figura* with its full metaphorical sense. The *lemma* made explicit a "condition", fulfilled which has as a "consequence" what was expressed in the image:

> In this respect, the ingenious drawing of Plantin's noble mark is worthy of praise. We see here a compass, one arm of which is held fixed, while the other transcribes a circle, that is, the figure which symbolizes perfection; with this is the epigraph 'Labore et Constantia', the two things that, above all others, ensure perfection in a work. It is thus possible to understand both work and constancy as an expression of the protasis [i.e. the compass], without this needing to be broken in the apodosis [i.e. the motto].[9]

Pietrasanta also saw this metaphorical transfer as the key to the pertinence of the mark as a whole with respect to the printing profession. Producing perfectly printed books, entirely free of errors, was at the time a very demanding activity, requiring extreme attention, deftness, strength and endurance. When Peter Paul Rubens designed Plantin's mark, he incorporated the allegorical figures of Hercules and Constancy into the ornamental frame he had added to the central motif,[10] thereby accentuating the transfer of the ethical message evoked by these figures to the technical action which was portrayed in the central image.[11] Similarly, in the portrait Hendrick Goltzius (1558–1617) made of Plantin for the *Epigrammata Funebria*, the printer is shown with his left hand

---

9   "Ita etiam laudem promeretur schema ingeniosum Nobilis Typographiae Plantinianae: Circinus vidilicet, altero pede insistens, altero circulum describens; hoc est, figuram quae est simulacrum perfectionis, cum hac Epigraphe, Labore et Constantia, quae duo ad opus perfectum inprimis conferunt. Etenim tam labor, quam Constantia, quasi propria locutione de Protasi et de ipso circino intelligi possunt; neque in Apodosim necessario transgrediuntur", in: Pietrasanta, *De symbolis heroicis libri IX*, pp. 382–383.

10   Erasmus declared in his *Adagia*, that the printer's work is a kind of herculean *labor: Erasmes de Rotterdam, Les Adages* (Paris: Les Belles Lettres, 2011), t.2, 1001; further indications in Anja Wolkenhauer, *Zu schwer für Apoll. Die Antike in humanistischen Druckerzeichen des 16. Jahrhunderts* (Wiesbaden: Harassowitz, 2002), p. 124f.

11   Peter Paul Rubens, *Design for the Emblem of the Plantin Press*, pen and brown ink and brown wash, 206 × 277 mm, ca 1628–1630 (Antwerp, Museum Plantin-Moretus, TEK 391). This design was never actually used as a mark by Plantin or his successors: see Anne-Marie S. Logan and Michiel Plomp, *Peter Paul Rubens: The Drawings* (New York: Metropolitan Museum of Art, 2005), pp. 181–182. Rubens did, however, provide other printers with designs which were actively used: Joannes Keerbegius, for example (1627), based on the sign that hung outside Keerbegius's press, *In de gulden sonne* (*In the golden sun*), and Jan van Meurs (1630): see Salviucci Insolera, *L'Imago primi saeculi* (*1640*), p. 166.

FIGURE 10.2   Hendrick Goltzius, *Portrait of Christopher Plantin*, 1581–1585. Copper engraving, 20,4 × 13,4 cm
© RIJKSMUSEUM, AMSTERDAM, RP-P-1884-A-7748

resting on a closed book, while with his right, he uses a compass to trace a circle, around which his motto, 'Labore et Constantia', is inscribed (fig. 10.2).[12]

Thus, while the book evokes his profession, the mark assumes here one of the *impresa*'s specific roles, namely to express and promote the sitter's innermost values and moral principles, in one word.[13] The inclusion of the printer's mark in both an erudite book and a portrait clearly indicates the importance of this graphic sign in sixteenth-century culture. Pietrasanta made no bones about placing Plantin's mark on an equal footing with *imprese* admired and debated in intellectual spheres.[14] His analysis of it drew directly, for example, on the theories that Paolo Aresi (1574–1644) exposed in his work *Imprese sacre*,[15] notably, the notion of "metafora continuata" (continued metaphor),[16] employed by Aresi to designate the idea of transferral from the graphic part of the *impresa* to its owner or referent.

Already, the earliest marks, which appeared towards the end of the fifteenth century, often figured coats of arms or blazonry held up by animals and/or worked into complex vegetal décors – a classic and well known example being that of the Parisian printer Jean Petit.[17] This use of heraldry clearly referred back to the kind of "emblemising" which characterised manuscript books from the third century on.[18] This omnipresence of heraldry in manuscripts throughout the Middle Ages – in every possible paratextual form – contributed not only to diffuse this cultural phenomenon, but also actively to shape the way symbols were perceived and used.[19]

---

12 Johannes Bochius, *Epigrammata funebria ad Christophori Plantini manes. Cum nonnullis aliorum ejusdem argumenti elogiis* (Antwerp: widow Christophe Plantin and Jan Moretus I, 1590) (USTC 406863). See Friedrich Wilhelm Hollstein, *New Hollstein. Dutch & Flemish etchings, engravings and woodcuts 1450–1700, Philip Galle* (4 vols, Amsterdam: Sound & Vision Publishers, 2001), IV. 162. See also Mark McDonald, *The Print Collection of Cassiano dal Pozzo. I: Ceremonies, Costumes, Portraits and Genre* (Royal Collection Trust, 2017), cat. n. 1603.

13 On the specificities of the Italian *impresa* and the French *devise*, as well as the evolution of both terms, see Donato Mansueto, 'The Impossible Proportion: Body and Soul in Some Theories of the *Impresa*', *Emblematica*, 11 (2001), pp. 5–29.

14 Pietrasanta, *De symbolis heroicis libri IX*, p. 166 *et passim*.

15 Paolo Aresi, *Imprese sacre con triplicati discorsi illustrate & arricchite a' predicatori, a' gli studiosi della scrittura sacra* (3 vols., Milano: Pacifico Da Ponte's heirs and Giovanni Battista Piccaglia, 1625), I. 83, *passim*.

16 Aresi, *Imprese sacre*, p. 83: "trasportata dalla cosa figurata al portatore dell'impresa".

17 Petit's marks can be dated from 1511 onwards. See Davis, *Devices*, pp. 371–375.

18 Laurent Hublot, 'L'emblème et le livre, entre appropriation et représentation', in Karin Ueltschi (ed.), *L'univers du livre médiéval. Substance, lettre, signe* (Paris: Honoré Champion, 2014), pp. 257–285.

19 Hublot, 'L'emblème et le livre', p. 273 *et passim*.

A SURVEY AT THE HEART OF THE *EMBLEMATIC ERA* 185

The present analysis focuses on the influence of emblems and closely-associated genres like the *impresa* on the typographic mark. Emblems constituted a literary genre that began to flourish in the second third of the sixteenth century. Characterised by an iconotextual composition, their accomplished form is generally considered by today's specialists to correspond to the tripartite arrangement of title, image and epigram exemplified by those found in the book of emblems by the Italian jurist Andrea Alciato (1492–1550).[20] Our focus on emblems is prompted by their structural affinity with printers' marks (which almost always combined an image and a motto), but also by the extraordinary success emblems met with from the mid-sixteenth century through to the end of the seventeenth – a success so marked that Daniel Russel has termed this period *aetas emblematica* (Emblematic Era).[21] This study is inspired by Daniel Russel's methodology exploring the ways of emblematic forms "may well provide a bridge between allegory, the dominant symbolic and rhetorical form of late medieval culture and new type of metaphor that begins to take shape with European romanticism".[22]

Scutis (Peter Schoeffer, Mainz, 1473), *armis* (Michael Wenssler, Basel, 1478), *signum* (Johann Veldener, Louvain, 1473), *symbulum* (Erasmus speaking of Aldus's mark)[23] are the words habitually used by printers themselves to refer to these woodcuts. French printers usually distinguished the terms 'mark for the *figura*, and 'device' for the *motto*, that seems to explicit a proto-emblematic lexicon, as also employed by Geoffroy Tory in his *Champ-fleuri* (1529):

> Aldus the Roman ... had his hieroglyphic mark, but he had not invented it. I now want to declare my own device and mark ... made as I thought and imagined, by speculating on its moral sense, in order to give some advice to printers and booksellers to follow and keep as an example for their inventions.[24]

---

20 The first illustrated edition of Alciat's book is: Andrea Alciato, *Emblematum Liber* (Augsburg: Heinrich Steyner, 1531) (USTC 701368).

21 Daniel S. Russell, *Emblematic Structures in Renaissance French Culture* (Toronto: University of Toronto Press, 1995), p. 9.

22 Russell, *Emblematic Structures*, p. 10.

23 See Davis, *Devices*, pp. 12–23.

24 "Alde le Roman ... auoit sa marque Hyeroglyphique, mais il ne lauoit pas inuentee. Ie veulx ici declarer ma Deuise et Marque ... faicte comme ie lay pensee & imaginee, en y speculant sens moral, pour en donner aucun bon amonestement aux imprimeurs et libraires de par dezca, a eulx exercer & employer en bonnes inuentions", in Lothar Wolf, *Terminologische Untersuchungen zur Einführung des Buchdrucks im französischen Sprachgebiet* (Tübingen: De Gruyter, 1979), p. 66.

These marks used by printers, as well as by merchants, artists or others craftsmen to distinguish their work or property were a symbolic portrait and tended to be directly linked to their lives, the professional and personal aspects with which they were often closely entwined.

Mauda Bergoli-Russo's study of the network of printers whose marks incorporated the image of the phoenix or its variants provides an interesting example of this.[25] The phoenix network spread right across Europe, from Venice (where numerous examples used by the Giolito De' Ferrari family, active in Venice between 1536 and 1606, and by Domenico Giglio can be found), to Trino in the Piedmont region of Northern Italy, Lyon (where the symbol was adopted by the printer Barbaus), and right through to Barcelona. The links between the members of this network were complex, sometimes resulting from family connections, as was the case of the Stagnino family of Trino, which adopted the symbol in 1536, and sometimes involved publishing contracts or exchanges, common contacts, and even underhand transactions such as counterfeiting.

Other common bases for what were generally referred to as "canting marks" directly linked to the owner were printers' initials and monograms, puns on names. The mark invented by Guillaume de La Rivière, Plantin's nephew and an employee active in Arras from 1591,[26] for example, incorporated a river (fig. 10.3).

The motto that accompanied this image, *Madent a flumine valles* (the valleys are flooded by the river / La Rivière), can be understood, via the pun on the printer's name, as an allusion to the printing profession and, more specifically, to the mission that La Rivière set himself, namely to render fertile the lands where his books were dispersed. This example, among others, reveals how the fashion for emblems penetrated different forms of language. Indeed, the composition of the text and the image invented by La Rivière is not only a mnemonic picture used as a means of marketing, but is more than that it expresses, like an emblem composition, embodying the moral wisdom the printer claimed to possess.

---

25   Mauda Bergoli-Russo, *L'impresa come ritratto del Rinascimento* (Napoli: Loffredo, 1990), chapter 2: "Cento anni (1520–1620) di trattazioni teoriche sulla impresa e sull'emblema: l'Italia nei suoi rapporti con la Francia", p. 31 *et passim*. For the complexity of the relationships that existed between printers whose marks were based on a similar motif see some examples gathered in the chapter 'Les marques sur les pages de titre', in Jean-François Gilmont and Alexandre Vanautgaerden (eds), *La page de titre à la Renaissance : treize études suivies de cinquante-quatre pages de titres commentées et d'un lexique des termes relatifs à la page de titre* (Turnhout: Brepols, 2008), pp. 155–209.

26   Dirk Imhof, "Between Philip II and William of Orange: The Correspondence of Christopher Plantin (ca 1520–1589)", in Jeanine De Landtsheer and Henk J.M. Nellen (eds), *Between Scylla and Charybdis: Learned Letter Writers Navigating the Reefs of Religious and Political Controversy in Early Modern Europe* (Leiden: Brill, 2010), pp. 217–232 (p. 229).

FIGURE 10.3   Guillaume La Rivière's mark, the wide river, in Maximilien de Wignacourt, *Discours sur l'estat des Pays Bas, auquel sont déduictes les causes de ses troubles et calamitez et leurs remèdes* (Arras: Guillaume de La Rivière, 1593)
© UNIVERSITY OF GENT

2   The Printer's Mark as a Medium of the Catholic Message

La Rivière's astute sense of self-fashioning should certainly be recognised in his decision to modify his mark when, in 1629, he went into partnership with his son, Jean-Baptiste de la Rivière, whose presses, also in Arras, were located at the sign of the "Bon-Pasteur" (The Good Shepherd) (Fig. 10.4).[27]

In the modified mark, the rural landscape is replaced by a cityscape; on the hilltop from which the view is seen, a shepherd protects his sheep from

---

27   The father-son partnership continued until 1634: Achmet Héricourt (comte d'), Zéphir François Cicéron Caron, 'Recherches sur les livres imprimés à Arras', *Memoires de l'Academie d'Arras* (Arras: Veuve Degeorge, 1849), vol. 24, pp. 221–222; 234–288; 306–330.

FIGURE 10.4   Guillaume La Rivière's mark, at the address of The Good Shepherd, from the dictionary compiled by Ferdinand van der Haeghen, *Marques typographiques des imprimeurs et libraires qui ont exercé dans les Pays Bas, et marques typographiques des imprimeurs et libraires belges établis à l'étranger* (2 vols., Ghent: C. Vyt, 1894), II. 8

a menacing wolf, while on the wide river below, a boat in full sail evokes plentiful catches.

The biblical allusions contained in this scene are further insisted upon by the figure of Christ situated in the foreground of the image – simultaneously the Good Shepherd and the mystical lamb, whose blood was destined to fill the sacrificial chalice.[28] Around the oval frame of the image runs the motto *Bonus pastor animam suam dat pro ovibus suis* (The Good Shepherd gives his life for his sheep). The scene also refers to the renewal of the sacrifice of Christ in the sacrament of the Holy Communion, as confirmed by the Council of Trent, as well as the apostolic mission of the pope and the Catholic Church.

---

28   In the story of the Good Shepherd (*Jn*, 10:1–21), Christ identifies himself as a responsible shepherd, whose duty, he claimed, was to bring together and guide his sheep, to look out for those who went astray, and lay down his life to save his flock. The boat evokes the miraculous catch of fish related in the *Gospel of Luke* (*Lk*, 5: 1–11).

A SURVEY AT THE HEART OF THE *EMBLEMATIC ERA*   189

The refined semantic message of this new mark did not, however, render redundant the personal motto of Guillaume de La Rivière, *Madent a flumine valles*. On the contrary, inscribed on a banderol hung from the cornice framing the scene and metaphorically linked to the landscape, this motto continued to indicate the motivating ideals behind the printer's commercial activity.[29] La Rivière's mark *Madent a flumine valles* appeared for the first time in 1593 below the title of a book by Maximilien de Wignacourt, written in praise of the king's action against "heretics".[30] The books printed by La Rivière included important contributions to the campaign aimed at reconquering errant souls. Among these was Pedro de Ribadeneira's biography of Ignatius of Loyola,[31] which, published in 1607, two years before Ignatius's beatification, furnished elements liable to promote the cult of the founder of the Society of Jesus and thus favour a positive response to his requested canonisation. Also noteworthy in this respect are several polemic and apologetic works by the Jesuit Louis Richeome (1544–1625) – in particular, *Le panthéon huguenot...*,[32] and *Le pèlerin de Lorette*,[33] both dedicated to Henry IV and Catholic-press bestsellers in their day – and other major works of what Henri Bremond has termed "devout humanism".[34] In fact, from the beginning of the father and son partnership in 1629, the production of the La Rivière firm tended to focus heavily on books dedicated to religious subjects, the life of saints, and specifically Jesuit literature: epigrams, devotional works, one of Kostka's letters, etc.[35]

---

29   The banderol is connected with the vignette via a quartered medallion figuring initials that we have not been able to identify. A catalogue of the books issued from the presses (highly diverse) of these two Arras printers, father and son, is contained in 'Recherches sur les livres imprimés à Arras', pp. 233–287.

30   Maximilien de Wignacourt, *Discours sur l'estat des Pays Bas, auquel sont déduictes les causes de ses troubles et calamitez et leurs remèdes* (Arras, Guillaume de La Rivière, 1593) (USTC 4179).

31   Pedro de Ribadeneira, *La Vie du B. père Ignace de Loyola fondateur de la Compagnie de Jésus. […] Nouvellement augmentée d'une bonne partie, qui manquait aux précédentes impressions* (Arras: Guillaume de la Rivière, 1607) (USTC 1119569).

32   Louis Richeome, *Le pantheon Huguenot decouvert et ruiné contre l'aucteur de l'Idolatrie papistique, ministre de Vauvert, cy devant d'Aigues mortes* (Arras: Guillaume La Rivière, 1610) (USTC 6901319).

33   Louis Richeome, *Le Pélerin de Lorette, voeu à la glorieuse vierge Marie, mère de Dieu, pour Monseigneur le Dauphin* (Arras: Guillaume La Rivière, 1611) (1st ed. Lyon: Pierre Rigaud, 1607).

34   Henri Brémond, *Histoire littéraire du sentiment religieux en France depuis la fin des guerres de Religion jusqu'à nos jours* (12 vols. Paris: H. Odelin, 1916–1936), I.19–67.

35   Caron, 'Recherches sur les livres imprimés à Arras', pp. 233–287.

All in all, for commercial reasons, printers' marks frequently reproduced or drew on the signs that hung outside their presses or shopfronts, also events like marriages and the relocation of presses often led to the modification of marks, as indeed the simple desire to keep up with new fashions and tastes. This was the case with Plantin's mark, the compass which, as mentioned, originated in the address of his press in Antwerp, situated 'at the Golden Compasses'. As we have tried to show in the case of the Plantin, whose richly symbolic mark was rooted in the address of his press, howsoever banal the origins of a given mark or the motivations behind its evolution, these factors in no way prevented the symbolic sense of an image from being optimised as a means of self-fashioning and self-promotion. For commercial reasons Plantin, as other cautious printers, did not expresses a religious message in his mark, he also abandoned his previous more explicit marks with a vine winding around a tree with the mottos 'Christus vera vitis' (Christus, the true vine) and the one more committal still: 'Exerce imperia et ramos compesce fluentes' (Exercise severe dominion over them, and check the loose straggling boughs).[36]

It is precisely the way printers used their marks to promote themselves and their enterprises that leads us to question their role in the transmission of ideological, political and religious ideas – a question rendered all the more relevant in light of the way books and images were mobilised in the Spanish Low Countries as part of the Catholic Counter-Reformation.

3 Relationships between Emblems and Printers' Marks in the Low Countries

In undertaking an iconological analysis of the marks of printers active in the Spanish Low Countries in the late sixteenth and early seventeenth century, our aim is to establish for this region what Anja Wolkenhauer calls a "cartography

---

36 See Hubert Meeus, 'The Evolution of Printer's Device in the Southern Low Countries up to 1600', in Anja Wolkenhauer, Bernhard F. Scholz (eds), *Typographorum Emblemata. The Printer's Mark in the Context of Early Modern Culture* (Berlin/Boston, De Gruyter, 2018), pp. 77–100 (p. 93). I have not been able to benefit from the studies of this important volume which remained unpublished when I finished this paper, nevertheless I wish to thank Mrs Anja Wolkenhauer for her insightful reading and comments on this research. See also Anja Wolkenhauer, "Sisters, or Mother and Daughter? The Relationship between Printer's Marks and Emblems during the First Hundred Years", in Wolkenhauer, Scholz (eds), *Typographorum Emblemata*, pp. 3–25.

A SURVEY AT THE HEART OF THE *EMBLEMATIC ERA*   191

of knowledge".[37] The identification of the sources which inspired these marks and contributed to their symbolic sense depends on our understanding of the cultural spheres in which printers and readers moved. It is only by mapping these cultural spheres that we can hope to fully comprehend the messages conveyed through this iconotextual medium. Giuseppina Zappella, in her study of the marks of Italian printers active in the sixteenth century, showed that these marks drew on a wide variety of iconographical sources, ranging from mediaeval heraldry and bestiaries to contemporary artistic production.[38]

The Spanish Low Countries was a land rich in visual media, constantly replenished by a thriving illustrated-book industry.[39] Printers were perfectly placed to draw inspiration from the wide variety of art forms disseminated through engravings. These notably included contemporary paintings. The mark chosen by Toussaint Leclerq, for example, a printer working 'at the sign of Saint Ignatius', in Lille, and specialised in the printing of Jesuit literature,[40] was closely based on an engraving by Schelte Bolswert, itself based on a drawing by Rubens, made to celebrate the canonisation of Saint Ignatius in 1622 and showing the founder of the Jesuit Company of Jesus in the act of contemplating his chosen monogram: IHS (Iesus Hominum Salvator).[41] Similarly, the success of emblems was very quick to spread; their influence in the Low Countries

---

37   Anja Wolkenhauer, 'Printers' marks in scholarly research – overview and questions', in Michaela Scheibe, Anja Wolkenhauer (eds), *Signa Vides – Researching and Recording Printers' Devices*. Papers presented on 17–18 March 2015 at the CERL Workshop hosted by the National Library of Austria (Vienna-London: Consortium of European Research Libraries, 2016), p. 12.

38   Giuseppina Zappella, Le marche dei tipografi e degli editori italiani del Cinquecento. Repertorio di figure, simboli e soggetti e dei relativi motti (2 vols., Milano: Editrice Bibliografica, 1986).

39   On illustrated books in the Low Countries, see among others: Karen L. Bowen and Dirk Imhof, *Christopher Plantin and Engraved Book. Illustrations in Sixteenth-Century Europe* (Cambridge: Cambridge University Press, 2008).

40   Besides numerous light works of a devotional nature, Toussaint Leclercq, active in Lille between 1640 and 1665, printed major bibliographical works by Antoine Sanderus and Claude Doresmieux. See Louis Trénard, *Histoire des Pays-Bas français: Flandre, Artois, Hainaut, Boulonnais, Cambrésis* (Toulouse: Privat, 1974), p. 274; Sébastien Afonso, *Imprimeurs, société et réseaux dans les villes de langue romane des Pays-Bas méridionaux (1580–ca 1677)* (Unpublished PhD: Free University of Brussels, 2016), pp. 346–347.

41   Schelte Bolswert (after Peter Paul Rubens), *Saint Ignatius de Loyola and Saint Francis Xavier*, 1622, etching, 34.7 × 25.2 cm. See *Hollstein's Dutch and Flemish Etchings, Engravings and Woodcuts* (72 vols., Amsterdam: Menno Hertzberger 1950), III. 239.

was already perfectly apparent in the sixteenth century. Towns like Antwerp, Louvain and Douai, where the emblem culture – widespread in all solemnities as in architectural decors – and the printing industry were flourishing, all contributed to the success of emblems throughout Europe.[42] It was notably in the Low Countries that important emblem-promoting works like the *Imago Primi Saeculi* (Antwerp, 1640) were published – in this case, linked to the centenary of the foundation of the Society of Jesus.[43]

We are not currently in a position to produce exhaustive results, but a preliminary survey of the Southern Low Countries, as well the outlying area in the Dutch Republic, has enabled us to question the strategic uses of typographic marks throughout the Low Countries. The presentation of the results of our analysis of the Spanish Low Countries as a whole will be followed up by specific case study: the work and career of the printer Balthazar Bellère I, active in Douai between 1590 and 1639. At present, the tools necessary to carry out a thorough analysis of the marks of printers in the Southern Low Countries are largely insufficient. Our research so far has drawn principally on the compilation of printers' marks published by Ferdinand van der Haeghen (1830–1913) in 1894 (used essentially by bibliophiles and collectors, this work is a compilation rather than a veritable catalogue)[44] and the catalogue of marks published by Louis-Catherine Silvestre (1792–1867) in 1867.[45] Unfortunately, neither of these two works contain graphic reproductions suitable for serious study: marks are often trimmed down, crowded together on the pages

---

42   See note 7 and, more specifically: John Manning, Karel Porteman, Marc van Vaeck (eds), *The Emblem Tradition and the Low Countries* (Turnhout: Brepols, 1999). This is also confirmed by Milazzo's contribution in the present volume (chapter 5).

43   *Imago primi saeculi Societatis Iesu a Provincia Flandro-Belgica eiusdem Societatis repraesentata* (Antwerp: Balthasar Moretus, 1640) (USTC 1003318). Among the numerous studies dedicated to this work: Salviucci Insolera, *L'Imago primi saeculi (1640)*; John W. O'Malley (ed.), *Art, Controversy, and the Jesuits: The Imago Primi Saeculi (1640)* (Philadelphia: Saint Joseph's University Press, 2015).

44   Ferdinand van der Haeghen, *Marques typographiques des imprimeurs et libraires qui ont exercé dans les Pays Bas, et marques typographiques des imprimeurs et libraires belges établis à l'étranger* (Ghent: C. Vyt, 1894) 2 vol.. See also Frank Vandeweghe and Bart Op de Beeck, *Drukkersmerken uit de 15de en de 16de eeuw binnen de grenzen van het huidige België/ Marques typographiques employées aux XVe et XVIe siècles dans les limites géographiques de la Belgique actuelle* (Nieuwkoop: De Graaf, 1993); G. van Havre, *Marques typographiques des imprimeurs et libraires anversois* (2 vols., Antwerp-Ghent: J.E. Buschmann, 1883).

45   Louis-Catherine Silvestre, *Marques typographiques ou recueil des monogrammes, chiffres, enseignes, emblèmes, devises, rébus et fleurons des libraires et imprimeurs qui ont exercé en France* (Paris: P. Jannet, 1867).

A SURVEY AT THE HEART OF THE *EMBLEMATIC ERA* 193

and accompanied by minimal information, generally nothing more than the printer's name, the city his press was located in and approximate dates of activity.[46] In providing the basis for a preliminary iconographic inquiry, these works have, however, allowed us to identify a number of cultural trends and tendencies marking the development of marks used by printers active in the Spanish Low Countries in the late sixteenth and early seventeenth century, to observe the variations in certain popular motifs, and to begin to inventory the diverse emblematic sources that contributed to inspire these distinctive iconotextual devices.

Firstly, Andrea Alciato's book of emblems, *Emblematum liber*, the most widely-published and well-known work of its kind at the time, notably provided the source of inspiration for several printers' marks. The first authorised edition of Alciato's book was printed in Paris by Chrestien Wechel in 1534. The first editions to appear in the Spanish Low Countries were printed in Antwerp from 1556 by Plantin, over the following decade, some 25 editions were produced in Paris, Lyon, Antwerp and other printing centres, many of which issued from Plantin's presses.[47]

One printers' mark which drew directly on Alciato's book of emblems is seemingly that of Jan van Turnhout, active in 's-Hertogenbosch: the mark, together with the date 1555, appears in a book issued from Turnhout's press (Table 10.1, nr 2).[48] The emblem it drew on figured in Wechel's 1534 edition of

---

46 Further research on the subject would be greatly facilitated by a repertory of marks based on a similar model to recent works such as Peter van Huisstede and J.P.J. Brandhorst's *Dutch Printer's Devices 15th–17th Century*, published both as a book and a CD ROM: Peter van Huisstede and J.P.J. Brandhorst, *Dutch Printer's Devices. 15th–17th Century: A Catalogue* (3 vols., Nieuwkoop: De Graaf Publishers, 1999) (from now on: 'DPD'). On other online database projects, see Wolkenhauer, *Signa Vides*, pp. 176–179.

47 The very first edition of Andrea Alciato's *Emblematum Liber* was published in Augsburg in 1531 without the author's permission. The illustrations, unplanned by Alciato, were by Hans Schäufelein. Adams, Rawles, Saunders, *A Bibliography of French Emblem Books*, entries F.001-072 cover early French editions of Alciato. The 1534 edition that Wechel published in Paris under the title *Emblematum libellus* was re-worked and carefully corrected by Alciato and provided with higher quality illustrations: Andrea Alciato, *Emblematum libellus* (Paris: Chrestien Wechel, 1534) (USTC 185363). For an analysis and a list of Alciato's editions by Plantin Press see Arnoud Visser, 'Why dis Christopher Plantin publish Emblem Books?', in Adams and van der Weij, *Emblems of the Low Countries*, pp. 63–78. On Alciato's cultural influence in Europe and containing a rich bibliography, see Anne Rolet, Stéphane Rolet (eds), *André Alciat (1492–1550): un humaniste au confluent des savoirs dans l'Europe de la Renaissance* (Turnhout: Brepols, 2013).

48 *DPD*, nr. 0858.

Emblematum libellus; the image figures Mercury's caduceus between the horns of Almathea, accompanied by the motto *Virtuti Fortuna Comes* ('Good fortune attendant on virtue'). Jan van Turnhout adopted both image and motto. The same emblem also inspired the mark of Wechel himself.[49] In this case, however, Wechel added two hands emerging from clouds holding the base of caduceus which is decorated at the top with wings evoking the Mercury's hat (Table 10.1, nr. 2). Wechel's modified version was in turn taken up by another printer, Pierre Bellère I, located 'In de Scilt va Bourgoignen' ('at the Shield of Burgundy') in Antwerp. In the works Bellère printed between 1575 and 1576, he introduced a further modification by changing the motto to *Fructus Concordiae* ('Fruit of Concord'), in order to underline the idea of concord evoked by the two hands supporting the caduceus. This mark, amongst others, was used by the Bellère family of printers, active in both Antwerp and Douai, until 1646.[50] This example illustrates not only the considerable influence of books of emblems, in particular that of Alciato, on printers' marks, but also the way certain printers' marks became models for others, and, importantly, the way printers modified and adjusted their iconographic and textual models to suit their own particular aims and requirements in terms of image and self-promotion, using emblematic language.

During the same years, another of Alciato's emblems was being used by the French printer Anthonis Maria Bergagne, based in Louvain (Table 10.1, nr 3) who published among others, many writings of Adam Sasbout from Delft, a Franciscan theologian and teacher in Louvain.[51] The emblem figures a lion accompanied by the very evocative motto 'Nec quaestioni quidem cedendum' ('Do not yield even to torture'). Bergagne adopted the image, as is attested by works printed from 1550 on.[52] His heirs also continued to use the mark with

---

49 Further enriched by the addition of Pegasus above the caduceus, the mark of Chrestien Wechel, bookseller-printer, active in Paris between 1522 and 1554, continued to be employed by Andreas Wechel (active in Paris, 1554–1573) and his heirs in Frankfurt. See Guy De Tervarent, *Attributs et symboles dans l'art profane: Dictionnaire d'un langage perdu (1450–1600)* (Geneva: Droz, 1997), pp. 154–155.

50 On the printing industry in Douai, see Afonso, *Imprimeurs, société et réseaux*, pp. 51–58.

51 Andrew Pettegree, Malcolm Walsby, *Netherlandish Books (NB)* (2 Vols.): *Books Published in the Low Countries and Dutch Books Printed Abroad before 1601* (Leiden: Brill, 2010), p. 1201 et passim.

52 Desiderius Erasmus, *Een sermoon van de barmherticheyt Gods* (Louvain: Anthonis Maria Bergagne, 1550) (USTC 408643).

A SURVEY AT THE HEART OF THE *EMBLEMATIC ERA* 195

minimal modifications to the animal[53] which also appears carrying a shield bearing a quatre-de-chiffre.[54]

A foray into the Dutch Republic, generally Calvinist in terms of religious leaning, brought to light certain territorial variants, one of which being that inventors of marks in these provinces tended to favour books of emblems by Protestant authors as sources of inspiration. The bookselling towns of Leiden, Dordrecht and Amsterdam offer interesting examples in this respect. Among these is the mark used by Joannes Maire (1603–1657), son of Antoine Maire, also a printer, based first in his hometown of Valenciennes and then, from around 1584, in Leiden.[55] Joannes Maire's mark features a peasant digging over the earth, bathed in the rays of the sun; inscribed in the circle of the sun is the Hebrew word "אֲדֹנָי", (pronounced "Adonai") signifying the name of God; the scene is framed by a laurel branch, a palm frond and the motto *Fac et spera* (Do and Hope). This same mark was in fact used throughout the entire seventeenth century, and even afterwards, by various printers based in Dordrecht, like Jacob Cornelisz Braat (active in Dordrecht between 1643–1655) (table 10.1, nr 4).[56] It appears to have been inspired by one of the emblems presented by Gabriel Rollenhagen (1583–1619), jurist and protonotary affiliated to the Protestant chapter of the Cathedral of Magdeburg, in his book *Selectorum emblematum centuria Secunda* (published in 1613).[57] Bearing a similar image and the same motto, *Fac et Spera*, this emblem is explained in Rollenhagen's book by the following distich: '*Subditus esto Deo, mandato munere fugens, Et spera in miseris, et pete, rebus opem*' ('Obey God by accomplishing the tasks required of you; remain hopeful and seek [his] help in times of hardship'). This same mark

---

53   Vincentius Lerinensis, *Pro catholicae fidei antiquitate et veritate, adversus prophanas omnium haereseoon novationes liber elegantissimus ... additum est breve commentariolum, per Ioannem Costerium ...* (Louvain: Ex officina Anthonij Maria Bergagne, 1552) (USTC 408795).

54   *Instructie oft onderwijs daer op men sal verpachten, betalen, ontfanghen ende bestrecken de nieuwe imposten binnen Brabant opghestelt* (Louvain: Anthonis Maria Bergagne, 1554) (USTC 408852).

55   Otherwise known as Jean Maire, Jan Maire, Johannes Le Maire or Joannis Maire. See Ronald Breugelmans, *Fac et spera: Johannes Maire, Publisher, Printer and Bookseller in Leiden 1603–1657; A Bibliography of his Publications* (Houten: Hes & De Graaf, 2003).

56   See Breugelmans, *Fac et spera.*, p. 30; Paul Begheyn, *Jesuit Books in the Dutch Republic and its Generality Lands 1567–1773. A Bibliography* (Leiden: Brill, 2014), p. 124; David L. Weaver-Zercher, *Martyrs Mirror: A Social History* (Baltimore: Johns Hopkins University Press, 2016).

57   Landwehr, *Emblem and Fable Books*, pp. 689, 692. Rollenhagen was often inspired by emblem books.

was already used in Dordrecht by Cornelis van Dalen (1602–1664), and also by further printers in Leiden[58] and Amsterdam.[59] One mark more similar to the Rollenhagen's emblem figuring a woman with a spade was being used by the bookseller and printer Willemsz van der Beeck, from 1640,[60] a printer active in the Mennonite town of Hoorn. Another recurring motif used by Protestant printers was that of the allegorical figure of the *Christian Religion* drawn from the work of the French Calvinist theologian, Théodore de Bèze (1519–1605), entitled *Icones*.[61] One of the printers who employed this figure as a mark was Bruyn Harmansz Schinckel, based in Delft (table 10.1, nr. 5). In Bèze's book, the verses which accompany the figure of *Religio* describe it as evoking poverty and purity, in opposition to 'Triumphant Rome'[62]; they also explain the open book the figure contemplates and turns towards the reader, as an invitation to follow, like her, the true law, the Word of God.

As a rule, iconographic motifs tended to undergo fewer modifications in the hands of these Protestant printers than their Catholic confreres, their marks often remaining unchanged when passing from one generation to the next or following the sale or transfer of a workshop. A tendency which ran strongly through Protestant and Catholic regions alike, however, was that of heavily loaded title pages with rich arrays of conventional symbols: the many examples include the missals printed by Gilles Bauduyn in Arras (16th–17th c.),[63] the Bibles printed by David Jansz Van Ilpendam, in Leiden (1590–1649), and the publications of François and Pierre Foppens, active in Brussels (17th–18th c.), with their resplendent images of doves, symbol of the Holy Spirit, and ostensories.

---

58 *DPD*, nr. 0017; 0043; 0223; 0269; 1063; etc. There does not, however, seem to have been any contact between van Dalen and Cornelisz Brat, even though a certain overlapping is observable in their respective catalogues during these same years, including, for example, Van Braght's *Martyrier-Spiegel* or *Martyr's Mirror* (1660) and the works of the Jesuit Famiano Strada.

59 *DPD*, nr. 0217: Bouman family.

60 *DPD*, nr. 0274.

61 Alison Adams, *Webs of Allusion: French Protestant Emblem Books of the Sixteenth Century* (Geneva: Droz, 2003), esp. pp. 119–153. Alison Adams, 'The Emblemata of Théodore de Bèze (1580)', in Karl A.E. Enenkel and Arnoud S.Q. Visser (eds), *Mundus emblematicus: Studies in Neo-Latin Emblem Books* (Turnhout: Brepols, 2003), pp. 71–96.

62 Adams, 'The Emblemata of Théodore de Bèze (1580)', pp. 141–143.

63 See Achmet Héricourt (comte d') and Zéphir François Cicéron Caron, *Recherches sur les livres imprimés à Arras depuis l'origine de l'imprimerie dans cette ville jusqu'à nos jours* (Geneva: Slatkine Reprints, 1971) (1st ed. Arras: Veuve J. Degeorge, 1851–1853).

A SURVEY AT THE HEART OF THE *EMBLEMATIC ERA*

4   The Case of Douai: the Unicorn flying towards the Sun

Though Louvain and Antwerp were the most active centres of book production in the Spanish Low Countries, towards the end of the sixteenth century, many printers began to look to other cities to develop and consolidate their activity. One of the towns principally affected by this movement and whose printing industry consequently experienced a sudden boom was Douai. With its rich and long-standing tradition of manuscript production linked to its numer-ous monastic institutions, Douai provided a particularly fertile ground for the installation of new presses. Added to this was the fact that Counter-Reformation zeal stirred up by the Council of Trent had led many Jesuits to flock to the town to swell the ranks of an ambitions enterprise: the reconquering of those erring souls who had been tempted away from the Roman Church – a mission which clearly called for typographical assistance. Finally, the demand for printers was also the result of the town's exceptional number of pedagogical institutions, including the university, founded in 1562 by Philip II.

Both the university authorities and the city's magistracy offered newly arrived printers financial help in setting up and getting their activity off the ground. Shortly after the opening of the university, Jacques Boscard (table 10.1, nr 7) and Jean Bogard (table 10.1, nr 8)[64] both left Louvain for Douai (respec-tively in 1563 and 1564). In 1590, the printer and bookseller Balthazar Bellère I arrived from Antwerp (where his father operated as a printer and member of the Guild of Saint Luke between 1553 and 1595) and set up shop in the "rue des Écoles". This thriving industry made Douai one of the most important intel-lectual bastions of the Counter-Reformation in the Low Countries.[65] Both the nature of the works published and the dedications they carried – often penned by the printers themselves and addressed to members of the town's clergy and superiors of religious establishments in its vicinity – attest very clearly the printing community's militant involvement in the Catholic cause. Bellère even explained the motivations behind his publishing choices directly to his readers:

> This is why, Reader, in the miserable times of the present day, when her-esy attacks us from without, and our own vices from within, and the jus-tice of God everywhere present, I wanted to share with you this work, in which you will find remedies for all evils.[66]

---

64   Silvestre, *Marques typographiques ou recueil des monogrammes*, 324–325, 960, 1128.

65   Afonso, *Imprimeurs, société et réseaux*, pp. 111–170.

66   "C'est pourquoy, Lecteur au temps miserable du iourd'huy, où l'hérésie nous combat du dehors, et nos vices au-dedans, et la justice de Dieu partout, je t'ai voulu faire pan de

The marks used by printers active in Douai also express this mission that they consigned to their publications.[67] That of Pierre Auroy (or Avroy) (active in Douai, 1604–1631), jointly inspired by the address of his press – 'at the Golden Pelican' – and one of the emblems in Hadrianus Junius's *Emblemata* (1565),[68] would have been easily recognisable at the time as a symbol of Christ and the Holy Communion (table 10.1, nr 9). The mark of Pierre Borremans (active in Douai, 1603–1616), figured the Apostles Saint Peter and Saint Paul. That of Jean de Fampoux (active in Douai, 1621–1652) combined an image of the Holy Spirit – again taken from the sign which hung above his press – with the motto 'Vincitur fama virtutibus' (Virtues Overpower Fame). Among the many other examples, let us mention Laurent Kellam I, active in Douai from 1603 until his death in 1613, following his expulsion from England around 1586 and subsequent apprenticeship as a printer in Louvain. Kellam's mark, once again based on the sign that hung outside his premises, figured the Passover Lamb, which he seemingly intended to be understood as an allusion to the sacrifice of a man exiled on account of his ideas, particularly since this was the mark he used in the works he printed in English translation and had smuggled into England.[69]

In this arsenal of symbols, the various marks employed by Balthazar Bellère I represent particularly refined examples. Bellère was highly prolific as a printer: over 700 editions printed in Douai between 1598 and 1639 bear his name and he was the favoured printer of both the university and the Jesuit community.[70] This represented a privilege that he readily acknowledged. In 1622, for example, Bellère and Jean Bogard (whose daughter Bellère married that same year) paid for a pyramid, in honour of the saints Francis-Xavier and Ignatius of Loyola, as

---

cest œuvre, où tu trouveras les remèdes de tous les maulx", in: Francisco Arias, *L'usance de la confession et S. communion, translaté par un père de la mesme compagnie*, (Douai: B. Bellère, 1602) (USTC 1116593). Epistle to the Reader, cited in Olivia Sauvages, "L'Age d'or des libraires douaisiens sous les Archiducs", in Claude Bruneel, Jean-Marie Duvosquel, Philippe Guignet and René Vermeer (eds), *Les "Trente Glorieuses" (circa 1600–circa 1630). Pays-Bas méridionaux et France contemporaine. Aspects économiques, sociaux et religieux au temps des archiducs Albert et Isabelle.* Proceedings of the colloquium held at the University Charles-de-Gaulle – Lille 3, 22–23 March and 5 October 2007 (Brussels: Archives et Bibliothèque de Belgique, 2010), pp. 249–258 (p. 258).

67   For the marks of printers active in Douai see van der Haeghen, *Marques typographiques*, II. *passim*; Silvestre, *Marques typographiques*, II. *passim*.

68   Hadrianus Junius, *Emblemata* (Antwerp: Christopher Plantin, 1565) (USTC 401188).

69   See Afonso, *Imprimeurs, société et réseaux*, p. 341.

70   Afonso, *Imprimeurs, société et réseaux*, pp. 315–316.

A SURVEY AT THE HEART OF THE *EMBLEMATIC ERA*   199

part of the ephemeral décor created to celebrate their canonisation.[71] Bellère
used several different marks incorporating various mottos: 'Fructus concordiae'
(Fruit of Concord); 'Studio et perseverantia' (With zeal and perseverance); 'Eo
omnia unde' (All things go to where they are from); 'Labore et perseverantia'
(With work and perseverance), both the latter inscribed around a circle traced
by a compass, recalling Plantin's mark[72]; 'Vanitas et omnia nihil' (Vanity and all
is nothing)[73]; and 'Venema Pello' (I Drive out Venom).

The last motto, together with the image which it accompanied, represent
the ultimate synthesis of Bellère's professional ideals. The image was that of a
unicorn plunging its horn into a pool of water; the motto indicated this action
as one of purification (table 10.1, nr 10). The mark as a whole was inspired by
one of the *imprese* contained in Paolo Giovio's *Dialogo dell'imprese militari*.[74]
This *impresa* belonged to a certain Bartolomeo d'Alviano, captain in the service of the Oursini family, who had it blazoned on his war standard in order
to warn off his enemies, whom he termed 'corrupters'. Bellère, conceiving his
own spiritual mission as a form of conquest, seemingly appreciated this military dimension to the emblem's history, since, on the first page of certain of his
publications – for example, 'In Hoc Signo vinces'-, he had the image of a standard, bearing the motto, worked into his mark. This militarised evocation of the
legendary power of unicorn to purify water thus became a way of affirming the
power of the book industry in the fight against heresy.

The analogy between venom and heresy, as indeed that between pestilence and heresy, had in fact been a commonplace since the Middle Ages

---

71   Sauvages, 'L'Age d'or des libraires douaisiens', p. 249. Such acts of generosity of the part of
      printers towards religious establishments were frequent, notably in Douai, as observed by
      Afonso, *Imprimeurs, société et réseaux*, pp. 292–293.

72   John Jones, *Sacra memoriae ad scripturas divinas in promptv habendas memoriterqve
      ediscendas accommodata / per E.D.M. Leandrum de S. Martino ... Anexa est Conciliatio
      locorum scripturae specie tenus pugnantium olim edita per Seraphinvm Cumiranum ...
      & nunc per succinctam epitomen explicata ab eodem R.P. Leandro de S. Martino* (Douai:
      Baltazar Bellère, 1623) (USTC 1118041); Jean Mauburne, *Rosetum exercitiorum spiritualium
      et sacrarum meditationum ... nunc recens ultra omnes alias editiones, verius, emendatius
      & distinctius edidit & castigauit R.P.M. Leander de S. Martino ...* (Douai: Baltazar Bellère,
      1620) (USTC 1117822).

73   On the title page of the book Gregorius I, *Operum. Scholia in eundem sacramentorum
      librum quae in Romana editione desideratur* (4 vols., Douai: Baltazar Bellère, 1615) (USTC
      441267).

74   Gabriele Simeoni, *Dialogo dell'imprese militari et amorose di monsignor Giovio vescovo di
      Nocera et del signor Gabriel Symeoni fiorentino. Con un ragionamento di messer Lodovico
      Domenichi, nel medesimo soggetto. Con la tavola* (Lyon: Guillaume Rouillé, 1559), pp. 66–67
      (USTC 116043).

and was still being actively exploited in devotional and predicatory literature. Jesuits, in particular, cultivated the image of heresy as a pestiferous monster, notably through theatrical and collegiate spectacles.[75] Bellère obtained the patronage of the Company of Jesus in 1593. This had a notable impact on both his career and the politico-spiritual mission of the Jesuits, now able to count on one of the most productive printing workshops in the Spanish Low Countries. It also had a direct impact on the typographical mark in the works which issued from the Bellère press: the place hitherto occupied by Bellère's personal mark now tended to be reserved for the monogram of the Company of Jesus: IHS (table 10.1, nr 10). Although the Ignatian monogram, systematically present on all the architectural property of the Jesuit community, was not, strictly speaking, a typographical mark, it now managed to gain access to one of the most important contemporary conveyors of publicity: the title page of the printed book. As the primary symbol of the militant action of the Catholic Church, the Jesuit monogram represented the universal spiritual ideals to which Bellère adhered. Specialists in the arts of language, the Jesuits were also quick to exploit emblems in their apostolic and pedagogical mission.[76] So, to come back to the words of Pietrasanta, it can fairly be said that, through their collaboration with the printing industry, the Jesuits managed to fully exploit the "force and nature" of the emblem. With respect to Bellère, the Ignatian *impresa* figuring the monogram inscribed within the circle of the sun became what the archivist and palaeographer Pierre Gheno has termed a "deferential mark", that is an emblem referring to a person or institution under whose protection or patronage a printer placed himself in conducting his business, as opposed to the more common "referential mark", i.e. referring to the printer himself.[77] This type of deference, also attested by the relatively common practice of displacing the printer or bookseller's personal mark from the title page in favour of the *impresa* of a religious order, not only facilitated immediate recognition of the religious leanings of the author and the content of the work, but also promoted the circulation of certain images and the ideas that they conveyed.

---

75 For the *typus haereseos* ('image of heresy') see the study presented by Walter S. Melion on Jean David's *Veridicus Christianus*. In the book, the allegory of heresy is developed by the depiction of a plague-ridden house being purified in the background. For the image of heresy in Jesuit festivals, see Rosa De Marco, *Le Langage des fêtes jésuites dans l'ancienne assistance de France (1586–1643)* (Turnhout: Brepols, forthcoming), currently consultable as a Ph.D. dissertation of the University of Burgundy – Franche-Comté.

76 The literature on this subject is extremely abundant. For a general appraisal of the question, as well as the bibliographical databases currently available: Daly, Dimler, *The Jesuit Emblem, passim*.

77 Pierre Gheno, 'Les marques typographiques en France des origines à 1600', *Cultura*, 33 (2014), pp. 75–95.

5   Conclusions

Typographical marks constitute melting pots of traditions and cultural references shared by a wider group of iconotextual forms including *imprese* and emblems. The various types of iconotext prevalent during the sixteenth and seventeenth century drew on a very rich and deep pool of sources including heraldry, Christian symbolism, numismatics, paremiology, epigraphy and even Egyptology. The extremely complex nature of the compositions which resulted require them to be studied as a distinct form of art, characterised by specific semantic and syntactic rules. While this study concentrates primarily on iconographic motifs and themes, it also necessarily takes into account the rules of composition governing the respective placing on image and motto, notably, as suggested by Anja Walkenhauer, the *dispositio* of the constituent elements of marks when they appeared on title pages.[78] Indeed, the deeper analysis of manipulation of text, the inclusion of Christian iconography and the combination of both in the printers' devises may contextually reveal the use of marks as *medium*. The comparison between some catholic marks and emblems from Protestants auteurs which seem quite close, suggests a teleological debate (see for example table 10.1, nr 8). The graphic part of marks, often enigmatic and thought-provoking, must surely have pricked the curiosity of all those who had occasion to browse through books at the time: scholars, of course, but also censors, booksellers, peddlers, etc. The mark encouraged an active reading. In the same way, printers sometimes favoured in their mark the use of rebuses: the mark of the brothers Jean and Antoine Lagache, based in Arras, for example, substituted the first two letters of their surname with the symbol for the musical tone 'la'; this appeared on a stave, followed up by the subsequent letters. Marks often appeared on the first pages of books. The earliest ones were generally affixed to the colophon along with the legal and commercial mentions attesting the authenticity of the work and the identity of its author, printer and diffuser; later, they increasingly figured on the title page, where their role as promoters of the commercial image and excellence of the printer was reinforced by rich and seductive ornamentation. The examples we have considered here have allowed us to observe the transition from an essentially self-referential to a more deferential use of marks among printers active in the Spanish Low Countries, that is, a tendency to insist less on personal professional excellency and more on collective ideals and missions linked to the politic-religious context of the times.

---

78   Wolkenhauer, 'Printers' Marks in Scholarly Research, pp. 7–26.

In the "Emblematic Era", printer's marks relate to the extraordinary success of emblems, contributing to the spread of knowledge with the resulting impact on ways of thinking between the late sixteenth and the end of the seventeenth century. The familiarity of printers and their readers with emblems, together with their recognition of their efficacy as conveyors of information and ideas, caused the invention and interpretation of typographical marks to develop into a veritable science. The importance of these marks in the history of books thus lies not only in their legal and commercial function, but also in the way they acted as highly condensed expressions of the cultural and ideological context in which the books they figured in were produced.[79] The eighteenth century still recognised this function of the mark:

> The ardour of beliefs, the nobility of character, the harsh demands of an honoured profession, its perils, faith in the immortality of thought are reflected around the mark [...]. Its legends, an intimate expression of these sometimes persecuted men, often bear the imprint of a sort of ascetic philosophy, of a spirit of stoic renunciation in favour of the study of science, which adds much to the interest of the mark.[80]

A more comprehensive study of the marks of printers active in the Southern Low Countries is required and would be greatly facilitated by the creation of more comprehensive catalogues and high-performance study tools. For the moment, we hope to have been able to pinpoint some of the characteristics of these distinctive text-image amalgams in printer's marks – variable and apparently inconstant, but clearly capable of conveying extremely complex and influential messages at the heart of the reformations of the Western Christianity.

---

79   The development of illustrated title pages which sometimes incorporated marks also emphasises this aspiration to condense in allegorical form the contents of books on a single page. See Karl Josef Höltgen, 'Emblematic Title-Page and Brasses', in Karl Josef Höltgen, *Aspects of the Emblem: Studies in the English Emblem Tradition and the European Context* (Kassel: Edition Reichenberger, 1986), pp. 91–140. See also, in this book, Annelyse Lemmens's contribution (chapter 12).

80   "L'ardeur des croyances, la noblesse des caractères, les sévères exigences d'une profession honnorée, ses périls, la foi en l'immortalité de la pensée se traduisent à l'entour de la marque [...]. Ses légendes, expression intime de ces hommes souvent persécutés portent souvent l'empreinte d'une sorte de philosophie ascétique, d'un esprit de renoncement stoïque au profit de l'étude de la science, qui ajoutent beaucoup à l'intérêt de la marque.": *Essai typographique et bibliographique sur l'histoire de la gravure sur bois, faisant suite aux costumes anciens et modernes de César Vecellio* (Paris: Ambroise Firmind Didot, 1863), pp. 196–197.

A SURVEY AT THE HEART OF THE *EMBLEMATIC ERA* 203

TABLE 10.1 An attempt to systematically assess the influence between emblems and printers' marks in the Low Countries (16th–17th century)

Nr.	MARK[a]	EMBLEM[b]
1	 *Labore et Constantia* Christophe Plantin, Moretus Antwerp (1557–1866)	 Silvestro Pietrasanta, *De symbolis heroicis libri IX* ... (Antverpiae: Plantiniana B. Moreti, 1634) Emblem: *Labore et Constantia* 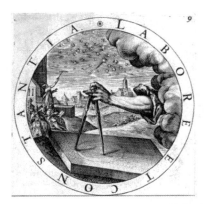 Gabriel Rollenhagen, *Gabrielis Rollenhagii selectorum emblematum centuria secunda* (Utrecht: Crispin van Pass, Arnhem: J. Janson, 1613) Emblem: *Labore et Constantia*

a The marks come from: Ferdinand van der Haeghen, *Marques typographiques des imprimeurs et libraires qui ont exercé dans les Pays Bas, et marques typographiques des imprimeurs et libraires belges établis à l'étranger* (2 vols. Ghent: C. Vyt, 1894); Peter van Huisstede and J.P.J. Brandhorst, *Dutch Printer's Devices. 15th–17th Century: A Catalogue* (3 vols., Nieuwkoop: De Graaf Publishers, 1999). To dating the activity of the printers: CERL Thesaurus on line (https://www.cerl.org/).
b For the emblems, we the Glasgow Library for the authorisation to publish.

TABLE 10.1 An attempt to systematically (*cont.*)

Nr.	MARK	EMBLEM
2	 *Virtuti Fortuna Comes* Jan (I) van Turnhout 's-Hertogenbosch (1527–1569) DPD, nr. 0858.  Chrestien Wechel  Paris (1495–1554) *Concordia Fructus* Pierre Bellère I Anvers (1562–1600)	 Andrea Alciato, *Emblematum libellus* (Paris: Chrestien Wechel, 1534) (USTC 185363) Emblem: *Virtuti Fortuna Comes*

TABLE 10.1 An attempt to systematically (cont.)

Nr.	MARK[a]	EMBLEM[b]
3	 Anthoni Maria Bergaigne Louvain (1552–1563)	 Andrea Alciato, *Livret des Emblemes* (Paris: Chrestien Wechel, 1536) (USTC 1056) Emblem: *Nec quaestioni quidem cedendum*
4	 *Fac et Spera* Cornelissz J. Braat Dordrecht (1643–1655)	 Gabriel Rollenhagen, *Gabrielis Rollenhagii Selectorum emblematum centuria secunda* (Utrecht: J. Janssonium, 1613). (USTC 1514844) Emblem: *Fac et Spera*

TABLE 10.1 An attempt to systematically (*cont.*)

Nr.	MARK	EMBLEM
5	 *Religio Christiana/ Religion Chrestienne* Bruyn Harmanszoon Schinckel Delft (1588–1625)	 Theodore de Bèze, *Emblemata* from his *Icones, id est verae imagines virorum doctrina simul et pietate illustrium* [...] *quibus adiectae sunt nonnullae picturae quas Emblemata vocant* (Geneva: Jean de Laon, 1580) EMBLEMA XXXIX.
6	 *Constantiam mihi Deus rebus malis des et bonis*[c] Jean Janssonius Arnhem (1588–1664) DPD 1637: Jacobsz Zoeteboom in Zaandam (from 1640); in Amsterdam Jacobsz Schipper (from 1639) and the bookseller Jan van Hilten (1626–1654)	 Georgette de Montenay, *Emblemes ou devises chrestiennes* (Lyon, Jean Marcorelle, 1567) (USTC 92436) Emblem: *Maxima non confundit justificat Christus*

---

c The reference to the Constancy appears in *Propter Constantiam* in *Devises et emblemes anciennes et modernes tirées des plus celebres Auteurs* (Amsterdam: Daniel de la Feuille, 1691).

TABLE 10.1   An attempt to systematically (*cont.*)

Nr.	MARK[a]	EMBLEM[b]
7	 *Summis Negatum Stare Divum* (Great things don't last forever) Jacques Boscard Douai (from 1563–1578)	 Georgette de Montenay, Emblemes ou devises chrestiennes (Lyons: Jean Marcorelle, 1567) Emblem: *Cui Gloria*  Gabriel Rollenhagen, *Nvclevs Emblematum Selectissimorum* (Cologne: de Pas; Arnheim: Jansson, 1611) (USTC 1506812) Emblem: *Non uno sternitur ictu*

TABLE 10.1 An attempt to systematically (*cont.*)

Nr.	MARK	EMBLEM
8	 *Cor rectum inquirit scientiam*[d] Jean Bogard Douai (from 1574)	 Gabriel Rollenhagen, *Nucleus emblematum selectissimorum* (Cologne: De Passe, 1611) Emblem: *Cor rectum inquirit scientiam*
9	 Pierre Auroy Douai (1602?–1631)	 Hadrianus Junius's *Emblemata* (Antwerp: Christophe Plantin, 1565) Emblem: *Quod in te est, prome*

---

d Guy De Tervarent, *Attributs et symboles dans l'art profane: Dictionnaire d'un langage perdu (1450–1600)* (Genève: Librarie Droz, 1997), p. 132) suggests to see in this motto a game of words: « Cor-rectum » (corrected) which is the ideal of a printer. A similar mark is used at the same time by other printers, in Lyon and in Rouen (see Silvestre, 417, 1128).

TABLE 10.1 An attempt to systematically (*cont.*)

Nr.	MARK	EMBLEM
10	 *Venena Pello* Balthazar Bellère 1 Douai (ca. 1590–1639; 1640)  IHS: *Monogram of the Society of Jesus*	 Paolo Giovio, Gabriele Simeoni, *Dialogo dell'imprese militari et amorose di monsignor Giovio, vescovo di Nocera : con un ragionamento di messer Lodovico Domenichi nel medesimo soggetto ...* (Lions: Guglielmo Roviglio 1559). Emblem: *Venena Pello*

TABLE 10.1 An attempt to systematically (*cont.*)

Nr.	MARK	EMBLEM
11	 Jean de Spire Douai (1643–1645)	 *Emblemata Politica : In aula magna Curiae Noribergensis depicta; Quae sacra Virtutum suggerunt Monita Prudenter administrandi Fortiterque defendendi Rempublicam, Petrus Iselburg Excudit* (Nürnberg: Peter Isselburg, 1617) (USTC 2055664) Emblem: *Spiritus, durissima coquit*
12	 *Semper in motu* Johannes Janssonius Amsterdam (1608–1664)	 Justus Amstelod Reifenberg, *Emblemata Politica* (Amsterdam: Johannes Janssonius, 1632) (USTC 1030558) Emblem: *Sic sphaera movetur*

A SURVEY AT THE HEART OF THE *EMBLEMATIC ERA* 211

TABLE 10.1 An attempt to systematically (*cont.*)

Nr.	MARK	EMBLEM
13	 Jean van Zuren Haarlem (1517–1591)	 Hadrianus Junius, *Emblemata* (Antwerp: Christophe Plantin, 1565) Emblem: *Boni adulterium*. (*Ad Ioannem Zurenum Harlem*)
14	 *Propinquior* Jooste van Colster Leiden (1614–1619)	 **Scipione Bargagli,** *La prima parte dell'imprese di Scipion Bargagli* ... (Venetia, Francesco de' Franceschi, 1589)[e] Emblem: *Propinquior*

e This impresa appears on the Title page, at the place of the printer's mark. Its meaning sums up the program of the book.

TABLE 10.1 An attempt to systematically (*cont.*)

Nr.	MARK	EMBLEM
15	 *Ardus qua Pulchra* Adrien van Wiyngaerden Leiden (1641–1673?)	 Barthélemy Aneau, *Picta poesis* (Lyons: Macé Bonhomme, 1552) (USTC 151179) Emblem: *Studiorum Contentio*
16	 *Qui va piano va sano/Paulatim* Jean van Gelder Leiden (1660–1683)	 *Devises et emblemes anciennes & modernes, tirâees des plus celebres auteurs, oder, Emblematische Gemèuths-Vergnèugungbey Betrachtung siben hundert und funffzehen der curieusesten und ergèotzlichen Sinn-Bildern, mit ihren zustèandigen teutsch-lateinisch-franzèosisch- und italianischen Beyschrifften* (Augspurg: Verlegs Lorentz Kroniger and Gottleib Gèobels, 1695) Emblem: *Paulatim, paulatim*

A SURVEY AT THE HEART OF THE *EMBLEMATIC ERA* 213

TABLE 10.1 An attempt to systematically (*cont.*)

Nr.	MARK	EMBLEM
17	 *Ars nutrit orbem perpetim* Hendrik Aertssens Antwerp (1612–1658)	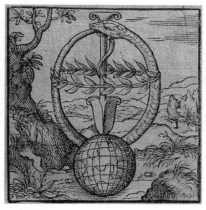 Hadrianus Junius, *Emblemata* (Antwerp: Christophe Plantin, 1565) Emblem: *Gloria immortalis labore parta*
18	 Martinus II and Philippus Nutius II Antwerp (1564–1586)	 *Devises et emblemes anciennes & modernes, tirâees des plus celebres auteurs, oder, Emblematische Gemèuths-Vergnèugungbey Betrachtung siben hundert und funffzehen der curieusesten und ergèotzlichen Sinn-Bildern, mit ihren zustèandigen teutsch-lateinisch-franzèosisch- und italianischen Beyschrifften* (Augspurg: Verlegs Lorentz Kroniger and Gottleib Gèobels, 1695) Emblem: *Dives Indoctus*

TABLE 10.1 An attempt to systematically (*cont.*)

Nr.	MARK	EMBLEM
19	 Jean van Brecht Bruxelles (1581–1587)	 Andrea Alciato's *Los Emblemas* (Lyons: Macé Bonhomme for Guillaume Rouille, 1549) Emblem: *Que qualquiera invençion es muy antigua*
20	 *His nititur Orbis* Jean et Luc van Meerbeeck Bruxelles (1622–ca. 1633)	 *Emblemata Politica* (Nürnberg: Peter Isselburg, 1617) Emblem: *His nititur Orbis*

TABLE 10.1 An attempt to systematically (*cont.*)

Nr.	MARK	EMBLEM
21	 *Ut Litterae immortalitate pari* Jean Van Waesberghe Antwerp (1561–1589) Rotterdam (1589–)	 Andrea Alciato, *Emblemata* (Lyons: Macé Bonhomme for Guillaume Rouille, 1550) Emblem: *Ex literarum studiis immortalitatem acquiri*
22	 *Studys Immortalitatem Acqvirimus* Dirck Dircksz Dordrecht (1643–1660)	 Andrea Alciato, *Les Emblemes* (Geneva/Cologny: Jean II de Tournes, 1615) Emblem: *De l'estude immortalité s'acquiert*

CHAPTER 11

The Counter-Reformation and Its Rebranding through Images: The Frontispieces of Books Printed in Antwerp

Annelyse Lemmens

No less excellent, pleasant and wonderful than the things seen above (in addition to others in this city), is the magnificent printing office of Christopher Plantin, King's Printer: his business is worthy of honour and memory, especially since we never seen one like this in Europe.[1]

∴

Questioning the impact of books and prints for the Catholic Reformation in the Low Countries cannot be made without evoking the importance of a city like Antwerp, both for its printing activity and its strategical position in the religious conflict. The 'Golden Age' the city enjoyed during the sixteenth century was in particular due to the vibrant harbour and commercial activities. In this context, the printing industry soon became prosperous, though, peculiarly, it attracted less an academic public than learned men of diverse horizons.[2]

---

1 "Moins excellente, agreable et merveilleuse que tout ce que dessus (outre d'autres moin-dres estant en ceste ville) n'est celle magnifique Imprimerie [...] par Christophle Plantin Imprimeur du Roy : l'entreprise duquel est digne de loz et mémoire, d'autant qu'on ne sçait point jusqu'à present on n'en voye de pareille en toute l'Europe", Lodovico Guicciardini, *Description de touts les Pais-Bas, autrement appelés la Germanie inferieure, ou Basse Allemagne* (Antwerp: Christophe Plantin, 1582), p. 170 (USTC 430657).

2 There was no university at Antwerp in the 16th century. About the diversity of books pub-lished in Antwerp, see Maurice Sabbe, *La vie des livres à Anvers aux XVIᵉ, XVIIᵉ et XVIIIᵉ siècles* (Brussels: Musée du Livre, 1926), pp. 5–94; Léon Voet, *L'âge d'or d'Anvers. Essor et gloire de la Métropole au seizième siècle* (Antwerp: Fonds Mercator, 1976), pp. 209–212; Werner Waterschoot, 'Antwerp: Books, Publishing and Cultural Production Before 1585', in *Urban Achievement in Early Modern Europe: Golden Ages in Antwerp, Amsterdam and London* (Cambridge: Cambridge University Press, 2001), pp. 233–248. On the more particu-lar influence of the religious freedom on the market, see Francine De Nave, 'La réforme et

---

© KONINKLIJKE BRILL NV, LEIDEN, 2023 | DOI:10.1163/9789004510159_012

THE COUNTER-REFORMATION AND ITS REBRANDING THROUGH IMAGES   217

Supported by the international traffic that flowed through the harbour and the influx of cosmopolitan traders in the city, the printers and publishers could sell their books in large quantities throughout a large part of the world. But what contributed the most to their international fame was their ability to produce books of exceptional quality both in their contents and in their appearance. Constantly challenged by the changing economic stakes, some printers began to specialise their production during the second part of the sixteenth century, as did, for instance, Christophe Plantin who made illustrated book his trademark.[3]

One of the masterpieces of the *Officina Plantiniana* is the *Descrittione di tutti i Paesi Bassi* by Lodovico Guicciardini (1521–1589), issued in 1581 in an Italian version and in 1582 in a French one.[4]

While the Florentine author became famous for his original work – his 'atlas', published in 1567, was the first detailed description of the Low Countries ever made – Plantin on the other hand distinguished himself thanks to the attention he paid to the quality of the images and the general presentation of the book. Already recognised as a fine printer, Plantin showed here his talents as a publisher by not simply reproducing the work of his predecessors but publishing his *Descrittione* in folio-size with engraved and etched images.[5] Though the emphasis on illustrations is what makes the greatness of this edition, the project was particularly ambitious due to the cost of the engravings and the

---

l'imprimerie à Anvers', *Bulletin de la Société d'Histoire du Protestantisme belge*, 10:3 (1985), pp. 85–94; Francine de Nave, Dirk Imhof and Gilbert Tournoy, *Antwerpen, dissident drukkerscentrum. De rol van de Antwerpse drukkers in de godsdienststrijd in Engeland (16de eeuw). Tentoonstelling in het Museum Plantin-Moretus te Antwerpen 1 Oktober-31 December 1994* (Heule: Snoeck, 1994).

3 In the 1570s, Christophe Plantin was one of the first amongst Antwerp's printers to publish books with engravings and etchings instead of woodblocks. See Karel Lee Bowen and Dirk Imhof, *Christopher Plantin and Engraved Book Illustrations in Sixteenth-Century Europe* (Cambridge: Cambridge University Press, 2008), p. 38.

4 Lodovico Guicciardini, *Descrittione di tutti i Paesi Bassi, altrimenti detti Germania Inferiore* (Antwerp: Christophe Plantin, 1581) (USTC 407847). The *editio princeps* was realized by Willem Silvius in 1567 (in Italian) (USTC 405351) and 1567 (in French) (USTC 27799).

5 Instead of reusing Silvius's woodblocks (as did Sebastian Henricpetri in his Basel's edition of 1580), Plantin ordered new engravings and etchings that fitted the large scale of the book. Despite the importance of images for this book, we do not know all the artists responsible for it. For instance, the first introductory plate – the allegory of the Low Countries – was designed by Crispin van den Broeck and engraved by Abraham de Bruyn. As the three other introductory pages are engravings too, some attribute them to the same artists. For the views of cities and maps, we can suppose the collaboration of Peeter van der Borcht, the circle of Frans Hogenberg of Cologne, and his assistants Ferdinand and Ambrosius Arsenius. See *PP*, nos. 1277–1278.

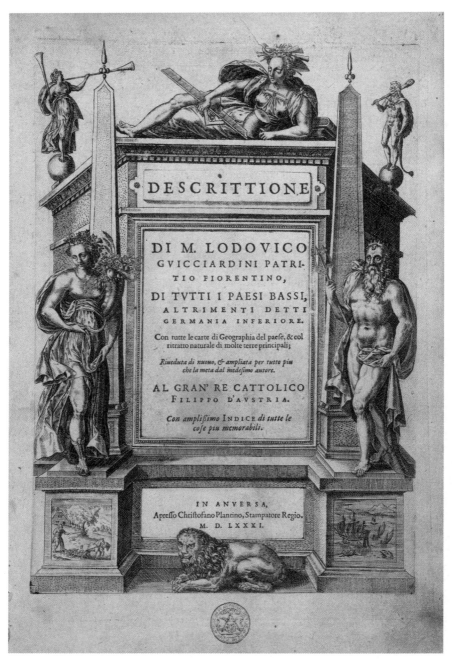

FIGURE 11.1 *Engraved title page*, Lodovico Guicciardini, *Descrittione di tutti i Paesi Bassi, altrimenti detti Germania Inferiore* (Antwerp: Christophe Plantin, 1581)
© PLANTIN MORETUS MUSEUM, ANTWERP, A1342

THE COUNTER-REFORMATION AND ITS REBRANDING THROUGH IMAGES 219

complicated context in which it had to be sold.[6] An attempt to optimise sales is doubtless the reason why Plantin marketed two different versions of the *Descrittione*, with and without plates, till 1582.[7] However, Plantin's project must have been above all connected to the expectations of the readers.[8]

In this regard, the four introductory plates play an important role in the reception of the book and the fame of the printer. The first image, an allegory of the Low Countries, gives a synthetic vision of the purpose of the book: as it is praised in the introductory poems, this composition highlights the benefits that the sea and the rivers bring to the country.

In this way, the page functions as a general summary of the purpose of the book and anticipated the conception of the frontispiece as defined much later.[9] The second engraving is a more classical title plate where the title is inserted in an architectural frame [Fig. 11.1]. This edifice gives the book directly a humanistic 'textura', rooted in the acceptation of the book as a monument dedicated to the author's memory and fame.[10] The personifications that are

---

6   The political and religious wars had affected the commercial activities in Antwerp by the end of the century. See Léon Voet, *The Golden Compasses. A History and Evaluation of the Printing and Publishing Activities of the Officina Plantiniana at Antwerp* (2 vols., Amsterdam: Vangendt – London: Routledge & Kegan Paul – New York: Abner Schram, 1969–1972), II. 459–460.

7   There was a significant difference in price between the variants: 7 guilders or 140 stuivers for the illustrated text; 2 guilders 10 stuivers, or 50 stuivers, for the text alone. Moreover, Christophe Plantin tried (unsuccessfully) to buy the former woodblocks used by Silvius in 1567 to prevent any other – cheaper – issue. See Bowen and Imhof, *Christopher Plantin*, pp. 198–199; Max Rooses & Jan Denucé (ed.), *Correspondance de Christophe Plantin* (9 vols., Antwerp: J.E. Buschman – Ghent: A. Hoste, 1883 [I]; Ghent: A. Hoste – The Hague: M. Nijhoff, 1885 [II]; Antwerp: De Nederlandsche Boekhandel – The Hague: M. Nijhoff, 1911–1918 [III–IX]), VI, no. 864; Maurice Van Durme, *La correspondance de Christophe Plantin. Supplément à la correspondance de Christophe Plantin* (Antwerp: De Nederlandsche Boekhandel, 1955), no. 149.

8   The customers of Plantin were local as well as international. To ensure his success, Plantin could rely on a network of booksellers across Europe. See Bowen and Imhof, *Christopher Plantin*, pp. 194–200, 208–210.

9   During the sixteenth and seventeenth centuries, the frontispiece was primarily considered as "the first page where stands the engraved title inserted in an image that represents the 'frontispiece' of a building", as defined in Antoine Furetière, *Dictionnaire universel contenant généralement tous les mots françois tant vieux que modernes et les termes de toutes les sciences et des arts* (3 vols., The Hague-Rotterdam: Arnout and Reinier Leers, 1690), II. 918. It is only from the nineteenth century that it will be defined as an engraving placed in front of title, which summarises the purpose of the book. Nevertheless, such engravings appear already in the seventeenth century. See Louis Marin, 'Les enjeux d'un frontispice', *Esprit créateur*, 27: 3 (1987), pp. 49–50.

10   On the ideal of the 'book as monument' during the humanist period and its legacy, see Albert Labarre, "Les incunables: la présentation du livre", in Roger Chartier and

FIGURE 11.2   *Frontispiece*, Lodovico Guicciardini, *Descrittione di tutti i Paesi Bassi, altrimenti detti Germania Inferiore* (Antwerp: Christophe Plantin, 1581)
© PLANTIN MORETUS MUSEUM, ANTWERP, A1342

THE COUNTER-REFORMATION AND ITS REBRANDING THROUGH IMAGES 221

placed on the architecture play also an important role in the support of the author, the book and the publisher. At the top, Geographia praises the greatness of the author, reinforced by the presence of a Gallic Hercules – who allies strength and virtue – and a representation of Fame. In the central part of the page, Ceres – left – and Neptune – right – are an allegorised vision of the content of the book: they translate the splendours of the Low Countries in the same manner as the first plate. It should be noted that the special use of personifications and deities in this engraving was an attempt to translate the special interest of an erudite readership who was attracted by their classical aura and their didactic capacity to evoke concepts.[11] The 'Leo Belgicus' that stands at the bottom of the page is another example, where the lion became a metaphor of the country, intentionally placed close to the address of the printer and publisher, and therefore lauded. The same reasoning applies to the last two engravings – two triumphal arches dedicated to the Seven Provinces and to Philip II of Spain – that ensured that Plantin's endeavour would be appreciated by the authorities.[12]

The introductory parts of the book and especially the frontispiece thus form a place of celebration dedicated to the text, its author and the printer-publisher. The frontispiece is also the privileged place of a strategy of action on the public in the service of a better reception of the text and a more pertinent reading.[13] Leaning from this experience, Catholic reformers not only used books as a means to deploy their thought but also explored the possibilities offered

---

Henri-Jean Martin (eds), *Histoire de l'édition française* (4 vols., Paris: Promodis, 1983–1986), I. 197; Olivier Deloignon, 'À la lumière des pages. Formes et fonctions de l'ornementation typographique au XVIᵉ siècle', in Ralph Dekoninck etc. (ed.), *Questions d'ornements. XVᵉ–XVIIIᵉ siècles* (Turnhout: Brepols, 2013), pp. 101–112; Anthony Grafton, *Commerce with the Classics: Ancient Books and Renaissance Readers* (Ann Arbor: University of Michigan Press, 1997), pp. 37–43; Otto Pacht, 'Notes and Observations on the Origins of Humanist Book Design', in Donald James Gordon (ed.), *Fritz Saxl. 1890–1948. A Volume of Memorial Essays from his Friends n England* (London: Thomas Nelson and Sons, 1957), pp. 184–194; Anne Réach-Ngo, 'De l'espace du livre à l'espace de l'œuvre: la consécration du fait littéraire à la Renaissance', in Alain Milon and Marc Perelman (eds), *Le livre et ses espaces* (Paris: Presses universitaires de Paris, 2007), pp. 63–84; Margaret M. Smith, *The Title-Page. Its Early Development. 1460–1510* (London: The British Library – New-Castle: Oak Knoll Press, 2000), pp. 15–23.

11   Elizabeth McGrath, 'Humanism, allegorical invention and the personification of the continents', in Arnout Balis, Carl Van de Velde and Hans Vlieghe (eds), *Concept, Design and Execution in Flemish Painting 1550–1700* (Turnhout: Brepols, 2000), p. 46.

12   Karen Lee Bowen and Dirk Imhof stressed the specific use of engraving for the four illustrations of the paratext, as their quality was a manner of strengthening the fame of the printer. See Bowen and Imhof, *Christopher Plantin*, p. 197.

13   Gérard Genette, *Seuils* (Paris: Seuil, 1987), pp. 7–8.

by frontispieces. It is all the more relevant given that Tridentine Reform gave unprecedented importance to images to the extent of setting them up as elements of distinction of the Roman Church. As it is often suggested, images were related to a lot of questions that were fundamental for Christian religion.[14] Nevertheless, the prime interest of the post-Tridentine communities was the 'power of images', in particular their rhetorical use. As Louis Richeome wrote in his treatise on images, "the things we hear can touch us gradually, the things we see can move us deeply"[15]: rather than value the pleasure of the eye, the images participate fully in the process of knowledge acquisition.[16] Capable of fixing the doctrine as well as making the dogmae a sensitive matter, they educated, helped remembrance, incited worship and supported meditation. Because of these functions, images were true allies of reform: they were tools

---

14   "La querelle des images renvoie à tant de questions fondamentales, comme l'Incarnation, la Présence réelle, le rôle de l'écriture et de la Prédication, les œuvres et les mérites, l'intercession des saints ou de la Vierge, qu'elle constitue très vite un excellent révélateur des choix confessionnels" ("The quarrel of images refers to so many fundamental questions, such as the Incarnation, the real Presence, the role of writing and preaching, works and merits, the intercession of saints or the Virgin, that it becomes very quickly an excellent indicator of denominational choices"), in Olivier Christin, 'La querelle des images au temps des Réformes', *Revue d'histoire moderne et contemporaine*, 43:2 (1996), p. 369. More widely, see Olivier Christin, *Une révolution symbolique. L'iconoclasme huguenot et la reconstruction catholique* (Paris: Les éditions de Minuit, 1991).

15   "Les choses que l'on oyt esmeuvent lentement. Les choses que l'on voit penetrent vivement", Louis Richeome, *Trois discours pour la religion catholique. Des miracles, des saincts, et des images* (Bordeaux: Simon Millanges, 1597), p. 483 (USTC 3690).

16   "Les images donc nous sont utiles, premierement pour la facile & preignante instruction, qu'elles nous donnent. La facilite est, que par leurs couleurs & lineaments exterieurs, en un clin d'oeil elles nous iettent dedans l'esprit la cognoissance de mile choses, qui ne pourroyent passer par l'oreille de long temps: car estant l'oeil un sens fort capable, & approchant de la vivacite de l'esprit, il regoit & comprend son obiet vistement, & tout a la fois, au lieu que les autres sens le tirent a parcelle, & par morceaux, & de tant plus tardivement, qu'ils sont plus bas & terrestres ... de la vient la peinture par ses couleurs & lineamens visibles, peut avec grande facilite instruire l'esprit" ("the images are thus useful, firstly for the easy and vivacious instruction they gave us. The ease is that, with their colours and shapes, they put in our mind the knowledge a thousand things that could not be remembered for a long time with the ears: because the eye is a sense with a high potential, and similar to the liveliness of the mind, it understands and receives his object quickly and at once, while the other senses understand only per parcel, per pieces and more slowly, because they are simpler and more earthly ... in this way painting, with its colours and visible lines, can easily educate the mind"), Louis Richeome, *Trois discours pour la religion catholique. Des miracles, des saincts, et des images* (Bordeaux: Simon Millanges, 1597), pp. 483–484 (USTC 3690).

THE COUNTER-REFORMATION AND ITS REBRANDING THROUGH IMAGES 223

that could imprint more deeply by impressing the senses or adding to the discourse the weight of emotions which enables a real conversion.[17]

The considerable promotion of the visual arts that accompanied the Catholic Reform was particularly striking in Antwerp where the efforts of the religious *Reconquista* affected politics interests and the needs of the commercial activities, at a crucial juncture. There, the necessity for the Roman Church to convert and strengthen the Catholic faith – Antwerp was indeed considered as the 'last bastion of Catholicism' – gave birth to numerous projects among which the refurnishing of churches and the reconstruction of buildings were maybe the most impressive.[18] During the reign of the Archdukes Albert and Isabella (1598–1621), the more forceful policy emphasised the potential impact of the printing industry.: It allowed for a more effective implementation of the Counter-Reformation in the Low Countries, and facilitated the launch of large projects that helped to revive the market of the book. In this way, as Brussels became the centre of political publishing, Antwerp became the centre of religious printing.[19] Moreover, the widespread installation of Jesuit colleges – from 1575 in Antwerp – encouraged the publication of textbooks and diverse books of devotion. The establishment of numerous orders in and around the city was also a source of renewal, while the reorganisation of the parishes under bishops Laevinius Torrentius (1587–1598) and Willem Van Bergen (1598–1601), and their support for the training of priests, was the mainspring for the publication of books of meditation, hagiographic narratives, or varied texts connected

---

17 The 25th session of the Council of Trent (1563) reaffirmed the legitimation of representations while asserting the necessity of appropriateness, suitability and clarity. For an analysis of this specific decree, see Antoine Fabre, *Décréter l'image ? La XXV* e *Session du Concile de Trente* (Paris: Les Belles Lettres, 2013). More generally, the influence of the Council on the use of images is discussed in Frédéric Cousinié, *Le peintre chrétien. Théories de l'image religieuse dans la France du XVII* e *siècle* (Paris: L'Harmattan, 2001), pp. 75–105.

18 Jos Andriessen, 'Rétablissement du catholicisme et Contre-Réforme', in Karel Van Isacker and Raymond Van Uytven (eds), *Anvers. Douze siècles d'art et d'histoire* (Antwerp: Fonds Mercator, 1986), p. 183. More widely, we can refer to the works of Marie Juliette Marinus, *De Contrareformatie te Antwerpen (1585–1676): kerkelijk leven in een grootstad* (Brussels: Koninklijke academie voor wetenschappen, letteren en schone kunsten van België, 1995) and Alfons K.L. Thijs, *Van Geuzenstad tot katholiek bolwerk. Maatschappelijke betekenis van de Kerk in de contrareformatorisch Antwerpen* (Turnhout: Brepols, 1990).

19 Peter C. Sutton, 'Les Pays-Bas espagnols', in Peter C. Sutton and Marjorie E. Wieseman (eds), *Le siècle de Rubens* (Antwerp: Fonds Mercator – Paris: Ludion, 1994), pp. 108–117; Werner Thomas, 'Andromeda Unbound. The Reign of Albert and Isabella in the Southern Netherlands, 1598–1621', in Werner Thomas and Luc Duerloo (eds), *Albert & Isabella. 1598–1621. Essays* (Turnhout: Brepols, 1998), pp. 1–13.

to the liturgy.[20] This bulk of activity especially affected printers who received commissions for editions of great literary 'monuments'.

1 The Catholic Reformation: Definition of the Roman Faith through the Printed Book

The establishment of a strong Catholic order in the Low Countries as well as throughout Europe was not a simple matter. Though the decisions taken at the Council of Trent were often elusive, they gave the first guidance for a redefinition of the Catholic faith. Against the protestants' 'sola scriptura' (and their strong philological bent), one of the first preoccupations of the papacy was to provide Catholic worship with unique tools, that is official liturgical books as well as an official version of the Bible. Along with papal inquiries, the works developed by the religious orders were nevertheless those that had the greatest impact on Catholic worship and its definition. The publishing of numerous texts dealing with theology was, of course, at stake. But the novelty lay in the edition of books specifically related to the education and devotion of the 'noviciates', then aimed at a more popular readership.[21] Every order had, of course, its own specificities, but they all embraced the Roman directives in terms of the contents and layout of the books.[22] Considering a microcosm such as Antwerp allows us to highlight the phenomena of emulation between these various orders (in particular in the visual aspects of the book) and thus help us to understand how a "catholic identity" could be built in the Low Countries.

The first step of this scheme consists in the legitimisation of the Roman position. With this in mind, several fundamental works were issued such as, for instance, the *Annales ecclesiastici* directed by Cesare Baronius (1538–1607),

---

20 Andriessen, 'Rétablissement du catholicisme', pp. 183–188; Thijs, *Van Geuzenstad tot katholiek bolwerk*, pp. 43–45.
21 Wilhelm Ribhegge, 'Counter-Reformation Politics, Society and Culture in the Southern Netherlands, Rhineland and Westphalia in the First Half of the 17th Century', *Humanistica Lovaniensia. Journal of Neo-Latin Studies*, 49 (2000), pp. 177–183.
22 Numerous bodies of control were set up in the context of the Counter Reformation. On this topic, see for instance Gigliola Fragnito (ed.), *Church, Censorship and Culture in Early Modern Italy* (Cambridge: Cambridge University Press, 2001); Jennifer Helm, *Poetry and Censorship in Counter-Reformation Italy* (Leiden: Brill, 2015) and André Puttemans, *La censure dans les Pays-Bas autrichiens* (Brussel: Librairie Falks Fils, 1935). On the layout of the book, our doctoral research on the frontispieces made in Antwerp between 1585 and 1650 show a clear standardisation of the models used from 1585 onwards.

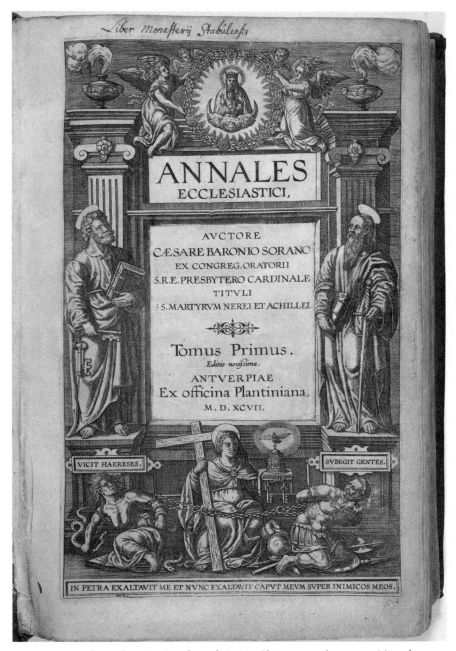

FIGURE 11.3   Cesare Baronio, *Annales ecclesiatici a Christo nato ad annum 1198* (12 vols., Antwerp: Officina Plantiniana, 1597–1607): engraved title page
© PLANTIN MORETUS MUSEUM, ANTWERP, 2–173.1

which consisted of twelve volumes that explored the history of the Church from its origins to 1198.[23]

The genesis of this monumental contribution was very long. Encouraged by Philip Neri (1515–1595), the original oral presentations of Baronius served as a basis for further research on the history of the Church.[24] Inspired by the philological works of the humanists, this required a time-consuming study of ancient texts whose purpose was to thwart the Protestant vision according to which Tradition was a degeneration of worship in apostolic times.[25] Describing history with scholarly methods was not only a way to fight Protestant heresy but also a means to give the Roman Church a strong and defendable basis. Started in the 1570s, the *Annales ecclesiastici* were finally printed by the Vatican Press upon the request of Pope Sixtus V in 1588. Its considerable success meant that it was reprinted, translated and summarised several times. Plantin's special interest in this work ensured that it was rapidly reprinted in Antwerp in 1589. This masterpiece then reached a larger readership particularly in the Netherlandish market where it became a weapon of choice to influence the mentalities and consciousness of contemporaries.[26]

The work's objectives are perfectly encapsulated in the frontispiece – the same plate was used for the editions of Rome and Antwerp – by the patterns used. Designed in Rome and signed 'M.G.F.', this image was structured by an architectural frame which was reminiscent of humanist practices: it was

---

23 Cesare Baronio, *Annales ecclesiastici a Christo nato ad annum 1198* (12 vols., Rome: Typographia Vaticana, 1588–1607) (USTC 812356).

24 The *Annales ecclesiastici* were undertaken under the inspiration of Philip Neri, when Baronius was still his assistant at the Congregation of the Oratory in Rome.

25 The *Annales ecclesiastici* were conceived as a reply to the *Centuriæ Magdeburgenses*, a set of thirteen volumes dedicated to the History of the Church. Redacted under the supervision of Mathias Flavius Illyricus – a fervent Lutheran – on the basis of trustworthy sources, these texts were used to legitimate Protestantism. This latter was presented as a restoration of the primitive Church, whereas the Roman Church appeared to be a gradual degeneration of the original worship. Ciriac K. Pullapilly, *Caesar Baronius. Counter-Reformation Historian* (London: University of Notre Dame Press, 1975), pp. 49–52; Manfred Sellink, '5. Caesar Baronius, Annales Ecclesiastici', in Francine De Nave (ed.), *The Illustration of Books Published by the Moretuses* (Antwerp: Plantin-Moretus Museum, 1996), p. 92; Giuseppe Scavizzi, *The Controversy on Images from Calvin to Baronius* (New York: Peter Lang, 1992), pp. 181–185.

26 The correspondence of Christophe Plantin indicates that the printer played an important role in the Antwerp's edition of the *Annales ecclesiastici*. So, as was the case in the context of the *Descriptio* of Guicciardini, the printer remained an important actor. See *Correspondance de Christophe Plantin*, nos. 1346, 1396–1397; Van Durme, *Supplément*, no. 208; Karen L. Bowen and Dirk Imhof, '18.257 Impressions of a Plate', *Print Quarterly*, 22:3 (2005), pp. 268–270. On the more general importance of historical publications for the Roman Church, see Ribhegge, 'Counter-Reformation Politics', pp. 179–180.

THE COUNTER-REFORMATION AND ITS REBRANDING THROUGH IMAGES   227

notably used for the corrected editions of ancient texts and then for some scholarly contributions, the architectural elements bringing the Classical 'textura' thanks to which the printed book acquired its dignity during the sixteenth century.[27] Indeed, through a process of adaptation of rhetorical rules to the order of the book, their appearance worked as a 'decorum' that reflected the ideal of suitability between the visual and the understandable. Therefore, the Classical aesthetic emphasised the prestigious status of the text and its correct use.[28] In the context of the Counter-Reformation, this humanistic legacy was, of course, revised because the goal was less to please the tastes of the supposed readership than to convince them of the authority of the Roman Church. Consequently, the frontispiece of the *Annales* preserved the rhetorical principle by which the text and its appearance were 'consubstantial'. This aura of the past nature of the text was further reinforced by the general structure of the image, the frame that underlined the limits of the text and gave it an appropriate space located beyond the margin.[29] As long as writing can preserve the spoken word from oblivion, the book perpetuates its content through the ages. As if it were a case, the 'book as object' protected and built the legitimacy of the text which, because it was in a different and unchanging reality, can lay claim to being an incontestable authority.[30] As if to reinforce the obviousness and the rightfulness of Catholic Tradition, the title plate also included some characters such as Peter and Paul who reminded the reader of the origins of the Church and Papacy. The personifications of Paganism and Heresy enchained at the bottom of the image seem to supervise the interpretation of historical facts described and commented inside the book. Finally, the representation of

---

27   Trying to restore the antique *bonæ litteræ*, the humanists used books as a means to educate their contemporaries and the future society. See Anthony Grafton, 'Le lecteur humaniste', in Guiglielmo Cavallo and Roger Chartier (eds), *Histoire de la lecture dans le monde occidental* (Paris: Seuil, 1997), pp. 239–240.

28   Grafton, 'Le lecteur humaniste', pp. 217–229; Rudolf Hirsch, *Printing, Selling and Reading. 1450–1550* (Wiesbaden: Otto Harrassowitz, 1974), pp. 72–73; Pacht, 'Notes and Observations', pp. 184–194; Smith, *The Title-Page*, pp. 15–23.

29   Victor Stoïchita, *L'instauration du tableau. Métapeinture à l'aube des temps modernes* (Geneva: Droz, 1999), pp. 87–88.

30   François Bougard, 'Mise en écriture et production documentaire en occident', in *L'autorité de l'écrit au Moyen Age (Orient – Occident)* (Paris: Publications de la Sorbonne, 2009), pp. 13–20; Llewellyn Brown, 'Espace du livre, espace du sujet', in Alain Milon et Marc Perelman (eds), *Le livre et ses espaces* (Paris: Presses universitaires de Paris, 2007), pp. 19–34; Michael T. Clanchy, *From Memory to Written Record. England 1066–1307* (Oxford: Blackwell, 1993), pp. 145–148; Henri-Jean Martin, *Histoire et pouvoir de l'écrit* (Paris: Albin Michel, 1996), pp. 84–91; Laurent Morelle, 'Usages et gestion de l'écrit documentaire (Occident, VIe–XIIe siècle): quelques considérations sur l'acte écrit', in *L'autorité de l'écrit*, pp. 117–126.

Ecclesia at the top of the frame works as a kind of visual dedication, asserting once more the greatness of the Roman Church.

Adopted in the context of religious publications, this type of frontispiece became a standard of Antwerp publishing activity. Another famous example can be found in the *Evangelicae historiae imagines* (1593) and the commentaries published under the title *Adnotationes et meditationes in Evangelia* (1594).[31]

Both composed by the Jesuit priest Jerónimo Nadal (1507–1580) and published posthumously, the *Evangelicae* and the *Meditationes* consist of 153 folio-size plates that narrate the life of Christ, and were completed by a set of spiritual exercises intended to guide the meditation of the votaries.[32] The complicated negotiations that accompanied the publication of this work certainly reveal its importance for the Jesuit order. Ignatius de Loyola himself was thought to have commissioned Nadal to make an 'evangelical instrument' where illustrations dominated content.[33] This interest in illustration concurred with the Tridentine commitment to sacred images as 'agents of spiritual reform'. However, these images raised problems in the process of publication because they required great precision and quality in their rendering.[34] Originally sketched in the 1560s by Nadal with the help of several artists, the models had been reworked several times, including at an advanced stage of the

---

31   Jerónimo Nadal, *Evangelicæ historiæ imagines ex ordine Evangeliorum, quæ tot anno in Missæ Sacrificio recitantur, in ordinem temporis vitæ Christi digestæ* (Antwerp: s.l., 1593) (USTC 402295); and Jerónimo Nadal, *Adnotationes et meditationes in Evangelia quæ in sacrosancto Missæ sacrificio toto anno leguntur* (Antwerp: Martinus Nutius, 1595) (USTC 413154).

32   Max Rooses, 'De plaatsnijders der Evangelicæ historiæ imagines', *Oud Holland*, 6 (1888), pp. 277–288; Adrien J.J. Delen, *Historie de la gravure dans les Anciens Pays-Bas & dans les Provinces Belges des origines jusqu'à la fin du XVIᵉ siècle. Deuxième partie. Le XVIᵉ siècle, les graveurs-illustrateurs* (Paris: De Nobele, 1969), pp. 150–155.

33   A letter of Nadal from 1573 attests that the author was already working on the project of the *Evangelicæ*. In 1575, it seems that the book was almost complete and a proof was sent to the Netherlands in 1576 for the printing. Due to the wars, this version was never printed and Nadal began a revision of the text from 1577 with the help of his assistant Zonhovius. The text was finally approved in 1579. Also, it is obvious that Nadal worked on the layout of the images from the beginning of the project. See Thomas Buser, 'Jerome Nadal and Early Jesuit Art in Rome', *The Art Bulletin*, 58 (1976), pp. 424–425; Maj-Brit Wadell, 'The *Evangelicæ historiæ imagines*: The Designs and their Artists', *Quaerendo*, 10 (1980), pp. 279–292.

34   The correspondence of Plantin shows how complicated the research of qualified engravers had been. It seems that for this reason, Plantin eventually abandoned the project. So, the Jesuits of Antwerp themselves payed for the publication of the *Evangelicae* (1593) – without any mention of place and printer. Then the *Adnotationes* were published in 1594 by Maarten Nutius. See Rooses, 'De plaatsnijders', pp. 277–288.

FIGURE 11.4 Jerónimo Nadal, *Evangelicae historiae imagines ex ordine Evangeliorum, quae tot anno in Missae Sacrificio recitantur, in ordinem temporis vitae Christi digestae* (Antwerp: s.l., 1593): frontispiece
© PLANTIN MORETUS MUSEUM, ANTWERP, A 3808

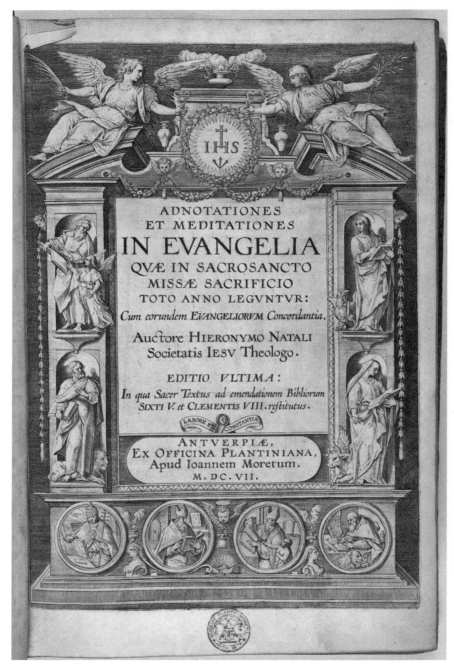

FIGURE 11.5   Jerónimo Nadal, *Adnotationes et meditationes in Evangelia quae in sacrosancto Missae sacrificio toto anno leguntur* (Antwerp: Martinus Nutius, 1595): engraved title page
© PLANTIN MORETUS MUSEUM, ANTWERP, A 555

THE COUNTER-REFORMATION AND ITS REBRANDING THROUGH IMAGES 231

publishing process, which certainly reflects the caution of the Jesuits toward images.[35]

It was also in the context of the publication process that the two frontispieces – for the *Evangelia* and the *Adnotationes* – were designed. Indeed, this kind of 'paratext' was above all an element linked to the work of the publisher rather than an initiative that came from the author, a least in the sixteenth century. We do not know exactly who was responsible for the design of these two images, but we can assert that they were made expressly for this project under, certainly, the supervision of the Jesuit authorities given the attention they paid to the illustration. For the *Evangelicae*, the publishing project of 1586 contained a preparatory sketch for the frontispiece, which had been finally reworked by Maarten de Vos and engraved by Hieronymus Wierix.[36] Unsurprisingly, this frontispiece contained an architectural frame as already seen in the example of the *Annales* of Baronius. Nevertheless, instead of the title – here located at the bottom of the structure –, the centre of the image featured a representation of the Christ in a manner that reminds us of the monumental altars that became popular during the Counter-Reformation. Similarly, the *Adnotationes* adopted an architectural structure that surrounded the title and, in this fashion, underlined the limits of the sacred and places it at the right distance from the beholder.[37] The addition of side characters – the Evangelists on the left and right and the four Fathers of the Church at the bottom – reinforces the orthodoxy of the text: the great figures invoked are the trustees of the Apostolic Tradition and their presence attests to the text conformity with their teaching. Therefore, as with the example of Baronius, the frontispiece does not only express the sacred *ethos* of text and book – as with humanist practices; it also uses the 'teaching power' of images to convince the reader of the sacred nature

---

35 The first sketches were made with the help of Livio Agresti, then reworked and completed by Giovanni Battista Fiammeri. During the years 1580, the models were reworked by Bernardino Passeri. Wadell, 'The *Evangelica historiæeae imagines*', pp. 279–292.

36 Marie Mauquoy-Hendrickx, 'Les Wierix illustrateurs de la Bible dite de Natalis', *Quaerendo*, 6 (1976), pp. 28–34.

37 We do not have any information about the genesis of the frontispiece of the *Adnotationes*. Nevertheless, the use of niches and medals to insert the characters suggests a Netherlandish conception; instead of large figures as we find in the example of Baronius, the evangelists are placed in niches and the four Fathers of the Church in medals. This structure can be linked to the altars that we still find at the end of the sixteenth century in Antwerp. Also, the collaboration of the Wierix brothers for the engraving of the plates in the book and the similarity with some following realisations could indicate their contribution. See for instance the frontispiece of Henricus Adriani, *Niewe legende oft d'leven, wercken, doot, ende miraculen ons liefs heeren Iesu Christi met sijn lieve heylighen* (Antwerp: Hieronymus Verdussen and Ian Van Keerberghen, 1593) (USTC 413066).

and orthodoxy of the text. In this way, the figures of the saints placed on the architecture must be understood as arguments which assert from the very first page the process of rhetorical demonstration.

2   The Conquering Image During the Early Seventeenth Century:
      Jan David's *œuvre*

The slow transfer of the frontispiece from the position of an 'exordium' – which gives a positive message to the reader – to that of an introduction or preface met with particular success within the framework of the polemical literature that flourished from the beginning of the seventeenth century. Indeed, the proximity of Antwerp to Protestant territories and the need for Catholic authorities to strengthen the Roman faith made the fight against heretics all the more important. This focus on a common enemy that reinforced the cohesion of Catholic ranks was relayed by clerical activities such as catechism and preaching. Moreover, the involvement of publishers, artists and authors in the Chambers of Rhetoric created in Antwerp a microcosm where a more 'constructed' criticism could emerge.[38] One of the main protagonists of this trend was Jan David (1545–1613), a Jesuit father engaged on multiple grounds: polemicist, preacher and teacher, his written work is as considerable as it is varied.[39] More specifically, he is recognised as the initiator of the Jesuit emblematical literature of the Southern Low Countries.[40]

His first success was the *Veridicus Christianus*, an illustrated catechism published in Antwerp in 1601.[41]

---

38   Arie-Jan Gelderblom, Jan De Jong and Marc Van Vaeck (eds), *The Low Countries as a Crossroads of Religious Beliefs* (Leiden: Brill, 2004), pp. 44–45.

39   L. Geerts-van Roey and Jos Andriessen, 'Pater Joannes David s.j. (1546–1613)', *Ons Geestelijk Erf*, 30 (1956), pp. 113–155; Roger Mols, 'David Jan', in *Dictionnaire d'histoire et de géographie ecclésiastiques* (32 vols., Paris: Letouzey et Ané, 1912–2018), xiv, col. 1485–1490. For the bibliography of Jan David, see Ferdinand Van der Haeghen, *Bibliotheca Belgica. Bibliographie Générale des Pays-Bas* (2nd ed., 7 vols., Brussels: Culture et civilisation, 1964–1975), ii. 69–74. For an analysis of the polemical works of David, see Jos Andriessen, *De Jezuïeten in de Nederlanden en het Prinsbisdom Luik (1542–1773)* (Brussels: Brussel Algemeen Rijksarchief, 1991), pp. 149–151.

40   The Jesuits generally used the 'ars symbolica' for its large audience, especially in the context of education and predication. See Ralph Dekoninck, '*Ad imaginem*'. *Statuts, fonctions et usages de l'image dans la littérature spirituelle jésuite du XVIIe siècle* (Genève: Droz, 2005), p. 287; Anne-Elisabeth Spica, 'L'emblématique jésuite', *XVIIe siècle*, 237 (2007:4), pp. 633–639.

41   Jan David, *Veridicus Christianus* (Antwerp: Jan Moretus I, 1601) (USTC 1009429). The Latin edition of 1601 was followed by a Dutch edition in 1602 under the title *Christelijcken*

FIGURE 11.6 Jan David, *Veridicus Christianus* (Antwerp: Officina Plantiniana, 1601): engraved title page
© KATHOLIEKE UNIVERSITEIT LEUVEN, LEUVEN, BRES-R5A14986

234   LEMMENS

While this book is often described as an emblem book, the images were generally used as a pedagogical tool. If it is true that the general layout of the pages recalls that of the *emblema triplex*, the images only play a descriptive and synthetic role that help the reader to memorise the text and its purpose. The latter is developed in a classic dialectical way where chapters successively describe the heretics, the good Christian and then a sum of Christian truths that will help the reader to strengthen his faith. Presented as a shield which could reach the 'comprehending readers' as well as the 'ruder minds',[42] the *Veridicus Christianus* opens on a frontispiece which can, in turn, summarise the entire scope of the work by illustrating the Psalm 34.12: "Come, my children, listen to me; I will teach you the fear of the Lord". Far from forgetting the architectural tradition and the use of exempla – here David and John the Baptist – Jan David brings to the foreground the teaching dimension of the image: while its visual display unveils the presence of the 'monument', the scene represented addresses more thoroughly the intellect of the reader-viewer and thus gives him an overall understanding of the book.

A couple of years later, Jan David pursued his catechetical work with the publication of a second emblem book, the *Occasio arrepta, neglecta*, where he managed to convert a pagan idol (*Occasio*) into a personification of Opportunity, the occasion of doing good.[43]

Inscribed in the continuity of the *Veridicus Christianus*, this book must be understood as an invitation to become a true follower of Christ that means seizing every opportunity of imitating him. Indeed, the original school play describes in twelve parts the meeting of a group of youths with Time and Opportunity and their fate according to the attitude they show towards the latter – Salvation for the *prudentes* and Damnation for the *imprudentes*. For the purpose of the book, David transformed the parts of the play into twelve chapters. Each of them opens with an engraving that summarises the argument developed afterward in the written commentary; each chapter then concludes with an *oratio* fitting the meditative purpose of the book. Besides the

---

Waerseggher. De principale stucken van t'Christen Geloof en leuen int cort begrijpende (Antwerp: Jan Moretus I, 1602) (USTC 1035931).

42   The preface to the reader explains the author's thought: 'so that the comprehending reader could catch the text with the eye, whereas the incapable and ruder minds at any rate could watch it by view'. The English translation can be found in Werner Waterschoot, 'Veridicus Christianus and Christeliicken Waerseggher by Joannes David', in Ralph Dekoninck and Agnès Guiderdoni (eds.), '*Emblemata sacra'. Rhétorique et herméneutique du discours sacré dans la littérature en images* (Turnhout: Brepols, 2007), p. 528.

43   Jan David, *Occasio arrepta, neglecta, huius commoda, illius incommoda* (Antwerp: Jan Moretus I, 1605) (USTC 1003460).

FIGURE 11.7 Jan David, *Occasio arrepta, neglecta, huius commoda, illius incommoda* (Antwerp: Officina Plantiniana, 1605): engraved title page
© PLANTIN MORETUS MUSEUM, ANTWERP, A 1205

introduction of a narrative frame, the development of the subject is similar to that of the *Veridicus*, with a dual presentation of the Good and the Bad, followed by some Christian Truth. The images are used to help the reader-viewer to memorise, meditate and enliven the 'lesson'.[44]

The use of literal illustrations perfectly matches the informative and educational powers that were given to images in the context of the Counter-Reformation. Furthermore, the pleasing collaboration of the author with the engraver Theodoor Galle (1571–1633) allowed the creation of a frontispiece that not only reveals the existence of a valuable book – by the use of a traditional architectural frame, as in the example of the *Descrittione* of Guicciardini – but also describes the content and makes it understandable. The portal surrounding the title is covered by roundels and panel-like sections that comment and diffract the subject. On both sides, the panels show a literal representation of *Occasio* seized (at the left) and shirked (at the right). Following the logic of amplification, the tree roundels on top of the page detail the idea of the seized opportunity, which is doing the right thing (*Occasio rei*) at the right place (*Occasio loci*) and at the right moment (*Occasio temporis*). As an antithesis, the panel at the top illustrates the rout of the Psylli, having selected the wrong time, place and course of action.[45] In the lower parts of the image, the representation of Jael killing Sisera on the left (Judges, 4.18–22) and, as a counterpoint on the right, a view of an unguarded citadel still expounds the binomial opportunity seized-missed. In conclusion, the two little panels inserted at the bottom of the page still insist on the "benefits of occasion seized" (*Occasionis arreptae commoda*) through an allegory of abundance and the "misfortunes of missed opportunity" (*Incommoda neglectae [occasionis]*).

---

44   The engravings used in the *Occasio* were first published without the text under the title *Typvs occasionis in qvo receptæ commoda, neglectæ vero incommoda, personato schemate proponvntvr* (Antwerp, Theodoor Galle, 1603) (USTC 1008752). Intended for Jesuit collegians, they were used at first as support for play and were then enriched by texts in the context of the *Occasio's* publication. Peter M. Daly and G. Richard Dimler, *Corpus Librorum Emblematum. The Jesuit Series* (Toronto: University of Toronto Press, 2005), I. 151, no. 145A; Dekoninck, *Ad imaginem*, pp. 296; Walter Melion, 'Figured Personification and Parabolic Embodiment in Jan David's *Occasio arrepta, neglecta*', in Walter Melion and Bart Ramakers (eds), *Personification. Embodying meaning and emotions* (Leiden: Brill, 2016), pp. 371–432; Manuel Insolera and Lydia Salviucci Insolera, *La spiritualité en images aux Pays-Bas méridionaux dans les livres imprimés des XVIe et XVIIe siècles* (Leuven: Peeters, 1996), pp. 145–147.

45   According to Herodotus, the Psylli were a Libyan tribe which suffered from the aridity of their country. Having held council, they decided to go to war, but they were caught by the wind and swallowed up by the sand. Herodotus, *Histoires* (10 vols., Paris: Les Belles Lettres, 1932–1955), IV. *Melpomène* (transl. Ph.-E Legrand), no. 173, p. 183.

THE COUNTER-REFORMATION AND ITS REBRANDING THROUGH IMAGES 237

The frontispiece warns the transitory aspect of opportunity; however, it does not mention the integration of the theme in the spiritual journey of the reader as the general preface precise it.[46] Despite this gap, the image puts a hermeneutic to the text as it defines and explains the general purpose of the book. The use of an "inlaid" architecture certainly addresses a Flemish sensibility already noticed in the frontispiece of the Nadal's *Adnotationes*. Nevertheless, the use of compartmentalised spaces serves here the specific understanding of the book.

3 Conclusion

The period of the implementation of the Counter-Reformation in the Low Countries was marked by the translation of the triumphal architectures that made the greatness of the humanist books to the religious sphere. As it appeared to initially be a Roman initiative, it was quickly adopted by local religious groups and artists. This reinforces what Paul Philippot wrote about the structure of the altars as they appeared after the Council of Trent:

> the forms imported from Italy [...] spread as demonstrative signs of allegiance to Rome. They mark the expression of a kind of *imprimatur* onto the frontispieces of books, they express Roman orthodoxy at the entrance of reorganized churches, but also at the entrance of the Beguine convents, they represent a sign of access to Faith, to modes of devotion as well as the modes of knowledge that the Church agreed on.[47]

The success of this Roman 'fashion' rests not only on the earning of a visual model able to highlight the inner nature of the text. It also concerns the use of images as 'tools' that can 'speak' for themselves. Images can take part in the discourse developed through the text: at first, personifications and biblico-historical characters were thus used as means to resume the general goals of the author – fighting heresy, legitimate Tradition or reunite the reader

---

46 Jan David, *Occasio*, fols. 2–3 [*praefatio ad lectorem*]. Walter Melion gave a translation of this particular purpose of the book: "to behave fitly, according to condition and degree, lest they neglect the God-given occasion of doing what is right; and so, in this explanation of *Occasio*, it seemed appropriate to construe each of the pictorial *schemata* in such a way as to be useful to every single person", in Melion, 'Figured personnification', p. 388.

47 Paul Philippot, Denis Coekelberghs, Pierre Loze and Dominique Vautier, *L'architecture religieuse et la sculpture baroques dans les Pays-Bas méridionaux et la principauté de Liège. 1600–1770* (Liège: Pierre Mardaga, 2003), p. 35.

with the Truth of Evangelical Times. Like this, in a complicated context of political and religious transformations, the book contributes to the revaluation of the laws of society and, instead of being a means of enacting transmission, becomes a basis for the new or renewed identities.[48]

The 'second' moment of the Catholic Reform stands out by the development of more and more descriptive frontispieces. If they generally conform to the first *imprimatur* of the Roman Church, they took advantage of the inner possibilities of images, which was to show the deep meaning of the text and the book thanks to the immediacy of sight. The frontispiece became therefore a true visual preface that embodied the classical 'introductio' of a speech, where the matter was not only to put the reader in a specific state of mind before the reading, but also to introduce the reader to the dynamic of reading through a visual device that describes the theme. In this way, the use of an 'emblematical mode'[49] allowed the creation of a space where the several functions of the frontispiece meet, drawing attention, arousing interest, creating a desire and finally pushing to take action.

---

48   Benito Pelegrìn, 'Le Baroque et l'infini. Architectures de l'esprit, édifications de l'âme', in Sebastian Schütze [first name of the editor] (ed.), *Estetica Barocca* (Rome: Campisano, 2004), pp. 47–59. This question is more widely treated in the book of Peter Burke, *A Social History of Knowledge from Gutenberg to Diderot* (Cambridge: Polity, 2000).

49   On the 'emblematical mode', see Peter Maurice Daly, 'Modern Advertising and the Renaissance Emblem Modes of Verbal and Visual Persuasion', in Karl Josef Höltgen, Peter M. Daly and Wolfgang Lottes (eds), *Word and Visual Imagination. Studies in the Interaction of English literature and the Visual Arts* (Erlangen: Universitätsbund Erlangen-Nürnberg, 1988), p. 350.

CHAPTER 12

Thesis Prints Dedicated to Archduke Leopold William of Austria, in the Service of the *Pietas Austriaca*

Gwendoline de Mûelenaere

1 Introduction

The Habsburg dynasty, which ruled the Southern Netherlands in the Early Modern period, governed in accordance with the principles of the *Pietas Austriaca*. These principles included the adoration of the Virgin Mary, the veneration of the Holy Cross, the Saints and the Eucharist, and the affirmation of Christian virtues. The expression *Pietas Austriaca*, from Baroque literature, was chosen as the title of a foundational study published by Anna Coreth in 1959.[1] The author gives the following definition of the term: "*Pietas Austriaca* was the piety – understood as a virtue of rulers – of the house of Austria's sovereigns of both the German and Spanish lines. The special meaning of this term was based on the conviction that God had given the house of Austria a certain mission for the empire and the church, because of the religious merits of its ancestors, or, more particularly, of the great ancestor Rudolph of Habsburg".[2] *Pietas Austriaca* does not refer to Austria as a geopolitical concept, but rather, it relates to the House of Austria. The term denotes the religious and political ideology according to which the strictly Catholic Habsburgs governed one of the largest empires in Europe.

In the introduction to Coreth's book, William Bowman insists on the fact that "*Pietas Austriaca*, with its strong belief in the real power and presence of the divine in religious practices and persons, was 'the' guiding principle of the Habsburgs. In other words, Habsburg rulers did not engage in acts of piety primarily as public rituals (although they certainly were that as well), but because they genuinely believed in the political and even military efficacy of performing these acts".[3] Far more than being just a propagandist instrument

---

1 Anna Coreth, *Pietas Austriaca* (West Lafayette: Purdue University Press, 2004).
2 Coreth, *Pietas Austriaca*, p. XXII.
3 William D. Bowman 'Introduction', in Coreth, *Pietas Austriaca*, p. XII.

© KONINKLIJKE BRILL NV, LEIDEN, 2023 | DOI:10.1163/9789004510159_013

240 DE MÛELENAERE

of symbolic or rhetorical effects in the eyes of the Habsburg monarchy, *Pietas Austriaca* played a significant role, from Rudolph I onwards, in establishing the family's political legitimacy and in reinforcing its sovereignty.[4] The monarchs acted as advocates of faith with the intention of gathering together the multiple territories to be ruled in a "religious and well-disciplined unity".[5] *Pietas Austriaca* resulted in the progressive establishment of an iconographic tradition based, among other things, on legends[6] and historical events, on religious practices and on respect for Christian virtues,[7] as well as on the recycling of characters and episodes from classical mythology and literature, adapted to the Catholic Faith.[8]

Although *Pietas Austriaca* is expressed under varied guises and in diverse contexts, it is nonetheless necessary to identify the personal intentions of prominent representatives of this particular form of intensely visible piety.[9] The ceremonial prints dedicated to Archduke Leopold William of Austria,

---

4 Bowman 'Introduction', in Coreth, *Pietas Austriaca*, p. XIII.

5 Vesna Cunja Rossi, *I Gesuiti, Trieste e gli Asburgo nel Seicento* (Trieste: Minerva, 2005), p. 109.

6 For instance, according to the dynastic legend, the origins of the Habsburgs' success date back to an episode in the life of Rudolph, Count of Habsburg, who is reported to have demonstrated his piety by giving his mount to a priest holding the viaticum.

7 For example, Werner Telesko studied the iconography of an illustrated broadsheet designed around the figure of Ferdinand II. Dating from 1636, the illustration stages the veneration of the Holy Cross. Telesko notes the recurrence of some characteristic features within the imperial iconography. Those 'fixed components' are among other items borrowed from the catalogue of virtues of Ferdinand II, as recorded by Wilhelm Lamormaini in 1638 (Werner Telesko, 'Transmediality in Early Modern Printmaking in the Example of a Broadsheet on Emperor Ferdinand II (1578–1637)', in Federico Italiano and Michael Rössner (eds), *Translation: Narration, Media and the Staging of Differences* (Bielefeld: Transcript Verlag, 2012), p. 149).

8 An essay by Marie Tanner shows the many ways the Habsburgs tried to link their past to their present situation and employed historical events to consolidate their political position by laying claim, in this case, to the glory of Ancient Rome. See Marie Tanner, *The Last Descendant of Aeneas: the Hapsburgs and the Mythic Image of the Emperor* (New Haven: Yale University Press, 1993).

9 Werner Telesko, 'The Pietas Austriaca. A Political Myth? On the Instrumentalisation of Piety towards the Cross at the Viennese Court in the Seventeenth Century', in Herbert Karner, Ingrid Ciulisovà and Bernardo J. Garcia Garcia (eds), *The Habsburgs and Their Courts in Europe, 1400–1700. Between Cosmopolitism and Regionalism* (Louvain: KU Leuven, 2014), p. 177, note 2. For instance, Luc Duerloo has shown how Archduke Albert expressed the *Pietas Austriaca* throughout his regency of the Low Countries: Luc Duerloo, 'Pietas Albertina. Dynastieke vroomheid en herbouw van het vorstelijke gezag', *Bijdragen en mededelingen betreffende de geschiedenis der Nederlanden*, 112 (1997), pp. 1–18; 'Archducal Piety and Habsburg Power', in Thomas Werner and Luc Duerloo (eds), *Albert and Isabella (1598–1621)*. *Essays* (Turnhout: Brepols, 1998), pp. 267–283.

IN THE SERVICE OF THE PIETAS AUSTRIACA 241

governor of the Spanish Low Countries from April 1647 to May 1656, seem
particularly relevant in this matter, since they use piety and Christian virtues to affirm princely authority.[10] This paper will investigate thesis prints,
whose tradition appeared at the end of the sixteenth century and developed
in seventeenth-century Europe. These illustrated broadsheets and booklets
were printed within the framework of academic disputations in universities
or in Jesuit colleges and summarised the conclusions to be defended. Such a
practice needs to be considered within the broader context of the Catholic
reconquest of the minds, a core mission of the institutions of higher education
in the Southern Netherlands. The prints abound in personifications, attributes, symbols, emblems, *imprese*, sacred figures or portraits of prestigious
ancestors, *exempla* and textual insertions. This essay will examine more specifically how these languages of various kinds were used as modes of transmission for political and religious messages, beyond the academic subject in the
strictest sense.

2   **Leopold William of Austria, Military Commander and 'Vir Sapiens'**

Leopold William of Austria (Graz 1614–Vienna 1662) was the son and brother
of the Emperors Ferdinand II and Ferdinand III, respectively. Raised at the
court of Spain, Leopold William was devoted to following an ecclesiastical career. Between 1625 and 1655, he was invested with several bishoprics
(Passau, Strasbourg, Halberstadt, Olomouc, and Wrocław). In 1642, he was
nominated Grandmaster of the Teutonic Order. This pious man remained
very attached to the Company of Jesus throughout his entire life, and this
earned him the reputation of being a Prince of the Church. Later, Leopold
William became military commander of the imperial army when he was
called upon to take up this position by his brother in 1639, during the period
of the Thirty Years' War. After his troops had suffered a series of defeats,
Leopold William took on the regency of the Southern Low Countries, in the
name of Philip IV. On the eve of the Peace of Westphalia, the war against
the Northern Provinces was not the Archduke's priority. His focus was on
fighting against France, and he won several military victories between 1647

---

10   An exhibition catalogue dedicated to the Archduke in 2003 contains several of those
       prints: Jozef Mertens and Franz Aumann (eds), *Krijg en kunst. Leopold Willem (1614–1662),
       Habsburger, landvoogd en kunstverzamelaar* (Bilzen: Landcommanderij Alden Biesen,
       2003).

FIGURE 12.1 Cornelis II Galle, *Portrait of Archduke Leopold William of Austria crowned by two angels*, ca. 1652. Engraving, 26,7 × 17 cm
© RIJKSMUSEUM, AMSTERDAM, RP-P-1904-380

IN THE SERVICE OF THE PIETAS AUSTRIACA 243

and 1652. However, the lack of financial support from Spain prevented him from succeeding in his undertaking. Finally, Leopold William gave up his role of governor of the Southern Low Countries on 9 May 1656 and returned to Vienna.

In 1645, the political and economic situation of the Spanish Low Countries was significantly weakened by the ongoing conflicts. Leopold William's arrival in Brussels in 1647 therefore provided hope to the population.[11] Once there, the Archduke gave a new impulse to the production of courtly art and he built a major collection of paintings,[12] which today forms the core of the Kunsthistorisches Museum in Vienna.[13] The abundant graphic production – thesis prints,[14] emblematic exhibitions (*affixiones*) of pupils in Jesuit colleges,[15]

---

11 Karel Porteman, *Emblematic Exhibitions (affixiones) at the Brussels Jesuit College (1630–1685). A Study of the Commemorative Manuscripts (Royal Library, Brussels)* (Turnhout: Brepols, 1996), p. 104.

12 Among the extensive literature on this subject, the following references may be consulted: Adolf Berger, 'Inventar der Kunstsammlungen des Erzherzogs Leopold Wilhelm von Osterreich', *Jahrbuch der kunsthistorischen Sammlungen des Allerhochsten Kaiserhauses*, 1 (1883), part 2, pp. LXXIX–LXXXV; Margret Klinge and Ernst Van Claerbergen (*et al.*), *David Teniers and the Theatre of Painting* (London: Paul Holberton, 2006); Renate Schreiber, *"Ein Galeria nach meinem Humor": Erzherzog Leopold Wilhelm* (Vienna: Kunsthistorisches Museum, 2004); Barbara Welzel, 'David Teniers II and Archduke Leopold Wilhelm', in Katlijne Van der Stighelen (ed.), *Munuscula amicorum: Contributions on Rubens and his Colleagues in Honour of Hans Vlieghe* (Turnhout: Brepols, 2006), pp. 631–644.

13 When Leopold William left for Vienna in 1656, his collection consisted of 517 Italian paintings and 880 Flemish and German Old Master paintings. See Marleen Forrier, *Autour de J. Brueghel l'Ancien, P.P. Rubens, A. Van Dyck: l'art et les artistes aux Archives de l'État* (Brussels: Archives Générales du Royaume, 1999), p. 94.

14 Leopold William himself defended a thesis, as indicated by the list of books he owned, drawn up in 1647 (n° 486): *Exercitatio Physica diffensa a Ser.^{mo} Archiduca Leopoldo Guilielmo. Tom. 2*. This indicates that the Archduke was acquainted with this academic practice. The inventory of his library also cites another thesis (n° 609): *Duodecim Conclusiones Christianae Philosophiae* (Gottfried Mraz and Herbert Haupt, 'Das Inventar der Kunstkammer und der Bibliothek des Erzherzogs Leopold Wilhelm aus dem Jahre 1647', *Jahrbuch der Kunsthistorischen Sammlungen in Wien*, 77 (1981), pp. XXXIX and XLI). I am grateful to Grégory Ems for bringing this source to my attention.

15 Karel Porteman noted that the peak of *affixiones* in the Brussels College was reached under the rule of Archduke Leopold William, (Porteman, *Emblematic Exhibitions*, p. 28). Of the nine Jesuit exhibitions organized during the government of Leopold William, four were dedicated to him: those of 1647, 1649, 1650, and 1651 (Grégory Ems, *L'emblématique au service du pouvoir. La symbolique du prince chrétien dans les expositions emblématiques du collège des Jésuites de Bruxelles sous le gouvernorat de Léopold-Guillaume (1647–1656)* (2 vols, Louvain-la-Neuve: Presses universitaires de Louvain, 2016), I. 11).

ceremonial engravings,[16] frontispieces of books, portraits, etc.– which was dedicated to Leopold William, reveals a strong military context. The Archduke himself is systematically depicted in armour, holding a staff of command and wearing the cross of Grandmaster of the Teutonic order. All these documents, frequently related to contemporary events, testify to the high expectations raised by the Archduke's politics and military operations against France. They represent a real *propaganda* in his favour, promulgated by the Jesuits, among others.[17]

Eight thesis engravings addressed to the governor during his rule are documented.[18] All of them were conceived and executed on behalf of students belonging to the aristocracy. The dedications to Leopold William found within these engravings aimed at obtaining a position for the student concerned within the Archduke's administration or were a means to thank him for privileges already earned. René Vermeir explains that a large number of honorary positions at the court of the Archduke were assigned to members of the local nobility. The elites of the Southern Netherlands were able to participate in the glory of the monarchy, because the court of the general governor in Brussels depended on Madrid, and, as such, constituted a seat of Spanish power itself. The Brussels court encouraged cohesion and political integration within the Empire by granting honours and benefices. The court also exercised an important ideological role in the context of the Counter-Reformation and the numerous armed conflicts occurring at the time.[19]

---

16   A large engraving executed by Erasmus II Quellinus (Antwerp 1607–1678) and Schelte a Bolswert (Bolswert 1586-Antwerp 1659) in 1653 may be mentioned here. The engraving was given by the city of Ghent as a tribute to Leopold William. The composition celebrates the Archduke's victories over the French troops during the first years of his government. See Franz Aumann, '*Flandria liberata*. Een merkwaardige kunstprent in 1653 door de stad Gent opgedragen aan landvoogd Leopold Willem van Oostenrijk', in Jozef Mertens (ed.), *Miscellanea Baliviae de Juncis II. Verzamelde opstellen over Alden Biesen, Bernissem, Leopold Willem van Oostenrijk ...* (Bilzen: Historisch studiecentrum Alden Biesen, 2000), pp. 265–310.

17   Porteman, *Emblematic Exhibitions*, p. 105.

18   Some of these engravings were the subject of an analysis in a previous publication. See Gwendoline de Mûelenaere, 'Double Meaning of Personification in Early Modern Thesis Prints of the Southern Low Countries: Between Noetic and Encomiastic Representation', in Walter S. Melion and Bart Ramakers (eds), *Personification. Embodying Meaning and Emotion* (Leiden: Brill, 2016), pp. 433–460.

19   René Vermeir, 'Les gouverneurs-généraux aux Pays-Bas habsbourgeois', in Daniel Aznar, Guillaume Hanotin and Niels F. May (eds), *À la place du roi. Vice-rois, gouverneurs et ambassadeurs dans les monarchies française et espagnole (XVIe–XVIIIe siècles)* (Madrid: Casa de Velázquez, 2014), pp. 29–30. See also Catherine Thomas, *Le visage humain de*

IN THE SERVICE OF THE PIETAS AUSTRIACA 245

FIGURE 12.2　Petrus Clouwet after Jean-Baptiste Van Heil, *Universal Philosophy*, thesis frontispiece with a portrait of Archduke Leopold William of Austria, 1655. Engraving, 41,2 × 26,5 cm
© ROYAL LIBRARY OF BELGIUM, BRUSSELS, SI 11514

A thesis broadside, executed by Petrus Clouwet (Antwerp 1629–1670) after Jean-Baptiste Van Heil (Brussels 1609–1685) and dedicated to the Archduke, bears witness to such political stakes. In 1655, Claude Maximilien de Lannoy (?1636–?1678)[20] defended a thesis in universal philosophy at the college of the Abbey of Marchiennes in Douai, during an academic session supervised by Jesuit Father Egidius de Fraisne. The *promovendus* belonged to a noble Flemish family. De Lannoy's father Philippe (d. 1658) was a member of the war council, governor of Ypres and majordomo to Leopold William. As noted by Jozef Mertens, the origins of the de Lannoy family, the high ranking of the father in the army and at the court, and the career intentions of the son, resulted in this tribute engraving made on the occasion of a public disputation.[21] The de Lannoys had possessions in the Hainaut and in Flanders, areas that were under threat by French troops. The family expressed in this representation their gratitude to the victorious general governor, as well as their hope of seeing the Netherlands retain control of this border region.[22]

On the engraving, a head-and-shoulders portrait of Leopold William is placed in a medallion decorated with laurel. Around the portrait, five cupids hold illustrated cartouches associated with a motto and the names of the subject matters taught at the faculty of Arts, Metaphysics, Astronomy, Ethics, Physics, and Logic. At the same time, these emblematic devices correspond to Christian virtues represented by five women. Metaphysics (Christian philosophy) is symbolised by a radiant triangle with the Hebrew name of Yahve. A banderol indicates *Et sublimia divum* ("the upper spheres are also subdued to the Gods" – i.e. the Trinity).[23] The same triangle is presented by a winged Minerva to the left of the portrait of the Archduke. The lions on the goddess's helmet and sleeve, an attribute of Hercules, seem to allude to *Fortitudo*, or moral strength.[24] On the other side, a second Minerva, whose helmet is decorated with a dragon, holds an armillary sphere. This instrument, ubiquitous in

---

l'administration. Les grands commis du gouvernement central des Pays-Bas espagnols (1598–1700) (Brussels: Académie royale de Belgique, 2014).

20　Léon de Herckenrode, *Nobiliaire des Pays-Bas et du comté de Bourgogne, par M. de Vegiano* (4 vols, Ghent: Gyselynck, 1865), II, p. 1186.

21　Jozef Mertens, 'Thesisprent van Lannoy de la Motterie, opgedragen aan Leopold Willem', in Mertens and Aumann (eds), *Krijg en Kunst*, p. 248 (cat. II.3.18).

22　Mertens, 'Thesisprent van Lannoy de la Motterie ...', p. 248.

23　Mertens, 'Thesisprent van Lannoy de la Motterie ...', p. 247.

24　James Hall, *Dictionary of Subjects and Symbols in Art* (London: Murray, 1974), p. 193.

IN THE SERVICE OF THE PIETAS AUSTRIACA   247

frontispieces to scientific books at the time, alludes to Astronomy, but it could also be an attribute of Prudence, since it was used to discover the movement of celestial bodies, consequently enabling people to be guided prudently.[25] Likewise, the dragon was also associated with Prudence, by confusion with the snake, which was the traditional attribute of this cardinal virtue.[26]

In the emblem held by a putto in the engraving, a globe is associated with the words *Dominabitur astris*. This refers to the well-known adage *Vir sapiens dominabitur astris* ("The wise man will dominate the stars"). According to the medieval astronomer John of Saxony (Paris, active 1327–1355), studying the science of asters requires three virtues to which correspond the three terms contained in that adage: an unwavering tenacity (*vir*), a favourable disposition (*sapiens*), and an indifference to temporal wealth (*dominabitur astris*). The prologue of his Commentary of Alcabitius's *Liber isagogicus* states:

> The wise man will dominate the stars. In these terms, Ptolemy addresses three properties or conditions that the true philosopher and particularly the astronomer must have, according to three human kinds rejected by astronomy. The first condition is the stability of intention. The second condition is the ability of disposition. The third condition is the renunciation of earthly possessions. The first one corresponds to *vir*; the second one correspond to *sapiens*; the third one correspond to *dominabitur astris*.[27]

The astronomer is "a scholar who contemplates the sky, turns away from material goods, and conforms to Christian religion".[28]

---

25   Patricia Radelet questions the presence and meaning of the armillary spheres in several frontispieces of important treatises, including the *Opticorum* by François de Aguilón. See Patricia Radelet-de Grave, 'Un petit dessin vaut mieux qu'un long discours', in Patricia Radelet-de Grave (ed.), *Liber amicorum, Jean Dhombres* (Turnhout: Brepols, 2008), pp. 422–471, esp. pp. 431–438.

26   Guy de Tervarent, *Attributs et symboles dans l'art profane: dictionnaire d'un langage perdu (1450–1600)* (Geneva: Droz, 1997), pp. 184–185 and 418. Hall identifies the imaginary animal as an attribute to embodied Vigilance: Hall, *Dictionary of Subjects and Symbols*, p. 109.

27   Alcabitius, *Liber isagogicus seu Introductorium et Commentum Johannis de Saxonia* (Venice: E. Ratdolt, 1485), fols. ee4v–ee5r: "Vir sapiens dominabitur astris. In quibus verbis Ptolemeus tangit tres proprietates vel conditiones quas debet verus philosophus habere et maxime astronomus, secundum quas tria genera hominum ab astronomia repelluntur. Prima conditio est stabilitas intentionis. Secunda est habilitas dispositionis. Tertia est abdicatio terrene possessionis. Primam tangit cum dicit: vir. Secundam cum dicit: sapiens. Tertiam cum dicit: dominabitur astris".

28   Jean-Patrice Boudet, *Entre science et nigromance. Astrologie, divination et magie dans l'Occident médiéval (XIIᵉ–XVᵉ siècle)* (Paris: Publications de la Sorbonne, 2006), p. 291.

248   DE MÛELENAERE

In the median part of the engraving, three last putti present an attribute of Ethics: a horse bit and the motto *Domat omnia* ("He subdues all things")[29]; an attribute of Physics: a rosebush in bud and the inscription *Regum digna voluptas* ("A pleasure worthy of kings"); and an attribute of Logic: a key and the text *Patent his o[mn]ia* ("All things are accessible to them"). The three personifications in the lower part correspond to these three disciplines, whose attributes they repeat: one of them is about to bridle a horse; another, crowned, cultivates tulips in the background; and the last one, key in hand, is heading toward the door of a building.[30] These aspects can also denote Christian virtues: the horse bit is generally used to illustrate Temperance[31]; the garden is frequently associated with Wisdom; and the key – signifying logic in general – indicates access to Knowledge.

The allegorical language displayed on the engraving thus illustrates the subjects that were being defended, while referring to virtues attributed to the dedicatee: moral strength/*Metaphysica*, Prudence/*Astronomia*, Temperance/*Ethica*, Wisdom/*Physica*, and Knowledge/*Logica*. This visual process enables the candidate to praise the Archduke – the Latin dedication is inscribed within a cartouche topped with the coat of arms of the student's family – and at the same time, to display the learning the candidate had gained during his studies.[32]

3   With Strength and Softness

The Archduke's motto *Timore Domini* ("by fear of the Lord"), associated with the lion and the lamb, is often brought into play in the iconography of compositions dedicated to him. The animals occupy a prominent place in an engraving executed by Adrien Lommelin (Amiens 1618/1622–Antwerp 1673/1675)

---

29   This may be a reference to Daniel 2:40: "Et regnum quartum erit velut ferrum quomodo ferrum comminuit et domat omnia sic comminuet omnia haec et conteret" ("And the fourth kingdom shall be strong as iron: since iron breaks in pieces and subdues all things, and as iron that breaks all these, so shall it break in pieces and bruise").

30   Mertens, 'Thesisprent van Lannoy de la Motterie', pp. 247–248.

31   de Tervarent, *Attributs et symboles dans l'art profane*, p. 327.

32   "Ser[enissi]mo Principi Leopoldo Guilielmo Archid[uci] Austriae Belgarum et Burgund[iae] pro regi gubernatori &c. Vniversam Philosophiam d[at] c[onsecrat]q[ue] Claudius Maximilianus de Lannoy Comitis de la Motterij filius P[hilippus]" ("Claude Maximilien de Lannoy of the Counts de la Motterij, son of Philippe, gives and consecrates his thesis on universal philosophy to the Most Serene Prince Leopold William Archduke of Austria, Belgium and Burgundy, governor for the king etc.").

IN THE SERVICE OF THE PIETAS AUSTRIACA 249

FIGURE 12.3   Adrien Lommelin after Antoine Sallaert, *Synopsis theologica*, title page for a
thesis defended by Humbert de Precipiano, Jesuit college of Louvain, 1648.
Engraving, 39,3 × 24,1 cm
© RIJKSMUSEUM, AMSTERDAM, RP-P-1908-702

after Antoine Sallaert (Brussels 1594–1650) for a theological disputation in 1648.

The lion flanks the personification of Force (*Fortiter*), while the lamb accompanies that of Softness (*Suaviter*). The Virtues attributed to the governor are waving a sword and a palm leaf, respectively, above his medallion portrait. The dedication inscribed on the pedestal states:

> To Archduke Leopold William, governor of the Belgians and the Burgundians, *exemplum* of his ancestors imperators; winner peacemaker; while he defends the seven Christian sacraments, Humbert de Precipiano, baron de Soye, declares the oath of his lasting submission.[33]

The paradoxical formula *Victori pacifico* ("winner peacemaker"), highlighted at the centre of the base, is reinforced by the presence of an eagle holding a bolt of lightning and a dove carrying laurel leaves in the sky above.

At the top of the composition, the banderol placed below the Christological lamb proclaims: *Ex Ipso Et Per Ipsum Et In Ipso Sunt Omnia* ("Everything comes from him, and exists through him, and is for him").[34] Below that banderol, a terrestrial globe displays the location of several towns of the Southern Netherlands. Words engraved on the medallion announce that Leopold William is *Hannoniae liberatori Flandriae vindici* ("liberator of Hainaut and protector of Flanders"). The Archduke's first campaign against the French in 1647 had allowed him to take back the towns of Armentières and Comines, on the Lys, and briefly the town of Lens, as well as Landrecies in the South and Dixmude in the North. The capture of these cities resulted in a propaganda campaign glorifying the governor, namely through the art of engraving[35] and

---

33 "Leopoldo Wilhelmo Archiduci Belgii et Burgundiae gubernatori. Maiorum suorum Caesarum exemplo. Victori Pacifico. Dum VII Christ[iana] sacramenta propugnat Submissionis aetern[i] sacramentum dicit H[umbert] A Praecipiano Baro de Soye".

34 "Quoniam ex ipso et per ipsum et in ipso omnia ipsi gloria in saecula amen" ("Everything comes from him, and exists through him, and is for him. Glory to him forever, amen!"), in *Romans* 11:36.

35 Among these engravings, an anonymous production of 1647 is held at the Department of Prints and Drawings of the Royal Library in Brussels (SI 34509) and an engraving by Paul Pontius (Antwerp 1603–1658) after Frans Luyckx (Antwerp 1604-Vienna 1668) is held at the Prentenkabinet of the Museum Plantin-Moretus in Antwerp (inv. V/P 30).

IN THE SERVICE OF THE PIETAS AUSTRIACA   251

medals,[36] but also during the procession of the Holy Sacrament of the Miracle in Brussels in July 1647.[37]

The next engraving to be analysed in this essay is the title page to a dissertation, entitled *Synopsis theologica de sacramentis ecclesiae*, which was defended on 21 April 1648 in Louvain by Humbert Guillaume de Precipiano (Besançon 1627–Brussels 1711),[38] under the direction of Jesuit Father Ludovic de Schildere. The paper debated the Catholic Sacraments and was mostly based on texts from the Council of Trent.[39] The candidate took advantage of his disputation to recommend himself to the Archduke, who had a right of appointment to ecclesiastical positions in Burgundy.[40] De Precipiano was appointed the head of the Cistercian abbey of Bellevaux two years later, in 1650. He would then become bishop of Bruges in 1682, and archbishop of Malines in 1690.

The thesis booklet contains a long dedication and three laudatory poems celebrating the victories and peace brought by the Archduke. The two symbolical animals depicted in the engraving are naturally reused to serve as a main thread to the odes. Their titles describe Leopold William as *victor* and *pacificus*, and the subtitles are biblical quotations referring to the lion and the lamb:

Agno sacramentali Austriacae felicitatis authori. Ex Ipso, et per ipsum, et
   in ipso sunt omnia (reiterated in the subtitle);
Leopoldo victori. Leo fortissimus bestiarum ad nullius pavebit occursum.
   Proverb. 30v 30[41];
Leopoldo pacifico. Leo et ovis simul, morabuntur. Isaiae XI v7.[42]

---

36   About the medals made in honour of Leopold William as propaganda tools, see Mertens
      and Aumann (eds), *Krijg en Kunst*, pp. 143–144 (cat. I.1.4), 174–175 (cat. II.1.13), 322
      (cat. IV.1).

37   A triumphal arch celebrated the four recent victories of the Archduke at that time:
      *Armentieria expugnata, Cominia capta, Lens devicta, Landrecies Novae spes proxima
      palmae* (Mertens, 'De gehuldigde krijgsheer', in Mertens and Aumann (eds), *Krijg en
      Kunst*, p. 75).

38   Arthur C. De Schrevel, 'Précipiano (comte Humbert-Guillaume de)', in *Biographie nation-
      ale de Belgique*, vol. 18 (Brussels: Bruylant, 1905), cols. 204–216.

39   Jean-Jacques Van Ormelingen, 'Twee verdedigers van de sacramenten', in Mertens and
      Aumann (eds), *Krijg en Kunst*, pp. 259–260 (cat. II.3.28–II.3.30).

40   Frans Gistelinck and Serge Landuyt, 'Een Leuvense sacramententheologie aanzet tot
      een carrière vanuit Franche-Comté', in Mertens and Aumann (eds), *Krijg en Kunst*,
      pp. 258–259.

41   "The lion, mighty among the beasts, retreats before nothing", in Proverbs 30:30.

42   "The calf and the young lion will live together", in Isaiah 11:6.

In the poems, the lamb is compared to the Eucharist and becomes in this manner the sign of respect that Leopold William nurtured towards God. The Lord favours the Habsburg family in turn for their profound piety, as indicated in the verse 45 of the first poem: *arma regit Pietas*, it is piety that directs arms and leads to victory.

This political choice of display of Christian devotion is also expressed through the 'mirrors for princes' literature[43] addressed to Leopold William: firstly, the *Idea principis Christiano-politici*,[44] secondly, the Archduke's posthumous biography signed by the Jesuit Nicolas Avancini,[45] and thirdly, the *Princeps in compendio*.[46] The writing of this third treatise, published in 1632, is alternatively attributed to his father Ferdinand II, to his Jesuit confessor, Wilhelm Lamormaini, or even to a collaboration between the two of them.[47] The handbook intends to present to Leopold William a sovereignty ideal, which uses devotion as an instrument of power. Although not particularly original, this text nevertheless specifies the ideological foundations that inspired the court of Vienna, its propagandists and the image they wanted to convey of the Habsburgs.[48] The themes discussed in this literary genre are often inherited from a tradition that repeats them and makes them become conventional. This feature of the literature addressed to the prince explains the frequent parallelisms it is possible to establish from one text to another (examples are the model of the Christian prince, the call for prudence and justice, founded on biblical figures, or the fear for God as a source of power). A difference can, however, be

---

43 The metaphor of the mirror (which encourages awareness, correction, or imitation) resulted in the literary tradition of the 'mirrors for princes' or *Speculum principis*, political treatises aiming at serving as a guide to the education of a good sovereign. Usually dedicated to the prince himself, the text describes the ideal prince, his behaviour, his role and his situation in the world. See Einar M. Jónsson, 'Les "miroirs au prince" sont-ils un genre littéraire?', *Médiévales*, 51 (2006), pp. 153–166.

44 Diego Saavedra, *Idea principis Christiano-politici centum symbolis expressa* (Brussels: Jan Mommart II and François Vivien, 1649). This book, which was very successful, was first published in Spanish in Munich in 1640, and then in French in Paris in 1668.

45 Nicolas Avancini, *Le prince dévôt et guerrier ou les vertus héroïques de Léopold-Guillaume Archiduc d'Autriche* (Lille: Nicolas de Rache, 1667). A Latin edition had been issued two years earlier.

46 *Princeps in compendio. Hoc est Puncta aliquot compendiosa, quae circa gubernationem Reipubl. Observanda videntur* (Vienna: Gregor Gelbhaar, 1632). This text was published by Franz Bosbach in Konrad Repgen (ed.), *Das Herrscherbild im 17. Jahrhundert* (Munster: Aschendorff, 1991), pp. 79–114.

47 Ems, *L'emblématique au service du pouvoir*, pp. 101–102.

48 Jean Bérenger, 'L'historiographie à la cour de Vienne (XVe–XVIIe siècles)', in Chantal Grell (ed.), *Les historiographes en Europe de la fin du Moyen Âge à la Révolution* (Paris: PUPS, 2006), p. 117.

IN THE SERVICE OF THE PIETAS AUSTRIACA 253

FIGURE 12.4   E. de Boulonnois after F.A. Marienhof, "Serenissimo Principi Leopoldo Guilielmo pacis ac tranquillitatis publicae auctori", in P.D.F., *À son Altesse Leopolde Guillaume* [...] *panegirique* [...], s.l., ca. 1651, 16 pp., 24,5 × 37,5 cm
© ROYAL LIBRARY OF BELGIUM, BRUSSELS, VH 26.867 C

noticed between thesis prints and mirrors: the engraved broadsides function as praise of the dedicatee, whereas the mirror literature displays an ideal figure of a ruler, external to the prince, which the latter is invited to imitate.[49]

The formula *Fortiter et Suaviter* used in this engraving is staged in a plate executed around 1651 by Esmé de Boulonnois after F.A. Marienhof for a 16-page panegyric. French verses state: "Et le burin a fait en ce charmant visage/ un mélange pompeux de force et de douceur" ("And the burin made in this charming face/a glorious mix of strength and softness"), while the Latin title recognises in Leopold William the author of public peace and tranquillity. The governor is

---

49   Bérenger, 'L'historiographie à la cour de Vienne', p. 109 and 111. The stage plays written the Order also presented theologico-political plots praising the prince publicly. See Annick Delfosse, 'Quand la politique est conviée sur les planches. Spectacles, patriotisme et morale politique dans les collèges jésuites belges au XVIIe siècle', *Cahiers du Centre de Recherches en Histoire du Droit et des Institutions*, 29 (2008), pp. 33–55.

FIG. 12.5 AND 12.6　　Paul Pontius after Abraham van Diepenbeeck, Thesis of Claudius, Count of Collalto, dedicated to Archduke Ferdinand of Austria, University of Louvain, 1645. Engraving, 102,5 × 68 cm
© RIJKSMUSEUM, AMSTERDAM,
RP-P-OB-70.060 AND 061

IN THE SERVICE OF THE PIETAS AUSTRIACA 255

depicted walking over two soldiers that have been brought down and *Invidia*, serpent-haired figure of Jealousy. An eagle representing the Archduke is shown carrying an olive branch to the city of Paris. The text and engraving were created within the context of the Fronde (and, more precisely, of the 'Union des Frondes' in 1651), and they convey the desire for peace that the French population yearned for.[50]

The rotunda illustrated in the background of the engraving is probably modelled after a thesis broadsheet conceived by Abraham van Diepenbeeck ('s-Hertogenbosch 1596–Antwerp 1675) in 1645 and dedicated to the young prince Ferdinand of Austria (Vienna 1633–1654), future Ferdinand IV of Habsburg and nephew of Leopold William.

The dome of the building bears the title *Sacra caesarea domus Austriaca pietatis et iustitiae sedes Ferdina[ndea]* ("The sacred imperial Austrian House, seat of Ferdinand's faith and power"). Rays of light are breaking through the mass of dark clouds to provide light on the top of the cupola and on the Austrian coat of arms crowned by angels. Two Latin inscriptions complete this staging: *Caelo patet uni* ("[The *domus*] is open to one heaven")[51] and *caelestibus armis* ("with his heavenly armour").[52]

The design of the edifice was itself inspired by two engravings made by Theodore van Thulden ('s-Hertogenbosch 1606–1669) after Peter Paul Rubens (Siegen 1577–Antwerp 1640) for the *Pompa Introitus Ferdinandi*.[53] The *Temple of Janus* was erected on the occasion of the triumphal entry of Cardinal-Infant Ferdinand of Austria into Antwerp on 15 May 1635. The publication recounting this event was enriched with forty engraved plates.[54] Issued in 1641, following the death of the Cardinal, the *Pompa* commemorates, after some delay,

---

50   Mertens and Aumann, 'Propaganda: de vredestichter', in Mertens and Aumann (eds), *Krijg en Kunst*, pp. 214–215.

51   There is no subject in this sentence, but I suggest "the House of Habsburg", because of the inscription on top of the cupola representing the *Domus Austriaca*.

52   Virgil, *Aeneid* XII, 167.

53   John Rupert Martin, *The Decorations for the Pompa Introitus Ferdinandi*, Corpus Rubenianum Ludwig Burchard: An Illustrated Catalogue Raisonné of the Work of Peter Paul Rubens, t. 16 (London – New York: Phaidon, 1972), pp. 111–112 and 164, Fig. 59.

54   Caspar Gevartius, *Pompa introitus Ferdinandi Austriaci a S. P. Q. Antuerp. decreta et adornata; cum Antuerpiam auspicatissimo advento suo bearet, XV. kal. maii, ann. M.DC.XXXV* (Antwerp: Jan van Meurs, 1641), plate inserted between pp. 42 and 43. See Anna C. Knaap and Michael C.J. Putnam (eds), *Art, Music and Spectacle in the Age of Rubens: the Pompa Introitus Ferdinandi* (London: Harvey Miller, 2013). Rubens drew the title page. Rubens's designs of arches and stages recorded for that event were actually the work of Theodore van Thulden. See Julius Samuel Held, *Rubens and the Book. Title Pages by Peter Paul Rubens* (Williamstown, Massachusetts: Williams College, 1977), p. 18.

FIGURE 12.7 Theodore van Thulden after Peter Paul Rubens, *Temple of Janus*, in Caspar Gevartius (ed.), *Pompa Introitus Ferdinandi Austriaci Hispaniarum Infantis...*, Antwerp, 1641, pl. 117A
© RIJKSMUSEUM, AMSTERDAM, RP-P-OB-70.270

the governor of the Spanish Netherlands and member of the Habsburg family. The broadsheet commissioned by Claudius de Collalto (Mantua 1628-Brussels 1661),[55] an Italian noble studying at the University of Louvain, copies the upper

---

55   He had a career in the service of Ferdinand III, as cupbearer (as of September 1646) and then as chamberlain and aulic councillor of the emperor (Mark Hengerer and Gerhard

FIGURE 12.8   Theodore van Thulden after Peter Paul Rubens, *Portico of the Emperors* (Matthias and Ferdinand II), in Caspar Gevartius (ed.), *Pompa Introitus Ferdinandi Austriaci Hispaniarum Infantis...*, Antwerp, 1641, pl. 50A
© RIJKSMUSEUM, AMSTERDAM, RP-P-OB-70.262

part of the monument designed by Rubens. The statues faithfully respect the iconography of those drawn for the *Portico of the Emperors*, another decoration conceived by Rubens for the Joyous Entry of Ferdinand of Austria.[56] The set of twelve stone statues, executed after oil sketches by Rubens, was given to the Cardinal-Infant by the city of Antwerp. The statues were later exhibited in a gallery of the palace on the Coudenberg, where they were destroyed by fire in 1731.

In an in-quarto frontispiece dedicated to Leopold William and probably conceived for a thesis booklet,[57] similar visual strategies are exhibited to convey the ideas of power, strength, and piety that direct the ruler's actions.

Schön (eds), *Kaiser und Höfe. Personendatenbank der Höflinge der österreichischen Habsburger*, available at: <http://kaiserhof.geschichte.lmu.de/10388>).

56   However, even though Rubens was responsible for the design of the portico, the idea of a gallery of statues of emperors came from Gevartius (Martin, *The Decorations for the Pompa Introitus Ferdinandi*, p. 107).

57   This seems to point to the presence of heraldry in the lower left part of the composition, probably belonging to a student, and the references to astronomy, possibly one of the disciplines defended within the framework of a philosophical curriculum. Unfortunately, the plate provides neither any information about the student nor the defence made. The

FIGURE 12.9   Jacob Neeffs after Philippe Fruytiers, *Austriaco Burgundico*, title page for a thesis dedicated to Leopold William of Austria, undated (c.1647–1656). Engraving, 22,3 × 17,2 cm
© ROYAL LIBRARY OF BELGIUM, BRUSSELS, SI 28961

IN THE SERVICE OF THE PIETAS AUSTRIACA   259

An eagle and a crowned lion surround the heraldry of the Habsburg House on top of the architectural structure. The animals hold, respectively, a globe and an astrolabe. Each of these objects bears a reference to Virgil's *Aeneid*: firstly, *Imperium terris* ("[his empire will match] earth's power")[58] and secondly, *Famam qui terminat astris* ("whose fame ends with the stars").[59] Both phrases are reused by Hadrianus Barlandus in his *Chronica Brabantiae ducum* (1526). The historian praises Charles V as the new Augustus, and borrows and adapts from the *Aeneid*, resulting in the following formula glorifying the Roman Emperor: *Burgundus origine Caesar, imperium Oceano, famam qui terminat astris*.[60] The Habsburgs claimed to be descendants of the Trojans.[61] The imperial ideology that developed in the West, mainly in the sixteenth century under the impulse of the Habsburg dynasty, was built on the founding myth of Rome as narrated by Virgil.[62] In the engraving, the lion grips tightly in its left paw the flag of the Spanish Netherlands, adorned with a double-headed eagle and a cross of Burgundy. Emblem of the Burgundian heritage, as well of the opposition to France, this was used as the flag of the region under the Habsburg monarchy. Below the animals can be read the archducal titles *Austriaco* and *Burgundico*.

<hr />

     index card of this engraving held at the Royal Library in Brussels cites the title "Medallion with a Germanic emperor", maybe because of the Latin inscription *Imperium terris*. However, the portrait, the coat of arms of the Habsburgs and the motto *Timore Domini* clearly identify the person in the engraving as Leopold William of Austria. The engraving is not dated but it contains the signatures of the artists Philippe Fruytiers (Antwerp 1610–1666) and Jacob Neeffs (Antwerp 1610–after 1660).

58   "En huius, nate, auspiciis illa incluta Roma imperium terris, animos aequabit Olympo" ("Behold, my son, under his command [Romulus] glorious Rome will match earth's power and heaven's will"), in Virgil, *Aeneid* VI, 781–82.

59   "Nascetur pulchra Troianus origine Caesar, imperium oceano, famam qui terminat astris" ("From this glorious source a Trojan Caesar will be born, who will bound the empire with Ocean, his fame with the stars"), in Virgil, *Aeneid* I, 287.

60   Ari Wesseling, 'In Praise of Brabant, Holland, and the Habsburg Expansion: Barlandus's Survey of the Low Countries (1524)', in Dirk Sacré and Gilbert Tournoy (eds), *Myricae. Essays on Neo-Latin Literature in Memory of Jozef Ijsewijn* (Louvain: Leuven University Press, 2000), p. 231.

61   Telesko, 'Transmediality in Early Modern Printmaking', p. 151; Alphons Lhotsky, 'Apis Colonna: Fabeln und Theorien über die Abkunft der Habsburger: Ein Exkurs zur Cronica Austrie des Thomas Ebendorfer', *Mitteilungen des Instituts for Österreichische Geschichtsforschung*, 55 (1942), pp. 171–245. On the reception of Virgil by the Habsburgs, see Elisabeth Klecker, 'Emblemata Vergiliana in der Habsburg-Panegyrik', in Martin Korenjak and Karlheinz Töchterle, *Pontes I. Akten der ersten Innsbrucker Tagung zur Rezeption der klassischen Antike* (Innsbruck: Studien-Verlag, 2001), pp. 209–223.

62   Tanner, *The Last Descendant of Aeneas*, p. 1.

A medallion portrait of the Archduke is depicted at the centre of the engraving, and below that can be seen his personal emblem: a defenceless lamb seeks protection beneath the cross of Christ and finds itself faced with a threatening lion.[63] The motto *Timore Domini* seen overarching the cross comes from the Proverbs of Solomon: "Whoever fears the Lord has a secure fortress, and for their children it will be a refuge".[64] During this time, the fear of God was seen as a powerful shield in battle, and it was for this reason that Leopold William had made this motto his own.[65] From this oval emerges a cloud on which is displayed a sentence from the Gospel of Matthew (28:18): [*Et accedens Jesus locutus est eis, dicens,*] *Data est mihi omnis potestas* [*in caelo et in terra*] ("[Then Jesus came to them and said,] All authority [in heaven and on earth] has been given to me"). On each side of the Archduke's effigy, there are two cartouches, one illustrating a staff of command and the other a sword. They each bear a similar expression: *Auspicio grandi* and *omine fausto* ("under favourable auspices"). Finally, in the lower part of the scene, three putti hold attributes indicating the three kinds of power conferred to the governor. The inscriptions *civilis*, *ecclesiastic* and *militaris* are joined with crowns, a mitre, a cross, and staffs of command.

The watchword of the Archduke *Timore Domini* inspired the theme of a stage play written and performed by the Jesuits of Antwerp in his honour in 1648. The different parts of the play are structured around the qualities generated by the "fear of God": wisdom, abundance and glory.[66] All elements of the *motto* are freely outlined in the frontispiece of the *libretto*: lion and lamb surround the cross of the Teutonic Order, on which is affixed the coat of arms of Leopold William.

The eye of God, horse bit and laurel complete the reference to his motto. To summarise, this maxim frequently served as a source of inspiration for the Jesuits and their pupils, since it gave them the opportunity to present Leopold William, "the greatest of all Jesuit supporters among the regents",[67]

---

63 This principle guided the life of the Archduke and was used as the main theme in the biography and the funeral orations written in his honour. The motto is also regularly extolled in the Jesuit colleges of the Low Countries (Ems, *L'emblématique au service du pouvoir*, pp. 160–168). See also Karel Porteman, 'De vreze des Heren. Leopold Willem en zijn devies "Timore Domini"', in Mertens and Aumann (eds), *Krijg en Kunst*, pp. 251–252 (cat. 11.3.22); Porteman, *Emblematic Exhibitions*, pp. 106–107.

64 "In timore Domini fiducia fortitudinis et filiis eius erit spes" ("Whoever fears the Lord has a secure fortress, and for their children it will be a refuge"), in Proverbs of Solomon 14:26.

65 Ems, *L'emblématique au service du pouvoir*, p. 66.

66 Franz Aumann and Goran Proot, '260 acteurs voor de nieuwe landvoogd', in Mertens and Aumann (eds), *Krijg en Kunst*, pp. 172–173 (cat. 11.1.10).

67 Porteman, *Emblematic Exhibitions*, p. 28.

IN THE SERVICE OF THE PIETAS AUSTRIACA 261

FIGURE 12.10   Anonymous, *Timore Domini concessa divinitus Israeli sapientia, felicitas, gloria*
[…], frontispiece for the libretto of a stage play given to Leopold William of
Austria, Antwerp, 1648. Etching, 20,5 × 15 cm
© KU LEUVEN, TABULARIUM, INV. A 16018 N°5

262   DE MÛELENAERE

as a *Princeps christianus*, an ideal prince, who combined state responsibilities and Christian values.[68]

4   The Adoration of the Virgin

In addition to allegorical scenes promoting Christian virtues, numerous historians have highlighted the importance of the devotion to the Virgin as a tool used in the service of the Habsburgs, and of its militant role in religious conflicts.[69] Post-Tridentine Catholicism raises Mary to the status of triumphal figure. The Virgin experienced a resurgence in interest in regions where the Counter Reformation was having an effect, in particular, in the seventeenth-century Spanish Netherlands. Two forms of Marian piety emerged, one individual and the other, community-wide. On the one hand, the Virgin is instituted as a model of the good Christian, having at Her disposal the virtues of humility, obedience, faith and hope; and the devotion surrounding the Blessed Virgin encourages the faithful to behave like Her. On the other hand, the holy figure is recovered by the sovereigns from a perspective of ostentatious piety. She can then assume an ideological function by serving the interests of the authority.[70] In territories where the different denominations competed, "an almighty Virgin is presented to be seen and to be believed in".[71] Monarchies who wished to base their dominion on the Catholic religion and to defend their countries from war and Protestant threat emphasised the conquering and victorious qualities of the Mother of God.

With the help of church congregations, the Habsburgs promoted thus this Marian patronage as a pillar of their dynasty in the Southern provinces, which were transformed "at the same time in showcase and in bastion of the Catholicism renewed according to the Council of Trent".[72] Annick Delfosse even talks of a "Marian offensive strategy" introduced for kingly purposes.[73] The Virgin was established as a symbol of stability and political union in the stressful climate caused by the conflicts of the time (the Thirty Years' War

---

68   Ems, *L'emblématique au service du pouvoir*, p. 98.

69   Among these historians, see Coreth, *Pietas Austriaca*, pp. 45–80.

70   Annick Delfosse, *La 'Protectrice du Païs-Bas': stratégies politiques et figures de la Vierge dans les Pays-Bas espagnols* (Turnhout: Brepols, 2009), pp. 9–11.

71   Delfosse, *La 'Protectrice du Païs-Bas'*, p. 11.

72   Olivier Chaline, 'Les Pays-Bas espagnols au XVIIe siècle. Présentation', *Dix-septième siècle*, 3, no. 240 (2008), p. 395.

73   Delfosse, *La 'Protectrice du Païs-Bas'*, p. 149.

IN THE SERVICE OF THE PIETAS AUSTRIACA   263

firstly, and the territorial conquests of Louis XIII and then of Louis XIV) and by the existing underlying economic insecurity. The Marian personage plays a role similar to that of the princely figure in the forming of collective identities. Commitment to the Catholic religion and loyalty to the Spanish monarchy provided support for strengthening a sense of community in inhomogeneous 'Belgian' provinces.[74] Archdukes Albert and Isabella, later followed by the general governors sent by Madrid, complied with the example of the perfect Christian prince shaped by Tridentine political thought.[75]

This politico-religious context in favour of the Marian figure incited the promotion of the doctrine of the Immaculate Conception and the expansion of sodalities placed under Her patronage.[76] During that time, the image of devotion to the Blessed Virgin spread in engraved productions that presented Her as a guide for the Christian prince as well as a patroness for college students who wished to place themselves under Her protection.

The final broadsheet to be analysed in this essay is an intricate composition glorifying Our Lady of Mount Carmel and the devotion that the Archduke expressed to Her. Although not strictly speaking a thesis print, this example is very similar in both form and intention. This broadsheet approximates an oil on canvas by the same artist, *The Virgin of the Apocalypse*,[77] which was possibly a sketch for a thesis frontispiece as well.[78] Entitled *Decor Carmeli* ("Beauty of Carmel"), the one metre high engraving by Abraham van Diepenbeeck and Adrien Lommelin is held at the St Charles Borromeo church in Antwerp. A feigned drapery unfolds over almost the entire surface of the broadsheet, in

---

74   Delfosse, *La 'Protectrice du Païs-Bas'*, pp. 17–18.

75   Delfosse, *La 'Protectrice du Païs-Bas'*, p. 111.

76   For instance, Ferdinand III officially dedicated Austria to the Immaculate Conception in 1647: Jean Bérenger, *Histoire de l'empire des Habsbourg 1273–1918* (Paris: Fayard, 1990), p. 308. Seven years earlier, the monarch had registered with the *Sodalitas Major* of Louvain, devoting himself, his family and the Empire to the Virgin (Delfosse, *La 'Protectrice du Païs-Bas'*, p. 12).

77   The sketch *The Virgin of the Apocalypse* (oil on canvas in grisaille, 73 × 54 cm, ca 1650) comes from the archducal collection in Vienna but is currently held at the Palazzo Pitti in Florence (Galleria Palatina, inv. 1890, no. 1105). See Didier Bodart, *Rubens e la pittura fiamminga del Seicento nelle collezioni pubbliche fiorentine* (Florence: Centro Di, 1977), pp. 108–109, cat. 30; David W. Steadman, *Abraham van Diepenbeeck. Seventeenth-Century Flemish Painter* (Ann Arbor, Michigan: UMI Research Press, 1982), p. 99, fig. 42; Hans Vlieghe, 'Abraham van Diepenbeeck', in Paul Huys Janssen, Marc De Beyer, Axel Heinrich and Hans Vlieghe (eds), *Meesters van het Zuiden. Barokschilders rondom Rubens* (Ghent: Snoeck-Ducaju & Zoon, 2000), fig. 46 (cat. 23).

78   Didier Bodart estimates that the presentation of the subject, the dimensions of the work of art and the blank scroll held by two putti call to mind a composition for a thesis (Bodart, *Rubens e la pittura fiamminga*, p. 108).

FIGURE 12.11   Adrien Lommelin after Abraham van Diepenbeeck, *Decor Carmeli*, thesis (?) broadside dedicated to Leopold William of Austria, ca. 1650–1655. Engraving, 100 × 40 cm
ANTWERP, ST CHARLES BORROMEO CHURCH, © IRPA, INV. 57750

front of a classical architectural structure. The scene acts as a background for the depiction of numerous Carmelite Saints and Blesseds, clergymen and kings paying homage to the Virgin Mary. On two imposing columns are affixed cartouches recounting in text and image the lives of saints related to the

IN THE SERVICE OF THE PIETAS AUSTRIACA   265

Order.[79] At the bottom is a large cartouche welcoming the Latin dedication addressed to the Archduke and signed "Carmelus Belgicus strictioris observantiae". This cartouche is surrounded by two angels, *Actio* and *Contemplatio*, presenting the coats of arms of Leopold William and of the Carmelite Order. Carmelites considered the Blessed Mary as a perfect model of the interior life and of contemplation, to which they aspired, while the governor was seen to epitomise an active defence of faith.

Most of the figures portrayed in this engraving are accompanied by a letter, which corresponds to their name engraved in the long dedication in the lower part. The tapestry, supported by six putti, is divided into four registers. The first register depicts the appearance of the Blessed Virgin Mary to Saint Simon Stock (letter "I."). According to a medieval tradition, the Prior General of the Carmelite Order had a vision in Cambridge on 16 July 1251, during which the Virgin handed the saint a scapular (a religious brown habit) as a token of the divine favour granted to his Order. After Simon Stock come Blessed Francesco Lippi (V.), Saint Andrew Corsini (W.) and three kings, Edward, Louis and Henri (Aa.). To the left, Saint Albert of Trapani (H.) stretches his arms toward the Child Jesus. He is followed by Peter the Hermit (O.), Saint Cyril of Constantinople (Q.), and Saint Avertanus (R.). Saint Teresa of Avila (S.) and Mary Magdalene de'Pazzi (T.), elevated, offer the Virgin a lily and a heart. Above the Virgin, a banderol held by an angel quotes the *Ecclesiasticus*: "Et circa illam corona fratrum. Porrexit manum suam ...".[80]

In the second register, the prophet Elijah (K.) presents his flaming sword, followed by Saint Cyril of Alexandria (N.), Saint Anastasius (P.), Saint Agabus (M.), and two members of the Belgian Order (L. and D.). One of them is writing the name *Leopoldus* in an open book. Saint Peter Thomas (accompanied by a little cross and not a letter) pays homage to the Virgin, along with Angelus of Jerusalem (X.) and his brother, John Patriarch of Jerusalem (Y.) and V. Bertoldus (Z.), Ven. Francisca Ambrosia and Ven. Petro Angelio Cernovicchio.

---

79   S. Elisaeus, S. Ioannes Baptista, S. Enoch, S. Telesphorus, S. Dyonisius de Speluncis, S. Hilarion, S. Bertholdus primus; S. Cyrillus, S. Caprasius, S. Albertus, S. Brocardus, B. Ioannes Soreth, V. Ioannes à Cruce, Honorio tertio.

80   "In accipiendo autem partes de manu sacerdotum et ipse stans iuxta aram circa illum corona fratrum quasi plantatio cedri in monte Libano" ("When he received the portions of the sacrifice from the hands of the priests, himself standing by the altar hearth, crowned with the circle of his brothers, as a cedar of Lebanon is by its foliage"), in Ecclesiasticus (Syrach) 50:13; and "Porrexit manum suam in libatione et libavit de sanguine uvae, et fudit in fundamenta altarii odorem divinum excelso Principi" ("He stretched out his hand to the cup, and poured of the blood of the grape, he poured out at the foot of the altar a sweet-smelling savour unto the most high King of all"), in Ecclesiasticus (Syrach) 50:16–17.

Below, Saint Gerard of Nazareth (A.), D. Theodoricus Allemannus (B.), Angela of Bohemia (C.), Saint Berthold of Mount Carmel (E.) and Onuphrius (F.) hold five illustrated broadsheets, each depicting an appearance of the Virgin with Child to the faithful. The text distributed upon these posters quotes the words the Virgin addressed to Saint Simon Stock in his vision: "Most loving son, receive this Scapular of thy Order, a token of my confraternity, to thee and to all Carmelites; a privilege, in which who so dies shall not suffer everlasting fire. Behold the sign of salvation, safety in dangers, a league of peace and an everlasting covenant".[81] The last phrase (*Ego Mater Misericordiae Sabbatho liberatio eos*) refers to the Sabbatine privilege, the promise of liberation from Purgatory on the first Saturday after death, through the special intercession of Mary; or, in general, the promise that those in the Carmelite Order, who persevered in their vocation, would be saved. The last group of characters is made up of clergymen and temporal leaders. Emperor Ferdinand III (Bb.) is portrayed in the centre, while his brother Leopold William (Cc.), holding a staff of command, is depicted on the right hand side, facing the viewer.

This work of art was probably donated by the Discalced Carmelite Fathers of Ghent. With the support of Bishop Antoine Triest (Beveren 1576–Ghent 1657), the fathers had obtained authorisation in 1648 to settle in the city. They bought the Leeuwenhof (outbuilding of the former Prinsenhof of Charles v) the following year. Leopold William financed the property via a grant as of 12 December 1652.[82] It can be assumed that the engraving was intended as a gift to thank the governor for his financial support to the Order.

5   Conclusion

Within the universe of signs provided by Baroque culture, thesis broadsides dedicated to the Habsburgs account for the elaboration of a communicational strategy set up around their family. Numerous allusions to classical, mythological, biblical and historical sources are integrated within an allegorical framework aiming at legitimising the family's power. This mingling of literary references is a way of highlighting the Roman (imperial) as well as the

---

81   "Dilectissime Filii, hoc accipe tui Ordinis Scapulare meae confraternitatis signum, tibi et cunctis carmelitis privilegium, in quo quis moriens, aeternum non patietur incendium; ecce signum salutis, salus in periculis, foedus pacis et pacti sempiterni".

82   Charles-Louis Diericx, *Mémoires sur la ville de Gand* (2 vols., Ghent: Goesin-Verhaege, 1815), II. 664–669.

IN THE SERVICE OF THE PIETAS AUSTRIACA   267

Christian (sacred) roots of the dynasty.[83] The recalling of the ancestral origins
of the Habsburgs, which is constant in the iconography developed over generations, affirms that the dynasty were granted their power directly from God.
A certain ideological continuity can be observed in literary and artistic works
dedicated to the Habsburg family, through the use of recurrent patterns, stereotypes, and traditional *topoi*.

Therefore, if thesis engravings are original compositions, designed for specific circumstances and particular protagonists, the language they draw on is
not innovative. Means of persuasion include the association of the ruler to virtues of piety and justice, the parallelism drawn between him and legendary figures, the glorification of his ancestors, etc. Thesis prints belong to a larger and
well-known literary production (mirrors for princes, political treatises, theatrical performances to the glory of sovereigns) and visual production (student
emblems, almanacs, frontispieces to scientific books). The originality of these
engravings lies in the application of such allegorical and symbolic language to
the study fields taught at the educational institutions.

In Flemish thesis prints, the celebration of the Habsburgs is adapted to the
political, religious and military realities of the Southern Low Countries through
the evocation of the armed conflicts of the time and the fight against heretics.
Academic dissertations addressed to Leopold William of Austria bear witness
to the choice of display, and even of dramatization of piety, for political ends.
The faithful are invited to imitate the example of the Virgin, but also that of
the ruler devoted to Her.[84] In accordance with the ideal image of the Archduke
that the Jesuits wished to spread, the iconography designed for thesis prints
represents Leopold William as a *Miles Christianus* ('Christian soldier'), a prince
who faithfully respects the tenets of the *Pietas Austriaca* and combines state
responsibilities with Christian values.

During public disputations, these representations were projected within
the circle of courtiers of the Habsburg monarchy.[85] Such events provided the
promovendi – often young nobles – with an excellent opportunity to prove
their loyalty to the Spanish crown and their fidelity to the Catholic religion,
two ferments of social and political cohesion in the local elite.

---

83   Telesko, 'Transmediality in Early Modern Printmaking', p. 152.
84   Delfosse, *La 'Protectrice du Païs-Bas'*, p. 13.
85   Maria Goloubeva, *The Glorification of Emperor Leopold I in Image, Spectacle and Text*
      (Mayence: Philipp von Zabern, 2000), p. 2.

CHAPTER 13

The Iconography of the Last Supper in Géronimo Nadal's *Evangelicæ historiæ imagines*

Valentine Langlais

1   The Last Supper in the *Evangelicæ historiæ imagines*

The episode of the Last Supper, narrated in the four Gospels and in the First Epistle to the Corinthians, is composed of two distinct moments: the announcement of Jesus's betrayal and the institution of the Eucharistic sacrament.[1] This sacrament is established by Christ's Words "Do this in remembrance of me". Depictions of the Last Supper increased during the Middle Ages and they show one or the other of these moments.[2] From the middle of the sixteenth century, this biblical episode was increasingly illustrated in Netherlandish religious art. Preference was given to the sacramental supper: most of the images of the Last Supper depict Christ blessing the bread or the chalice. This was mainly due to the struggles between the Catholic Church and the Protestants about the sacrament of Eucharist.[3] In this context of religious conflicts, the renewed Catholic iconography of the Last Supper was used in defence and glorification of the Eucharistic sacrament and all that depends on it, such as the dogma of transubstantiation, the celebration of the mass as the renewal of Christ's sacrifice, and the Catholic liturgy. In this regard, Géronimo Nadal's *Evangelicæ historiæ imagines* offers a very uncommon illustration of the Last Supper, but one that was in keeping with the religious context of its publication.[4]

The *Evangelicæ historiæ imagines* was a devotional production overseen by the Spanish Jesuit Géronimo Nadal (1507–1580) and published in 1593 in Antwerp. The publication is composed by 153 plates illustrating episodes

---

1   Matthew 26:17–29; Mark 14:17–25; Luke 22:14–38; John 13:21–30; I Corinthians, 11:23–26.
2   Kees van der Ploeg, 'Iconographical aspects of the Last Supper in the Middle Ages', in Wim de Groot (ed.), *The Seventh Window: the King's Window Donated by Philip II and Mary Tudor to Sint Janskerk in Gouda* (Hilversum: Verloren, 2005), pp. 199–214.
3   Lee P. Wandel, *The Eucharist in the Reformation. Incarnation and Liturgy* (Cambridge: Cambridge University Press, 2006); Lee P. Wandel (ed.), *A Companion to the Eucharist in the Reformation* (Leiden: Brill, 2014).
4   Géronimo Nadal, *Evangelicæ historiæ imagines* (Antwerp: Martinus Nutius II, 1593) (USTC 402295).

© KONINKLIJKE BRILL NV, LEIDEN, 2023 | DOI:10.1163/9789004510159_014

GÉRONIMO NADAL'S EVANGELICÆ HISTORIÆ IMAGINES 269

from the Life of Christ, arranged according to the evangelical chronology. The plates were engraved by Flemish engravers, mainly the Wierix brothers, after the drawings of three Italian artists: Livio Agresti, Gian Battista, and Bernardino Passeri.[5] In 1595, this edition was followed by the publication of the *Adnotationes et meditationes in Evangelia*.[6] Here, the images are arranged according to the liturgical order from the *Missale Romanum*, and are accompanied by annotations and meditations written by Nadal himself.[7] This text is composed by commentaries and detailed descriptions of the space and time in which the illustrated episode took place.

Among the 153 engravings, a group of four plates depicts the episode of the Last Supper according to four distinct moments. They were engraved by Hieronymus Wierix after Bernardino Passeri's drawings, and are numbered from 100 to 103. They were inserted as a group in the *Evangelicæ historiæ imagines*, and then in the *Adnotationes et meditationes*. They have the same tripartite pattern as the other engravings of the *Evangelicæ historiæ imagines*: the engraving centres on the illustration of the biblical episode and is framed by the title in the upper part and the captions in the lower part.[8] pPlate n° 100 (p. 217),[9] *Feria V. Maioris Hebdomadæ*, depicts the 'Sabbat of May', and more precisely the *Cœna legalis*, that is to say the 'Supper according to the Law', which is the celebration of the Passover by Christ and his apostles (Fig. 13.1).Plate n° 101 (p. 221), *Cœna communis, et Lavatio Pedum* illustrates the 'Ordinary supper and the Washing of the feet' (Fig. 13.2). Plate n° 102 (p. 225), *Sanctissimi Sacramenti, et Sacrificii Institutio*, represents the 'Institution of the Sacrament and the most Sacred Sacrifice', namely the institution of the Eucharistic sacrament (Fig. 13.3) and, finally, plate n° 103 (p. 229), *De Gestis post sacram Communionem*, shows the 'Gesture after the Holy Communion', that is the announcement of the Jesus's betrayal and the gesture designating Judas (Fig. 13.4).

---

5 Maj-Brit Wadell, 'The Evangelicae Historiae Imagines: the designs and their artists', *Quaerendo*, vol. 10, n°4, 1980, pp. 279–291; Pierre-Antoine Fabre, 'Quelques éléments pour une théorie jésuite de la contemplation visuelle', in Alain Tapié (ed.), *Baroque, vision jésuite: du Tintoret à Rubens* (Paris: Somogy, 2003), p. 29; Ralph Dekoninck, 'Ad imaginem': statuts, fonctions et usages de l'image dans la littérature spirituelle jésuite du XVIIe siècle (Geneva: Droz, 2005), pp. 235–239.

6 Géronimo Nadal, *Adnotationes et meditationes in Evangelia quæ in sacrosancto missæ toto anno leguntur ...* (Antwerp: Martinus Nutius II, 1595) (USTC 40334).

7 Dekoninck, *Ad imaginem*, p. 233.

8 Dekoninck, *Ad imaginem*, pp. 245–247.

9 The pagination of the plates mentioned in this article are from Nadal's *Adnotations et meditations*.

FIGURE 13.1   Johannes Wierix after Bernardino Passeri, *Feria v. Maioris Hebdom*, 1593, woodcut, 232 × 145 mm
© RIJKSMUSEUM, AMSTERDAM, RP-P-OB-67.223

FIGURE 13.2   Johannes Wierix after Bernardino Passeri, *Cœna commvnis, et Lavatio Pedum*, 1593, woodcut, 232 × 145 mm
© RIJKSMUSEUM, AMSTERDAM, RP-P-OB-67.224

FIGURE 13.3   Johannes Wierix after Bernardino Passeri, *Sanctissimi Sacramenti, et Sacrificii Institvtio*, 1593, woodcut, 232 × 145 mm
© RIJKSMUSEUM, AMSTERDAM, RP-P-OB-67.225

GÉRONIMO NADAL'S EVANGELICÆ HISTORIÆ IMAGINES 273

FIGURE 13.4   Johannes Wierix after Bernardino Passeri, *De Gestis post sacram Commvnionem*, 1593, woodcut, 231 × 144 mm
© RIJKSMUSEUM, AMSTERDAM, RP-P-OB-67.226

274 LANGLAIS

Such a division is unique in the iconography of the Last Supper. Even though these episodes exist independently of each other, no iconographical cycle in the Low Countries presents these four moments together. Some sixteenth-century Flemish altarpieces present the Passover as the prefiguration of the Last Supper,[10] while others juxtapose the Washing of the Feet and the Eucharistic supper.[11] In the second half of the sixteenth century in Italian painting, when Bernardino Passeri received a commission for the *Evangelicæ's* drawings, some artworks gathered these two events in a single composition.[12] In the field of illustrated religious books of the sixteenth century, it seems that only Alardus Amstelredamus's *Passio Domini nostri Iesu Christi*, published in 1523 and illustrated by Jacob Cornelisz van Oostsanen, presents two moments of Christ's Last Supper.[13] One engraving illustrates *Christ and the apostles celebrating the Passover* (Fig. 13.5), and another depicts the *Institution of the Eucharistic sacrament* (Fig. 13.6).[14] In other devotional books published at the same time as the *Evangelicæ Historiæ Imagines*, the Last Supper is illustrated by one engraving focused on the institution of the Eucharistic sacrament or on the announcement of Jesus's betrayal, as in Benito Arias Montano's *Humanæ Salutis Monumenta*, first published in 1571.[15]

The *Evangelicæ historiæ imagines* is considered as the foundation of the Jesuit illustration, and its iconography is in accordance with the new iconographical instructions from the Council of Trent.[16] However, one can wonder

---

10   Dieric Bouts, *Triptych of the Holy Sacrament*, 1464–1468, oil on panel, 180 × 150 cm, Leuven, Saint Pieter Church; Jan Gerritsz. Dey, *Triptych of the Holy Sacrament*, 1570, oil on panel, 210 × 169 cm, Culemborg, Elisabeth Weeshuis Museum (Inv. 0570–0203).

11   Master of the Adoration von Groot, *Triptych of the Last Supper*, 1500–1525, oil on panel, 117 × 156,5 cm (Brussels, Royal Museums of Fine Arts of Belgium, Inv. 6908); Michiel Coxcie, *Triptych of the Holy Sacrament*, 1567, oil on panel, 279 × 454 cm (Brussels, Royal Museums of Fine Arts of Belgium, Inv. 42).

12   Livio Agresti, *The Last Supper*, 1571, fresco, Roma, Oratorio del Gonfalone; Benedetto Caliari, *The Last Supper and the Washing of the feet*, 1582, oil on canvas, 282 × 366 cm, Venice, Convento dei Canonici Lateranensi; Cesare Nebbia, *The Washing of the feet* and *The Last Supper*, 1590–1599, fresco, Roma, Chiesa della Trinità dei Monti.

13   Alardus Amstelredamus, *Passio Domini nostri Iesu Christi, sive scopus meditationis Christianæ, ex optimis quibusque poetis Christianis, iisque vetustissimis concinnatus* (Amsterdam: Doen Pietersz, 1523) (USTC 420881).

14   James Clifton, Walter S. Melion (eds), *Scripture for the Eyes. Bible Illustration in Netherlandish Prints of the sixteenth Sixteenth Century* (New York: Museum of Biblical Art – London: D. Giles, 2009), pp. 64–65.

15   Johannes Wierix, after Pieter van der Borcht, *The Last Supper*, 1571, etching, 114 × 73 mm, London, The British Museum (1875,0710.116) in Benito Arias Montano, *Humanæ Salutis Monumenta* (Antwerp: Christophe Plantin, 1571) (USTC 401487).

16   Dekoninck, *Ad imaginem*, pp. 232–233; Maj-Brit Wadell, *Evangelicæ Historiæ Imagines: Entstehungsgeschichte und Vorlagen* (Göteborg: Acta Universitatis Gothoburgensis, 1985);

GÉRONIMO NADAL'S EVANGELICÆ HISTORIÆ IMAGINES 275

FIGURE 13.5   Jacob Corneliszoon van Oostsanen, *Christ and the apostles celebrating the Passover*, 1523, woodcut, 110 × 78 mm
© THE BRITISH MUSEUM, LONDON, 1859.0709.2865

FIGURE 13.6 Jacob Corneliszoon van Oostsanen, *The Institution of the Eucharistic sacrament*, 1523, woodcut, 110 × 78 mm
© THE BRITISH MUSEUM, LONDON, 1859.0709.2865

GÉRONIMO NADAL'S EVANGELICÆ HISTORIÆ IMAGINES

why Géronimo Nadal chose to divide the Last Supper in four distinct moments rather than follow the iconographical tradition of the sixteenth century? Two factors can explain the choice made by Nadal and the illustrator. First, the *Evangelicæ historiæ imagines* were conceived in the 1550s, at the same time as the Council of Trent (1545–1563). During the Council, the Catholic sacrament of the Eucharist was at the heart of several sessions because it was one of the most polemical subjects of the struggle between the Catholic Church and the Protestants. The Council of Trent confirmed the dogma of transubstantiation, rejected by all Protestants, and the liturgy surrounding the celebration of the mass.[17] Three Jesuit theologians participated in the Council, and their presence showed the implication of the Society of Jesus in the protection of the Catholic faith against the Reformation.[18] Since the foundation of the Society, Jesuits were attached to the Holy See by a fourth vow of obedience to the Pope, and they undertook to defend the Catholic faith, and, therefore, the Eucharistic sacrament.[19] Second, Nadal's text followed the publication of the *Spiritual Exercises* by Ignatius of Loyola (1548), which is why it is generally considered as a figurative translation of the *Spiritual Exercises*.[20] As we will see, the four engravings follow the same division of the episode as that made by Ignatius of Loyola in his meditation upon the Last Supper, and some details are very close to the reading of this event by the Jesuit father. In this way, the choice of four engravings for one episode usually summarised in one image or two, is influenced by the religious context, both by the debate on the sacrament of the Eucharist and by Jesuit theology and the publication of Loyola's *Spiritual Exercises*. Furthermore, this approach offers an iconography as orthodox and faithful as possible to evangelical texts. This respect of the biblical

---

Pierre-Antoine Fabre, *Ignace de Loyola: le lieu et l'image. Le problème de la composition de lieu dans les pratiques spirituelles et artistiques jésuites* (Paris: J. Vrin, 1992); Paul Rheinbay, *Biblische Bilder für den inneren Weg. Das Betrachtungsbuch des Ignatius-Gefährten Hieronymus Nadal* (Egelsbach: Hänsel – Frankfurt: Hohenhausen, 1995).

17 Norman P. Tanner (ed.), *Decrees of the Ecumenical Councils* (2 vols, London – Washington: Sheed and Ward – Georgetown University Press, 1990) II, pp. 693–701: Session XIII [11 October 1551]: 'Decree concerning the most holy sacrament of the Eucharist'; Session XXII [7 September 1562], 'Teaching and canons on the most holy sacrifice of the mass', pp. 732–736. Wandel, *The Eucharist*, pp. 226–227.

18 The Jesuits Pierre Favre, Diego Lainez and Alonso Salmeron participated in the Council of Trent on request of the pope Paul III. Wandel, *The Eucharist*, p. 220.

19 John W. O'Malley, *Saints or Devils Incarnate? Studies in Jesuit History* (Leiden: Brill, 2013), pp. 38, 40.

20 Pierre-Antoine Fabre, 'Les *Exercices spirituels* sont-ils illustrables ?', in Luce Giard, Louis de Vaucelles (eds), *Les Jésuites à l'âge baroque, 1540–1640* (Grenoble: J. Million, 1996), pp. 197–209; Fabre, 'Quelques éléments', p. 29.

story is possible through the multiplication of scenes illustrated in one engraving and thanks to letters, which refer to captions in the lower part of the plate. The Jesuits' faithfulness to the Bible served to legitimate their positions, as well as those of the Catholic Church, on the question of the Eucharistic sacrament, the dogma of transubstantiation, the Catholic liturgy and the celebration of the mass. In showing Christ's gesture in detail, they sought to demonstrate that Catholic faith, doctrine and liturgy followed Christ's teaching and action, unlike the Protestants. In this way, the four engravings of the Last Supper in the *Evangelicæ historiæ imagines* actively engaged in the defence of the most polemical sacrament during the religious dispute between Catholics and Protestants, the Eucharistic sacrament.

To explain how these four plates sought to defend the Catholic Eucharistic sacrament, I first want to examine the four engravings and show how close their iconography is to biblical texts whilst remaining original in comparison to the traditional iconography of the Last Supper. Second, I shall explain how the four plates are dependent on each other and form a narrative unity, following Ignatius of Loyola's reading of the Last Supper. Finally, I shall demonstrate how the four engravings, together with the annotations and meditations, form a coherent and didactic discourse that sought to demonstrate the validity of the Catholic Eucharistic sacrament.

2 The Iconography of the Last Supper

In the plate n° 100, four little scenes serve as the prelude to the main episode, which represents the celebration of the Passover. Scenes A and B are barely visible through the opening on the outside on the left side (Fig 13.1). According to the three synoptic Gospels, they illustrate the moment when Christ asked to his disciples to prepare the Passover.[21] Two of them, Pieter and John, go to Jerusalem and follow a man, the water carrier, for the preparation of the Passover.[22] In the background, on the right, the two apostles are at the 'Sion Mountain' and are asking to prepare the Passover 'C'. On the other side of the wall, on the left, the main room opens onto the kitchen where the Passover is being prepared: the lamb, on a spit, is being cooked in a large fireplace 'D'. These four little scenes come before the main episode, that is, the celebration of the Passover by Christ and his apostles 'E'. Christ is celebrating the Passover according to the rite of the Ancient Law, as indicated in the subtitle 'Cœna

---

21   Matthew 26:17–18; Mark 14:13; Luke 22:7–11.
22   Mark 14:13; Luke 22:10.

GÉRONIMO NADAL'S EVANGELICÆ HISTORIÆ IMAGINES   279

legalis'. Jesus and his disciples are standing around a table. Judas is already recognisable through his purse, hanged to his belt. A plate with the Pascal lamb and unleavened breads are on the table. The thirteen men hold a pilgrim's stick, evocating the Flight from Egypt by the Jews.[23] The Pascal lamb, the standing position of the celebrants and their pilgrim's stick are usual in the iconography of Christ celebrating the Passover, as in van Oostsanen's engraving (Fig. 13.5), and in the illustrations of the Passover according to the rite of the Ancient Law.[24]

The next engraving, n° 101, illustrates two episodes: a common supper 'A', which takes place in the background, and the Washing of the feet 'D' (Fig. 13.2). According to John's Gospel, it is during the supper of the Passover that Christ rose to wash feet's apostles and then, once he had returned to His place, announced the betrayal.[25] The title of the plate and the caption 'A' refer to a *Cœna communis* ('ordinary supper'). Ignatius of Loyola alludes to a supper, taken by Christ after the Passover and before the Washing of the Feet.[26] Later, the Jesuit theologian Cornelius a Lapide in his *Commentaria in scripturam sacram*, published in Antwerp in 1616 and known as the *Great Commentary*, offers this interpretation of this common supper:

> Observe that Christ partook of a triple supper with His disciples, the ceremonial, the ordinary supper, and the Supper of the Eucharist. In families of ample means, the lamb being insufficient to satisfy the hunger of so many persons, there usually followed the ordinary supper, at which they ate other kinds of meat. And so Christ washed the feet of the Apostles after the two former suppers and before the third.[27]

Thus this ordinary supper is the one depicted in the background, behind the Washing of the Feet. During this supper, according to John's Gospel, Judas is

---

23   Exodus 12:11: 'And take your meal dressed as if for a journey, with your shoes on your feet and your sticks in your hand: take it quickly: it is the Lord's Passover'.

24   For example, Hendrick Assuerusz van Montfoort, *The Passover*, 1564, oil on panel, 32,5 × 46,5 cm (Zwolle, Heino, Museum De Fundatie); Harmen Jansz. Muller, after Gerard van Groeningen, *The Passover*, 1567–1570, etching, 210 × 287 mm (Amsterdam, Rijksmuseum, Inv. RP-P-1904–3364).

25   John 13: 1–12.

26   Ignatius of Loyola, *Spiritual Exercises*, in Georges E. Ganss (ed.), *Ignatius of Loyola. The Spiritual Exercises and selected Works*, (New York, Mahwah: Paulist Press, 1991), pp. 167.

27   Cornelius a Lapide, *The Great Commentary of Cornelius a Lapide* (trans. by Thomas W. Mossman) (8 vols., London: John Hodges, 1908), VI, p. 44. Alan J. Hauser etc. (eds), *A History of Biblical Interpretation, vol. 2. The Medieval through the Reformation Periods* (Grand Rapids: Eerdmans, 2009), p. 439.

already possessed by the Devil.[28] To evoke this possession and the betrayal, letters 'B' and 'C' of the captions tell the dialogue between Christ and Judas, using the texts of Matthew and Mark's Gospels.[29] Christ explains that the traitor is the one who will put his hand in the plate with Him. The main scene is the Washing of the Feet 'D'. As in many examples illustrating this episode, Christ and Peter are talking, because the apostle refuses to allow Christ to wash his feet 'E'.[30] Finally, Christ is putting on His mantel and seems to go back to the table 'F'.

The next two plates, n° 102 and 103, illustrate the two more usual moments of the Last Supper: the institution of the Eucharistic sacrament (Fig. 13.3) and the announcement of the betrayal (Fig. 13.4). In the plate n° 102, two scenes are depicted. The first one is in a medallion in the upper part of the engraving: Christ and his disciples have just finished the ordinary supper 'A', and this moment arrives immediately before the main scene 'B'. Although the title of the plate is the 'Institution of the Sacrament and the most Sacred Sacrifice', the engraving does not illustrate Christ instituting the sacrament in blessing bread or wine, but He is offering the Communion to the apostles. The paten and the chalice on the table remind the institution of the sacrament and the liturgy of the mass.

The last plate, n° 103, depicts the 'gesture after the Holy Communion', being the announcement of the betrayal and the designation of Judas (Fig. 13.4). The main scene follows immediately the institution of the sacrament of the Eucharist and the Communion of the Apostles. Christ announces that one of them will betray Him, and then He gives a morsel of bread to Judas 'A', 'B', who, troubled by the devil, leaves the Cenacle 'C'. He is guided by the devil, seated on his head. In the medallion, after Judas's departure, Christ teaches the apostles and explains to them the necessity of his future sacrifice 'E', according to John's Gospel.[31] In the background of the plate, Christ and the eleven apostles leave the Cenacle to go to the Garden of Gethsemane 'F'.

---

28   John 13:2.

29   Matthew 26:23; Mark 14:20.

30   Lambert van Noort, *The Washing of the Feet*, 1560, oil on panel, 125 × 198 cm (Antwerp, Koninklijk Museum voor Schone Kunsten, Inv. 449); Crispijn de Passe the Elder, after Maarten de Vos, *The Washing of the Feet*, c.1584, etching, 186 × 154 mm (London, The British Museum, Inv. F,1.195); Adriæn Collært, after Maarten de Vos, *The Washing of the Feet*, c.1590–1600, etching, 181 × 222 mm (San Francisco, Fine Arts Museums of San Francisco, Inv. 1963.30.12490).

31   John 13, 14.

GÉRONIMO NADAL'S EVANGELICÆ HISTORIÆ IMAGINES

3 The Narrative Unity

These four plates show the same unity of time and place, marked at the beginning and at the end by a movement: Christ and the apostles' arrival at Jerusalem and in the host's house in the first plate 'A', 'B', 'C', and their departure for the Garden of Gethsemane in the last plate 'F'. Between these two movements, the four episodes are depicted in the same room, seen from different angles. Steps at the foreground or at the background, outward openings and door frames, accessories like the dresser or lights, are the same in each plate. Furthermore, some details from the different plates connect the events between them. In plate n° 100, the twelve stools at the background on the left are the same as in plate n° 101 and announce the Washing of the Feet of the next plate. This episode is remembered in engraving n° 102 with the same stools on the right while, at the foreground, the pilgrim's sticks left on the steps remind the Passover. In plates n° 102 and 103, the medallions remind or announce past or future events. The one in plate n° 102 shows the end of the common supper, and links plate n° 101 to the Eucharistic supper. In plate n° 103, the medallion announces the subject of the next three engravings, Christ's teaching. The four plates form a narrative unit, within which the different episodes take place in the same place, during the same evening and involve the same characters.

The representation of the four moments of the Last Supper and the different details that connect the plates between them rest probably upon Ignatius of Loyola's *Spiritual Exercises*. The four moments of the different plates correspond to Ignatius of Loyola's detailed description of the Last Supper in his *Exercises*. In the exercises of the First Day of the third week, entitled *How Christ our Lord went from Bethany to Jerusalem to the Last Supper inclusively*, Ignatius explains:

> The first Prelude is to survey the history. Here it is to recall how Christ our Lord sent two disciples from Bethany to Jerusalem to prepare the supper, and later went there himself with his other disciples; and how, after eating the Paschal Lamb and finishing the meal, he washed their feet and gave his Most Holy Body and Precious Blood to his disciples; and further, how he addressed his farewell discourse to them, after Judas had left to sell his Lord.[32]

In the second contemplation, Ignatius of Loyola suggests that:

---

32   Ignatius of Loyola, *Spiritual Exercises*, p. 167.

If someone wishes to extend the time spent on the Passion, in each contemplation he or she should take fewer mysteries. That is, in the first contemplation only the Supper; in the second, the washing of the feet; in the third, Christ's institution of the Holy Eucharist; in the fourth, his farewell discourse to his apostles; and so on through the other contemplations and mysteries.[33]

Ignatius of Loyola proposes the same division in the part 'The Mysteries of the Life of Christ our Lord'.[34] The four engravings of the Last Supper illustrate every episode mentioned by Ignatius of Loyola, even those which were rarely or never depicted, such as the departure from Bethany to Jerusalem, the common supper, and Christ's teaching after the Eucharistic supper. The multiplication of scenes in a same plate enables a very detailed representation of the biblical text and allows them to remain true to Ignatius of Loyola's *Exercises*.

Whether Nadal's *Evangelicæ historiæ imagines* was an illustration of Ignatius of Loyola's *Spiritual Exercises* has been the subject of debate.[35] Even if the *Evangelicæ historiæ imagines* is not an illustration of the *Exercises* in the strict sense of the term, Nadal's book follows closely the different meditation's steps offered by the Jesuit Father, and proposes a similar approach. The illustrations take their roots in the biblical text and they guide the faithful on the devotional way, "using a methodological pilgrimage very similar in fundamental conception to the *Exercises*", as Gauvin A. Bailey writes.[36] In this way, the *Evangelicæ historiæ imagines* provides very faithful illustrations to the episode of the meditation, and in every plate the image and the text are indivisible from each other. Thanks to the multiplication of scenes, letters and captions, the four plates of the Last Supper propose the most faithful, almost literal, adaption of the biblical texts.[37] Through this process, Christ's gestures and words are as 'dissected' to legitimate Catholic faith and liturgy against Protestant attacks.

---

33   Ignatius of Loyola, *Spiritual Exercises*, p. 171.

34   Ignatius of Loyola, *Spiritual Exercises*, pp. 192–193.

35   Fabre, 'Les *Exercices spirituels* sont-ils illustrables?', pp. 197–209; Fabre, 'Quelques éléments', p. 29.

36   Gauvin A. Bailey, 'Italian Renaissance and Baroque Painting under the Jesuits and its Legacy throughout Catholic Europe, 1565–1773', in Gauvin A. Bailey etc. (eds.), *The Jesuits and the Arts, 1540–1773* (Philadelphia: Saint Joseph's University Press, 2005), p. 126.

37   Dekoninck, *Ad imaginem*, p. 246.

GÉRONIMO NADAL'S EVANGELICÆ HISTORIÆ IMAGINES

4 The Defence of the Catholic Faith

The Jesuits use the fidelity of the images to the biblical texts to demonstrate that religious rites of Catholic Church came directly from their reading of the Bible and of Christ's Words. First, starting the Last Supper's cycle with the Passover serves to show how the Catholic mass stems from the Jewish ceremony and how it is the achievement of the Ancient Law (Fig. 13.1). In the 'meditati' which follows the plate, Nadal relates Christ's Words. Christ explains:

> These ceremonies are divine, and because of that they must be respected before to be abolished, even by me who don't want to destroy the law, but to accomplish it.[38]

Then, the text reminds the reality of Christ's sacrifice, compared with the sacrificed Lamb during the Passover, in order to defend the doctrine of the Real Presence:

> They do that those who deny your Body, who deny your Blood, who deny with a sacrilegious mouth your presence in the Holy Sacrament. They say the Eucharist symbolises, but does not contain Christ, that it does not show the thing itself, but symbolises only Christ's Body and Blood.[39]

The *Adnotationes et meditationes* emphasises the link between the lamb, sacrificed and eaten during the Passover, and Christ, sacrificed on the Cross, and whose Body and Blood are incarnate in the bread and wine and given under these species during the Catholic mass. The presence of the Passover at the beginning of the Last Supper's cycle reminds to the faithful that the Eucharistic sacrament does not symbolise Christ's sacrifice but it is the renewal of this sacrifice: as the Jews which reproduce the sacrifice of the lamb during the Passover, the Christians repeat the sacrifice of Christ during the mass.[40] In this

---

38 "Divinæ errant illæ ceremoniæ, ac propterea ante abrogationem observandæ, etiam à me, qui veneram non ut legem foluerem, fed ut adimplerem: veni enim ut figuram, in qua posita erat lex ego perficerem, significatum exhiberem legis, umbram mea præsentia depellerem", in Géronimo Nadal, *Adnotationes et meditations*, p. 219.

39 "Hoc faciunt qui tuum corpus, qui tuum sanguinem, qui te sacrilego ore negat esse in venerabili Sacramento. Significat, inquiunt, non continent Chriftum; non reipsa exhibit, sed significat duntaxat corpus Christi & sanguinem Eucharistia", in Géronimo Nadal, *Adnotationes et meditations*, p. 220.

40 On the relationship between the Passover and the Last Supper, see Enrico Mazza, *L'Action eucharistique : origine, développement, interprétation* (Paris: Edition du Cerf, 1999), pp. 21–47.

way, Nadal emphasises the reality of the transubstantiation and justifies this dogma.

The next subject is the Washing of the Feet (Fig. 13.2). This ceremony instituted by Christ is respected by the Roman Church. Every year, during the Maundy Thursday, the pope and the clergy repeat Christ's gesture. This liturgical tradition is criticised and ridiculed by the Protestants. Calvin, in his commentary on John's Gospel, expresses his opinion about this rite used in the Catholic Church:

> Moreover, whereas they [the papists] ought to have followed Christ, they became Apes rather than followers. They ordaine every yere a publike washing of the feete as is were upon a stage: so that they thinke that they have fulfilled the bare and vaine ceremonie excellently: when they have done this they suffer themselves freely to contemne their brethren.... Neither doth Christ in this place commende unto us a yeerely ryte: but hee commaundeth us to bee readie during our whole life to washe the feete of our brethren.[41]

Against these Protestants attacks, the Council of Trent and the Jesuits justify the ceremony of the Washing of the Feet. The *Catechism of the Council* uses this episode to point out the necessity for the faithful to be purified and in 'state of grace' to receive the Communion:

> It may appear that that preparation is very necessary, the Example of our Savior ought to be proposed. For before he gave his Apostles the Sacraments of his Body and Blood, although they were already clean, he washed their Feet, that he might declare that all diligence is to be used, that there be nothing wanting to us, to the highest integrity and innocence of Soul, when we go about to receive these sacred Mysteries.[42]

The Jesuit Peter Canisius (1521–1597), in his *Great Catechism*, insisted on the historical reality of this rite, and explained its equivalence to the baptism.[43] Later, Robert Bellarmine (1542–1621) used this episode to emphasise that a person

---

41 John Calvin, *A Harmonie upon the three Evangelists, Matthew, Mark and Luke with the commentarie of M. Iohn Calvine: faithfully translated out of Latine to English, by. E.P. Whereunto is also added a commentarie upon the Evangelist S. Iohn, by the same authour* (London: Thomas Dawson, 1584), p. 314 (USTC 509925).

42 *The Catechism for the curats compos'd by the Decree of the Council of Trent* (London: Henry Hills, 1687), p. 225.

43 Peter Canisius, *Le grand catéchisme*, (1554) (2 vols., Paris: Louis Vivès, 1873), II. 244.

who receives the sacrament without confession, receives it unworthily.[44] This episode between the Passover and the Communion of the Apostles underlines the necessity to be purified to receive the Eucharistic sacrament. This plate is in support of the defence of the Catholic rite of the Washing of the Feet, and it also implies the presence of Judas during the Eucharistic supper and the Communion. Indeed, Judas sits at the end of the row, in the background of the room. We can recognise him thanks to his purse, which he holds before him. Again, this detail probably comes from Ignatius of Loyola's *Exercises*, since Ignatius indicates that Christ "washed his disciple's feet, even those of Judas".[45] Judas is hence purified and ready to receive the Eucharistic sacrament.

Although the title of plate n° 102 is the 'Institution of the Sacrament and the most sacred sacrifice', its subject is the Communion of the Apostles (Fig. 13.3). Christ is giving a morsel of bread to one of the apostles. Usually, when Christ is seated at a table and offers bread to one of his disciples, it is Judas and the episode is the announcement of the betrayal.[46] But here, Judas is seated in the foreground, and there is a clear distinction between the Communion in plate n° 102 and the announcement of the betrayal in the last plate. Two other examples commissioned by Jesuits show the same choice to depict Christ giving Communion to one of his disciples: plate n° 141 of the *Evangelicæ historiæ imagines* illustrating the 'Supper at Emmaus' (Fig. 13.7), and the *Last Supper* painted by Rubens for the Jesuit church of Antwerp, known thanks to the oil sketch (Fig. 13.8).[47] This Rubens's painting belongs to a larger decorative program designed by Jesuit Fathers. As with the others paintings of the church, it was the result of a close collaboration between the painter and the Jesuit Fathers and reveals the concerns of the Company.[48]

---

44   Robert Bellarmine, *De Sacramento Eucharistiæ, Controversia Generalis*, (2 vols., Ingolstadt: David Sartori), II. 1588–1593.

45   Ignatius of Loyola, *Spiritual Exercises*, p. 192.

46   The iconography of the Communion of the Apostles exists in an independent way and shows Christ standing in front of the altar and giving the hosts to the apostles kneeling: Justus of Ghent, *The Communion of the Apostles*, 1472–1474, 331 × 335 cm, tempera and oil on panel (Urbino, Galleria Nazionale delle Marche).

47   Anna C. Knaap, 'Meditation, Ministry, and Visual Rhetoric in Peter Paul Rubens's Program for the Jesuit Church in Antwerp', in John W. O'Malley etc. (eds), *The Jesuits: Cultures, Sciences and the Arts, 1540–1773* (2 vols, Toronto: University of Toronto Press, 1999–2006), II. 166.

48   Knaap, 'Meditation, Ministry, and Visual Rhetoric', pp. 157, 160–161. A copy of the original contract for the ceiling paintings, specifies what subjects Rubens with the help of his studio, is to execute for the vaults in the galleries, where is the *Last Supper*. See John Rupert Martin, *The Ceiling Paintings for the Jesuit Church in Antwerp* (Brussels: Arcade, 1968), pp. 213–219.

FIGURE 13.7 Johannes Wiei, after Pieter van der Borcht, *The Last Supper*, 1571, etching, 114 × 73 mm
© THE BRITISH MUSEUM, LONDON, 1875.0710.116

FIGURE 13.8   Antoine II Wierix after Bernardino Passeri, *Eodem die apparet Iesvs dvobvs discipvlis evntibvs emavnta*, 1593, woodcut, 233 × 146 mm
© RIJKSMUSEUM, AMSTERDAM, RP-P-OB-67.265

The depiction of Christ giving Communion, a choice which seems proper to the Jesuits, underlines several points of the religious practice of the Jesuits and the Catholic Church concerning Communion. First, the illustration of the Communion instead of the institution of the Eucharistic sacrament underlines the necessity to receive frequently the Eucharistic sacrament. During the sixteenth century, the Catholic Church and several religious orders incited the faithful to receive Communion more frequently than during the Middle Ages.[49] The Company of Jesus was the order that defended this practice with

49   Michael W. Maher, 'How the Jesuits used their Congregations to promote Frequent Communion', in John P. Donnelly etc. (eds), *Confraternities and Catholic Reform in Italy,*

the most insistence.[50] As in *De Imitatione Christi* (*The Imitation of Christ*), Ignatius of Loyola recommended a frequent Communion and praised the profits of this practice to achieve spiritual perfection.[51] In the eighteenth annotation of his *Exercises*, Ignatius encouraged the faithful "if possible, to reception of the Eucharist every two weeks or, if better disposed, weekly."[52] Following Ignatius of Loyola, other Jesuits incited frequent Communion, as Cristobal de Madrid in his book *De frequenti usu sanctissimi Eucharistiæ sacramenti libellus*.[53] The necessity to receive Communion frequently is probably at the core of the choice of Christ's gesture in this plate. Moreover, this engraving is the only one of the cycle to show three steps parallel to the bottom edge of the image. In the three other plates, either no step is present in the image (Fig. 13.1), or steps make possible the movement of the characters (Fig. 13.2) or one step enables Judas's departure (Fig. 13.4). In plate n° 102, the three steps at the foreground offer an entrance to the Cenacle and to Christ's table (Fig. 13.3). They are an invitation made to the reader to enter in the image and to receive Communion, like the apostles. In the plate n° 141 (Fig. 13.7) and in Rubens's *Last Supper* (Fig. 13.8) steps are also placed at the foreground of the image. In this way, the association between Christ's gesture of Communion and the steps in the foreground probably works like an invitation to meditate on the importance of Communion and on its frequent reception. The image invites the reader to receive the Eucharist directly from Christ's hand, like the apostles or the disciples at Emmaus.

Secondly, plate n° 102 shows how Catholics receive Communion (Fig. 13.3). The apostle who receives the sacrament bows his head and holds his hands in prayer, to show his humility and respect of the sacrament. Furthermore, Christ put the morsel of bread directly in his mouth. Again, the same attitude is adopted by the disciple in the engraving of the 'Supper at Emmaus' (Fig. 13.7). If this gesture has no scriptural source, it illustrates the way to receive the sacrament in the Catholic Church: Christ's gesture is the same as the priest's one when he is giving the Communion to the faithful during the mass. For

---

  France and Spain (Kirksville: Thomas Jefferson University Press, 1999), pp. 75–96, esp. pp. 75, 78.

50 John P. Donnelly, 'The New Religious Orders, 1517–1648', in Thomas A. Brady, Heiko A. Oberman, and James D. Tracy. (eds), *Handbook of European History, 1400–1600: Late Middle Ages, Renaissance and Reformation*, (2 vols, Leiden: Brill, 1994–1995), II. 284–315; Maher, 'How the Jesuits', pp. 75, 78; O'Malley, *Saints or Devils*, p. 169.

51 Maher, 'How the Jesuits', p. 77; O'Malley, *Saints or Devils*, p. 168.

52 Ignatius of Loyola, *Spiritual Exercises*, p. 126.

53 Cristobal de Madrid, *De frequenti usu sanctissimi Eucharistiæ sacramenti libellus* (Roma: Tipografia del Collegio Romano, 1557) (USTC 839449).

GÉRONIMO NADAL'S EVANGELICÆ HISTORIÆ IMAGINES   289

example, in Canisius's *Great Catechism*, the Eucharistic Communion is illustrated by a priest, standing before the altar, putting the host in the mouth of one of the kneeling communicants.[54] This behaviour is specific to Catholics, since Calvinists receive the bread in the hands without bowing.[55] Plate n° 102 fulfils a pastoral function in showing the proper way to receive Communion, on the model of Christ and apostles.

Thirdly, the plate implies that Judas also receives Communion from Christ. The presence of Judas during the Eucharistic supper is accepted by Catholics. Ignatius of Loyola underlined that "when the supper was finished, Judas went out to sell Christ our Lord".[56] Cornelius a Lapide, in his *Commentaries*, also explained "that Judas was present at the Passover and the Eucharist, and that he did communicate with the rest of the Apostles, is the common opinion of all other Fathers and Doctors ...", and then he used evangelical texts to prove this statement.[57] In his book about the religious iconography *Treatise on Sacred Images*, Johannes Molanus defended this conviction. He gave some details concerning the iconography of the Last Supper and explained that an image of this episode must show that Christ gave the sacrament to all the apostles, including Judas.[58] In plate n° 102, Judas is seated at Christ's table and is waiting to receive Communion, as the other apostles. Furthermore, in plate n° 103, the paten is empty and the chalice is no longer on the table (Fig. 13.4). This evolution underlines the fact that Jesus denounced Judas and announced his betrayal only after the Communion of all apostles. In the last image, Christ does not give a host to Judas, but a morsel of bread unblessed.

---

54 Petrus Canisius, *Institutiones Christianiæ Pietatis seu Parvus Catechismus Catholicorum*, (Antwerp: ex officina Christophe Plantin, 1575), pp. 40–41 (USTC 406289). Illustration in Lee P. Wandel, 'Catechisms: Teaching the Eye to Read the World', in Feike Dietz etc. (eds.), *Illustrated Religious Texts in the North of Europe, 1500–1800* (Farnham: Ashgate, 2014), figure 2.12, p. 72.

55 John Calvin, *Van dat scuwen der afgoderie, valschen godsdienst, ende gheueynstheyt, een seer fijn ende christelijck onderwijs* (*On avoiding idolatry, false worship and hypocrisy*) (Anvers: Theophilus Brugensis, 1554) (USTC 404228); Wandel, *The Eucharist*, p. 199; Koenraad Jonckheere, *Antwerp Art After Iconoclasm: Experiments in Decorum, 1566–1585* (Brussels: Marcatorfonds, 2012), pp. 169–174.

56 Ignatius of Loyola, *Spiritual Exercises*, p. 193.

57 Cornelius a Lapide, *The Great Commentary*, III, p. 167.

58 "Dans la plupart des peintures de la communion des apôtres, treize fragments, c'est-à-dire treize parts de pain azyme, sont représentés, un fragment dans la main du Seigneur et douze dans la patène, pour signifier que lors de son dernier repas le Sauveur, Notre-Seigneur, a distribué le sacrement de son corps aussi bien à lui-même, qu'à tous les apôtres, Judas compris.", in Johannes Molanus, *Treatise on Sacred Images* (Leuven, 1594), trans. by François Boespflug, *Le Traité des Saintes Images* (Paris: Cerf, 1996), book IV, chap. 17, p. 523.

290   LANGLAIS

Even though plate n° 102 illustrates the Communion of the Apostles and caption 'B' does not repeat the Eucharistic words of the institution, the reference to the institution of the Eucharistic sacrament is not absent from the plate (Fig. 13.3). Pierre-Antoine Fabre suggests that the engraving infers the Eucharistic words through the transition between the medallion and the main scene, as if the medallion was given to be eaten as the host offered by Christ to his apostles.[59] The reader can reconstitute the intermediate section, when Christ says the words instituting the Eucharist, by looking first at the medallion and then at the main scene. Nadal repeats Christ's Words, and underlines at the same time the dogma of transubstantiation:

> He takes in his hand the whole bread, He thanks God the Father, and He blesses, breaks, gives to the apostles from his hand the salutary host ... Here are the sacred words He uses: This is my body: through these words, He ensures that the substance of bread turns into the substance of his body, that is to say He makes transubstantiation ... In the same way, after taking the chalice, He ensures that the substance of wine turns into the substance of his blood, that is to say He makes transubstantiation.[60]

Plate n° 102 summarises the main issues linked to the Eucharistic debate: the Eucharistic Communion and the way to receive it, the necessity to receive the sacrament frequently, and the dogma of transubstantiation. Finally, we can also observe in this plate that a figure of the devil is placed before Judas's knees. This detail is uncommon in the iconography of the Last Supper, yet there are two contemporary examples which show also a monstrous creature near Judas. They are two etchings, one engraved by Philipps Galle after a drawing by Jan van der Stræt, a Flemish artist working in Florence (Fig. 13.9), and the other by Hieronymus Wierix after Otto van Veen (Fig. 13.10).

---

59 "Tout se passe donc comme si cet énoncé était produit dans l'articulation des deux images, comme si c'était le médaillon lui-même qui, comme l'hostie que Jésus tend à ses apôtres, se donnait à être consommé; comme si cette articulation offrait l'image à la consommation de celui qui la regarde, dans sa présence réelle, au-delà de sa représentation – la représentation de l'instant immédiatement antérieur à la célébration eucharistique", in Fabre, "Quelques éléments", p. 36.

60 Accipit in manus panem integrum, gratias Patri Deo agit, benedicit, frangit, dat Apostolis de manus sua salutarem hostiam. Sed interea dum hæc facit, poft benedictionem, antequam ad fractionem venire, adhibet divina illa verba: Hoc est corpus meum: quibus verbis fecit, ut panis fubftantia in corporis fui fubstantiam coverteretur, hoc est transsubstantiaretur ... Similiter accepto calice fecit, ut substantia vini in sanguinis sui substantiam mutaretur, idest transsubstantiaretur..., in Géronimo Nadal, *Adnotationes et meditations*, p. 225.

FIGURE 13.9   Pieter Paul Rubens, *The Last Supper*, 1620, oil on panel, 43,8 × 44,1 cm
© THE ART MUSEUM, SEATTLE, 61.66

This iconographical detail illustrates John's Gospel, when it is said that Satan entered into Judas after Christ gave him the morsel of bread.[61] In the annotations, Nadal explains the devil had already fills Judas with his force during the common supper. Then, when Judas receives the bread, the devil controls him with more violence and torments Judas's soul and body. In the last plate, the same devil is seated on Judas's head, and he leads the traitor with a thin cord. This detail shows the whole domination and possession of the apostle by the devil. This unprecedented detail is perhaps inspired by the medieval representations of the Synagogue blinded or lead by the devil.[62] The similarity between the Synagogue blinded and Judas shows that Judas, like the Jews, turns away from the true religion and the true faith, Christianism. Again, Cornelius a Lapide offered an explanation of Judas's possession by the devil:

---

61   John 13: 27.
62   *Ecclesia (Church) and Synagoga (Synagogue)*, c.1230, stone, South Transept Portal, Cathedral of Strasbourg.

FIGURE 13.10   Philips Galle after Jan van der Straet, *The Last Supper*, 1585, etching, 198 × 269 mm
© BOIJMANS VAN BEUNINGEN MUSEUM, ROTTERDAM, LI966/56-3

Notice here in the case of Judas how a man who deserts Christ is palpably deserted by Christ, and when deserted is attacked by Satan – possessed by him, and, when possessed, hurried into every crime, and then into the abyss. Just as Judas from an apostle became a devil, so Lucifer from the fairest of angels became the darkest of evil spirits, – as the sourest vinegar is made from the sweetest wine, and the heretic – Luther, for instance – nay, the heresiarch, is made from the monk.[63]

In this way, like the Synagogue and the heretics – Luther and the other Protestants – Judas turns away from Christ and from the true religion, Catholicism and the Roman Church.

---

63   Cornelius a Lapide, *The Great Commentary*, VI, p. 66.

5 Conclusion

Together, these four plates, through images, captions and commentaries, are absolutely in agreement with Jesuit theology and teaching, and with Catholic precepts defended and reaffirmed by the Council of Trent. The division of the Last Supper in four distinct illustrations, connected by some visual means, is a way to illustrate this founding episode of the Christian Church with a lot of details, but from the Jesuit point of view. Indeed, if illustrations are faithful to evangelical texts, in one hand, in other hand some details are proper to Catholic interpretation, like Christ's gesture for the Communion of the Apostles. Otherwise, the association of very detailed images to texts of captions, annotations and meditations, insists on the historical character of the Eucharistic supper, as the achievement of the Passover, the first mass performed by Christ, and the institution of the dogma of transubstantiation. Through an analytical and exhaustive narration of all events which form the Last Supper, an approach possible thanks to the format of the illustrated book, the *Evangelicæ historiæ imagines* forges links between the historical episode and the temporal religious life, in order to show that dogmas and religious rites of the Jesuits, and more largely of the Catholics, come directly from Christ's words and actions, unlike Protestants religious practices. This approach corresponds to the ideology and pastoral function of the Society of Jesus, which wants to establish its evangelical project relying on Christ's teaching and the apostolic mission.[64] In this way, through a renewed iconography of the Last Supper, Nadal's publication aims to spread Jesuit and Catholic teaching about the sacrament of the Eucharist in the context of the reconquest and the Catholic reform.

---

64   Bernadette Majorana, 'Images et culture de mission', in Alain Tapié (ed.), *Baroque, vision jésuites : du Tintoret à Rubens* (Paris: Somogy, 2003), p. 40; Knaap, "Meditation, Ministry", p. 166.

Index

Books and Prints at the Heart of the Catholic Reformation in the Low Countries (16th–17th centuries)

Africa   140, 175
Agabus, saint   265
Agresti, Livio   269
Alardus Amstelredamus   274
Albert v, duke of Bavaria   93
Albert vii, archduke of Austria   2, 23–24,
    32, 36, 44, 61, 139–140, 155–156, 158–159,
    164–166, 175, 223, 263
Albert of Louvain, prince-bishop   38
Albert of Trapani, saint   265
Albertus Magnus   161, 166, 172
Alciato, Andrea   61, 64, 77, 185, 193–194,
    204–205, 214–215
Aleandro, Girolamo   31
Allen, William, cardinal   90
Alps   117, 133, 149
Álvarez de Toledo, Fernando, duke of
    Alba   88
Alviano, Bartolomeo d'   199
America   25, 34, 149, 175
Amiens   89, 248
Amsterdam   132, 195–196, 206, 210
Anastasius, saint   265
Ancxt, Marie   20
Angela of Bohemia, saint   266
Angelus of Jerusalem, saint   39, 265
Angoulême   85
Anthoine, family   23–24, 27–30, 33, 38
Anthoine, Hubert I   23, 28–29, 34, 40
Antwerp   2–5, 9–11, 13–14, 16–21, 31, 37, 40,
    46–49, 54–55, 59, 61–66, 70–71, 77,
    81–82, 95–99, 106, 120, 128, 130–131,
    135–140, 146, 148, 150–151, 153, 157, 160,
    171, 174–175, 179, 190, 192–194, 197, 216,
    223–224, 226, 228, 232, 246, 248, 255,
    257, 260, 263, 268, 279, 285
Arenberg, dukes of   34
Aresi, Paolo   184
Arias Montano, Benito   67, 274
Aristotle   161
Arlotto, Piovanno   162

Armentières   250
Arras   82, 90, 99, 173, 186–187, 196, 201
Arsenius, Ferdinand   117–119, 123–124, 127–128
Arsenius, Gualterus   117
Artesia   82
Asia   175
Augsburg   47, 73–75
Auroy, Pierre   198, 208
Austria   25, 72, 239
Avancini, Nicolas   252
Averoult, Antoine d'   144–146
Avertanus, saint   265

Balinghem, Antoine de   168
Bargagli, Girolamo   181
Barlandus, Hadrianus   259
Baronius, Cesare   224, 226, 231
Basel   72–74, 185
Bauduyn, Gilles   196
Bavo, saint   135
Beatrice of Nazareth   162
Bedmar, Alfonso de la Cueva-Benavides y
    Mendoza-Carrillo, marquis of   147, 149
Beeck, Willemsz van der   196
Beke, Maria Vander   140
Bellarmino, Roberto, cardinal   126, 284
Bellerus, Balthazar I   192, 197–200, 204
Bellerus, Gaspard I   20
Bellerus, Joannes   50
Bellerus, Marie   15
Bellerus, Petrus I   15–17, 20, 194, 209
Bellevaux, abbey of   251
Benedict, saint   163
Berckmans, Lynsken   20
Bergagne, Anthonis Maria   194
Bergen, Willem van   223
Bergerac, treaty of   84, 87
Bergeron, Pierre   37
Bernard of Clairvaux, saint   157
Berthold of Mount Carmel, saint   266
Besse, Pierre de   167–169

Beyerlinck, Laurentius 174–175
Bèze, Théodore de 196
Binet, Étienne 99, 168
Bogard, Jean 51, 197–198, 208
Bohemia 136, 153, 266
Bohemian crisis 3, 131, 139, 141, 151, 153
Bolswert, Schelte 191
Borcht, Peeter vander 49
Borremans, Pierre 198
Boscard, Jacques 87, 197, 207
Boucher, Jean 151
Boulonnois, Esmé de 253
Bourgeois, Jacques 93
Braat, Cornelisz Jacob 195, 205
Brabant 41, 95–96, 99, 102, 104, 105, 116, 130, 135, 153, 259
Brahe, Tycho 109–111
Brazil 173
Brueghel, Jan II 158
Bruges 95, 251
Bruneels, Olivier 29
Bruno, Giordano 167
Brussels 2, 23–44, 95, 98, 101, 105, 114, 116–117, 120, 125, 128, 135, 139–140, 146–147, 152, 169, 171, 196, 223, 243–246, 250–251, 256
    Coudenberg Palace 23, 257

Calais 85
Calvin, Jean 2844
Cambrai 51, 81, 82, 91–92, 99, 157, 168, 173, 175
Cambridge 265
Camus, Jean-Pierre, bishop 99, 162, 168
Cannes 160
Capel 88
Carafa, Pier Luigi 180
Catherine de' Medici, queen of France 84
Caymox, Balthasar 74
Ceres 221
Cernovichio, Pietro Angelo 265
Charenton 171
Charles V, Emperor and king of Spain 31, 91, 259, 266
Christian of Brunswick 134–135
Cicero 160
Clarisse, Rogier 136
Clavius, Christoph 3, 101–102, 106, 108, 110–111, 113–114, 117, 120–121, 126, 128

Clouwet, Petrus 246
Collalto, Claudius de 254, 256
Cologne 26, 60, 72, 92, 146, 168, 174–175, 180, 207–208
Comines 250
Commers, Elisabeth 20
Constantinople 146, 265
Cordier, Bernard 15
Corsini, Andrea, saint 39, 265
Costerius, Henricus 54
Costerus, Franciscus 46
Croÿ, Charles III de 34
Cyril of Alexandria, saint 265
Cyril of Constantinople, saint 265

Dalen, Cornelis van 196
Damery, Léonard 101, 115–119, 122, 125
Daneau, Laurent 86, 97
Danzig 60
David 142
David, Jan 4, 61–62, 64, 66–77, 159, 170–173, 175, 232–234
Davity, Pierre 149
De'Pazzi, Mary Magdalene, saint 265
Della Faille, Joannes 106, 136–137
Della Faille, Martin 137
Delft 194, 196, 206
Democritus 159, 164, 167–170, 175
Denis the Carthusian 40
Des Freuz, René 92
Deventer 176
Diepenbeeck, Abraham van 254–255, 263–264
Diericx, Volcxken 11
Dixmude 250
Dordrecht 195–196, 205, 215
Dordt 83–85, 87
Douai 1, 32, 51, 81–83, 87–95, 99, 105, 140, 168, 171, 173, 192, 194, 197–198, 207–210, 246
Dresseler, Jan 52
Drexel, Jeremias 76
Du Carroy, Jean 85
Du Moulin, Pierre 171

Einhard Charlemagne 164
Eisengrein, Martin 92–94
Elizabeth, queen of England 134, 151, 153

INDEX
297

Engelgrave, Henricus 76
Enghien 34
England 85, 87–88, 134, 198
Erasmus 185
Ertborn, Anna van 14–17, 21
Escaut 63
Escobecques 89
Estella, Diego de 169
Eucherius 160

Faber, Johannes 106, 142–143
Fampoux, Jean de 198
Farnese, Alexander, duke of Parma 27–28, 46, 61, 94, 153
Ferdinand II, emperor 141, 241, 252
Ferdinand III, emperor 241, 266
Ferdinand IV of Habsburg, archduke of Austria 254–255, 257
Fernandez de Eyzaguirre, Sebastian 40
Fiesole 162
Flavius, Johannes Christophorus 169
Fleurus, battle of 133
Florianus, Johannes 98
Folch de Cardona y Borja, Felipe, marquis of Guadalest 39
Foppens, François 196
Foppens, Pierre 196
Forster, Gaspar 60
Fraisne, Egidius de 246
France 3–4, 25, 33, 51, 55, 81–82, 87, 89, 94, 99, 134, 146, 165, 168, 241, 244, 259
Francis of Assisi, saint 165, 173
Francis-Xavier, saint 39, 198
François de Sales, saint 40, 99, 161–163
François de Valois, duke of Alençon and Anjou 84
Frankfurt 72, 135
Frankfurt, fair 47, 52, 55, 59, 63–67, 72–74, 77
Frederick V of the Palatinate 151
Freiburg 46–47, 73

Galilei, Galileo 101, 103–105, 110–111, 113, 117, 120, 122, 126–129
Galle, Cornelis II 58
Galle, Philips 55, 62, 290
Galle, Theodoor 54, 57, 62, 64, 68, 70–71, 74, 236
Garasse, François 171, 175

Gattinara, Mercurino 31
Gaverelle, Jan de 139, 141, 147
Gavre, Baudouin de 91
Gazet, Angelin 159, 173–174
Gemma Frisius 116–117, 121–122
Gemperlin, Abraham 47
Geneva 83–84, 86, 176
Genoa 138
Gerard of Nazareth, saint 266
Germany 25, 74, 87, 129, 133
Geydert, Joann Christoph 174
Ghent 40, 87, 89, 95, 114, 135, 140, 171, 266
Giglio, Domenico 186
Giles of Orval 38
Ginderhoven. Martin van 56
Giolito De' Ferrari, family 186
Giovio, Paolo 199, 209
Girard, Christophe 171
Giunta, Jeanne 12
Goes, brothers van der 137
Goltzius, Hendrick 182–183
Gonzaga, Charles, duke of Nevers 146
Gramaye, Jean-Baptiste 33
Gracián de la Madre Dios, Jerónimo 39
Grassi, Orazio 126
Gratiani, Gaspar 133
Graz 72, 127, 241
Gregory I, pope 176
Gregory XV, pope 39
Gregory the Great, saint 176
Greuter, Mattheus 125
Grienberger, Christoph 108, 111, 113–114, 116, 121, 125–128
Gudula, saint 135
Guicciardini, Lodovico 217–218, 220, 236
Guillard, Charlotte 11
Guînes 85
Guldin, Paul 127
Gummarus, saint 135

Haarlem 149, 211
Habbeke, Gaspar Maximilien van 39
Habsburg, family 1–3, 30, 33, 72, 81, 83, 87–88, 91, 131, 133–139, 146, 150–151, 153, 155–157, 162–163, 168, 170, 175–176, 239–240, 252, 256, 259, 262, 266–267
Hainaut 82, 91, 246, 250
Halberstadt 241

298 INDEX

Halle   35
Hamont, Michiel van   27–28
Heidelberg   72
Heil, Jean-Baptiste van   246
Heilbronn   142
Henríquez, Crisóstomo   25
Henry III, king of France and Poland   83–84, 91
Henry IV, king of France and Navarre   83, 152, 189
Heraclitus   167–169
Hercules   151, 153, 182, 221, 246
Hilarius, saint   160
Hillen, Margriete   15–16
Hoeymaker, Ferdinand de   29–30
Hoorn   196
Hugo, Herman   76
Hungary   75
Huy   169

Iberian Peninsula   14
Ignatius of Loyola, saint   39, 161, 189, 191, 198, 228, 277–279, 281–282, 285, 288–289
Ilpendam, David Jansz van   196
Immerseel, Willem van   137
Ingolstadt   47, 49, 72, 93, 127
Ireland   134
Isabella Clara Eugenia, archduchess of Austria   2, 23–24, 32, 36, 39, 44, 61, 139–140, 155–156, 158–159, 164, 166, 175, 223, 263
Italy   101, 105, 129, 133, 146, 186, 237

James Matamoros, saint   136
Jeghers, Christoffel   59
John (Danck) of Saxony   247
John Patriarch of Jerusalem, saint   265
Joseph, François Leclerc du Tremblay, father   147
Junius, Hadrianus   61, 64, 198, 204, 211, 213

Kellam, Laurent I   198
Kepler, Johannes   110–111, 126
Kirchhausen   136
Klarenstein, Matthias Arnoldin von   141
Kortrijk   62
Kostka, Stanislas   189
Krakow   60, 74–75

Lagache, Antoine   201
Lagache, Jean   201
La Marck, Erard de, prince-bishop   31
Lamormaini, Wilhelm   252
Landrecies   250
Lannoy, Claude Maximilien de   246
La Noue, Guillaume de   85
Lapide, Cornelius a   279, 289, 291
La Rivière, Guillaume de   186–189
La Rivière, Jean-Baptiste de   187
Launoy, Matthieu de   3, 81–89, 91, 93–99
Leclerq, Toussaint   191
Leiden   46, 61, 195–196, 211–212
Leipzig   72, 74
Lens   250
Lérins   160
Lesteens, Guilielmus   16
Leopold William, archduke   4, 239–246, 250–261, 264–267
Leuven see Louvain
Liborius of Paderborn, saint   135
Lindanus, Willem, bishop   142
Liefrinck, Mynken   48, 50
Lierre   105, 135
Liesvelt, Jan van   19
Lippi, Francesco   265
Lipsius, Justus   17, 35, 136
Lommelin, Adrien   248–249, 263–264
London   132
Louis IX, king of France, saint   162, 165
Louis XIII, king of France and Navarre   167, 263
Louis XIV, king of France and Navarre   263
Louvain   1, 28, 31–32, 38, 82, 89, 95, 105–106, 120, 125, 140, 153, 169, 175, 185, 192, 194, 197–198, 205, 251, 256
Luther, Martin   292
Lyon   12, 160, 171, 186, 193, 206–207, 212, 214–215
Lys, river   250

Madrid   149, 244, 263
Madrid, Cristóbal   288
Maelcote, Jean van   105
Maelcote, Odo van   3, 101–130
Magdeburg   135, 195
Maigret, Georges   169
Main   63, 72
Mainz   72, 185

INDEX 299

Maire, Antoine 195
Maire, Joannes 195
Makeblijde, Lodewijk 40
Manutius, Aldus 185
Margaret of Parma 140
Marienhof, F. A. 253
Marliano, Luís, bishop 31
Martin, saint 164
Mechelen 31, 40, 135, 251
Mechelen, Lucas van 163
Medici, family 44
Meerbeeck, Jan van 25, 29–30, 39, 214
Meerbeeck, Lucas van 29, 38–39, 214
Melander, Joannes 53
Mercury 132, 194
Merulus of Rome 176
Meteren, Emanuel van 149
Mexico 138
Minerva 246
Minières, Jean de 85
Miraeus, Aubertus 33, 139–141, 147, 151
Molanus, Joannes 153, 289
Moldavia 133
Mommaert, family 27, 30, 40
Mommaert, Jan I 27, 29–30, 39–40, 152
Mons 28, 82, 91
Moreau, Anne 16
Moretus, family 59–60, 67, 70, 74
Moretus, Balthasar I 1, 57–59, 71, 136, 180
Moretus, Balthasar II 46, 57–58
Moretus, Jan I 17–19, 47, 49–50, 53–56,
    58–59, 61–65, 70–71, 76
Moretus, Jan II 64
Mouronval, Jan de 87–89, 93

Nadal, Jerome 4, 68–69, 228, 237, 268–269,
    277, 282–284, 290–291, 293
Namur 82
Nantes, edict of 81
Natalis, Hieronymus 62, 64–66, 68, 70,
    77
Neckar 72
Neptune 221
Neri, Philip, saint 39, 226
Ninove 170
Norbert, saint 135–136
Numan, Philip 38, 162, 226
Nuremberg 72–74
Nutius, Martin 62, 67

Olomouc 73, 241
Onuphrius, saint 266
Oostsanen, Jacob Cornelisz van 274–276, 279
Ortelius, Abraham 56
Oursini, family 199

Padua 113, 129
Palatinate 72
Paradin, Claude 181
Paris 3, 11, 16, 44, 52, 63–64, 71, 82–85,
    87–88, 90, 92, 94, 117, 123–124, 146, 152,
    169, 171, 184, 193, 247, 255
Passau 241
Passeri, Bernardino 269–274, 287
Paul V, pope 141, 148
Pauwijns, Elizabeth 20
Pennetier, Henri 3, 82–83, 85
Pepermans, Jan 29–30, 39
Peretti Damasceni, Francesco, prince of
    Venafro 121
Peru 138
Peter the Hermit 265
Peter Thomas, saint 2655
Petit, Jean 184
Petrus Canisius, saint 2, 40, 46–60, 142–143,
    284, 289
Philip II, king of Spain 23, 31, 43, 90, 92, 105,
    152–153, 197, 221
Philip III, king of Spain 147
Philippines 149
Piedmont 76, 186
Pietrasanta, Silvestro 179–184, 200, 203
Pionius, martyr 174
Pius V, pope 142–143
Plantin, Christophe 1–2, 15, 17–19, 46–55,
    58–64, 179–184, 186, 190, 193, 199, 203,
    208, 211, 213, 216–221, 226
Plantin, Martina 18
Plantiniana, Officina 9, 12, 14, 19, 38, 57–64,
    66, 70, 73, 136, 172, 217
Plutarch 165
Poitiers 171
Poland 60, 75, 146
Pont-à-Mousson 73
Potitus, martyr 176
Prague 135
Precipiano, Guillaume Humbert de, baron of
    Soye, archbishop 250–251
Puteanus, Eryicius 169–170

300   INDEX

Quellinus, Erasmus II   58

Rabelais, François   171, 175
Reynolds, William   151
Rhine   72
Rhineland   133, 153
Ribadeneyra, Pedro de   152, 189
Richelieu, Armand Jean du Plessis,
    cardinal   147
Richeome, Louis   99, 168, 189, 222
Rivière, Jeanne   17–19, 21–22
Robat, Victor   91–92
Rockocx, Nicholas   137
Roelofs, Anna   92
Roermond   142
Rojas Sarmiento, Juan de   116, 121–122
Rollenhagen, Gabriel   195–196, 203, 205,
    207–208
Rombout, saint   135
Rome   3, 31, 101, 110, 113, 116–117, 120–121,
    124–127, 129–130, 141, 176, 196, 226, 237,
    259
Rosweyde, Heribert   160
Rubens, Peter Paul   136, 182, 191, 255–257,
    285, 288, 291
Rubens, Philip   136
Rudolph I of Habsburg, king of
    Germany   239–240
Rykel, Denis, *see* Denis the Carthusian

`s-Hertogenbosch   47, 193, 204, 255
Sabina, martyr   174
Sailly, Thomas   144–146
St Gall   127
Saint-Omer   82
Sallaert, Antoine   249–250
Sallust   139
Sambucus, Joannes   61, 64
Sanderus, Antonius   33, 38
Sardinia   149
Sartorius, David   47, 49
Sasbout, Adam   194
Saxony   72
Schedelius, Christophorus   60
Scheiner, Christoph   116, 126–127
Scherpenheuvel   38
Scheyfve, Claudio Christoval   40
Schildere, Ludovic de   251

Schinckel, Bruyn Harmansz   196
Schleidorn, Joannes Christophorus   174
Schoeffer, Peter   185
Schoevaerdts, Govaerdt   29–30, 40
sConincx, Arnout   15
Scotland   87, 134
Scott, Thomas   134, 153
Scribani, Carolus   64, 139–141
Scribani, Hector   140
Severus, Sulpicius   164
Seville   138
Sicily   149
Sigismund III Vasa, king of Poland and grand
    duke of Lithuania   75
Simeoni, Gabriele   181
Simon Stock, saint   265–266
Simons, Petrus, bishop   62
Sixtus V, pope   149, 226
Sonnius, Michel I   52, 64
Sonnius, Michel II   55
Soto, Andreas de   39–40
Spain   14, 25, 50, 59, 61, 71, 138–140, 148–149,
    241, 243
Stagnino, family   186
Stapleton, Thomas   89–90, 92
Steelsius, family   14–17
Steelsius, Frans   15–17
Steelsius, Gillis   16–17
Steelsius, Joannes I   14–15
Steelsius, Johanna   15, 17
Steelsius, Magdalena   15
Steelsius, Yda   15
Stöffler, Johann   116, 121–122
Strael, Martine van   29
Stræt, Jan van der   290, 292
Strasbourg   72, 241
Sueyro, Emanuel   139, 141, 147
Surius, Laurentius   92

Tacitus   139
Tanchelm   135
Teresa of Ávila, saint   39, 162, 265
Theodoricus Allemannus   266
Tholon   149
Thomas Aquinas, saint   158, 161, 166
Thomas of Jesus, saint   39
Thulden, Theodore van   255–257
Tilius, Thomas   98, 100

INDEX

Titelmans, Franciscus   143
Torrentius, Laevinius   223
Tory, Geoffroy   185
Tournai   84, 87–90, 92, 99, 106, 151–152
Trautmansdorf, Maximilian von   141
Trent, Council of   1, 188, 197, 224, 237, 251, 262, 274, 277, 284, 293
Trier   72
Triest, Antoine, bishop   266
Trino   185
Turnhout, Jan van   193–194, 204

Valenciennes   84, 90, 173, 195
Vedelius, Nicolas   176
Veen, Otto van   290
Veken, Nicolaas van der   15
Veldener, Johann   185
Velpius, Catherine   23
Velpius, family   23–24, 27–30, 33, 38
Velpius, Rutger   23, 27–29, 34–35, 41–43, 115
Vendeville, Jean, bishop   92–93
Venice   76, 126, 186
Verdussen, family   1, 16
Verdussen, Hieronymus I   20
Verdussen, Hieronymus III   16
Verepaeus, Simon   47, 49–50, 142, 144
Verhoeven, Abraham   131–132, 134–135, 139, 150–151, 154
Verstegan, Richard   151, 171
Vienna   75, 241, 243, 252, 255
Vincent of Beauvais   173

Vinck, Pierre   41, 43, 116
Virgil   259
Visch, Carolus   25
Vivien, François   29–30, 40
Vos, Maarten de   231

Walloon provinces   3, 5, 82, 90
Wechel, Chrestien   193–194, 204–205
Wenssler, Michael   185
West Indies   134
Westphalia, Peace of   241
White Mountain, battle of   137
Wierix, Antoine II   287
Wierix, Hieronymus   231, 269, 290
Wierix, Johannes   269–273
Wignacourt, Maximilien de   189
Willer, Georg   47, 74
William of Orange, stathouder   89
Worms   72
Worms, edict of   31
Wouters, Engele   20
Wouters, Hendrik   96
Wouwere, Mechtelt van den   20
Woverius, Johannes   136
Wrocław   241
Würzburg   72–73

Ydens, Étienne   24, 40–44
Ypres   62, 171, 246

Zurich   73–74, 123